This book is due for return on or before the last date sh

e Education

LESSONS IN CLASS

A fresh appraisal of Comprehensive Education

Dick Copland

TUPS Books

© Dick Copland 1998

Published by TUPS Books
30 Lime Street, Newcastle upon Tyne NE1 2PQ

Typeset by Sumner Type, London SE22
Printed by Trade Union Printing Services, Newcastle upon Tyne

A C.I.P. catalogue record for this book is available from the British
Library

ISBN: 1 901237 060

CONTENTS

PART V   POWERFUL FORCES: extraordinary happenings

PART VI   COMPREHENSIVE EDUCATION: key to the future

Foreword
by Caroline and Tony Benn

Ryhope is a school few will have heard of unless they live in Sunderland. What's more, it was closed over ten years ago and its headteacher, Dick Copland, has now retired.

What makes it so important is that it sums up the experience of thousands of schools trying to give young people the best education possible during an era when so many ordinary schools were determined to implement comprehensive education in the 1970s; and then in the 1970s and 1980s, typical of so many more enduring the 'inconsistencies, impracticalities and injustice' of governments systematically seeking to destroy the comprehensive principle upon which schools like Ryhope had based themselves.

As we know, that principle has survived, and today comprehensive education remains the experience of the great majority of young people attending school in Britain — no small thanks to the work of teachers like Dick Copland, whose meticulous records of his years at Ryhope have enabled him to reconstruct that school's experience within the historical context of education for ordinary people over the last 150 years.

Copland combines local and national educational developments with detailed accounts of the development of Ryhope's curriculum and teaching policies and its interaction with its local community from the day of its formation as a comprehensive school in 1969 right up to the eve of the 21st century. Every aspect of education in schools is covered and shows that the comprehensive principle is the only basis upon which education for everyone can possibly be built in a democracy.

The main drama of the book concerns the last struggle when the school was made the target of local and national conservatives in the 1980s — particularly in relation to its decision to abandon corporal punishment.

The record of public denigration, combined with sustained 'crisis' reporting from the areas's powerful newspapers about the possible effects on 'discipline', plus rationalising activity from a local authority looking for a school 'to close', bring home to us the obstacles so many ordinary schools had to face when trying to sustain progress in an era of prejudice, 'market'-driven change, quangocratic rule and continuing government determination to undermine comprehensive education.

Ryhope was blessed with a headteacher who did not sink quietly to rest, but chose instead to fight to the end — and far beyond — and in so doing turn a turbulent neighbourhood drama into a fine story of commitment that will long survive within the local folk memory of a community that supported him in his efforts.

This then is a story of Everyschool written by a head who makes his observations on the basis of long experience within the classroom, wide reading in the theory of educational practice, and a deep social commitment to a democratic community life for everyone. It is educational common sense that is powerfully documented and far outlives the puny forces that brought down the school itself.

April 1998

Preface

Lessons in Class: a fresh appraisal of Comprehensive Education examines how the full range of teaching and associated activities in school relate to the nature of the comprehensive system itself. It is intended for all who are interested in the development of public education and its impact on society.

Education is, by its nature, a political activity, so this aspect is implicit throughout and addressed specifically from time to time. Emphasis is on the secondary years but there is shared experience with the primary and post-16 stages. Policies and events are set against a background of personal experience whilst aspects of social history help to place educational ideas in context. Part V is an extended commentary on a set of remarkable local and national circumstances — political in essence — which influenced events in one particular school. Today, different circumstances produce their own constraints and opportunities which must always be taken into account when analysing developments.

A coordinated and coherent approach to decision making, both at school and national level, is essential and, with this in mind, developments during forty years of comprehensive education are related to the potential of the system to meet the constantly increasing aspirations of people today. The book provides starting points for discussion, assumes no specialised knowledge, keeps jargon to a minimum and explains any specific terms that are used. A few of the most common are described in 'Terminology Explained' (p 361). The book aims to help non-specialist readers to gain in confidence on educational matters, especially with regard to how young people learn, so that they can more readily assess the impact of current developments. The need for active support for comprehensive education has never been greater and, throughout the book, lines for development as well as campaigning points are suggested.

Every day, people of all ages and occupations make significant contributions to the development of comprehensive education. Many are school students, parents or teachers; some are education experts or members of local communities and a few become activists when the need arises. During my career in schools, I had the pleasure and privilege of meeting and working with a lively, helpful and stimulating cross-section without whose ideas and energy this book could not have been written.

It would be invidious to select individuals for commendation but I hope that those reading these pages will recognise aspects in which they were involved and the influence which their work, actions and perseverance had on events and activities. Here I must not forget those who saw it as their special mission to induct me into the ways, life and language of the north east. Together with the support of my close family, such actions greatly influenced my thinking and, whilst naturally accepting full responsibility for all decisions within my spheres of responsibility, I remain widely indebted.

Maurice Levitas, formerly of Neville's Cross College of Education in Durham, read an early version of the manuscript and gave encouraging and detailed comment while my wife, Joyce, has provided practical assistance, patience and support throughout. Finally I wish to thank Clare Cowen of Sumner Type and Dave Temple of Trade Union Printing Services (TUPS) for their encouragement, forbearance and expert advice in the publishing field.

Reponsibility for the content and opinions in the book is entirely mine.

D.C.
April 1998

Introduction

The arrival of Sir Keith Joseph at the Department of Education and Science during Mrs Thatcher's first Conservative government marked a turning point for the role of the Secretary of State in educational planning. With the full approval of the cabinet he set about studying what actually went on inside state schools with a view to changing it.

Government departments, local authorities, trade unions, churches and pressure groups of various kinds had all been active in the field of education over many decades. Elected representatives planned for buildings and resources, increases in higher education places, the introduction of comprehensive education, extended welfare services, and more and better qualified teaching and non-teaching staff working under improved conditions of service. However, the Labour Party, in particular, spent little time with what actually went on in educational establishments, what school students did during their working hours and the values that were transmitted to them. Yet a nation's education system helps to determine prospects of personal fulfilment as well as reflecting and contributing to society's values, so it was certainly not lack of importance which inhibited interest in the internal working of schools. It perhaps suited many to go along with a popular belief that education was specialised and complex so that only those who had training and direct experience were qualified to assess the issues. Nothing could be further from the truth. Hopefully, this book will help to demystify some of the apparent complexities of education and enable readers to appreciate the significance of their own experience and aspirations. As ideas in education and their implications become more accessible, so there will be wider recognition of the potential for major improvements when informed people and organisations work together collaboratively.

Part I sets the scene by looking at the role of public education seen from different perspectives while Part II examines the educational and political context in which comprehensive education was established. It includes references to research and events whose significance for today is often overlooked. Part III is concerned with how non-selective principles can be transformed into effective practice whilst Part IV draws on experiences at a specific school to examine the process of establishing an appropriate environment and ethos in all aspects of a school's life. Part V describes a sustained attempt to change the course of this school and analyses the nature and significance of the attacks and responses to them. Finally, Part VI relates concepts and experiences already considered to current issues and identifies priorities for campaigning.

I
SETTING THE SCENE:
political, historical and social influences

1
Role of Public Education

Public education has evolved, and continues to evolve, under the influence of powerful forces representing differing, and often opposing, views of the role of education in society. As a result there are anomalies and inconsistencies which make it easy to misunderstand issues and thus to misjudge strategies and tactics for advance. Education legislation since 1979 provides a powerful incentive to work for deeper public awareness of key issues and this introductory chapter aims to uncover some underlying principles.

Ideas and ideals

Societies develop systems of education to support their economic and political objectives. Throughout the period of state education in Britain the tenets and requirements of the capitalist system have had a major influence in our schools and institutions — but not an unchallenged one.

Nineteenth-century mining community

A village classroom, one summer day in 1876, may seem a remote spot from which to commence an examination of the aim and purpose of public education. In fact, it could hardly be more revealing:

'OH HAPPY ENGLISH CHILDREN!' was a song taught to the school children of Medomsley, a Durham pit village, on 19th July 1876. Inspectors of schools had instructed that eight new songs were to be learnt every term and this was one of them. That summer morning singing may have sounded like a music lesson but it was not; the music was merely the medium, the words were what mattered and their message was about social stability.

This is the opening paragraph of a fascinating article ' "Oh Happy English Children!": Coal, Class and Education in the North East' which appeared in *Past and Present* (Colls, 1976:75). The article describes how, in the first half of the 19th century, miners educated their own children. This was much to the alarm of the coal owners such as Lord Londonderry until help arrived in the form of village schools urgently introduced by the authorities. Colls explains:

> 'Knowledge is Power' headed the frontispiece of *The Miners' Advocate* and there we have it: while owners' education after 1844 was taught to deprive power, miners' self-education before 1844 was taught to attain power. (p 77)

The author notes:

> The coalfield schools which first shuffled into existence during the 1850s and after ... were in fact about the business of re-education; they constituted a massive exercise in trying to shift the nascent loyalties of children away from the community which would nurture them and the men and women who had borne them. (p 75)

Just before the coalfield schools 'shuffled into existence', Seymour Tremenheere, the Children's Employment Commissioner for the district could find only two colliery owners who were attempting to fulfil the approved aims for education in their communities:

> Londonderry was praised for his educational projects toward 'enlightening and forming the minds of the rising generation'. (p 94)

while:

> Lady Londonderry has good schools established in all her collieries ... Her workpeople have never struck for wages; [her schools] are the leaven by which the mass are kept civil, obedient and well conducted. (p 96)

Colls refers to widespread fears among the better off:

> A mellowing bourgeois generation ... frightened itself ... into visions of a revolution which was not its own. (p 97)

He goes on to show that public education was meeting any such challenge with efficiency:

> Popular education ... was factual, utilitarian and harmless. 'Useful Knowledge' was re-defined for the pit community into lists of memorized facts; immediate relevance was replaced by formal categories of scholarship taught at the lowest level; Labour Value and the Rights of Men were replaced by 'Object Lessons' on Autumn and A Tree, and morality lessons on carelessness and industry. (p 97)

'Formal categories of scholarship' presumably meant the three R's with relevance confined to mundane and subservient activities. Relevance as an abstract expression is meaningless, as we must always ask 'relevance for what and for whom?' Colls summarises the situation:

> The collieries' 'Happy English Children' were the unwitting actors in a grand design to improve efficiency, break 'Idle Monday', pacify a troubled district, erode cultural loyalties and, as Lady Londonderry was promised, to see 'a more intelligent and efficient body of workpeople springing up around you'. Such was the motive and the policy of education in the colliery districts of Northumberland and Durham up to 1870 and beyond it. (p 98)

Today, social and political situations are outwardly different but there remain many parallels. For example, phrases like 'intelligent and efficient' are subject to interpretation according to context just as they were a century and a half ago. Conservative governments in the 1980s and '90s also believed that education must play a key role in creating appropriate attitudes and conditions for the type of economic and social relations which they saw as appropriate to a market economy. Proponents of their Education Acts were, therefore, also about the business of re-education. Apparently worthy aims to improve standards and efficiency must always be examined critically to see whether the methods proposed are in the interests of all young people or only of a privileged minority.

The Times *(1854) and* Sunday Telegraph *(1979)*

The Times newspaper, in 1854, believed in straight speaking. A leading article in that year, reproduced in full by Paul Corrigan (1979), urged an end to disputes about the respective role of church and state in education. This formed part of an influential campaign stressing the necessity for universal public education as an antidote to revolutionary ideas among the people:

> While we are disputing which ought to be considered the most beneficial system of education, we leave the great mass of the people to be influenced and formed

by the very worst possible teachers. Certain teachers, indeed, could be called instructors for evil ... In 1850 Harney's *Red Republican* has published in full 'the Communist Manifesto' supporting every revolutionary movement against the existing social and political order of things, and calling on working men of all countries to unite; the National Reform League was campaigning for nationalisation of land, atheism was being actively propagated. In the very heart of the apparently well-ordered community enough evil teaching was going on to startle, if not alarm, the most firm-minded. Systems the most destructive of the peace, the happiness and the virtue of society, are boldly, perseveringly, and without let or hindrance, openly taught and recommended to the acceptance of people with great zeal, if not with great ability. (p 31)

The Times saw the way forward in terms remarkably similar to the underlying assumptions of much of the legislation on education and training appearing in the 1980s. Only the words and jargon are different:

Let the wise and the good, offer to the people a beneficial education in place of this abominable teacher. (p 32)

A free translation of the last sentence might have read: 'Let the landowners and capitalists offer to the working class an education beneficial to the former in place of the dangerous ideas being picked up by working people from informal education in their own communities, workplaces and associations.' Those in the last century in positions of power and influence who supported the provision of education by the state had a clear class perspective. They called publicly for the indoctrination of bourgeois values to induce acceptable (ie docile) attitudes by the working class and to ensure maintenance of the economic and social order. Today, explicit appeals to class solidarity are rarely necessary and Conservative cabinet ministers with no experience of state schools, either through their own or their children's education, are served and supported by senior civil servants many with similar backgrounds. They know little of the needs of the majority of the young people in our state schools and even less of their untapped potential. Nevertheless, they fear unknown consequences if this talent is encouraged to develop to the full. From time to time, however, events sharply increase people's political awareness and understanding.

One such period was the so-called 'winter of discontent' in 1978/9 which involved workers in many industries. Peregrine Worsthorne, then associate editor of the *Sunday Telegraph* (1979), wrote a leading article which touched on education:

What possible justification can there be in allowing mere porters and caretakers, who can contribute so little, to interfere in the work of surgeons and teachers, who contribute so much.

In the following week, *Labour Weekly* (1979), later closed down as an 'economy measure', drew attention to the article and referred to Worsthorne's views:

He worries that this blunt language might embarrass some of his more 'socially sensitive' readers who believe that 'even porters and caretakers' deserve to be treated with respect. 'Fine' he says, 'so long as these courtesies do not disguise the truth: that surgeons are *superior* to porters and caretakers *inferior* to teachers' [his words and emphasis].'In the old days' says Mr. Worsthorne, 'this would not have needed saying, since porters and caretakers knew their place'. If these distinctions are blurred, he says, there is a danger that 'the populace starts getting delusions of grandeur, and the elite delusions of inadequacy' ... This can only be put right when those in positions of power and influence 'once again develop the will to rule, which in turn can happen only when they are convinced, as their predecessors once were, of their right to rule'.

Affinities with *The Times* leader a century earlier stand out clearly whilst, in recent years, the actions of a succession of ministers responsible for education and youth and adult training schemes demonstrated that the 'will to rule' had not lost momentum.

Elementary Education Bill

The Elementary Education Bill of 1870 marked an important step forward. It provided for publicly funded school places where existing provision, mainly by the churches, was inadequate. This was the first step towards the establishment of universal, free and compulsory elementary education finally achieved with the Education Act of 1902. The 1870 Act was introduced into the House of Commons by W E Forster whose speech is published in full in J Stuart Maclure's (1968) *Education Documents of England and Wales 1816-1967.* Despite its undoubted achievements, the state scheme was confined to the elementary education 'chiefly of the working classes' (p 102). A limited objective certainly but no deterrent to subsequent campaigning which led eventually to 'secondary education for all' in the Education Act of 1944[1]. After describing the provisions of his Act, Forster stated his priorities in the concluding part of his speech.

Three matters of national importance depended 'upon the speedy provision of elementary education'. Firstly:

> Our industrial prosperity ... If we leave our work-folk any longer unskilled, notwithstanding their strong sinews and determined energy, they will become over-matched in the competition of the world. (p 104)

Secondly:

> Our national power. Civilized communities throughout the world are massing themselves together, each mass being measured by its force; and if we are to hold our position among men of our own race or among the nations of the world we must make up the smallness of our numbers by increasing the intellectual force of the individual. (p 105)

In other words, elementary education will provide the basis for strengthening our military effectiveness to protect and expand our dominant position among the world's imperialist powers. Forster's third concern was to maintain:

> The good, the safe working of our constitutional system ... Now that we have given them political power we must not wait any longer to give them education. (pp 104-105)

Forster's concerns were widely held.[2] Fears of social unrest and even revolution were prevalent and the words 'we' and 'them' place in perspective any thoughts that public education arose chiefly as the result of a benign liberalism on the part of those who wished to share their own opportunity for a fuller and richer life with the less fortunate. Frank Booton (1985), in a book entitled *Studies in Social Education: Work with Youth 1860-1890*, describes a continuous public debate for fifty years concerning what to do with the 'working classes'. He explains that liberal minds were much exercised with the question of their 'improvement'. Forster's considerations rarely come to the attention of student teachers where initial training courses now have time for only a few hours, if any, on the history of education.[3] When I commenced my post-graduate course for a teaching certificate in 1949, history of education was a main subject. Our text book contained summaries of the main provisions of the 1870 Act but no mention of Forster's speech. This was typical of the time so perhaps the issues were considered unsuitable or, at least, irrelevant topics for those about to enter the public education service. Today, the education system is seen as necessary to ensure 'safe working' for a social system with ever widening disparities between the hopes and expectations of the privileged and those for whom the prospect of satisfying work and job security are but a dream.

Educational opportunities for working people today are vastly more extensive than envisaged in 1870. They have been won by determined and organised effort and must be continually defended and extended. The Education Reform Act of 1988 was intended as a mechanism to reintroduce selection in education but in less direct ways than through a prescribed selection process. Earlier attempts to reimpose selective schools at Solihull and elsewhere in the early 1980s were successfully resisted by the strength of popular opposition. Indeed, in 1983, the parents of Solihull twice rejected schemes to bring back grammar schools. The ill-fated City Technical College (CTC) scheme, later abandoned, and the slow take-up of grant maintained status (opting out) were obvious attempts to introduce a multi-tier system of schools. However, the more 'popular' proposals for local management of schools (LMS) and for open enrolment require equal scrutiny and awareness. The former is portrayed as letting those most closely involved take the decisions and the latter as widening parental choice. These may sound progressive but contain provisions which have the potential to be even more effective in differentiating students and causing anxiety to teachers who can no longer be assured that their conditions of service, prospects for promotion and job security are negotiated and monitored democratically both nationally and at local authority level. Unlike the CTC and grant maintained schemes, LMS applies to almost all schools and any negative tendencies will be widespread (Chapter 17).

Two headteachers

Teachers, heads and governors have contrasting views of the aims of the public education service and individuals can have considerable influence. Here is a reference in full for a student who left a secondary modern school in Sunderland in July 1968, one year before it was amalgamated to form part of a new comprehensive school:

> The above pupil has followed for four years a course of remedial instruction as befits his intelligence, ability and attainment. His health is good. I would recommend him for work of a practical and repetitive kind and would be pleased to answer any specific enquiries about him.

We can be pleased that the young man's health was good but there is no doubt about his position in society as perceived by his headteacher. An extreme example, no doubt, but used here to draw attention to the countless opportunities in school life — through comments, attitudes or the provision of educational opportunities for selected students only — to convey to many young people, especially of working class, and/or Afro-Caribbean background, a view of their place in society. On the other hand, aims have nowhere been better and more succinctly set out than by P E Daunt (1975), former headteacher of a comprehensive school in Sussex. In his book *Comprehensive Values* he puts forward as a 'guiding and defining principle of comprehensive education', the view that:

> The education of all children is held to be intrinsically of equal value. (p 16)

Such a principle should apply throughout the public education service and is the criterion by which each clause of government legislation needs to be judged.

Her Majesty's Inspectors

In September 1993 the recently established and powerful quango Ofsted (the Office for Standards in Education) licensed its first competitive inspection teams. Prior to that (indeed since 1839) the performance of schools was monitored through liaison and inspection by a group known as Her Majesty's Inspectors. Over the years their views and opinions helped to determine aims and objectives and their title was meant to imply independence from the Department for Education and its predecessors. More realistically, it identified HMIs, as they were popularly known, as an influential force in the monitoring and control of state education. HMIs have drawn attention to deficiencies in buildings, staffing and resources, and have been concerned for the welfare of school students. To some degree they championed the cause of more relevant and purposeful teaching and certainly kept a close eye on the transmission of moral and political values. Far from being independent, however, their own perspectives, which naturally influenced their opinions, drew heavily on the consensus approach of senior members of the civil service. In the mid-1970s the Department of Education and Science (1977) published the first of a series of 'Matters for Discussion' booklets produced by the inspectorate. Its title was *Ten Good Schools: A Secondary School Enquiry* and the introduction commences:

> This informal small-scale survey of some aspects of the life and work of ten secondary schools was carried out in the summer term of 1975 to test whether generalisations could be made about the factors that contribute to success in secondary education. (p 5)

This worthy aim led one to read on expectantly but, sadly, hopes were not fulfilled. In highlighting some of the 'characteristics that might be emulated' in one unidentified school 'deemed to be successful', the inspectors state:

> It would be difficult to single out for particular appraisal any one aspect of the school. Indeed the school's strength and character seem largely to lie in the overall evenness of its virtues: the commonsense, goodwill, decency, moderation, patience and tolerance that control everyone's actions. If nothing hits the heights spectacularly, nothing approaches anywhere near the depths: and the whole commands great respect and considerable admiration. (p 12)

The words are more subtle than those used in the last century but sentiments are strikingly similar implying precisely the same docility and acceptance of authority as was envisaged by many who supported the Education Act of 1870. If 'Knowledge is Power', as *The Miners' Advocate* proclaimed, then students at this school were missing out. 'Overall evenness' is a recipe for being exploited, not for human progress; school students should be entitled to learn that all who have succeeded in making a contribution, however small, towards a better society have done so through collaboration and organisation, through education and campaigning, and through perseverance in the face of indifference or hostility. Old style HMIs were not just inspectors in a narrow sense of the term. Part of their brief was to draw the attention of teachers and administrators to examples of good practice in the schools they visited. Whilst they may have been successful in certain fields, the booklet contains several commendations which reflect highly questionable values. For example, in a second comprehensive school, there is an even more explicit comment on the importance attached to conformity by school students and thus, also, by their parents:

> The success of the school is attributable to the well-ordered environment established as a result of a consensus of outlook of staff and pupils: there is an absence of tension because all know the objectives and agree upon them. Under the leadership of the headmaster, a stable and exceptionally competent staff keep their work under critical review: they are imaginative and flexible in outlook and

willing to adapt, yet clear that professional standards must be maintained. In consequence, the needs of all types of pupil are given proper consideration: the opportunities for the ablest and the interested to develop their talents are good and the nonconformists are treated with a firm sympathy which seeks to help them to achieve the best of which they are capable. (p 10)

Here, conformity is to be with 'professional' values though others might infer that what is meant is 'conservative and conventional'. The patronising attitude to non-conformists could hardly be put more clearly and one may ask: how many attributes, seen as essential by many in adult life for personal fulfilment as well as social and political advance, come under this classification in our schools? The views of HMIs therefore, whilst worthy of scrutiny and consideration, were seriously limited as indicators of what should be done in a local or national situation. But whatever doubts there may have been about HMIs, it is incredible that they should have been replaced by market orientated teams responsible only to a quango and linked with schools only for the few days of an inspection.

Southall Black Sisters

There is no shortage of evidence to show that racism is widespread in education taking various forms which mirror the wider context. As well as direct racism through patronising remarks, threat, harassment and negative assumptions about learning prospects, it is necessary to critically examine apparently positive initiatives such as multiracial (or multicultural) education and anti-racist policies. However well intentioned, many — perhaps most — contain racial assumptions. Southall Black Sisters (1990) make the point in *Against the Grain* a publication (not specifically concerned with education) prepared to mark their tenth anniversary:

> We have always argued that we will not remain confined within our 'traditions' and 'culture'. Today in the public mind they are narrowing even more so that the only legitimate identity is a newly constructed religious one. (p 4)

A contributor, Gita Sahgal, reports an early encounter with a journalist:

> Was she not aware that the black women didn't wish to be regarded as persons with problems? ... That was social worker speak and they were not going to be pathologised by the state. (p 14)

The number of black children in state schools categorised as having learning difficulties is a source of considerable concern to many black parents but Hannah Siddiqui sees no solution in segregated schools:

> Separate schools seek to segregate and control my sexuality, limit my world vision and curb my aspirations, to destroy my chances of higher education or of a chosen career. Indoctrination which prepares me for my role as a good Muslim wife and a mother. A school which keeps me in ignorance of the alternatives. (p 62)

She adds:

> The fundamentalists are supported by the state, the multiculturalist and the liberal anti-racist lobby. (p 62)

It is impossible, with two or three quotations, to do justice to this illuminating publication which, amongst other themes, shows how easy it is, even for people of goodwill, to accept regressive stereotyping.

Research studies show that a relatively high proportion of black school students are in the bottom streams of comprehensive schools where these exist and that numbers in so-called 'pupil referral units' for students with behavioural problems are unduly weighted with black students. An early authoritative report from Nottinghamshire County Council Education Department *Pupil Exclusions from Nottingham Secondary Schools* (Nottinghamshire, 1991) covers the school year 1989/90. It shows that although only 3.2% of the secondary school population was classed as Afro-Caribbean, this group accounted for almost 28% of all exclusions (p 27). Compared with a previous survey in 1988, the results show that 'the proportion of exclusions involving black children has increased' (p 28). Patsy Hunter, parent of a former school student in Nottingham and active in the city's Afro-Caribbean Family and Friends Centre, believes 'Black families now feel desperate about the apparent failure of the state education system' (*The Times Educational Supplement*, 1991b). Maureen Stone (1995) in her sociological study *The Education of the Black Child in Britain* also addressed this theme:

> The community, parents and children are sufficient guardians of the black cultural inheritance. Schools have to be about something else ... if you really want to reduce educational and racial inequality, the best way is by providing your pupils with the skills and knowledge they need to make their own way in the society in which they live. (p 6)

She rightly adds:

> This is a hopeful message, and an encouraging one. (p 6)

So much in this field needs to be done and the number of teachers fully committed is still much too small. They work at best in an indifferent environment and need massive support if a major change in outlook is to be achieved. In 1990, in the final Statutory Orders laid before Parliament for National Curriculum English, all references in the English Working Group's recommendations that school students should read from 'a range of cultures' were cut from the statements of attainment. *The Times Educational Supplement* (1990a) reported that efforts to force a debate were blocked by government whips while the government also announced changes in regulations under of the 1966 Local Government Act which allowed local authorities to fund a range of initiatives in multicultural education. As *The Times Educational Supplement* (1990b) reported: 'Money will no longer be given for programmes aimed at raising achievement through multicultural approaches'.[4] In a further report (*The Times Educational Supplement*, 1990c) it was confirmed that race advisory posts may be scrapped and that 'money will in future only be available for promoting the use of English. Schools and local authorities will have to compete for money on the basis of clearly defined short-term projects which they must then monitor'. By 1996 funding was part of the Single Regeneration Budget of local authorities and restricted mainly to providing teachers of English as a second language. However, the new Labour government has pledged itself to reverse the latest round of Conservative cuts in funding.

Continuing racist and fascist actions provide a stark reminder that the task of furthering the progressive aims of our public education system must encompass the needs and aspirations of all its citizens.

History and sociology of education

The strands of thought considered so far represent a selection of items which I have found helpful in clarifying thoughts and ideas. They are, of course, a very selective sample but help to demonstrate that study of the history of education is essential for a realistic understanding of the present. In this respect, Professor Simon's four-volume *Studies in the History of Education* (Simon, 1965, 1974a, 1974b and 1991) are outstanding in scholarship and readability. They provide both a broad sweep of the ideas and changes that have occurred during the period and also much revealing and illuminating detail. For example, in the second volume, *Education and the Labour Movement 1870-1920*, the author shows that the movement fought to abolish fees, humanise school discipline and further the development of rational and secular education; it also led campaigns to improve the health and social conditions of the young. Not surprisingly, however, Simon notes that:

> Objectives were rarely fully gained, but it was this movement which began to force the pace of educational development. (p 161)

In recent years the pace has been forced from a different direction and to an extent previously undreamed of. With little regard for the long term needs of the majority of school students, much recent legislation reintroduces inequalities and anomalies which are becoming increasingly visible both to professionals and to the public. The main thrust of current policy fails to address itself to the demands of an education based on the equal value of each child and student.

Study of the sociology of education provides further insight into ideas and ideals though there are pitfalls and lines of thinking to be avoided. Maurice Levitas (1974), formerly a senior lecturer in the sociology of education, provides an informative critique in his book *Marxist Perspectives in the Sociology of Education*. He notes that culture can be defined as the whole way of life of an entire society with its 'elements of values, beliefs, knowledge, mutual expectation, interaction within and between institutions' (p 5). Noting, also, that human beings are 'capable of coping with a wide and changing range of activities' he emphasises that the combination of the two ideas — a high human capacity for variation in response together with the culture concept — should help teachers to:

> take a constructively optimistic standpoint in regard to the educability of children. (p 6)

He draws attention to a requirement for successful teaching:

> What is transmitted to children, deliberately and unconsciously, by people, by their surroundings, by events, and what is acquired by them, is their culture. Having all become carriers of the culture of their society, they consolidate from each other, in their play and other forms of peer group interaction, that culture. Thus it follows that teaching, to be effective, must have regard for culture already acquired. (p 7)

Nevertheless he sharply criticises ideas of the so-called 'relativists' and their 'new directions' in sociology. Their ideas, fashionable in some academic quarters from the early 1970s, claimed that narrow cultural horizons among working class students and restricted codes of language (involving a limited range of words and concepts) were to be treated as equally valid with what were described as 'middle class' modes of thought and expression. Teachers, portrayed as 'middle class', were urged not to deprive students of their 'own' culture.

Such thinking led some well-meaning teachers, anxious not to blindly assume the validity of their own values, to restrict the educational opportunities of working class students by setting learning tasks within narrow cultural and intellectual limits. Such a policy further handicapped those it was supposed to help and at the same time, as Levitas points out, gave credence to streaming and other forms of selection. Certainly, all educators must start from where their learners are, recognise the contribution each can make and in no way destroy feelings of security. But a prime aim of education must be to challenge and extend experiences and to develop skills and critical faculties — a theme developed in later chapters.

Power and influence

Progressive aims can only become realities if they are supported with the means to defend gains and implement development. Ultimate authority is based on popular support yet for long periods, not least in the post-war decades, the mechanism of control of the public education service was rarely discussed explicitly by those working for its advancement. No matter how convincing the arguments for education of equal value, first steps to its realisation must be to assess the strengths and weaknesses of the forces concerned and to organise support for action. Here, after reference to the role of parents and to the influence and needs of school students, we look at the part played as major supporters of public education by trade unions and the Labour Party.

Parents

Parents come from all parts of the class and social spectrum. As the process of decision making by market forces has been promoted and gathered momentum, the concerns and aspirations of the influential have had an increasing effect at all levels of policy making. The majority of parents are not, however, members of organised groups except when an issue such as a proposed school closure leads to local action. The involvement, influence and contribution of parents is discussed, both explicitly and implicitly, throughout the book.

School students

School students, understandably, have little collective power, although the effect of their day to day interaction with their teachers is not to be under-estimated. Occasionally a school council with elected student members has an opportunity to participate in important matters affecting conditions of work and curriculum though it is significant that the Education (No 2) Act of 1986 required the removal of student governors in the few cases where they existed. Various bodies are directly involved in the welfare of school students. These range from local education authorities, governing bodies and teacher unions to parent-teacher associations, broadly based organisations such as advice centres and the Council for Civil Liberties and pressure groups such as the highly successful Society of Teachers Opposed to Physical Punishment.[5] The Education Reform Act had nothing to say on the welfare of school students though, ultimately, parents have recourse to the courts. However, this in no way replaces the need for recognised conditions and entitlement for students in school, a function undertaken among adults by trade unions and professional associations. Conditions vary greatly from school to school and between local authorities but the following points are worthy of consideration by all who are in positions of responsibility:

- Are prospects for some students pre-determined by selection into streams and bands and how are such decisions arrived at? Almost invariably such practices perpetuate educational inequalities.
- Are certain subjects and options, particularly in the later stages of secondary school, denied to students who are considered unsuitable and what recourse has a parent to appeal? The original entitlement of almost all school students to the national curriculum was a positive feature in this respect but was soon whittled away.
- Are there instances of humiliating or degrading punishment? Fortunately these are much rarer since the abolition of corporal punishment which became effective in state schools from August 1987.
- Are the arrangements for considering serious disciplinary matters

scrupulously fair and impartial? The 1986 Education (No. 2) Act required local authorities to establish safeguarding procedures for parents and teachers before a suspension is confirmed. All arrangements need to be monitored and linked to a national code for the promotion of good order in school[6] which, in turn, will require effective and well resourced help and guidance for parents and young people when difficulties arise.

- Is there adequate shelter during school breaks in cold and windy weather?
- Do students receive excessive amounts of compulsory homework with varying penalties for default?
- Do school clothing requirements imply institutional and impersonal attitudes? Historically, uniforms stemmed from the public schools where they supported class based social attitudes. Required more generally they can place individual students and parents under moral and financial pressure and, as a result of the enforcement process, adversely affect teacher-student relationships.[7]

There is a lack of public awareness of many of these issues and the examples show that much remains to be done.

Trade union movement

The Trades Union Congress has a small general education department which has produced constructive documents on a range of educational matters. The following example is taken from its evidence to the Newsom Inquiry into the education of 13 to 16 year olds of 'average or less than average ability' (Trades Union Congress, 1962):[8]

> Their education ... must assume that their environment can be changed, and will inevitably change significantly during the lifetime of today's young people.
> (p 166)

The point is still relevant. 'Can be changed' implies organising and acting corporately, an activity which certainly does not figure in national curriculum thinking. Notes of comment submitted by the Trade Union Congress (1977) on the Labour government's consultative Green Paper *Education in Schools* continued the theme:

> The schools are failing to raise the quality of democratic life by not providing the foundation young people need to understand the issues: and, equally important,

to develop the skills they need to participate in the decision making processes that already exist in their communities and are developing in the workplace. The truth is that most young people leave school politically and economically illiterate. (p 347)

The TUC identified as 'the greatest single issue':

> To identify the proper role for schools in preparing young people to play their part in maintaining social progress ... In the TUC's view the next generation has a right to demand that they are properly equipped to meet such challenges not least in respect of being able to make accountable those political, industrial and general economic forces which shape their lives. (p 347)

The Trades Union Congress (1980) approved a motion moved by the National Union of Teachers which referred to the 'Government's attempt to gain central control of educational spending and of the curriculum' and instructed its General Council to form an alliance 'similar to that which brought about the 1944 Education Act' (p 453). A year later this initiative became The Educational Alliance involving thirty affiliated unions and other organisations such as the Campaign for the Advancement of State Education (CASE). The Alliance operated with a measure of success in some regions but has never had the impact of the Council for Educational Advance set up in 1942 with the TUC as a major partner in an active campaign to raise public awareness prior to the introduction of the 1944 Education Act. In 1991, the TUC withdrew its servicing and convening role as part of a series of economy measures, and the Alliance agreed to merge with the still functioning Council for Educational Advance. In the north east in 1993 the organisation held a training day on how to campaign against school opt-out proposals and ran successful courses for school governor trade unionists providing a distinctive input and generating a corresponding response. Clearly there is an important role for such activities.

The TUC, as part of its campaign around the Education Reform Bill (the basis of the 1988 Act), produced several issues of 'Education Briefing' and unions such as the National Association of Local Government Officers (NALGO) and the National Union of Public Employees (NUPE), both now part of UNISON, produced training courses and excellent briefing packs on the implications for their members of the Education Reform Act. Useful as these various developments were, however, it remains a fact that, overall, there has been little effective trade union influence, even in periods of a Labour government, on the daily life and work of the schools and the transmission of values in the public education system.

National Union of Teachers

Teacher unions have exercised considerable influence on the aims and practice of public education. They are industrial unions in the sense that they are based on a single 'industry' and this is one of their main sources of strength. Some of this influence is clearly at risk in so far as local management of schools and grant maintained status (opting out) may result in a change to 'company' bargaining based on individual schools. The oldest of the teacher unions is the National Union of Teachers which was established in 1870 as the National Union of Elementary Teachers (dropping 'elementary' in 1888). Until the amalgamation of the National Association of Schoolmasters and the Union of Women Teachers to form the NASUWT in the early 1970s, the NUT was the only union open to all teachers, including headteachers, without distinction of sex, professional status or type of state school taught in. For over two decades the union conference has on several occasions instructed its executive to explore possibilities of amalgamation with the NASUWT the other TUC affiliated teacher union but so far, regrettably, without success.

Throughout its history the NUT has demonstrated concern for the education service as a whole which it has seen as important for the interests of its members as well as essential in its own right. In this respect the NUT has campaigned for comprehensive education, nursery schools, smaller classes and the provision of adequate resources of manpower and materials. In 1970 its Conference voted to affiliate to the TUC — a considerable achievement when one considers the political affiliations of teachers at that time. A survey undertaken by *The Times Educational Supplement* and *The Times Higher Education Supplement* (1974) entitled 'Teachers in the British General Election of October 1974' showed that while Labour obtained 39% of the vote nationally, only 26% of teachers voted for them. The survey also considered the replies of teachers to a number of key questions including their opinion on the elimination of grammar schools (an essential part of Labour's policy as comprehensive education was extended). 70% were opposed to this reform and the survey commented:

It really is a massive vote, by all sectors of the profession, against one of the principal trends of educational policy over the last ten years. (p 19)

A similar number (71%) considered the raising of the school leaving age to be a mistake. This was another Labour backed reform which, at the time, had just seen the first full year groups staying on to age 16. The authors of the survey conclude:

> We are dealing with a profoundly Conservative profession. It is also a conservative one. Not only does it have a tendency to vote Conservative in preference to any other party, but it also strongly resists change. (p 33)

No doubt the 1997 general election would yield a very different result. Six weeks before that election a poll carried out for the NUT and reported, together with other survey material, in *The Times Educational Supplement* (1997a) showed 59 per cent of teachers intending to vote Labour compared with 49 per cent of the general public. Support for the Conservatives among teachers was half that of the public. Nevertheless, in 1970, the NUT, despite a more progressive than average membership, risked loss of membership on affiliating to the TUC though in the event this proved to be very small.

Annual Conferences of the NUT have been noted for free expression of opinion and the ability of delegates to mete out summary justice, through balloting, if they detect complacency or inefficiency in actions and recommendations from the Executive. Each conference, however, has its share of negative issues and comments which remind all committed to the advancement of state education that there is no cause for complacency. The Conference of 1978, for example, revealed important constraints on union policy making. Its newspaper *The Teacher* (1978a) reported a debate concerning control of the curriculum. One delegate proposed an amendment which:

> instructed the Executive to initiate and participate in a TUC inquiry into the state of education ... It was not good enough for teachers to isolate themselves from the trade union movement and say that what was taught in schools was their exclusive preserve.

This seemed straightforward enough but another delegate replied:

> It would be in total contradiction of Union policy to agree to the call for a TUC inquiry. The basic, fundamental point is that we as the professionals are the only ones competent to make curricular decisions.

Similar viewpoints had been widely and strongly held by many teachers for decades. It was rarely challenged from inside or outside the education service until the arrival of the Conservative government of 1979. An executive member, opposing the amendment, endorsed the thinking:

> The Union has experienced the greatest difficulties with the TUC education committee, particularly over matters which were Union policy, and the General Council were the last people the Union should go to on the basis of their past performance on educational issues.

A sweeping statement in view of the TUC's longstanding support for state education but the amendment was none the less defeated. It was not the only example that year of antipathy to associating too closely with TUC policies. Under a headline in the same issue of *The Teacher* 'School Campaigns against Race Hatred Approved' a delegate, arguing that the Union's policies on racism were not effective enough, commented: 'It was lamentable that the Union could not even support the TUC policy on race'. In its following edition *The Teacher* (1978b) gave an account of a debate on women at work. The report commences 'Conference decided not to support the TUC charter for women at work after it was warned that such support would tear the Union apart'. Although there were strong voices in favour of support, the problem appeared to centre around the right to family planning and abortion which was included in the charter.[9]

These examples illustrate problems, help to guard against complacency and emphasise the need for effective organisation. In contrast to such difficulties most NUT conferences also produced significant achievements. During the 1980s, members successfully challenged traditional attitudes in a variety of policy areas. At the 1982 Conference, for example, a motion was carried which not only called for the abolition of corporal punishment but also instructed the Executive to mount a campaign on the issue. This welcome development was in sharp contrast to the situation four years earlier when the *Sunday Telegraph* (1978) could report from the Annual Conference of the National Association of Schoolmasters Union of Women Teachers:

> A TUC policy document calling on the Government to ban the cane in schools in England and Wales has been withdrawn for discussion as a result of protests by the teachers' unions which had not been consulted.

Successive conferences have supported progressive policies on salaries, conditions of service, inter-union cooperation and a wide range of educational issues which contribute to the unity of the service and its members. Members have been willing to take industrial action in the principled support of union policies and, despite limitations at times arising from over-cautious leadership on the one hand and divisive ultra-left activities on the other, solidarity has been of a high order helping to strengthen support and deepen understanding of the issues among both teachers and the wider public.

Labour Party

At several periods during this century the Labour Party campaigned for and provided schools and resources on a reasonably generous scale at both national and local level. All too often, however, Labour saw such developments as the near completion of the job instead of the basis for a start and for decades there has been an urgent need to tackle the key question of the transmission of values. Apart from the General Strike, the year 1926 should be notable in labour history for the education motion which was debated at the party conference (Labour Party, 1926). Among other matters, it called for a Workers' Committee of Inquiry:

(b) to prepare recommendations on the best methods of teaching and of securing true discipline in school.

(c) To prepare a report as to how far the present books, pictures and other materials used in schools, and the predominant methods of teaching and disciplining children, foster a bourgeois psychology, militarism and imperialism: and as to how far, under a workers' administration, this might be counteracted and a proletarian attitude towards an outlook on life might be cultivated.

This was to be the last occasion for over fifty years at which a motion concerned with what went on within schools was debated at the Labour Party conference. Not until 1980, in which a composite motion was passed containing a one line commitment to abolish corporal punishment, was a motion of this kind to appear again. No such errors of omission were made by Conservative governments after Sir Keith Joseph became Secretary of State for Education and Science in 1981. For example, concerns expressed in the 1926 resolution apply with equal force to the government's advice to the working group it set up to prepare the scheme for history in the national curriculum. This advice aimed to foster ideas in school students justifying Britain's imperialist role in history though naturally the word 'imperialism' was not used. In this case the worst was avoided thanks to a mainly educational lobby but, as the Northern Region Education Alliance pointed out in its submission on the working group's interim report 'There is little evidence that school students will learn that men and women, corporately campaigning and organising together, have shaped the course of history and are doing so today'.[10]

Such considerations were missing, too, in the Labour Party's (1993) Green Paper *Opening Doors to a Learning Society* although this discussion document contained general statements worthy of support. For example all will agree that 'At the heart of effective learning and teaching is the quality of the curriculum' (para 4.17) but the question of what is meant by quality is not discussed. Any organisation claiming a meaningful influence on the aims and values of popular education must be actively involved at national and local level on matters which affect these issues as well as on organisation, accountability, provision and resources. Resources are not discussed at all in the Green Paper nor do comprehensive schools receive a single mention! Since then, new plans, often ambiguous with regard to selection, were outlined in *Diversity and Excellence* (Labour Party, 1995) and, soon after the general election, in the White Paper *Excellence in Schools* (Department for Education and Employment, 1997). These embrace some of the most divisive actions of Conservative governments in recent years.

First-class education for all

As we shall see in future chapters, the arrival of comprehensive education called into question many educational, social and political assumptions. Achievements by the schools gained wide public support but attacks followed quickly in an attempt to turn this support against key features of the new development. Much of the opposition was based on rumour and innuendo although some was associated with genuine problems arising from such a radical change.[11] The attacks were only partially successful as the rejection of Solihull's plans to reintroduce selection showed but, inevitably, there was some loss of confidence and the threat remains very real. Indeed education legislation from the 1980s was designed to replace the comprehensive aim of a first class education for all, regardless of background, with a shopping list of schools providing varying facilities and prospects for their 'products' (ie the young people who attend them). A centralised and authoritarian method of control was the centre piece of policy despite a veneer of parental choice, parent governors and local management of schools. Accompanied by insensitive criticism of teachers and teaching methods such policies inevitably restrict opportunities for genuine learning by the majority of school students and especially those with working class backgrounds.

Indeed, despite all the advances in state education since 1870, there has been a lack of vigilance in defending important gains, and weaknesses in nurturing and extending them. As the 1970s unfolded, this neglect left state education vulnerable and exposed to the divisive intentions of the legislation of the 1980s and '90s. After a decade and a half of intense and systematic misrepresentation of its potential and significance for ordinary people, the strategy of Conservative governments was ever more clearly to dismantle and privatise state education. However, legislation for such a purpose is a flawed and imperfect instrument. It comes with a full quota of inconsistencies, impracticalities and injustice because it does not address the real needs of ordinary people. This leaves open the opportunity for effective action based on increased understanding by a wider public of educational principles and practice. The successful boycott of school testing in the summer of 1993 uniting teachers, parents, governors and school students is a good example.

Educational values have now become high profile and explicit but for much of the lifetime of state schooling it has been easy to present education as 'non-political' and a matter of consensus. It is necessary, therefore, to use every opportunity to open up awareness and understanding of the educational process including its political significance. State education is an achievement of the people and, whilst educational initiatives alone cannot bring about fundamental changes in society, the converse is also true: advances in working and social life, especially during an era of new technology, cannot proceed far without parallel developments in education. We need to understand and explain as widely as possible, therefore, precisely why state education is such an achievement and thus raise public expectations for the future.

We commence with a look at ideas of intelligence, ability and capacity for learning.

II
COMPREHENSIVE EDUCATION
IN CONTEXT

2

Human Abilities and the School System

For a generation of school students the system of schooling in this country was based, in part, on a theory of intelligence. Its best-known product was the 11-plus, an examination which dominated the educational prospects of individuals. Although the theory is long since discredited its influence on our education system continues today in the escalating moves towards greater selection both between and within schools. New ideas concerning human intelligence supported growing evidence from the classrooms that an overwhelming majority of young people were capable of surprising achievements in depth and understanding providing they had the opportunity and incentive. This chapter describes the metamorphosis in thinking which provided such a strong basis for the introduction of comprehensive education.

Intelligence

Growth of an idea

In 1905, a French researcher, Alfred Binet, published a set of thirty questions to be used with children from the age of three upwards. He tried out the questions and found that, on average, a five year old could answer so many, a seven year old rather more and so on. Then he took a step which was to have an unexpected and far reaching influence on generations of school children and their families. He defined a concept which he called mental age — and he 'measured' it. If a four year old answered as many questions correctly as the average number answered by five year olds then Binet said that this child had a mental age of five, a year in advance of its actual age. Other children had mental ages below their actual age. So began a succession of events which was to give a great impetus to all with inclinations to classify children at the drop of a hat. Over the years a succession of terms like 'slow', 'backward', 'two years retarded' and 'D-stream material' (as well as their positive counterparts) became everyday terms in school staffrooms and the wider educational environment. What's more their accuracy could be 'proved' — with a test! Enthusiasm for the tests abounded and, as early as 1914, the idea that Binet's questions measured inherited characteristics had been introduced although Binet, himself, reacted strongly against what he considered an unwarranted escalation of his idea. A statistical term called intelligence quotient or IQ, soon to be dreaded in homes throughout the country, entered the vocabulary. IQ compared mental and actual age as a percentage. For children who scored exactly the average score, their mental and actual ages were equal so their IQ's were 100 (ie mental age 100% of actual age).

Between the wars education above the age of eleven was provided mainly in elementary schools and fee paying grammar schools with local authority scholarships to the latter for those who could not afford the fees. Bradford, in 1919, was the first education authority to use mental tests and, by the 1930s, they were in widespread use as part of the procedure for choosing pupils for scholarships. They were more sophisticated than Binet's and claimed to measure IQ, with an IQ of about 125 necessary for success. The full intelligence testing story is a remarkable one with flawed concepts appearing to give the divisive system of elementary and grammar schools an educational, as opposed to political, justification. The use of IQ tests for scholarships was seen by many as a progressive move discriminating less against working class children than the methods they replaced. The latter usually included an English essay, a notoriously subjective and class-orientated task, in which children were asked to write on subjects such as going away on holiday which were beyond the experience of most working class families.[1] Then would follow an interview before the headmaster or headmistress and other senior teachers. The interviews were not confined to the child only as parents were interviewed separately, no doubt to check that they accepted the ethos of the grammar school and had at least a grounding in the social graces and conventions.

Secondary education for all

During the second world war political awareness increased in the armed services and among organised workers and demands for better deals in housing, social security and education were irresistible. In 1944 R A Butler introduced an Education Bill which guaranteed secondary education for all — but, in practice, provided in more than one kind of school. The grammar schools were perceived to have by far the highest status and offered straightforward entry to the more prestigious jobs. Entry to the grammar school, however, depended on successful negotiation of an academic hurdle. When I commenced my teacher training in 1949 the school leaving age had just been raised from 14 to 15 and the measurement of intelligence had become an industry. The extent of this industry is referred to by V A Krutetskii (1976) in *The Psychology of Mathematical Abilities in School Children*. His revealing account commences with a review of the nature of children's abilities in the light of Soviet psychological and educational research. In a chapter critically summarising foreign work on the subject, he quotes a United States author (Goslin, 1963):

> It appears that between 150 million and a quarter of a billion standardized ability tests of many different kinds are being administered annually in the United States by schools, colleges, business and industrial firms, and government agencies, including the military services ... (p 10)

Large numbers of primary school pupils entered for the 11-plus tests so named because the pupils transferred to secondary school in the September after their eleventh birthday but before reaching the age of twelve. Those with birthdays in the summer months were still only ten when they took the examination which many parents saw as crucial to their life chances. Certainly the disparity in provision and opportunity in the different types of school was immense and bicycles were among the more popular incentives offered for success in the examination by anxious and ambitious parents. From the earliest age children became aware of the importance of the hurdle which was to come. In contrast, in 1936, the Soviet Union passed a law prohibiting the use of intelligence and mental tests and the selection of school students. If, in Britain, IQ tests had been simply an episode in history they might not have had much relevance to education today. In fact, the theory which underpinned the selection process interacted with deep-rooted popular opinions that children were born 'bright', 'thick' or 'average'. As a result, even in the immediate post-war years, separate schooling was accepted without serious opposition.

The 1944 Education Act did not lack words of inspiration. As an impressionable student, the secondary system seemed to me at the time to be logical, concerned for individual development and backed by lecturers, researchers and professors of apparently impeccable scholarship. I made notes at the lectures on intelligence testing and allocation procedures for selective schools. I read books, answered the exam papers and never, at the time, questioned the basis of the whole enterprise. I do not recall meeting any student or member of staff who did.

Age, aptitude and ability

After the war the grammar schools ceased to be fee-paying and allocation of places became the sole responsibility of the local education authorities who maintained them. Secondary modern schools, some purpose built but many developed from existing elementary schools, provided most of the 'secondary education for all' promised in the 1944 Act. So who went where? No problem according to a typical textbook of the time written by a professor of education. *The Psychological Basis of Education* (Peel, 1956) reflected widespread attitudes:

> It is primarily a question of aptitudes, on the one hand, for academic, abstract and bookish education and, on the other, for practical, constructive, creative, technical education. (p 155)

> In a footnote, the author adds: We have grouping according to the *quantity* of intelligence which each child has. This decides whether a child is fit for grammar (and technical) school or a secondary modern school. (p 155 footnote)

According to this line of thinking, all that had to be done to ensure correct allocation was to measure aptitudes and quantity of intelligence. Aptitude was a particularly useful word because of a frequently quoted section of the 1944 Education Act (Ministry of Education, 1944). This required education authorities to ensure that there should be 'sufficient schools in number, character and equipment' to provide for all students:

> such variety of instruction and training as may be desirable in view of their different ages, abilities and aptitudes and of the different periods for which they may be expected to remain at school. (p 16)

As for quantity of intelligence, that's what IQ tests were all about — or so it was assumed by the majority of education committees and officials who organised the tests, teachers who prepared candidates for them (or received them afterwards) and by parents and the pupils themselves. They were powerfully supported by educational psychologists but the results produced many anomalies.[2] True there was more than one theory of intelligence but most from the western world agreed that everyone had something called general intelligence. This term was not too clearly defined but it was held to be the single most important factor affecting success in school work. It was said to have the following characteristics:

- Fixed for each individual at the point of conception.
- Did not alter whatever the experiences of the child. This implied that general intelligence was largely unaffected by cultural and social background or by the effects of schooling.
- Could be measured with reasonable accuracy through appropriate tests.

So the stage was set. Everyone's educational prospects were fixed and the job of state school educators was to see that school students did not fall below their potential as measured by the IQ test. That of parents was to condition their offspring to accept the verdict of nature.

If students' abilities are known, why not group them accordingly and let teachers undertake the condescending and demoralising task of helping their charges to 'work to the best of their ability'? Indeed, the phrase 'pool of ability' was used to describe a more or less finite number of intelligent young people who might benefit from higher education. Karl Marx had pointed to the all-embracing effect of the class factor in human relations a century previously but, for a long time, there was insufficient realisation that the so-called tripartite system of grammar, technical and secondary modern schools helped to maintain existing class divisions. It therefore comes as no surprise to learn that measurements of intelligence designed by professionals showed the majority of middle class students scoring higher than their working class contemporaries. As Krutetskii pointed out:

> If the children of workingmen score lower on tests, on no account does this indicate that they are less gifted ... the conditions of life do not give full scope to the development of ability in workingmen's children. (p 17)

Self-evident today, one may think, but certainly not an issue which was allowed to intrude into the programme of studies of students of my generation.

Testing and differentiation

Great advances have occurred in the intelligence story in recent decades. A clearly written summary of developments following the collapse of the old theories is provided by David Pyle (1979) in *Intelligence: An Introduction*. This provides an optimistic view of human potential starting with a challenge to past orthodoxies. For example:

> Intelligence may not be fixed ... but flexible as children learn a whole array of skills. (p 19)

> Intelligence is not able to be directly measured. (p 19)

> IQ scores are affected by the cultural conditions of the community, and in particular there are strong associations with social class: the home background (especially the mother) and schooling experienced by the child can affect his development. (p 67)

These quotations are typical of many in his book which describes evidence showing that the old theory is totally discredited. One of the key developers of that theory, Sir Cyril Burt, was knighted for his research into intelligence testing. He died in 1971 at the age of 88, one of the most widely respected figures in British Psychology. A few years later evidence emerged which suggested that key aspects of his work had been fraudulent. Indeed, Richard Morris of St. Andrews University, speaking in a radio broadcast entitled 'The Burt Scandal', described him as 'a scientific criminal guilty of the worst of all scientific crimes, the falsification of experimental data'.[3] Since then, Burt has been vigorously defended in some quarters and several of the specific charges remain unproven. Whether or not Burt 'cooked the scientific books' to help prove that intelligence is inherited, his published results were very successful in this objective. But we must beware of holding an individual responsible for the excessive significance attached to intelligence tests. His work was simply reinforcing prejudices widely held throughout the western world. Krutetskii puts it bluntly:

> In capitalist countries testing serves the class interests of the ruling classes by proving that there is a low level of mental ability among workers' children and special giftedness among children of the ruling classes. (p 17)

Brian Simon (1971) in *Intelligence, Psychology and Education* refers to his experience when teaching in boys' schools after the second world war and observes:

> The school system appeared to be (as indeed it was) run on the assumption that no child could ever rise above himself, that his level of achievement was fatally determined by an IQ — 'his' IQ as it was generally thought to be. (p 15)

The national curriculum has provided a new impetus for testing and differentiation. The values, ideology and purposes of those leading this field — whether government ministers, members of task forces, civil servants or appointees to the diverse range of quangos administering education — all need special scrutiny. Compared with forty years ago, there is more widespread wisdom within the teaching profession concerning testing and its effects but many of us are still wary when the assessment of school students is under consideration. However well intentioned the motives — for example, to discover causes of difficulty so that appropriate help can be given — the results can so easily be put to misuse by people with quite different objectives. There is no doubt, however, that even today many people loosely accept the notion of fixed intelligence from birth. So, although the 11-plus is a thing of the past for most, but by no means all, children there has been no serious challenge to the widespread segregation of students within schools into bands, streams and sets. Students are allocated according to the results of tests, school records and teachers' opinions. Allocation to the groups is said to be based on 'ability' which, used in this way, is virtually interchangeable with 'intelligence' on the old and discredited theory. Pyle notes the educational consequences:

> Decisions about general ability and hypothetical levels of intelligence often mean that children are allocated positions in some rank-order. Those relegated to the lower divisions on such criteria can be 'damned' forever in educational situations ... this common practice does a grave injustice to the complexities and potentials of such children's minds. (p 19)

As purely biological (inheritance) theories of intelligence are questioned, so too must arguments to justify divisions in school be challenged. Pyle reminds us that:

> If we were to decide that intelligence was fixed from birth and few factors could be manipulated to alter this, then a teacher might decide that only bright children should be stretched ... many people today still have such thoughts ... because they are ignorant of the research over the last few years. (p 49)

and, a little later:

> Beliefs held by teachers about the concepts and nature of intelligence determine
> to no small extent the levels of achievement expected of pupils. (p 59)

Unfortunately, many teachers, politicians, administrators and governors are as ignorant of the results of modern research into the nature of intelligence as the wider public. Yet the research has major implications for the internal organisation of schools and expectations for their students. From the early 1980s, In-Service Training (INSET) for teachers greatly increased in scope yet one has to search very hard indeed to discover courses designed to help teachers work without setting and streaming. On the contrary, a blanket of silence has to all intents and purposes been drawn over significant research in this field. This is in marked contrast to an abundance of high profile courses concerned with aspects of school life directly concerned with government initiatives.

Conditions for learning

A fundamental task for every educator is to create conditions so that students can learn as effectively as possible. They should have the opportunity to increase their knowledge, skills and understanding in intellectual, aesthetic and practical activities so that they can develop a wide range of aptitudes and abilities. In this challenging but achievable task we need concepts which are more precise than 'intelligence'. Whilst it is a matter of observation that some students can understand a mathematical formula or grasp the essentials of a written argument more quickly and extensively than others, this example of intelligent behaviour is not the only kind. People with high academic qualifications often display a distinct lack of intelligence in many of their actions. Few would disagree with Pyle when he writes:

> However one defines intelligence, it must be seen as ... many-sided, not
> one-sided. This implies that people can be intelligent in many different ways ...
> and these ways probably develop with age from childhood to adulthood. (p 19)

We need terms and concepts which can be applied directly to the process of learning. 'Ability' used in its proper sense of competence and achievement in a specific action or activity is an example. As abilities are developed through the process of learning what are the conditions for success? Naturally these vary with the task in hand and the age and maturity of the individual learner or group. Certain questions, however, are relevant to all situations:

- Is the learner in a good mental and physical state?
  No one can learn effectively if they are worried, insecure, undernourished or see no purpose in the task in hand. Successful parents and teachers recognise the importance of getting children to want to learn and this, in turn, implies that home and school should be places where children feel secure and are recognised and respected for their own worth.

- Does the learner already possess related abilities so that he or she is ready to commence study in the desired direction?
  If not, preparatory work must be undertaken. Failure to ensure that all learners have essential preliminary information, skills and understanding is one of the most frequent causes of poor progress and lack of confidence in school.

- What are the difficulties involved in each learning activity?
  This is the crux of the problem as many learning tasks are much more complex than appears at first sight. 'It is easy if you know how' may be said about someone who has just gained mastery of an activity but for others, if essential prior knowledge is missing, the same problem can seem insuperably difficult; it does not, however, mean they are unintelligent. Teachers and parents need to identify the steps which must be mastered in a learning process and to devise methods and activities which help the learners to build on what they know. Strategies are needed to help each student to learn successfully and there must be opportunities for extra time to be spent on particular aspects. In learning to drive a car, one student may need extra practice on a three-point turn whilst another may experience difficulty in starting on a hill. Similarly, in learning a school subject, students need opportunities for supplementary work on topics causing difficulty.

- How will the teacher and student know what progress is being achieved?
  Sometimes the answer is obvious but throughout all stages of the learning process it is necessary to devise methods of assessment which reveal information to assist in planning the next stage and to identify the cause of any lack of understanding so that help can be provided. Monitoring of this kind forms an integral part of the learning process and is, itself, a skilled and sensitive operation. Success requires knowledge of the significance and reliability of methods of assessment and good sense as to when and how to apply the results and interpret

them to the student. Nothing is gained if a student is put off and best results are obtained when learners are kept fully informed; where possible they should be involved in planning the monitoring process. There is little in common with assessment procedures designed primarily to provide data for league tables.

Implications for teaching arising from these considerations are discussed in the section 'Effective Learning' in Chapter 6.

Performance of school students

Many more students in our schools fail to achieve realisable targets because of unfavourable conditions for learning than do so from so-called lack of intelligence. Certainly one can anticipate — in the absence of any scientific, systematic study of the whole learning process — that variations in the genetic make up of individuals endow some with greater natural potential for learning. Nevertheless the importance of any biological factors in the development of human abilities must be kept strictly in perspective. Pyle comments:

> Many teachers watch how children perform on tasks, and then guess at their future capabilities. This may be a very mistaken strategy, and one which might lead to gross underestimates of ability. (p 88)

Reasons for good or poor performance have much to do with whether or not the conditions for learning are favourable. This principle can be applied to a wide variety of situations, for example: the relative achievement of boys and girls in different school subjects; the ease or difficulty of specific topics within a subject and the guidance of individual students. Optimising the learning conditions is therefore an essential step before estimates can be made concerning future potential. Whilst one is unlikely to become a mathematical genius or an Olympic athlete without an appropriate combination of inherited genes it is also true, as the United States educationist John Holt (1964) said in *How Children Fail*, that almost all children:

> fail to develop more than a tiny part of the tremendous capacity for learning, understanding, and creating with which they were born and of which they made full use during the first two or three years of their lives. (p xiii)

Differentiation and segregation of students within schools leads to a dead end as far as widening opportunities are concerned. The real need is for a spectacular increase in the attention given to improving conditions for learning. True, this is neither a simple task nor a cheap one but it is urgent. As we have seen, the effects of selection can be devastating and, unlike the unlamented 11-plus, selection procedures are subject to no real democratic controls. To my knowledge rarely, if ever, were internal school selection procedures and their consequences monitored by education authority officers and inspectors, nor indeed did Her Majesty's Inspectors subject them to any rigorous examination and assessment. New arrangements for inspection by contracted teams seem unlikely to change the situation.[4] .

Developing abilities

Opportunity is essential if one is to develop one's abilities. Krutetskii observes:

> Abilities are not something fore-ordained once and for all: they are formed and developed through instruction, practice, and mastery of an activity. (p 4)

In other words: we learn by doing. If some people are denied the opportunity of doing things which others regard as important, they do not learn about them and may then be regarded as ignorant and unintelligent. Krutetskii emphasises the relationship between ability and activity:

> Ability is a dynamic concept. It not only shows up and exists in an activity but is created and even developed in it. (p 66)

Here we have the crux of the matter put in simple terms: human beings do not have some general ability which governs their learning prospects in virtually every task and justifies placing them in the A-band or the D-stream. Abilities are created and developed by an appropriate programme of mental and physical activities.

Nina Talyzina (1981), in her book *The Psychology of Learning,* described impressive work in the Soviet Union on stages of development of mental processes. These included initial familiarisation, development in a material form, the importance of external speech and, finally, internal assimilation as an act of the mind (pp 109-114). Near the end she writes:

> Because of its social nature man's psychic activity is transmitted from generation to generation not through biological heredity but through teaching activities and the assimilation by new generations of socially generated ... activity. (p 322)

The translation may be a little heavy and one may not wish to go as far as Talyzina in eliminating all biological factors but the message is clear:

teachers transmit ability! Of course they do when one thinks about it and, with this realisation, the school system is seen to be even more important than we imagined. The concept of developing abilities through learning experiences represents a tremendous advance from the pessimistic perspective derived from earlier theories. However, there remains much to be done while outmoded attitudes keep so many unaware of the potential for fuller human development in our society.

'Mixed ability'

Classes of students which represent a cross-section of a school year group are a natural entity of the school community. Bernard Barker (1986), former head of Stanground School, Peterborough made the point in *Rescuing the Comprehensive Experience,* a book which gives a valuable insight into problems and achievements in the development of comprehensive schools. He refers to:

> Classes constructed as a microcosm of the community are the most natural arrangement for a common school. (p 103)

Unfortunately such groups are commonly referred to as 'mixed ability'. This term has acquired connotations of social engineering when the reverse is actually the case; it is selection, often based on the most dubious of criteria, which falls into that category. The term is seriously misleading: 'ability' in the singular suggests that each member of the group has a single ability. In order to create a 'mix' one must presumably be able to measure, estimate or in some other way identify it. The expression thus gives unintended support to the old discredited theory of intelligence and, as a consequence, it makes natural groupings an easy target for reactionary opinions. I prefer 'non-selective' as a more accurate and informative description of both teaching methods and the groups themselves. Streams, bands and sets can then be distinguished as 'selective' which identifies their true character although their members represent a wide range of abilities, motivation and educational needs.

Expectations

Expectations have a crucial influence at all ages whether at home, school or at work and are one of the most important factors in determining the educational performance of young people. The expectations of teachers are important, as Pyle noted, and so are those of parents and the learners themselves. Attitudes of fellow students and social groups within society do much to condition the expectations of those most directly involved.

Research in the post-war decades emphasised the importance of factors such as social class, home background and schooling all of which influence expectations. In *The Home and the School* J W B Douglas (1964) reported the results of research into a large sample of children from all social classes and all regions of Britain born during one week in March 1946. When the children in the survey reached age 11 in 1957 the tripartite system was almost universal and the team analysed factors influencing whether or not a child went to grammar school. One factor examined was the effect of mothers' expectations especially for children whose scores on tests undertaken by the research team suggested that they would be borderline for grammar school places.

The results were remarkable:

> Those whose mothers want them to go to grammar school and stay there until they are seventeen get 11 per cent more grammar school places than expected, those whose mothers are undecided get 8 per cent fewer places than expected, and those whose mothers want them to go to secondary modern schools and leave early get 60 per cent fewer places than expected. (p 1)

The effect of social class on the same children was equally striking:

> Grammar school places are awarded at the age of eleven to 51 per cent from the upper middle classes, 34 per cent from the lower middle, 21 per cent from the upper manual, and 22 per cent from the lower manual working classes. (p 47)

These are just two of the results in the survey and, in total, they showed how far from being educationally fair (in the sense of selecting by academic potential) were the allocation procedures for grammar school places. The impact of the research helped to form the opinions of many progressive educationists at the time especially as the book was published just when moves towards comprehensive education were gaining momentum. Today, few student teachers are introduced to research of this nature on their initial training courses and the lessons here also remain largely 'forgotten'.

Junior school experience

Many of the children in Douglas' survey had attended junior schools which had two classes in each year group. At the time, these were almost invariably divided into two streams: the A-class and the B-class. The children were separated into the streams before the age of eight and Douglas and his associates investigated the effects of this very early selection.

First a myth was refuted:

> It was rare for children to change streams; over the whole three-year period the annual rate of transfer was 2.3 per cent and approximately the same numbers moved up as down. (p 113)

Teachers often justified streaming and setting by claiming that it is easy to move students from one stream to the other. This may appear true in theory but, as Douglas shows, teachers' estimates and recollections of the numbers of students who moved are greatly in access of the actual numbers involved. Details of the movements are interesting:

> The few children who moved from the lower to the upper streams are distinguished by having received superior care in early childhood ... The children who start in the upper streams and end in the lower tend to be those from large families who received poor care in early childhood ... (p 117)

However, it was the effects within streams rather than movements between them, that makes the survey so noteworthy. Tests of the children's performance were repeated at intervals:

> The children in the upper streams improve their scores ... and those in the lower streams deteriorate. (p 114)

The research team made a close survey of children who, at eight years, had the lowest test scores in the A-streams and those of the same age who had the highest scores in the B-streams. These were borderline children who, before being allocated to classes, must have scored very similarly on attainment tests. By age eleven, the situation was very different:

> In the upper streams it is particularly the children of relatively low ability who benefit ... In the lower streams, the brighter children show a greater average deterioration. (p 114)

The conclusion is inescapable. Selection is a lottery. The winners go forward and the losers are faced with a handicap which will become cumulative as their education proceeds. Douglas offers an explanation of these differences in performance:

> Once allocated, the children tend to take on the characteristics expected of them and the forecasts of ability made at the point of streaming are to this extent self-fulfilling. (p 115)

Subsequent research has confirmed the effect on school performance of expectations but self-fulfilling prophesies are still found in our schools. Estimates are made of students' potential which lead on to differential treatment of one kind or another. Those chosen for the five-star service produce better results. The chapter in *The Home and the School* which describes this work concludes as follows:

> Streaming by ability reinforces the process of social selection which was observed in the earlier chapters of this book. Children who come from well-kept homes and who are themselves clean, well clothed and shod, stand a greater chance of being put in the upper streams than their measured ability would seem to justify. Once there they are likely to stay and to improve in performance in succeeding years. This is in striking contrast to the deterioration noticed in those children of similar initial measured ability who were placed in the lower streams. In this way the validity of the initial selection appears to be confirmed by the subsequent performance of the children ... (p 118)

These and similar findings, together with the abolition of the 11-plus, provided a foundation for the reorganisation of junior school practice where, for two or three decades, streaming became the exception rather than the rule. Research with secondary age students also concluded that the educational and social environment of these students was highly significant.[5]

However, whilst many comprehensive schools established some non-selective groups, this was often for pragmatic reasons (for example, to get to know the students better or to reduce discipline problems) rather than in response to a non-selective rationale.[6] We examine the position in comprehensive schools in more detail in Part IV.

Class size

There is a very practical consideration to take into account when students are to be separated on selective criteria. Staffing and accommodation dictate that there have to be about 25 to 30 students in most classes and ultimately this requirement must dominate in selection and allocation procedures. It follows that some students of very similar performance or estimated potential will be allocated to a 'higher' group and some to a 'lower' one. If the expectations, rate of progress and course content are markedly different for the two groups they cannot be equally suitable for similar students who have been so completely separated. There is no solution to this dilemma within a selective system of grouping and this indisputable fact gave further impetus to non-selective teaching in both junior and comprehensive schools.

Developments in both junior and comprehensive schools over three decades have led to promising and successful strategies for learning in non-selective groups. Some of these developments are discussed in Chapters 6 and 7 and form a logical continuation of the work which has been described in the current chapter. For an overwhelming majority of young people in school, social and educational factors influence their progress more than their biological endowment. This is a message of optimism because the social and educational environment can be changed through human endeavour.

3

Arrival of Comprehensive Education

Growing realisation of the inadequacy and unfairness of the 11-plus examination coincided with increasing public awareness of the differences in educational provision for students in grammar schools compared with their brothers and sisters in modern schools. The introduction of comprehensive schools between the 1950s and '70s in most local authority areas was a considerable (though qualified) achievement and an essential step towards the development of a fully comprehensive system of education in content and spirit as well as in name. The educational history surrounding the coming of comprehensive education and its aftermath has been written about extensively and with fascination for all interested in politics and education.[1] This chapter is based on a few personal impressions to complement more scholarly accounts, recalling how it seemed at the time to an active practitioner.

Selective system becomes indefensible

Shortly before the general election of 1964, Labour Party leader Harold Wilson said 'The grammar schools will be abolished over my dead body', or words to that effect. Not a very inspiring comment for those of us who were working in secondary modern schools and looking forward to the coming of comprehensive education.

Failure in the grammar school

Riddings Secondary School opened as a new secondary modern school in Scunthorpe in 1958 with a mainly first year intake together with the first year of a new grammar school due to open in the area in 1960. Relations were cordial and joint activities flourished. At first the grammar school students were allocated randomly to their three classes but, after a year, the staff divided them into streams on the basis of first year performance and end of year examinations. A few working weeks later, as the staff were preparing their pre-Christmas end of term reports, grammar school teachers started referring amongst themselves to the 'dead wood' of the C-stream. This was a great shock to the modern school staff who had seen it as their prime duty to restore self-confidence in their charges after the shattering effect of 'failure' in the 11-plus examination compounded for many by a feeling of public humiliation. Yet the young people allocated to the grammar school C-stream — one third of the successes in the 11-plus — had obtained scores within the top 25%. Four years later, many of the modern school students who had scored somewhat less well in the same 11-plus did better in the General Certificate of Education (GCE) than these 'dead wood' students. Scarcely surprising in view of such low expectations for the latter.

Evidence that this was no isolated case can be found in the report of a research project into streaming in grammar schools undertaken four years later by Colin Lacey (1966). The school in which he did a case study also streamed students at the end of the first year with remarkably similar effects. After sixth months in the second year this bottom stream was already regarded as a difficult form to teach because, as he quotes two of his colleagues:

> 'They are unacademic, they can't cope with the work.'

> 'Give them half a chance and they will give you the run around.' (p 255)

Lacey had further discussions:

> Masters discussing 2C with me put it bluntly. 'There is not one boy in the class who has any sort of academic ability. In fact most of them shouldn't be in the school at all. It's not fair on them and it's not fair on the school.' Remarks of this sort were frequently made while talking to me in front of the class and were obviously audible to the front rows of boys, as well as to myself. (p 260)

The experience at Riddings and the events described by Lacey are examples of ways in which too many grammar schools created their own failures from among their intakes. For those who rebelled, a quick exit could be arranged and Riddings, in common with other secondary modern schools in the area, received a small quota each September of students transferring from neighbouring grammar schools. The reasons given were invariably concerned with difficulty in keeping up with the work. In fact, we found the majority to be quite capable intellectually but with behavioural problems which, with the development of more successful school careers in the modern schools, were often eliminated or markedly reduced. Brian Simon (1971), in the introduction to his book *Intelligence, Psychology and Education*, also describes changes in attitudes which he witnessed as a teacher in a boys' grammar school just after the war. Although the students were streamed A, B and C on entry, he refers to the joy of teaching the boys of all first year classes 'so infectious was their vitality and enthusiasm' (p 11). But these qualities were not to grow and develop with age and maturity:

> The lively boys I had known and enjoyed teaching in the first year C-stream had by the third and fourth year in grammar school become passive non-cooperators. Once among the selected few in the borough they were now 'the dregs' of this school and saw no reason to respect an institution that so degraded them. (p 13)

It was possible to deduce much about grammar school education of the time from the behaviour, attitudes and conversation of their students, parents and teachers. Criticisms of the system, however, were muted. Teachers were strongly discouraged from expressing any serious reservations whilst every attempt was made, for example through the termly report, to convince young people and their parents that any deficiency in their academic performance was entirely due to mental weakness and/or idleness and lack of application. There was no suggestion that 'could do better' might apply to the schools as well as the students whilst parents, many of whose children were first generation grammar school entrants, tended to quietly accept the situation. Above all, the schools were cushioned from criticism because of the career opportunities they opened out to all who accepted their methods and ethos. Many grammar schools also failed their students in a less obvious way: in a sense they were intellectually undemanding and did not sufficiently challenge even their most capable students. This more surprising problem arose from the type of work which was common at the time. Too much of it relied on taking notes, memorising the content of lessons and practising how to answer examination questions in a stereotyped manner. Simon observed some of the effects which went far beyond members of the C-stream:

> There was almost as great a difference between the A-stream of the fourth year and the eager 11-year olds I had once taught, insofar as classes had become

docile, passive, difficult to stimulate to anything but note taking of a kind related directly to preparation for examinations. (p 14)

Lacey's study also considered the full range of students in each year and he reports in similar terms noting that the behaviour of first-year boys is characterised by 'eagerness, cooperation with the teacher and a high degree of competition among themselves'. Whilst this type of enthusiasm was occasionally to be found in the second and third years, these classes were more likely to allow 'five or six people to do all the work' (pp 247-248). The author gave a fuller account of his work with additional interesting material in *Hightown Grammar* (Lacey, 1970). In defence of over emphasis on factual rather than inspirational teaching, it might be argued that public examinations required just such an approach allowing the schools no choice. But I never found this to be an acceptable excuse. In every type of school some teachers rose above the situation to the gratitude of the more discerning of their students as they provided stimulating and intellectually demanding lessons whilst still ensuring good examination grades. This showed that, given the will, constrictions of the examination system could, to some extent, be overcome. Unfortunately, in many grammar schools such teachers were in a minority — often a very small minority. Furthermore, whilst GCE questions and marking schemes were mainly of a routine nature, the examination boards came under pressure from the majority of teachers and schools if they set questions which diverged in any way from the conformity that had come to be expected.

These matters raise many questions involving curriculum, examinations and teaching methods which we shall address in subsequent chapters.

Unacceptable actions

A year or so after the 'dead wood' event, the parent of one of our students at Riddings came to see the headteacher in consternation. His younger child had been allocated to the new grammar school which was now open and he had attended a meeting for parents of new entrants the night before. They had been told by the headteacher of the grammar school: 'We think it best if your sons and daughters do not mix with children who attend the modern school'. The head's 'advice' was no casual remark as the teenage daughter of a member of the modern school staff found out. She often cycled to the grammar school and, one morning, met her cousin who was cycling in the reverse direction to the modern school. They stopped for a chat but must have been observed. When the grammar school student reached her destination in good time she was sent for by the senior mistress and told: 'You know you are not supposed to talk to modern school pupils'.

Similar authenticated stories were being told up and down the country and had a marked effect on parents and teachers alike. Many were able to see for themselves the difference in provision for the grammar schools: better teacher/student ratios even for those of the same age; better science laboratories and other specialist rooms, and more money allocated, per student, for goods, materials etc.

Modern school achievements

By the late 1950s modern school students were voluntarily staying on until age 16. Despite handicaps, they were achieving examination results which were often better than some of their colleagues who had gone to grammar school after taking the 11-plus. A striking example of the potential of young people came from Brumby Boys School, a secondary modern in Scunthorpe. The school admitted 120 students each year and entered some for GCE O-level examinations which, at that time had six grades of pass (1 to 6) and three grades below this (7 to 9). Four boys were successful in mathematics in 1962 out of 18 entered and many modern schools would have been pleased with this achievement. Then a teacher took over who believed that much more was possible. Here are the results for 1963:

Of 26 entered, 25 were successful with the other gaining a near miss grade 7. The successful results by grade were:

Grade	1	2	3	4	5	6
Number	11	4	1	-	7	2

This performance, outstanding at the time by any standards, was no flash in the pan; during the next five years the average annual figures for GCE mathematics were as follows: 19 candidates and 15 passes with two at grade 1 and two at grade 2. This from 'failures' at 11-plus in a subject regarded as difficult even in grammar schools and at a time when the leaving age was 15 and the total number of O-level passes in all subjects was much less than in GCSE today.

Parity of esteem

The 11-plus examination or allocation procedure, as it was usually referred to by the local education authorities who administered it, was taken by pupils in the last year of junior school. The purpose was to discover which pupils had the aptitude for grammar school education and most procedures involved the use of so-called intelligence tests. There were some curious results: for several years after the close of the second world war, Birmingham had grammar school places for about 10% of pupils in the city. Conveniently, the 11-plus procedures found that only 10% of Birmingham pupils could benefit by this form of secondary education. In parts of Wales, however, the grammar school provision, for historical reasons, was nearer 40%. No prizes for guessing that a relatively massive 40% of Welsh pupils, taking almost identical tests, were found to have the necessary aptitude.

Before 1944 grammar schools were open to fee-paying students and also to those from local elementary or 'council' schools who were successful in a scholarship examination.[2] As mentioned in Chapter 2, the 1944 Act arose as a response to popular demand for better social conditions after the war and guaranteed secondary education for all. The Act did not rule out developments on comprehensive lines and, as early as 1942, there was unanimous support for a resolution at the Labour conference supporting widespread experiments in this field. By 1950 the conference was calling on the government to implement a comprehensive policy. However, successive Labour Ministers of Education were opposed to the reform. Strongly supported by civil servants, they followed the recommendations of the notoriously biased Norwood report (Board of Education, 1943) to provide this universal secondary education in three varieties of school: grammar, technical and modern. At first modern schools provided between 80% and 90% of school places in most districts. With national problems of finance and resources this could, perhaps, have been justified as an interim measure on the grounds that a scarcity of specialist teachers and equipment could be concentrated in the grammar and technical schools. Justification on these grounds would, of course, have precluded acceptance of the so-called tripartite system as a long term policy. In fact, something quite different happened and the three types of school were promoted as equal but different. In a pamphlet *The New Secondary Education* (Ministry of Education, 1947a) the virtues of each type of school were skilfully described. Then came the crunch:

> The modern school will be given parity of conditions with other types of secondary school; parity of esteem it must achieve by its own efforts. (p 30)

Parity of conditions was never even remotely achieved and 'Parity of Esteem' became mere propaganda. Despite heroic efforts on the part of some modern school teachers, with the co-operation of their students and parents, to provide a really worthwhile education (and some modern schools created a working atmosphere second to none) the basic deception became increasingly clear to all. When Riddings Secondary School opened in 1958, I was in the hall as the head addressed the parents of new entrants. He described the buildings which combined architectural flair with the generous cost yard-sticks of the time. He outlined the forward looking educational provision that a young and enthusiastic staff had prepared, gave his support to homework as a means of helping the learning process and referred to the importance of parent-teacher cooperation. On finishing his well delivered speech, he asked for questions. The first was this: 'How do I get my child transferred to the grammar school?'

Public opinion grew steadily stronger and it was clear that parity of provision and esteem could only be realised with the abolition of the selective system. It is worth recalling, however, that *The Times Educational Supplement*, a journal noted more for its middle of the road views rather than revolutionary zeal, had stated in its edition of 15 December, 1945 (*The Times Educational Supplement,*1945):

> No greater mishap could overcome the new order in English education than that there should be established within it different grades of secondary school. And that is what inevitably different types of schools with different leaving ages would become: different grades of schools with superior or inferior social status and ... different exit ramps leading to different and exclusive levels in adult society.

By the mid-1960s both the National Union of Teachers and the Labour Party had accepted comprehensive education as official policy. Several Local Education Authorities, as different in social background and geographical location as the London County Council and the Isle of Man, had already opened or planned comprehensive schools. The LCC had played a leading role in planning and campaigning for comprehensive schools since before the war whilst, in rural areas, Conservative councils recognised the efficiency of the development. A number involved imaginative schemes, for example at Wyndham School in Egremont, Cumberland where I became deputy head a term before it opened in 1964.[3] In the following year, the Labour government issued a circular known as 10/65 (the 10th DES circular in 1965) which requested all local authorities to prepare plans for a comprehensive system of education and to submit them within twelve months. Unfortunately the circular had no statutory power and also permitted certain schemes of reorganisation which could scarcely be seen as genuinely comprehensive. Nevertheless 10/65 proved to be a benchmark in the development process and, in the following years, a large number of comprehensive schools were established.

Qualified victory

Comprehensive reform, although a little late in arriving, was still a famous victory though as a battle won in a campaign rather than an operation completed. It provided the opportunity for a re-examination of our whole concept of education not least in our understanding of how people learn (Chapter 6). This challenging and rewarding task was essential if the new schools were to go forward towards establishing 'parity of esteem' among all their students. Many schools aimed precisely in this direction but others appeared to base their organisation on fundamentally different priorities. Whilst problems arose because of the lack of a clear objective for the new schools, they gained in public support and attempts to return to selective systems in Solihull and elsewhere in the 1980s had to be abandoned after public protest. However, we must beware of thinking that we have ever had a fully comprehensive system in place. The co-existence of private schools excludes seven or eight per cent of the school population — a much higher percentage from families of wealth and influence — from participating in comprehensive education. Even within the state sector some local authorities successfully held out against reorganisation and retain selection at 11-plus in their areas today.

Internal selection

The question of selection within schools should have concerned successive Labour governments and local education authorities since the inception of comprehensive education. Its effects may be less obvious but no less damaging. Having created several thousand comprehensive schools in order to abolish the evils and unfairness of selection, the labour movement said, in effect, 'Job Done!' In reality nothing could have been further from the truth: the job had only just begun. For example, by the school year 1993-4 half of all comprehensive schools still retained at least some selection even in year 7, the first year of entry for most schools. This information, together with more detail given in Chapter 17, note 10, comes from an extensive survey by Caroline Benn and Clyde Chitty in *Thirty Years On: Is Comprehensive Education Alive and Well, or Struggling to Survive?* (Benn and Chitty, 1996).

Methods of selection have varied from school to school, sometimes from one year to another. Most are administered by teachers who are inexperienced in this complex and uncertain operation and most involve an element of 'professional judgment' from the primary and comprehensive school teachers concerned. This is a notoriously uncertain procedure with many research projects showing that teachers' opinions of their students' capabilities and potential are heavily weighted in favour of children from middle class backgrounds and favourable home circumstances. Unlike the 11-plus which it replaced, the present arrangements are rarely undertaken in any rigorous and objective manner; there is no right of appeal and it is a procedure totally without democratic control. No doubt some comprehensive schools use the results of the national tests, known originally as standard assessment tasks or SATs, set up under the 1988 Education Reform Act for allocation of new entrants to classes. Similarly, results of the tests at age 14 may be used to determine eligibility for the more prestigious options in the last two years of secondary education.

The fact that bands, streams and sets are now under one roof rather than in different schools is of little comfort. The result is to produce the same expectations of academic success, mediocrity or failure as in the system which comprehensive education replaced. Stuart Hall (1983), Professor of Sociology at the Open University, writing about the general thrust of social and educational policies in a paper entitled 'Education in Crisis', refers to:

> the brutal revival of vocationalism ... and the division of the world into 'hands' and 'brains', each with its own appropriate slot in the educational structure ... (p 3)

He continues:

> Inequality in education, has become, once again, a *positive* social programme
> ... The problem is that it is not matched on the other side by any corresponding
> vision.

Since then inequalities have increased with schemes for local management of schools favouring those in more prosperous areas. Lack of vision in education has a bearing on the question 'If selection between schools produced an outcry from the public, why has there been no similar call against selection within schools?'

Conditioning

Non-selection for grammar school was a fate which befell at least seventy five per cent of pupils in the public education service, many with parents very ambitious for their children. With fee paying in grammar schools abolished by the 1944 Education Act, there was no alternative for anyone who could not afford high independent school fees. Selection within schools was perceived differently. Streamed classes and ability sets had existed for years in all types of secondary school and attention had rarely been drawn to the negative effects. Also, selection within schools is more flexible and numbers of students in each band can be adjusted to meet parental pressures and aspirations.[4] In contrast the lowest bands of comprehensive schools contain a high proportion of students, including many from ethnic minorities, whose parents have already been conditioned to low expectations for their children.

Expectations are closely linked to the case for comprehensive education. Robin Pedley (1956), in his influential book *Comprehensive Education: A New Approach* referred to the expectations of people at the time of the 1944 Act:

> In 1944 ... the extension of secondary education to all children seemed an
> operation simple in principle if formidable in magnitude. People hoped by this
> means to secure two things: first, an equal chance with others for their own
> children to get to the top; and second, an end to the great cleavages between
> different types of school. (p 18)

So far so good. But what of parents' expectations after their children have entered a comprehensive school? Students who are capable of achieving qualifications necessary for medium and high status jobs can be strongly motivated in their school work. At the other end of the scale many families accept, more as a fact of life than through conscious reasoning, that their children are destined for the bottom rungs of the social ladder linked with inadequate training schemes, casual work and unemployment. Under these circumstances, a school can supply only limited incentives for a substantial number of its students. Those allocated to the lowest bands are all too likely to become self fulfilling prophecies for their teachers and parents who, in their different ways, identified them at an early age as low achievers. Despite this undoubted handicap, however, I have met an encouragingly wide acceptance of the ultimate value of education by parents and students in the 'lower' groups.

Fundamentals of comprehensive education

Comprehensive education, properly harnessed in the interests of all its students, can play a vital part in challenging socially based expectations of failure and thus help to liberate people from feelings of inferiority. There are two essential requirements:

A non-selective approach

First there must be a commitment towards the replacement of internal selection if equitable policies are to have a chance of lasting success. In 1974 Sunderland Local Education Authority produced an overall objective for its education service which included an admirable commitment to:

> Eradication of notions of inferiority and superiority as these may be created by selectivity both between and within schools.

Campaigning, explaining, listening and adapting are, of course, all essential if such a well intentioned aim is to receive wide public support and become organically rooted in the community. In Sunderland's case, there was no follow up and, when put to the test, much effort was spent in attempting to prove that the objective was either irrelevant or meant something else (Part V).

Research into the effects of expectation on performance, and into the catastrophic effects of streaming and setting was a factor which motivated comprehensive enthusiasts in the 1960s and '70s including many students preparing to enter teaching. Modern ideas of intelligence, outlined in Chapter 2, concentrate on human potential and, dispense with any justification for selection based on deep seated but outmoded ideas of a fixed level of intelligence for each individual. These research findings opened out a new range of possibilities based on comprehensive schools and, today, provide an optimistic outlook for human development and fulfilment involving a full measure of self-respect for all members of the community.

Despite the strength of this case, it might be argued that, if students are allocated to groups of about the same level of attainment, they will be easier to teach and are therefore more likely to make progress. The flaw in this argument is that students are never at the same level of understanding and attainment no matter how the class is organised — still less are they equally motivated. Teaching methods based on assumptions of equality of attainment and motivation are likely to produce boredom for some if the pace is to slow and feelings of incompetence among others if the pace is too quick. Teaching to 'the middle', as is sometimes advocated by teachers, is a less than inspiring guideline. The solution lies in the organisation of classroom work which exploits the possibilities for whole class, group and individual learning which are now available. In Chapter 6, we look at these and other promising initiatives which started in some of the developing comprehensive schools in the 1960s and the early '70s. We shall also examine how developments in our knowledge of the learning process and in the availability of new technology can be applied extensively in our schools. Time and resources must be deployed to facilitate learning as the priority for which administration and finance exist.

A curriculum for all

The second requirement for effective comprehensive education is an appropriate curriculum for the task in hand. A school for all implies a common, though not inflexible, curriculum and, in the next chapter, we examine some of the principles involved. To set us on our way, here is a remark, widely appreciated at the time, from Jerome Bruner (1972) who became well known in the field of education during the formative period of comprehensive education. In a book entitled *The Relevance of Education* he states boldly:

> Anything can be taught to anybody at any age in some form that is both interesting and honest. (p 32)

Commenting on a different political system, similar thoughts were expressed by Rudolph Bahro (1978) in *The Alternative in Eastern Europe:*[5]

I proceed on the assumption that the overwhelming majority of people have all
the faculties needed to acquire the necessary scientific and artistic general
education at an academic level. (p 290)

Splendid sentiments of hope and optimism!

4

Attitudes and Ideology behind the Curriculum

The school curriculum has far-reaching implications at classroom, school and national level yet, for many years, it was seen as a purely educational matter best left to the experts. Certainly there is unknown territory to explore and pitfalls to be avoided but also a wealth of educational principles and practice to act as a guide and inspiration. The basic ideas and issues are clear and straightforward, require no specialised knowledge and relate directly to values and aspirations in society. This chapter describes some of the educational, social and political factors which influence the development of all curricula and must therefore be taken into account when creating an appropriate curriculum for a truly comprehensive system of education.

What is the curriculum?

Students go to school to learn — but who is to learn what, by what means and for what purpose? These are questions of fundamental importance and the answers determine the programme of learning and teaching in every school. This programme, together with the values transmitted with it, makes up the school curriculum.

The opportunities and challenges of the curriculum are well illustrated by English which holds a key position in every school. The ability to read and write with confidence and accuracy is a much sought after skill so every English department aims to develop the level of literacy among its students together with their ability to communicate effectively. But English aims at so much more than good technique; it has a very special part to play in helping young people to develop the power to think for themselves and the confidence to express the results whilst, through the study of literature, students become acquainted with the thoughts and feelings of others. English, therefore, engages students in improving their skills and technique, developing their sense of self-worth and self-confidence and widening their horizons through access to our cultural heritage. It is clear that simplistic recipes for higher standards accompanied by ill-considered attacks on the competence and integrity of teachers are entirely counter-productive. Such an intricate and sensitive entitlement will be achieved by acknowledging the worth and nature of the task and providing encouragement and support towards ever greater effectiveness.

Every school curriculum implies answers to the questions What?, Why?, How? and for Whom? whether or not the issues have been openly discussed and debated. Here the under-rated contribution of educational drama illustrates the point that, from time to time, we may need to protect endangered species in the curriculum.[1]

Educational drama is a subject closely related to English. For example one of the objectives for drama at Ryhope School referred to 'exploring a variety of register, voice control and appropriateness of language' and another to 'developing the personality and maturity of the individual through concentration, self-discipline, self-expression, self-confidence, use of imagination, oral fluency and the ability to work independently and co-operatively'. The scope of the subject is far wider than the production of plays although there are shared skills and techniques. The teacher will have a variety of games and activities for group 'warm up' and to develop trust, concentration and so on. He or she may introduce a topic following prior discussion with the group or alternatively it may arise from an incident in literature or on television. Themes often concern relationships — in the family, at school or in society — relevant to the process of growing up but students are also introduced to wider challenges.

Members of the class develop and participate in activities around the issue and, through role-play, experience situations involving prejudice or moral conflict which help them to work out their own ideas and priorities. Indeed, educational drama provides unique opportunities for students to explore in a practical way their own thoughts, emotions and feelings, as well as those of others, and at the same time to develop their language and communication skills through group cooperation. Under sensitive and competent guidance the subject can do much to develop confidence and self-assurance in even the most shy and uncertain young person and should, like English, form part of the entitlement of all school students. In fact, drama did not even merit a mention in the Education Reform Act of 1988 and, although many schools continue to include drama in their programmes of study, it is becoming more difficult to ensure an adequate supply of well-trained and motivated staff in this challenging area of the curriculum.

Outside educational circles the What? Why? How? and for Whom? questions were rarely discussed. Not, that is, until the early 1980s when Sir Keith Joseph, Secretary of State for Education and Science, recognised their importance to his cause and an opportunity to control and influence educational developments in elitist directions. By blurring issues and obscuring the nature of the real choices to be made, it is possible to propose developments in the curriculum which appear plausible yet, while helping some students, reduce the opportunities and prospects of others. In a comprehensive system of education the curriculum must give practical realisation to the principle established by Daunt, quoted in Chapter 1, that every student is entitled to be considered as of equal value.

For whom should we plan the curriculum?

As we have seen in Chapter 2, research shows that almost everyone is mentally fitted for a full and liberating education in its widest sense. We must not assume, therefore, as advocated in many influential quarters, that a vital requirement is to provide differentiated curricula to match different 'abilities' of students. As a means of separating young people in preparation for their role in adult society, differentiation fits the bill admirably. It is no surprise that it is prominent in the national criteria for the GCSE and other public examinations; appears on the first page of the Education Reform Act (1988), and is official policy at the Department for Education and Employment. Rejecting differentiation does not preclude alternatives in the curriculum which are of genuinely equal status. It means, however, that we must consider the effect on students of not choosing, or being selected for, an option as well as the benefit to those who avail themselves of the choice. A decision concerning modern languages in the curriculum at Ryhope School illustrates the importance of the 'equal status' criterion.

In the 1970s, the precise place of modern languages in the curriculum presented problems in many comprehensive schools not least in the north east.[2] Languages are difficult to learn and need a high degree of motivation and sustained application if even a modest facility in communication is to be obtained. Where schools divided students into sets or ability bands, languages were usually confined to the upper groups but, at Ryhope, we had a programme of languages for all in the first three years (now compulsory under the national curriculum). On one occasion we decided that, for about a quarter of the students in our third year, we would provide additional lessons to develop basic skills in English as a more productive alternative than continuing with the main stream modern language course. The decision, taken as I thought on educational and caring grounds, was not a success. Several students inquired with feeling as to why they were being deprived of part of the programme of the comprehensive school of which, they reminded me, they were full members. Many regarded these alternative classes as 'drop out' groups and the morale of teachers and taught was low; after that experience, no forced differentiation occurred again.

The answer to the For Whom? question is straightforward: the curriculum is to be designed for all — with each individual equally entitled to a full status education.

What should we teach? how should it be taught? and why?

Answers to these questions (ie decisions concerning content, method and purpose) help to determine the quality of the education provided but we must appreciate that a decision concerning any one of them also affects the others. For example, the introduction of non-selective teaching methods (How?) to help realise comprehensive principles (Why?) must be considered in relation to content (What?) and will help to determine it.[3] An example of failure to consider all the factors occurs when the answer to one of the questions is given dominant status.

The content of school mathematics courses was long influenced by a 'top-down' approach: university mathematics departments demanded certain prior knowledge for acceptance to degree courses so A-level courses had to provide it although only a small proportion of A-level mathematics students went on to take degrees in the subject. Before commencing on A-level courses, students were judged to require particular knowledge from their O-level or GCSE work and so the chain went on. It affected all stages of secondary education and its narrowing influence could be detected in the primary sector. What would be the content of mathematics education in schools if the Why? and How? questions were allowed to stand equally beside What? Demand for the basics of numeracy, ie competence in the essentials of calculation and computation, remains assured. In today's society this includes understanding of statistics, graphical communication, computers and calculators, shape and pattern as well as traditional topics like decimals and percentages which figure so prominently in the media. In addition, students need time to gain confidence by exploring ideas and concepts through simple investigations — so mathematics education must not be overburdened with specialist topics of interest to a minority whose needs can be met in other ways.[4] Students should also learn of the human need throughout history for measurement and calculation and of its power and significance today. Thus, through studies in mathematics, they would widen their cultural perspectives and gain insight into the life and achievements of earlier societies.[5] University influence is less strong since the introduction of the national curriculum and this provides the opportunity for an unconstrained re-examination of the aims of mathematics teaching based on the principles and interactions discussed in this chapter.

Many improvements have been achieved over the years enabling teachers to teach in more relevant and satisfying ways but failure to appreciate the importance of relationships is a major source of misunderstanding; concentration on method or content in isolation can lead well intentioned teachers to produce results which, at best, are reduced in effectiveness but may even have outcomes opposite to those intended. Failure to place content and method in their full educational context produces inconsistencies which provide easy arguments in support of divisive alternatives. On the other hand, when inter-dependence is recognised and planned for, results are enhanced and likely to prove durable. The task is to see that the needs of all students are fulfilled under each of the headings.

The curriculum as a system

Fritjof Capra (1983) is a theoretical physicist who has written and lectured about the philosophical implications of modern science. In *The Turning Point* he outlines a systems view of life which looks at the world 'in terms of relationships and integration'. He explains:

> Instead of concentrating on basic building blocks or basic substances, the systems approach emphasises basic principles of organization ... Systemic properties are destroyed when a system is dissected, either physically or theoretically, into isolated elements. Although we can discern individual parts in

any system, the nature of the whole is always different from the mere sum of its parts. (pp 286-287)

Although Capra is mainly concerned here with biological and environmental matters his description of the systems approach suggests a constructive way of looking at the school curriculum. This also forms an inter-related system in which, without doubt, 'the nature of the whole is always different from the mere sum of its parts'. Adoption of this principle directs curriculum planning towards integrated and realisable objectives and away from a piecemeal approach as employed for the national curriculum. In its original form the national curriculum was not only unco-ordinated, but unworkable, and necessitated major adjustments to reduce content for students and workload for teachers to fit the time available. The results are now more viable but not necessarily more equitable and consistent with comprehensive principles.[6]

The hidden curriculum

Attitudes which underpin school policies and the values held by individual teachers and the wider community influence the perception of all learners. Young people are quick to understand what values are held to be important from the way things are said, the rules and regulations, teachers' reactions to day-to-day incidents and a hundred and one other indicators. This influence is sometimes referred to as the hidden curriculum and may be either progressive or retrograde but is never neutral. It thus requires the attention of all who wish to see the establishment of a truly comprehensive system of education in organisation and practice. The class values of society will always have a major influence in the hidden curriculum and, with market values emphasised in almost all aspects of educational life, this presents us with a special challenge.

As values transmitted through education have far reaching consequences, we next look at attitudes and ideology which help to determine the nature of the curriculum and its inter-relationships.

Attitudes and ideology

Attitudes to knowledge and learning

Attitudes to knowledge and learning are fundamental. People hold very different views on this matter, which affect their answers to the questions:

What?, Why?, How? and For Whom? One view is captured in two sentences by Bahro (1978):

> Young people ... sit in the hall below and are allowed to ask questions. The rostrum is occupied by people who already know the truth. (p 286)

This view reflects an attitude which assumes that the role of students is to obediently receive a transmitted truth. Learning is a very dull process under such circumstances and schools and teachers have long recognised the importance of actively involving their students in the learning process. Opportunities to investigate, question and contribute from experience provide deeper insight, motivation and relevance for students. Learning which involves shared experiences can lead beyond planned areas of study to give deeper, and sometimes unexpected, insights into the topic. When moral, political or religious questions arise, schools and teachers risk being unjustifiably accused of bias and indoctrination. Educational objectives covering this type of learning should, therefore, form part of school and college curriculum plans so that, with this necessary safeguard, teachers can involve their students with confidence in the learning process.

The ethos of the school as a whole has a major influence on attitudes to learning by staff, students and parents. Shortly after the close of the second world war, a secondary modern school, newly established under the 1944 Education Act, received a visitor. This was Vicars Bell (1950), head of an all-age village school and author of a book called *The Dodo: The Story of a Village Schoolmaster.* He chose the title to mark the imminent extinction of his species and his graphic descriptions provided memorable moments when, as a student in 1950, I listened to extracts read to us by an enlightened professor of education:

> In the period of my indecision and uncertainty I applied for an appointment to the Headship of a Secondary Modern School in the Midlands, and I was called up for interview. I met first the director of education for the county. He was a man very near to retirement. The honours which had come to him he had never struggled for. The publicity that he had suffered from was that which comes inevitably to sheer goodness of quality. I wanted at once to work under him, for I knew that he would see what I was trying to do. The buildings were well planned and seemed palatial after my own. We arrived at the school just as the classes were changing rooms. A bell rang. All the doors opened, and from each emerged a child. Each was meticulously neat and tidy, and almost identically dressed. Each had a small celluloid badge bearing the word 'PREFECT'. They stood like policemen, while the classes marched in silence down the corridors

which surrounded the quadrangle. At the corner, commanding a view of two corridors, stood a grown-up teacher. A soft hat set at a jaunty and vigilant angle proclaimed him to be The Teacher on Corridor Duty. The children passed smartly by. I looked at each face, and from one or two came a glance of recognition: 'Yes, I'm a human soul, too, really, in spite of appearances.' In a few moments the doors had shut, the sentinels had disappeared. Education was once more going on inside the classrooms. (p 165)

Practices as extreme as that described by Vicars Bell have long disappeared from our schools yet if any group of students perceives their school to be impersonal and authoritarian this inevitably induces, at best, a restricted attitude towards learning. The teacher in the classroom will work best within a school ethos which is friendly but not patronising, challenging and demanding but not paternalistic. In classes where a higher than average number of students come from socially deprived backgrounds and/or belong to ethnic minorities some teachers may feel uneasy or threatened and respond to their students with over-strict formality or by keeping a distance. When this derives, as it usually does, from lack of confidence rather than elitist attitudes, professional support backed by a positive school ethos can prove the key factor in rectifying the situation.

Values associated with public examinations also affect attitudes to knowledge and learning. Public examinations are an influential part of every secondary curriculum and act as an instrument of selection for more advanced courses and careers. However necessary this task may be we should remember that the more privileged always have a flying start. There are influential arguments for abandoning the concept of GCSE as a school leaving examination. Instead, it should be seen as a stage in a young person's development providing the opportunity to obtain credits which can be built on in the future. A development along these lines would certainly contribute to less divisive and competitive attitudes both within schools and outside them. Attitudes are also strongly influenced by methods of monitoring and assessing students' progress. This highly skilled activity, discussed further in Chapters 9 and 12, is distorted and trivialised by mandatory testing for league tables and the snap judgments they induce. Once again, as in the era of the 11-plus examination, many teachers feel compelled to distort their teaching to achieve higher test scores at the expense of broader and deeper understanding.

Political beliefs

Attitudes to knowledge and learning are closely associated with political beliefs and the school curriculum is a powerful instrument for expressing and transmitting values. As we saw at the start of Chapter 1 the coal owners of the last century provided education in order to thwart the efforts of miners to attain power through self-education. Three years after the October revolution in Russia, Lenin (1920) dealt with what to learn and how to learn. In his customary incisive manner he told an audience of young people that education could not succeed if it 'were restricted only to the classroom and divorced from the ferment of life'. To counteract some post-revolutionary feeling that a total break with the past was desirable and feasible, he emphasised that it was essential to distinguish between what was good in the old system from much which 'cluttered up the brain'. In Britain, in the 1960s and early '70s, there were also some well-intentioned but mistaken ideas concerning the use of distinctive topics and methods for the education of working class children. In the 1980s, Conservative governments commenced a major restructuring of state education one of whose thrusts was to try to dictate attitudes to the curriculum and thus gain access to the minds of the young. Bahro quotes an apt warning from a poet, Reiner Kunze:

People, we are going to teach you, so that you will remain ignorant (p 300)

So Durham miners, Conservative governments and the founder of the Soviet Union have all realised the relevance and importance of the school curriculum to their visions and objectives. So, too, have committed teachers and educationists in Africa, the West Indies and other developing countries where independence brought with it a legacy of books, curricula and teaching methods from a colonial past together with associated values and ideas. In 1968 I advised the government of St Kitts-Nevis-Anguilla in the West Indies on their plans for comprehensive education. In a sweltering infant classroom one morning I listened to the headmistress reading the children a story. 'Daddy' was returning home from the office to be received by 'Mummy' and a nice warm fire. The hidden curriculum was having a field day. Class distinction and sex stereotyping would have applied in any environment, but there was an additional message for those I was with: the implication of a superior culture to their own.

Many in St Kitts, in 1968, were reacting against the dearth of locally produced books and materials and, hopefully, the position has improved.

The influence of the previous British colonial presence was still very evident in the schools at that time. Corporal punishment was widespread and I remember, on one occasion, mildly remonstrating with the head of a secondary school concerning the curriculum. I referred to the excessively formal methods of instruction I had noticed. For example, teachers of English all seemed to find it necessary to pick out nouns and verbs and other parts of speech before starting to read a story. He told me that conditions in the schools represented a considerable advance from the days when, as a pupil, he played truant on Wednesday afternoons. This was the time for the moral education lesson. Two hundred children would assemble in a large classroom. The teacher would call out 'What is honesty?' The children were expected to reply, in unison, 'Honesty is the best policy' before moving on to the next stimulating exhortation!

The educational legacy of the past was evident everywhere but also an increasing realisation of its negative implications. Colonialism had been maintained by ideological as well as economic and military pressures leaving a corresponding urgency to replace all that 'cluttered up the brain'. In Britain, too, the importance of maintaining and developing the ideological initiative in educational matters has been demonstrated throughout the period of state education.

Religion

Collective school worship and religious education, first made compulsory in the 1944 Education Act, are divisive practices creating a conflict of values for both school students and teachers. Few parents, even the strongest advocates of a materialist philosophy,[7] withdraw their children from religious activities partly because they are rarely informed of their legal rights but also to avoid their children being singled out. Teachers exercising a similar right may risk being labelled uncooperative with all that entails for career and even job prospects. The unsatisfactory situation for families of non-Christian faiths has long been highlighted and the 1988 Education Reform Act has exacerbated their situation. Many ministers of religion, as well as church members, believe that the state should provide only secular education as in most other European countries. Indeed, among the most active supporters of the comprehensive ideal, both within and outside the schools, are to be found those with religious beliefs and those with secular views working closely and effectively together.

Nevertheless, the influence of religion on the ideology of the curriculum, actual and hidden, is not to be underestimated.

Motivation

Whatever decisions are made about the curriculum, and however favourable the attitudes of a school and its teachers to knowledge and learning, students need to be motivated before they can learn effectively. Motivation, therefore, is an important part of the art and technique (the How?) of teaching and influences method, content and purpose. Furthermore, it cannot be divorced from the social, ideological and material environment in which the learning takes place. In addition to immediate requirements in the classroom, we must therefore ask such questions as 'Are we encouraging our students to learn so that they can be obedient citizens and read the Job Centre notices?' Or, recognising that people can change society, are we helping them to prepare themselves for informed and responsible adulthood in which they can play an active part in determining the future?

In the classroom

However attractive on paper, school curricula are put to the test in the classroom and in the remainder of this chapter we aim to establish a basis for understanding specific issues of the curriculum whatever their context. The ideas to be considered are often obscured by a minefield of educational jargon, not least in official reports and publications. Parents and governors should never hesitate to question papers and hand-outs which are peppered with undefined terms. Their principal effect is to induce feelings of inadequacy among the readers who would have no problems in understanding the issues if they were presented in clear English.

Involving learners

In adult education classes, members enrol for courses as a result of personal needs and interests; as they proceed they often develop in understanding and consciousness far beyond their expectations at the start. Expert guidance, collaborative discussion with fellow students, shared experiences and independent study prove a powerful combination for effective learning. Similar experiences are possible from the earliest days at school; to any field of study each class member will bring a unique background of personal experience, knowledge and previously developed capabilities and it should be an important part of their school experience that there are opportunities to learn through both cooperative and independent activities. Today there are many excellent examples of varied and effective teaching approaches but there are also many teachers who are wary of considering the necessary changes. The art of classroom management is a sensitive one, not quickly acquired and proposals for change can induce fears that the quality of work and job satisfaction may, at least, temporarily diminish. There is the familiar situation where teachers — at their desks, the blackboard or the television monitor — are clearly visible as the focus of attention and 'masters' or 'mistresses' of the situation. Any diffusion of this scenario may seem to some as a threat to their authority rather than as an opportunity for student and teacher to learn together. In reality, authority which develops from shared experience is of a deeper and more lasting nature and teacher reluctance is often overcome by sharing experience among colleagues.

Where corporate activities and genuine inquiry are encouraged in the classroom there will often be a similar approach to wider issues. Together, they will influence the perception of a school and what it stands for but, as we have seen, this is open to misinterpretation. If, for example, a school tries openly to help its 'problem' students rather than to keep as quiet as possible about them, it may appear to be out of step. In the present climate, 'good schools' are not expected to have problems except of the most trivial and ephemeral kind, and most certainly they should never let the outside world know if something more serious occurs. Schools which have attempted openness have often been singled out for attack. An early example occurred at Prestolee Elementary School in Lancashire where cooperative and independent study in a state school operated in the 1920s and '30s.[8] The first case of a comprehensive school to receive full media attention occurred in the early 1960s[9] while, in the '70s and '80s, attacks on comprehensive schools differed from school to school according to local circumstances but had this in common: the recipients were trying to implement the comprehensive ideal in the interests of all their students, those from working class families equally with those from professional and middle class homes. Several of the target schools, discussed in Chapter 6, had outstanding achievements by any standards. Today, with open enrolment, spare school places and financing mainly by numbers on roll, the risks have never been greater even for the most modest deviations from the norm. Safer, in a climate of public ignorance, to stick to methods where the teacher is metaphorically 'on the rostrum' and students listen. Too bad if, in so doing, we teach and they 'remain ignorant'.

This dilemma needs to be seriously addressed. Whilst all young people are entitled to be protected from piecemeal and unco-ordinated innovation (and the concept of a national curriculum recognises this) they are equally entitled to much more than a 'safety first' education. We all learn rapidly, and often with excitement and enthusiasm, in unfamiliar and unexpected situations. Wise parents chart a course for their children between the extremes of over-protection and foolhardiness. Children who are first guided and then trusted in situations for which they are ready are the fortunate ones; much the same applies in school.

Wrong directions

Teaching strategies which include opportunities for collaborative and independent study are an important element in a young person's education but only, of course, if the learning objectives are achievable and desirable. 'Child-centred education' was a fashionable term at one time especially in primary schools. Teachers would often say to their secondary colleagues 'You teach subjects; I teach children' but this apparently innocent aphorism is based on flawed reasoning. To focus attention on the child at the same time as on the curriculum is essential. To imply that the curriculum is of relatively minor importance is, at best, a misunderstanding of its nature and, at worst, an abdication of responsibility.

Classroom activity directed towards the following objectives seems innocent enough:

> To educate the minds of the pupils and teach them to study, learn and assimilate and not merely to cram their brains with ... notes and facts and stock phrases in order to secure diplomas and degrees ... The school aims to educate the whole man: the physical, the social, the aesthetic, the religious, the intellectual aspects.

In fact, this statement was issued by Mussolini's Minister of Public Education soon after the fascists came to power in Italy in 1923. It is reproduced by Harold Entwistle (1979) in *Antonio Gramsci: Conservative*

Schooling for Radical Politics (p 80) and forms part of a major educational reform, one of whose requirements was:

> the organisation of elementary education along progressive lines. (p 78)

Similarly worded objectives were formulated at about that time for very different purposes by countries as varied in intention as the USA and the USSR. In Britain, the second Hadow Report *The Primary School* (Board of Education, 1931) stated its opinion that:

> The curriculum is to be thought of in terms of activity and experience rather than of knowledge to be acquired and facts to be stored. (para 75)

Words like 'progressive', 'activity', and 'child centred' are inadequate in themselves as guidelines if they can be applied in such different circumstances. They relate to the 'How' of teaching without involvement of the 'What' and 'Why'.

Identifying good practice

Advances in teaching method have made a major contribution to our understanding of the purpose and possibilities of the curriculum as a whole. The best of our primary school practice, built up during the 1950s and '60s, was based on the involvement of pupils in a variety of cooperative and independent activities, prepared and carefully monitored by teachers. With hindsight there are important lessons to be learned but the way forward cannot involve putting the clock back to an unrelieved diet of 'chalk and talk'. In the early days of comprehensive schools the expression 'resource based learning'[10] covered similar methods to those pioneered in primary schools and, throughout the century, we have had a variety of words and phrases to distinguish learning situations which involve active participation by students from those where the teacher mainly gives information or sets tasks to the class as a whole. In practice, teaching methods lie on a continuum rather than in mutually exclusive compartments. In the 1980s additions to the educational vocabulary stemmed from projects such as the Technical and Vocational Education Initiative funded through the Manpower Services Commission. The TVEI (Chapter 1, note 11) saw the potential in student centred learning methods. Their approach, backed by offers of unprecedented resources, appealed to many schools as the way ahead for at least some of their students. 'Negotiated curricula' and 'experiential learning' were prominent in speeches and reports. The former referred to regular negotiation between student and teacher and the latter to learning by experience — as the Hadow Report and Lenin both recommended — how else?[11] Even if the ideas are scarcely new, they sound worthy of approval and so they are — if learning objectives are clear and acceptable. This is not always the case.

Unsound or insufficiently thought-out teaching material can be presented in packages which are attractive to staff and students. The materials may involve learning activities which occupy and interest the class but whose content is narrow and indeterminate in scope. One so-called enterprise activity stemming from TVEI, with derivatives running today under the 'Education and Business Partnership' and other initiatives, involved students in exercises which simulated running a small business or factory. The project took place away from school and lasted a week. Real products were 'manufactured' and students played the roles of entrepreneurs, management, various grades of factory based employee, salespersons and trade union officials. The professional skills of the teachers responsible for the project were, doubtless, impeccable but who asked about their depth and breadth of knowledge of economic and industrial relations, let alone their views on issues such as trade union representation and negotiating rights? The attitudes of a team of teachers involved in such an activity are likely to have a considerable effect on values absorbed by the students both directly and through the hidden curriculum. Their experiences may be enlightening, but the question is: in what direction? Teachers may see such enterprises as a useful break from school routine for their students and an opportunity for them to learn about how industry works and to experience at first hand the 'life and social skills' (such as working in a team) which industry is thought to require from its employees. Popularity is an excellent motivator but, unless subjected to a rigorous analysis as far as content and purpose are concerned, it is not a sufficient condition for inclusion in the curriculum.[12]

By the early 1990s, projects and assignments were firmly back on the educational agenda after a partial eclipse in previous decades. Their new-found respectability stemmed directly, and in some ways surprisingly, from the syllabuses introduced by the new GCSE boards which provided the opportunity for a high content of course work[13] and also to the recommendations of several national curriculum documents. Project work motivated many students and the quality of work produced has been widely acknowledged.

In assessing the value of group and individual work, it is essential to relate methods to objectives. Teachers who work most actively for improvements in the curriculum quickly recognise the better motivation and depth of understanding when school students are actively engaged in the learning process. Nevertheless, there are times when direct instruction is efficient and the appropriate technique to use. Method, content and learning objectives must be planned together for optimum effect and we must avoid the trap of assuming a simple relationship of the type:

activity method = progress; direct teaching = reaction.

The inverse is equally limiting.

Freedom and choice

Curriculum responsibility

Teachers in Britain have long prided themselves with justification on their ability to motivate students and to make their lessons varied and interesting. For many years they attributed this, in part, to the degree of freedom they had in Britain compared with most European countries where curricula and textbooks were centrally prescribed. Nevertheless this freedom was always subject to constraints such as examination syllabuses, parents wishes, the requirements of the next stage of the educational ladder and the priorities of inspectors and advisers, headteachers and heads of department. Until the mid-1980s, however, the freedom of teachers to ultimately determine the curriculum was jealously guarded, not least by teachers' unions. Many feared that central direction would greatly reduce opportunities for teachers to provide relevant and stimulating work for their students.

Projects such as the TVEI added to the constraints on schools and teachers and, while providing some welcome opportunities, they also contained divisive and restrictive elements. Lord Young, an unelected Conservative Secretary of State for Trade and Industry, played a major part in TVEI developments. 'We must find a way to motivate the majority of young people who simply don't benefit out of the existing comprehensives with their watered down academic system' he writes in his autobiography thus betraying his hostile approach to comprehensive education (Young, 1990:90). His solutions involved technical and vocational education from the age of fourteen for many school students whilst, presumably, those aiming at the professions pursued an undiluted academic curriculum. Such polarisation leads inevitably to selection.[14]

Nevertheless by the start of the 1980s lack of a major curriculum input from outside the teaching profession had led to weaknesses and inconsistencies which provided the opportunity for the radical Right to seize the initiative. Whilst the expertise and experience of teachers concerning method and motivation is essential if insight and depth is to be given to the development of the curriculum, others have an equal right to a say because of its importance in shaping the future. Public education needs the support of informed democratic organisations working in conjunction with professionals to support stimulating and effective teaching and defend it against ill-motivated attack. Under teacher autonomy, it must be accepted that all was far from well. Teachers faced conflicting pressures in the classroom and it was all too easy for even the most conscientious and forward looking to sometimes take a short term view when planning the next day's lesson with immediate relevance and a busily occupied class taking precedence over longer term and deeper objectives.

Relevance and good sense

The need for relevance in the curriculum is often taken for granted. But relevance means different things to different people and depends on the context in which it is considered. Entwistle's book brings out an important principle in this respect: if we try to make all our teaching immediately relevant to our students by choosing topics within their existing sphere of experience, we shall, inevitably, abdicate an important part of our responsibility to them. For some students in secondary school, excessive emphasis was given to topics such as community studies, personal and social education, youth culture and projects based on hobbies and interests. Consequently, they did not have sufficient opportunity to be introduced to important branches of knowledge, culture, skill and aspiration which should be the right of every young person at school. This is not an argument for an unrelieved diet of academic school subjects and there is no reason why any or all of the topics above should not form part of a purposeful, well thought out and challenging educational programme. However, when drawing up schemes of work which involve a substantial input from students, it is necessary to keep in mind an analysis of the strengths and weaknesses in these experiences. Entwistle quotes Gramsci:

> When one's conception of the world is not critical and coherent but disjointed and episodic, one belongs simultaneously to a multiplicity of mass human groups. The personality is strangely composite: it contains Stone Age elements and principles of a more advanced science, prejudices from all past phases of history at the local level and intuitions of a future philosophy which will be that of a human race united the world over. (p 35)

Thus, there are promising elements in each person's background which should be developed and there are others which will need correction. Gramsci also makes a useful distinction between common sense and good sense. The former, he points out, contains both progressive and regressive elements and is therefore unreliable as a guide to educational philosophy:

> Common sense, then, is rooted in folklore but enriched with scientific ideas and with philosophical opinions which have entered ordinary life. Good sense is this 'healthy nucleus which exists in 'common sense' ... and which deserves to be made more ... coherent'. (p 35)

Over emphasis on the teaching of skills, as opposed to content, needs similar scrutiny. When acquisition of a skill helps a young person to achieve self-confidence and a sense of achievement, it is to be welcomed. If, on the other hand, 'skills based learning' represents little more than an attempt at immediate relevance for those who may feel disadvantaged in current circumstances then, almost certainly, there will be important omissions in their education including experience of 'the teacher as liberator' (note 8). In the secondary sector, the greatest scope for freedom of choice existed for teachers of 'non-examination' candidates in the lower streams of comprehensive schools — the very ones at highest risk of being sold short in their education. In contrast, public examination syllabuses and pressures for results have produced much less curricular freedom where academically able students are concerned and especially for those from the highest socio-economic groups. As Gramsci put it:

> The difficulty about espousing freedom as an educational aim is that freedom is essentially a negative concept, signalling an absence of restraint. (p 85)

Technical education and intellectual challenge

It is easy to assume that some natural barrier exists between academic and technical education. Arguments can then be made in support of differentiation in the curriculum by the provision of separate courses from the age of fourteen or so. This is a central point of criticism of schemes like the TVEI, at least in its original formation. Differentiation implies selection and school students should not be faced with choices which exclude them from major fields of learning. In reality, no natural barrier exists. The two branches of education are closely inter-related and this should be reflected in the curriculum of all school students from the earliest age. This principle was a welcome feature of the national curriculum as originally proposed but it will need to be defended. The impossibility of fitting the whole of the national curriculum in its original form into a school timetable of reasonable length — a revealing error from a government professing the importance of standards — means that some parts of the national curriculum have been squeezed or made optional. In the process of adjustment, we must retain the entitlement of all young people to a balanced education. The problem is particularly acute in the last two years of compulsory schooling (Key Stage 4) and, as usual, those with the greatest needs are also at greatest risk of being sold short. Entwistle notes that, for Gramsci:

> a major function of schooling is the development of intellectuals. (p 113)

But Gramsci's intellectuals were to be no narrow group of academics:

> By 'intellectuals' must be understood not those strata commonly described by this term, but in general the entire social stratum which exercises an organisational function in a wider sense — whether in the field of production, or in that of culture, or in that of political administration. (p 114)

Supervisors, technicians, shop stewards, trade union officials, political organisers and propagandists are all quoted as examples of people exercising responsibility. Today many other categories could be added and it remains just as important that intellectual activity is extended far beyond academic environments. Although Gramsci was considering the requirements of adult education at this point, his thinking has implications for our schools. All school students are entitled to be stimulated in an intellectual manner so that they are helped to develop their critical faculties. This applies equally to studies which are technical, scientific, literary, social or artistic and aesthetic. An education along these lines extending voluntarily into adult life is a worthy and attainable ideal. We must never underestimate the mental capacities of our students.[15]

Check-list for every school curriculum

The questions in the following check-list reflect the inter-relationships of the curriculum. With content, method, purpose and the key question of for whom? in mind, they are intended as a guide on which to base specific questions about existing or proposed curricula. They are intended as suggestions and starting points for teachers, governors, parents and all concerned with policy making; they are especially important when changes and modifications are proposed however minor or peripheral these may appear — or be made to appear.

- *If the curriculum as a whole is under consideration*:
    - Are aims and objectives in the classroom consistent with ethos and practice in the school as a whole?
    - Do the constituent parts complement each other so that common values are reinforced throughout the learning process?
    - Are teaching methods based on the principle that all students can develop their abilities through appropriate learning experiences?

- *If common learning experiences for all are being considered* (as they certainly should be in a comprehensive system of education):
    - Are content and teaching methods in accord with intended objectives?
    - What values and priorities do they indicate?

- *If alternative programmes of study for different students are recommended*:
    - Who chooses the subject or course for each student?
    - What will those who take each alternative miss? How important is this?
    - What values are transmitted to students and their parents by offering the choice?

- *For the public examination system which exercises such a great influence on the secondary schools:*
  - For whom is it intended?
  - Are syllabuses based on the real needs of students or are they designed 'top down' starting from the wishes of universities and employers?
  - Is it a unifying or dividing instrument? What are the effects on those who take the examination and on those who do not?
  - For students who will not take the examination, are equally satisfactory alternatives available?

Adaptation of the curriculum must be a continuous task if schools are to provide their students with practical and social skills, as well as formal qualifications, which enable them to meet with confidence the changing situations of everyday life. Adaptation certainly but not at the expense of basic principles for our students are also entitled to receive inspiration; to learn how to contribute collaboratively to the creation of a better future, and to have equal access to the cultural heritage of mankind.

5

Enhancing Educational Experience:
a plan for advance

The comprehensive ideal is an inspiring and practical one with the aim of full personal development for all. As part of this process we must ask whether any single school can provide all that is needed for each of its students. Suppose we could extend the range of opportunities provided by individual primary and secondary schools with a complementary programme of activities at local authority and regional level. Enhanced opportunities could give immense satisfaction and fulfilment to young people during their most formative years whilst results, in terms of achievement and personal satisfaction, would more than justify the costs involved. Indeed, large sums are currently raised in the independent sector to provide just such a variety of experience. In this chapter we first consider aspects of community education and examine educational thinking which has influenced the size of schools. These issues provide a background to proposals for enhancing the experience of all school students.

Community education

Expressions like 'community education' and 'community school' have a reassuring ring to them and one instinctively feels ready to support the worthy concepts which they represent even if a little uncertain as to their precise significance. Here we need go no further than the opening sentence of a statement of policy by the Community Education Association (1991):

> Education is a life long learning process, concerned with identifying and meeting the needs of individuals and their communities. It should lead to a common effort to improve everyone's quality of life. (p 5)

This statement is fully consistent with the principles of comprehensive education already discussed and such ideas have inspired some impressive comprehensive developments. From 1964 to 1969 I was deputy head of Wyndham School at Egremont (now in Cumbria), a purpose built community school financed with a contribution from the rural district council as well as the county education authority. The school served a wide and diverse area and the imaginative buildings included a high class swimming pool shared with the community; an attractive library serving school and public, and facilities for adult education. The staff was largely hand picked for the job.[1] Whilst most schools cannot match this provision, 'a common effort to improve everyone's quality of life' should involve all comprehensive schools and their communities.

Neighbourhood schools

In the formative years of comprehensive education, the idea of a neighbourhood comprehensive school, serving its local community and being an organic part of it, was widely accepted. It was in the minds of many who planned and implemented schemes in both rural and urban areas. When I taught in secondary modern schools in the 1950s and '60s it was taken for granted that each school served its own catchment area and, today, this is still the case for many primary schools. A government circular (Ministry of Education, 1947b) defined a comprehensive school as one which catered for:

All the secondary education of all the children in the given area ... (p 272)

Reference to a given area (or neighbourhood) is closely linked with the idea that comprehensive schools should serve their communities whether or not they are specifically designated as community schools. The main problem stemmed from the belief that a mix of social class and 'ability' in each school was essential. This objective often proved incompatible with house building policies which separated local authority housing for rent from private housing to buy. Some education committees tried to define the catchment areas of their schools to achieve such a mix but this was often very difficult and incompatible with the idea that schools could act as an educational and recreational focal points for large housing estates.[2] Brian Simon (1971) dealt with the implications of engineered mixes in the epilogue to *Intelligence, Psychology and Education*:

What therefore, is being said here is that to promote social harmony by helping social classes to understand each other ought to be one of the primary objectives of comprehensive schools; a modern version of the longstanding policy of using the schools system, by way of regulating organisation and content, as a means of social control. (p 271)

He saw the idea of all schools having such a mix as 'metaphysical' and the comprehensive of the future as a school:

serving a particular locality, one of a system covering an area as a whole. (p 272)[3]

We shall return later in the chapter to the far reaching implications of this observation but, first, we examine constraints on the size of comprehensive schools in order to assess how much flexibility there is for schools to match the varied sizes of actual communities.

Matching schools to communities

When comprehensive schools for the 11-18 range first appeared on the drawing board, it was commonly thought that they must be very large (up to 2000 or more on roll) in order to generate viable sixth form numbers. In many areas this was impossible and local education authorities met the problem in different ways. Some concentrated sixth form provision in one or more large schools, others introduced sixth form or tertiary colleges[4] whilst others again took advantage of new regulations allowing more flexibility in the age of transfer between schools. First, middle and upper schools made their appearance with transfer ages of 8 or 9 (first to middle) and 12, 13 or 14 (middle to upper) according to local circumstances. These alternatives were adopted only in a few areas and the 11 to 18 'all through' comprehensive school remained the largest group. In fact, 11 to 18 schools had numbers on roll ranging from two or three hundred to two thousand or more and, although schools achieved commendable successes with their sixth forms many, like those of all but the largest grammar schools, were comparatively small. There are many arguments against small sixth forms including the cost per student, restricted choice of curriculum and classes with numbers too small to generate stimulating discussions among members. Research evidence confirms that the majority of young people benefit by studying in a student environment alongside contemporaries taking a wide range of courses.

The educational and social benefit of such an environment is not to be underestimated and the case for post-16 education to be provided in tertiary colleges is a very strong one. Where established, they have proved popular with students, staff and parents.

Even if tertiary colleges had been universal, the question of school size would have remained because the case for large schools depended on two other factors. In the 1960s and '70s the majority of schools and local education authorities considered that a wide range of options for students in their last two years of compulsory education was essential. This also required a large size of school if the necessary teaching expertise was to be recruited and option groups were to be economical in size.[5] From the late 1960s there were dissenting voices which doubted the wisdom of too broad a menu and a few schools adopted a more common curriculum which ensured balance but still allowed students some choice. Twenty years later the proposal for a national (common) curriculum was widely welcomed. Unfortunately its rationale and structure were ill thought out and the original framework proved impracticable. Nevertheless, and despite concerns over moves towards a two-track approach separating academic and vocational routes, there is no wish to return to an extensive à-la-carte model.

One further factor contributed to thinking that large comprehensive schools were essential. This was the alleged need for several streams, bands or sets in each year group. As we have seen in previous chapters, such a policy is a danger to the healthy and progressive development of comprehensive education. All three arguments used to support a requirement for large schools are, therefore, either outdated or spurious but these are not arguments against large schools as such. Many have made notable contributions to educational thought and practice and several continue to be at the forefront of comprehensive school development. In the early 1970s opponents of comprehensive education often claimed that large schools were impersonal and that individual attention was impossible. Not only were such arguments contrary to the experience of the overwhelming majority of teachers, parents and students of the schools but critics failed to mention that among the country's largest schools were Eton College and Manchester Grammar School.

Constraints concerning size need not worry us unduly if we wish to emphasise the role of comprehensive schools in serving neighbourhoods and communities. Optimum size can be determined by local needs in conjunction with availability of buildings and other practical considerations. It follows that we can expect, and welcome, schools of different sizes as long as *equally high quality educational provision is available for all students*. Equally high quality needs examination in the context of the total needs of students in all schools, even the largest. In the next section we look first at some student needs in the internal environment of their schools and then examine opportunities for learning beyond school boundaries.

Enhancing provision

Internal environment

Up to the mid-1970s (a few years earlier in the primary sector) the majority of schools were full and all available space had to be used for teaching. This left negligible facilities for social and recreational activities and for personal study. Banishment to the playground before school and at break and lunchtimes except in extreme conditions is not acceptable. Young people huddling in porches on bleak 'outdoor' days does nothing to foster good relationships either among students or with staff. Most of the former note that, except for those on duty, conditions are very different for the adults (and perhaps the most senior students) inside. Those with sensitive, introspective or studious dispositions find being sent outside a particularly irksome and frustrating experience and one which maximises opportunities for bullying. Some improvement was possible in new schools where house and year rooms were provided but these usually had to double as teaching spaces. A decline in the birthrate, leading to falling school rolls, provided a missed opportunity to improve the quality of life for school students and with it their respect for the values of education. Decent conditions for relaxation are an entitlement and spare space in schools should be seen as an opportunity and challenge for architects and educators.

In the summer of 1985, Sunderland Local Education Authority issued proposals for the reorganisation of the borough's secondary education to meet government requirements for cost saving in the face of reduced intakes. As with most authorities, the requirements were seen, in part, as an arithmetical exercise to match school closures with an acceptable reduction in the number of school places. Sunderland did, however, take the opportunity to establish a tertiary system which extended the comprehensive principle to the 16 to 19 age range but the published proposals included no indication that spare teaching space in the 11 to 16 schools might be used for the educational and social benefit of their students. Ten years ago it was interesting to observe the physical changes which occurred immediately in two former schools re-designated as part of the tertiary college provision. Attractive and non-threatening entrances, carpets, curtains and blinds, soft décor, common rooms for students as well as major improvements and extensions to specialist facilities all led to a transformation of the buildings and contributed to the esteem in which the colleges are held. Younger students, well used to high standards at home, would undoubtedly respond to similar, if more modest, consideration. The Trades Union Congress (1962) made a similar point three decades ago:

> Facilities for private study, and some common room facilities for older students, might well add to the contribution which secondary schools might make to effective secondary education. (p 169)

Or, as Geoffrey Cooksey, first director of the highly respected Stantonbury Campus in Milton Keynes[6] put it in an interview with *The Times Educational Supplement* (1985):

> Carpets are curriculum tool number one.

A striking observation to focus attention on the relationship between the quality of learning and the physical and aesthetic conditions for school students.[7]

Beyond school boundaries

Within relatively recent times all local authorities have experience of providing services directly involving the education of school students. Examples include learning-to-swim classes, outdoor activities, musical instrument tuition, work experience schemes and activities related to TVEI and other initiatives.[8] Expanding this idea to embrace a total educational provision, drawing not only on local authorities but also on other organisations and resources in the district, could unleash the potential for each comprehensive school to serve the young people in its locality as part of, in Simon's words, 'a system covering an area as a whole'.

The Community Education Association's policy statement, referred to above, notes that:

> Learning programmes should not be constrained by institutional boundaries
> and rules but should be resourced from a variety of centres ...

So can we compensate for the inevitable limitations of any particular institution noting that the total teaching expertise and resources available within a district are far wider than those within an individual school? In the past the quality of local education authorities' services, despite restrictions due to underfunding, was often excellent but it is necessary to ask whether they were anything like sufficient in extent. The comprehensive ideal of full personal development for all still has wide public support but the aspirations of parents and school students do not remain static. The mis-match between what individual primary and comprehensive schools can offer and people's expectations has increased during the last three or four decades and almost certainly contributes to the increase in enrolments to independent day schools and to support for grant maintained status in more affluent areas. Learning programmes 'resourced from a variety of centres' could give immense satisfaction and fulfilment to young people during their most formative years yet the possibility has never, I believe, been seriously examined in this country. In July 1985, at the time of Sunderland's reorganisation plans, I wrote to the director of education as follows:

> I believe that the quality of education for pupils throughout the borough could
> be enhanced and standards raised if specialist centres formed an integral part of
> a comprehensive system for the 5-16 age range. Neither primary nor secondary
> schools can expect to have a sufficient range of specialist expertise and
> resources to be able to develop fully the whole range of interests and talents of
> all their pupils. This has been recognised in Sunderland for many years by its
> Borough wide, and widely respected music provision ... Examples of the kind of
> centre which would be beneficial to the education service include modern
> languages, arts and crafts, drama, sport, science and technology, English,
> humanities, environmental and computer studies. Such centres would, of
> course, be closely linked to the LEA's advisory and inspectoral service.

Events have moved on since then but the central argument remains valid and, if adopted, could be incorporated in the national curriculum.

Even the largest schools cannot expect to have experts in every aspect which may be of interest to at least some young people. Primary and secondary schools should be staffed by well qualified teachers in all the main areas of the curriculum and their work complemented by an extended service on a local authority and regional scale. Such a service must not be viewed simply as extra opportunities for the gifted using some central building, perhaps a former school, as a centre of excellence. Certainly one would anticipate excellent work, but arising as the result of a policy of access for school students dependent solely on interest, commitment and need and organised in a variety of ways of which the following are examples:

- Facilities for project work under the national curriculum.
- Activities and courses at various locations on topics such as those in the letter above and many more.
- Well qualified staff teams working both in the schools and at local centres, for example in performing arts.
- Increased support for students with special needs incorporated as part of the normal school provision.
- Cooperation with organisations and voluntary bodies to provide, for example, sports coaching and courses in first aid.
- Educational and financial support for gifted performers who may need training at unusual hours or to live away from home for part of the time.
- Short stay residential courses.
- Weekend and school holiday activities.

The possibilities are endless and, whilst the organisational challenges are not to be underestimated, there is already a wealth of experience in both schools and authorities for incorporating activities into school programmes. A proposal to enhance primary and comprehensive school experience is not a matter of starting from scratch but rather of creating a totality of educational experience for school students based on a fully comprehensive philosophy of education. Organised support for teachers continues to exist in all local education authorities and provides a service of research, advice, courses at local centres and school based work. It does not require a great step forward in imagination to extend this principle to school students.

Sources of ideas

During recent years several organisations and many local groups have implemented or campaigned for activities designed to help young people to benefit as much as possible from their school experience. The scope and scale of such activities covers a wide spectrum: 'Kids Club Network' and 'Education Extra' work for schools to remain open later with facilities available; the Princes Trust runs a network of study support centres; the Labour government's scheme for literacy classes during the school holidays is to be extended and repeated next year, and homework clubs run by local groups apparently abound.

No doubt many parents, teachers and well-wishers are involved throughout the country — mainly on a voluntary basis — but the kind of enhanced educational experience being suggested here would take its place as an integral part of the total educational provision and entitlement. John White (1997), professor of philosophy of education, has made radical suggestions for the compulsory school day. According to a report in *The Times Educational Supplement* (1997b) Professor White's idea came after a visit to the former Soviet Union where he saw children being taught in classrooms in the mornings and taking part in chosen activities in the afternoons.

In the spring of 1988 I visited the former German Democratic Republic for an education study tour.[9] Throughout its forty-years history the GDR provided complementary studies and activities for its school students as part of their educational entitlement. The compulsory period of education was based on ten-year comprehensive schools catering for ages 6 to 16. Many of these schools were in rural areas with 25 to 30 students in each year group giving a number on roll of about 300. Even in larger towns the schools rarely exceeded double this size so internal school selection was almost an impossibility even had it been thought desirable. All schools provided facilities for hobbies and further study groups which operated mainly in the afternoons using some of the school's teaching staff as well as other teachers, instructors and coaches for specialist activities. Towns and districts had centres staffed independently of the schools which provided programmes of activities during the day and at weekends. A booklet notes that 1.5 million — a very high proportion of the total school population — participated regularly in activities which included electronics and computer technology, mathematics, chemistry, astronomy, model railway construction, hiking, painting, music, literature, puppet shows, local history and a wide range of sporting activities.[10] Study of educational practice in another country can provide helpful insights and encourage re-examination of familiar practices but there are no readily transferable blueprints.[11] Nevertheless the GDR's contribution to a comprehensive system of education remains relevant today.

The task ahead

A fully comprehensive system, with teaching largely based on flexible, non-selective methods (Chapter 6) could form the basis of an effective and equitable programme of enhanced educational experience. Despite restrictions on local authority spending, there are also circumstances favourable to a major initiative. The comprehensive system is still largely in place, some of the spare teaching space in schools could be adapted for new activities and there is valuable experience in appropriate teaching methods.[12] Reciprocal feedback between school-based staff and teachers and instructors responsible for extra-school activities will be an important element in effectiveness and, given leadership and commitment, our primary and comprehensive schools, already achieving much, could develop as key elements of an extended comprehensive system, rich in variety, and with a strong community focus. Certainly the time is right for pilot schemes.

Failure to address the issue of mis-match between expectations and provision will lead to increasing fragmentation of our educational system. In contrast, the opportunity to enrich the national curriculum without overcrowding it, and for schools to collaborate rather than compete, would attract broadly based support. Parents want the very best for their children and, under an effective scheme, could have confidence that their local school, particularly if developed on community lines, would provide access to the widest possible range of mental, physical and creative activities organised and led by experts in their field. *The Times Educational Supplement* (1991e) noted that an independent boarding school for girls in Dorset was attracting custom with a 'Bring your own pony' offer whilst, near Brighton, crewing yachts is a popular weekend activity at Rodean independent girl's school. Whilst neither of these activities might immediately come to mind in everyone's list of priorities for the state sector, they vividly illustrate the serious attention which independent schools are giving to widening experiences and broadening the appeal of their schools to prospective students.[13] Students of state schools deserve no less and enhanced educational experience under the guidance and overall responsibility of local education authorities seems the way forward.

III
COMPREHENSIVE VALUES:
non-selective practice

6

Initiatives in the Classroom

The arrival of comprehensive schools gave tremendous encouragement to teachers who had recognised inherent limitations in much of the classroom practice common at the time. Many combined their knowledge and experience with energy and enthusiasm to develop greatly improved methods of teaching and learning. The work of these pioneers showed that the best of modern teaching techniques supported by imaginative deployment of teachers and teaching spaces made the placement of school students in bands, streams or sets unnecessary and counter-productive. Their work created the potential for a major expansion of non-selective teaching in our comprehensive schools. In this chapter we consider criteria for effective learning, examine what has already been achieved in schools and look ahead to future developments.

Effective learning

Learning should certainly be useful but also inspiring for the future. Sir David Attenborough made the point as incoming president of the British Association for the Advancement of Science in an interview with Ian Nash, science correspondent of *The Times Educational Supplement* (1991c):

> Science must not be seen simply as a way of making life better or increasing the Gross National Product ... I feel sorry for people who do not see science as romantic or cultural. It affects our lives in a profound way.

Sir David was not averse to utilitarian values incorporated as part of the learning objectives but told Nash:

> I suspect that the reason children don't take up science is because it is too
> methodical, grounded and pedestrian whereas it should change lives.

In an editorial, *The Times Educational Supplement* (1991d) commented:
'Changing lives is what real education is about'.

Pedagogy explained

What goes for science is equally applicable to other subjects. School
students will learn from example; and the examples set will depend on the
aims and methods of teaching. Learning is a highly complex and, thus,
fascinating process; a variety of evidence suggests that no two people learn
and organise their thinking in precisely the same way so there are no easy
solutions or remedies to improve the effectiveness of learning and
teaching. That said, it is essential to recognise that teaching is a science as
well as an art and to provide a high level of research into the psychology of
learning and into pedagogy.

Pedagogy sounds an old-fashioned word but in its sense of the science
of effective teaching it is a very useful one. It is used more widely on the
continent but its study in many countries including Britain, has fallen
behind. Because of this, we leave open the opportunity for individuals and
groups to come up with simplistic and negative solutions which receive
mass coverage in the media but whose main achievement is to blur the
issues for the public. This, in turn, tends to distance ordinary people and
prevent them from becoming the allies of teachers in the complex but
rewarding tasks ahead. Simon (1985) has drawn attention to the problem
in a chapter entitled 'Why No Pedagogy in England?' in his book *Does
Education Matter?* After tracing the 'actual death of pedagogy' during the
forty years when mental testing dominated the scene, he concludes:

> We can no longer afford to go on in the old way, muddling through on a largely
> pragmatic, or historically institutionalised, basis ... the conditions now exist for
> a major breakthrough in terms of pedagogy. (p 89)

'Why No Pedagogy?' should be essential reading in all colleges and
departments of education as well as on in-service training courses. It adds
powerful arguments against strands of current thinking which imply that
the majority of teacher training can be acquired 'on the job' at school
rather than through a balanced programme of theoretical study and
practical experience firmly based in education departments and colleges.

Although the theoretical side may have been lacking, many comprehensive schools from the start established commendable practice in their classrooms based on non-selective teaching groups. In this chapter, we look at some of these teaching strategies but commence with further examination of the conditions for effective learning which were outlined in Chapter 2. Here, we stress the pedagogical and resource implications.

Classroom essentials

As we saw in Chapter 2 it is essential to address basic considerations such as physical and mental health, a sense of security and the absence of anxiety of a personal, social or family nature. 'Hungry to Learn' is the title of a devastating report by Angela Neustatter for *The Times Educational Supplement* (1991a) outlining the realities of poverty and their effects on schooling. Others have stressed that, in school as elsewhere, attention must always be given to emotional (or affective) matters as well as to knowledge (or the cognitive domain) if children are to feel secure and confident.

Fears associated with the learning process itself can be very real and must be reduced to a minimum if we are to build up in our students the necessary self-confidence and motivation towards the task in hand. Adult and community education workers are particularly aware of the significance of these matters and try to minimise adverse effects on access to education by people who could benefit given the right encouragement. In schools, where access is compulsory, teachers know that the effect of changes in motivation and self-confidence on individual performance can be dramatic. One must, however, be wary of reducing underlying complexities to nebulous and subjective categories such as 'home influence'. The influence of the home is certainly significant but it needs considering with precision and detail; some teachers refer to 'poor home background' as if the label provided a universal explanation for lack of progress and absolved the school from further responsibility. This generalisation is particularly unfortunate for children whose economic and physical circumstances at home leave much to be desired but where love and care are of a high order. Here, teachers may note signs of poverty and assume that nothing can be done. Many of the influences on a young person go much wider than home circumstances and include peer group pressure, often associated with sex-stereotyping, which can have devastating effects on individuals. Also the hidden curriculum and its values, described in Chapter 4, will play an important part in the success or otherwise of the intentions of teachers and learners.

Favourable conditions in the classroom are equally essential and involve the quality of preparation, presentation, feedback and monitoring of work. For example, one cannot hope to learn something new effectively if essential background information and understanding is missing. I have often noticed when meeting a class in mathematics for the first time that some students are able to answer orally with depth and insight yet have a low expectation of their overall performance. This often turns out to be a case of gaps in knowledge and understanding rather than lack of mental facility.[1] Equally, one cannot hope to grasp new concepts in subjects as diverse as science, literature and design unless they are first presented in concrete form in a variety of situations and over a period of time. Eventually, with appropriate learning experiences, the concept will become an integral part of a person's mental store.

Occasionally, research or carefully observed classroom practice produces dramatic results. Adey (1991) and others at Kings College, London published a report showing major improvements in performance in several subjects in the GCSE after students had taken part in a course to develop thinking skills two or three years earlier. The thinking skills course was directly related to the subjects in which the students later did well but, despite this success, the researchers were unable to persuade the Department of Education and Science to fund further research. Fortunately the group was undeterred and set up an organisation called CASE (Cognitive Acceleration through Science Education) which supports an active network of professionals and arranges conferences and courses.[2] An earlier example where research pointed to the potential of soundly based techniques to develop the mental processes of all human beings is described by a Soviet educational psychologist, Nina Talyzina (1981) in *The Psychology of Learning*. She shows how students mastered complex concepts and processes as diverse as writing the Russian alphabet (for young children) through strategies in chess to being able to apply general principles to the setting up of machine tools (for apprentices). The educational methods she describes are based on first analysing each task to identify general principles and then to devise strategies of learning based on understanding of principles rather than memorising large amounts of data, specific to just one particular situation. Talyzina's work would make an excellent starting point for a major initiative in pedagogical research in Britain.

There remains much to be done if the implications of Bruner's challenging assertion (Chapter 3) concerning the educability of everyone in some appropriate form is to become a reality in everyday school practice. With an effective pedagogy we can help his statement to be realised for more of our students and enable them to meet their aspirations and develop their abilities more widely and fully. Truly effective learning must also include a natural progression throughout the different stages of learning, for example from primary to secondary. In the 1960s and early '70s, when comprehensive schools were introducing non-selective grouping into their early years, they were sometimes criticised for bringing too much change too quickly. It was often forgotten that non-selective grouping in the comprehensive schools actually removed an unnecessary change (and acute cause of anxiety) that had existed for too long as pupils moved from non-selective groups in the majority of junior schools to banding or streaming at secondary level.

Teachers and resources

In the state sector in 1946 there was one teacher, including the head teacher, for every 32 pupils in primary schools and 22 in secondary schools. By the time of the Education Reform Act (1988) these figures had improved to 22 and 15 respectively.[3] Naturally teachers aim to be more ambitious in the quality and variety of learning experiences which they offer young people but it is vital that the time and expertise they need to apply to the learning process is not whittled away by inefficient and time consuming administrative duties, particularly those associated with the national curriculum and assessment. There is no room for complacency with reports of oversized classes, especially at the primary stage, continuing to cause concern whilst the financial gain to schools who reduce teaching staff is a constant temptation to heads and governors. Substantial 'savings' can be made in the relatively expensive area of providing specialist help for students with special educational needs.

If teachers are to explore and develop the possibilities of non-selective grouping, they need imaginative initial and in-service courses and support in the classrooms. However, such advice and training can only be effective if teachers have the tools to do the job including an adequate supply of teaching and learning resources of the highest quality: books, library facilities, work and assignment sheets, videos, computer programs, reference and assessment material — all of a high standard in terms of design, production and user friendliness. Above all, materials, as well as courses, must be based on up-to-date practical and theoretical knowledge concerning the learning process. Developments in information technology provide an exciting, but still relatively untapped, source for releasing human potential through the learning process.

Support staff [4]

The supply and training of technician, clerical and other support staff has rarely been adequate. Most local authorities increased support staff as they introduced comprehensive schools in the 1960s and '70s but subsequent efforts to upgrade their strength and training were patchy at best and non-existent in many cases. In recent times clerical and financial staff have been augmented to cope with the increase of accounting, paperwork, and computer output resulting from local management of schools and the national curriculum. Important as these may be, they are only indirectly related to classroom practice.

The role of school librarians and technicians is a skilled and vital one if we are to extend and widen our learning strategies. Schools fortunate enough to have suitably trained librarians find their contribution to the task of encouraging school students to deepen and broaden their reading experience to be invaluable. The contribution and potential of technicians has long been recognised by teachers in subjects such as science and technology. Today most departments call on their services for assistance with video recorders and other audio-visual equipment. With publicity and communication skills to the fore and the opportunities provided by desktop publishing — a skilled and time consuming process — the expertise of suitably experienced technicians can make a major contribution in the preparation of informational material for parents, students and the wider community. Also, as teachers and technicians combine their expertise, desktop publishing greatly facilitates the production of resources for teaching and learning. The relationship of support staff to the learning process is, perhaps, most obvious at the youngest stages of learning where nursery nurses (or non-teaching assistants) work in the classrooms of nursery, infant and junior schools under the supervision of class teachers. The role of support staff in all types of school has not received the attention it deserves and urgent action is needed to upgrade salaries, status, training and career structure if our students and teachers are to benefit fully from the effective use of technological and other resources.

Non-selective grouping: a natural and practical arrangement

It is now time to see how non-selective grouping has worked out in practice. To do so we shall focus on schools which minimised internal selection as an essential first step towards achieving the wider goals of comprehensive education. The formation of non-selective classes requires no process of social or educational engineering in sharp contrast to streaming and similar practices. There, the allocation of students to classes involves tests and teachers' estimates of apparent ability, the results of which depend on many factors which cannot be allowed for and are known to be heavily weighted towards social class (Chapter 2). In contrast, and as we have seen in that chapter, Bernard Barker used the phrase 'natural arrangement' to aptly describe non-selective groups.

Need for flexibility

This natural arrangement must in no sense be rigid and restricting; the whole purpose of non-selective grouping should, on the contrary, be dynamic and permit reasonable flexibility to both teacher and student within the overall aims and objectives of a national comprehensive curriculum. Such a curriculum need not require every student to study in depth the text of a Shakespeare play or to learn a second foreign language; equally unacceptable would be a curriculum framework which denied an opportunity for extra depth of study solely on the grounds that all would not wish to avail themselves of it. However, no student should be excluded from a specific choice as a result of arbitrarily imposed criteria such as offering particular choices only to certain groups. Where choice is between subjects, it is relatively easy to accommodate through a system of options providing these maintain breadth and depth in the curriculum and are seen to be of equal status (Chapter 4).

Two examples: literature and mathematics

A different situation occurs where there are good educational reasons for offering choice within a single school subject, for example in the study of literature. Views differ concerning the most appropriate texts for school students and many schools 'solve' this problem by specifying different works for each set or band; the limitations of such a procedure are obvious but how can a choice be offered within a non-selective system of grouping? There are many possibilities and a most effective one was described by Shirley Williams (1991), deputy head of English at Highgate Wood Secondary School in north London. Her department had no streaming and, in an article 'English by Design', she outlined a series of choices offered by the English staff leading up to GCSE. Each student chose a total of eight modules during two years including prose, poetry and drama. The choice offered ranged from *Billy Liar* to *Julius Caesar* and from books by women writers to war poetry. 'Our examination results have improved, our pupils' attitudes to literature have changed, and our teachers are teaching material they know and like', she reported. Such a success story should be welcomed and built on but, predictably, there was a problem, this time stemming from the very top. Examination grades at Highgate Wood, as at many schools, were based on a rigorous assessment of course work rather than an end-of-course examination but John Major personally announced a government decision to abolish this widespread, popular and successful mode of examination in English. It remained to be seen whether the essence of the course could be retained under this restrictive and, essentially, élitist intervention.

Opportunities for students to gain a more advanced qualification in mathematics at age 16 have existed since the days of School Certificate before the war but often schools did not make use of these opportunities, even though some of their students could benefit, because of insufficient numbers in the year group with the necessary grasp of fundamentals to form a class of an economic size. We met this dilemma in the early 1970s at Ryhope School where teaching methods were also based on a non-selective framework (Copland, 1975). It is interesting to note that arrangements to meet the situation had organisational similarities with Highgate Wood's English literature work particularly in the use of teams of teachers. Although these were specific to a particular school at a particular period, they illustrate certain principles which remain important. Four non-selective tutor groups were timetabled together for mathematics in adjacent rooms. Each group had a teacher responsible for the overall progress of its members and these formed part of a team of five teachers in the fourth year and six in the fifth who were allocated for each lesson. This enabled the team to arrange for an additional teacher in the classroom, to take groups to a nearby mathematics laboratory (adapted from a former cloakroom by a buildings studies group) or to withdraw students from one or more tutor groups for a variety of purposes. These ranged from help for students experiencing difficulty to tutorials on a complex topic for the additional mathematics course. College students undertaking teaching practice supported by their tutors and prepared to work enthusiastically in a team, were welcome additions. Their contribution enabled a wider variety of work to take place and also for some team work to be introduced in the first three years of the school during the period of their practice.

This mathematics scheme applied to the school's first comprehensive intake and the results showed that the arrangement was capable of flexibility to meet the needs of individuals. A higher proportion than ever before gained a qualification in mathematics with thirty three obtaining a higher grade pass: 28 at O-level (grades 1 to 6) and five equivalent CSE grade 1's.[5] Nine students gained O-level mathematics early, either at the end of the fourth year or in November of the fifth year. At the end of the fifth year, four became the first ever students from the area to obtain additional mathematics at O-level. All four later gained degrees in mathematics, science or engineering.

Mathematics was certainly a good subject to illustrate the principles involved as, at the time, the subject was widely felt to require selective groups even from the first year. The experience showed that flexibility was practicable within a non-selective system of grouping and desirable. Under streaming or setting it would not have been possible to justify an express stream or top set for early O-level entry followed by an additional mathematics course.[6] A top set would have been either uneconomic in size or have contained many students likely to experience a growing sense of failure as they found it harder and harder to keep up. At the other end of the scale, our arrangements enabled those who had difficulties with mathematics to receive specialist help in a natural environment without being subjected to the indignity of membership of a bottom set, however efficient and caring the teachers might be. Unfortunately there are no statistics which can establish the efficacy of our approach in that direction — only perceptive reports concerning improved student morale from teachers who had taught the lowest groups in the past.

During these developments, two simple criteria emerged to distinguish group work in non-selective situations from setting:

• Special-purpose groups should be flexible in composition. Any student who wishes to join should be able to do so and, if he or she finds the work too hard or too easy, should be able to leave by mutual arrangement with the teacher.

- Membership of such groups should take up only a certain proportion of time so that, over a period, no individual gets more than a proper share of teacher-time. This precludes teaching a small number together on a semi-permanent basis.

These principles can be applied to a wide range of subjects and learning activities. An analysis of the organisational possibilities of non-selective grouping, supported by essential resources and in-service training, could lead to greatly increased flexibility for teachers and students. In too many schools this remains unexplored territory.

Comprehensive schools in the vanguard

Early in 1972, the BBC presented a series 'ROSLA and After' and an accompanying book (BBC, 1971) for teachers planning for the Raising of the School Leaving Age. This was before video recorders became widely available and the series was broadcast weekly just after the end of school. With Ryhope School's first comprehensive intake then in their third year, several of the staff watched and discussed the programmes as a source of ideas for fourth and fifth year planning. Week 7 turned out to be of special significance for our future policy. Sub-titled 'Team Teaching' it centred around the work of the fourth and fifth years at the Hedley Walter School in Brentwood, Essex. In place of streaming, all students followed a common curriculum and were prepared for GCE O-levels or CSE examinations. The latter provided the option of syllabuses devised and assessed by the school but subject to approval and modification by the examinations board. The board was also responsible for moderating school assessments to preserve parity of standards between schools. Known as Mode 3,[7] the scheme opened up many opportunities in the public examination system and had similarities with degree examinations at universities where a visiting examiner from another university provides the moderating function.[8]

At Hedley Walter, teams of teachers were teaching a group of subjects to half a year group at a time. They devised schemes of work involving an integrated approach to related subjects and introduced topics through a lead lesson or presentation given to all students. Individual work and group activities followed under the guidance of members of the team with the specialist knowledge of individual teachers readily available to all who needed it. The first four years at Hedley Walter were fully comprehensive and the percentage of students leaving at the statutory leaving age (then age 15) was smaller than average for the south east of England. The teachers, therefore, had experience of teaching a wide cross-section of students without streaming. Their work provided the starting point for us to pursue similar objectives at Ryhope School although, as our circumstances were different, the details of the solutions, described in Chapters 10 and 12, reflected this.[9]

We soon learned of other schools with similar objectives extending to their fourth and fifth years. One of the best known was the David Lister School, Kingston-upon-Hull's first comprehensive, under its dynamic headteacher Albert Rowe. The work of the school, based entirely on non-selective grouping, has been described by Rowe (1971) and its example was an inspiration. Several of the staff went on to pioneer work in senior positions in other schools. Derek Roberts (1982), for example, described briefly but lucidly the educational reasons why, on becoming head at the newly opened Campion School in Bugbrooke, Northamptonshire, he introduced non-streaming. He observes:

> Pupils who have been taught in mixed ability groups still manage eight or nine distinctions at Ordinary level and follow the traditional path to Advanced levels and University. (p 6)

These results are consistent with the view that sound teaching methods associated with non-streaming are no less advantageous for the most capable students as for anyone else. Unfortunately, the implementation of these principles at David Lister did not survive the retirement of its head. In March 1975 I attended a discussion for Sunderland headteachers on 'The Place of Languages in the Comprehensive Curriculum'. One of the speakers was G H Garner, Rowe's successor as head of David Lister. He commenced his remarks by saying that when he spoke of what was happening at the school, this referred to the last three years since he had been appointed. He made it clear that he did not wish to be associated with anything that had happened earlier, and it came as no surprise to learn that his contribution to the learning of languages was based on allocation to streams and sets.

Countesthorpe College, a 14 to 18 comprehensive school on the outskirts of Leicester, was built with independent and resource-based learning in view. It opened in 1970 and the staff immediately set about the task of turning principles into practice. Naturally there were problems on this frontier of pedagogical advance, but the College soon established a nation-wide reputation among educationists who saw its line of development as one of promise and excitement. Advertisements for teaching posts brought in hundreds of applications. During its formative period under the principalship of John Watts, it gained a high reputation among its parents and students despite intense efforts by reactionary local politicians and the local newspaper to discredit the aims and achievements of the college. The most capable students obtained excellent school examination and degree successes whilst those with learning difficulties received effective help based on individual teaching techniques. The needs of the majority in-between were no less to the fore in the priorities of the college. Its ethos of equal value fostered high self-esteem among its students and led to important developments in teaching method as well as in related matters of school organisation and management.[10]

The Sutton Centre at Sutton-in-Ashfield took a bold step to enter students exclusively for CSE examinations, most of them as mode 3 syllabuses. The centre staff felt that this would enable them to plan the curriculum as a whole and to cater for students of all abilities without streaming. At the same time they were confident that they could provide a full measure of depth and rigour for those who wished to pursue further education at the centre beyond 16.[11] The school made a most promising start but, again, there was both ill-informed and ill-intentioned criticism. The story of the Sutton Centre, describing its successes and the results of the attacks, is well documented in the education literature.[12]

Buckinghamshire provides an unlikely setting for a major success story:

> Stantonbury Campus is the progressive Milton Keynes comprehensive that has survived local doubt and criticism without provoking crisis, and now stands as a working model for visitors from all over the world.

This is the opening sentence of an article in *The Times Educational Supplement* (1985) which marked the retirement of Stantonbury's first director, Geoffrey Cooksey.[13] When fully established the number on roll rose to 3000 with a further 12000 adult users. The first 300 arrived in September 1974 and, seven years later, twenty seven of them went on to university or polytechnic. Nothing very surprising in that statistic alone but, unusually, ten of the twenty seven had obtained no more than three GCE O-levels at age 16. Many schools would have rejected them for A-level courses but their own determination together with an enlightened policy, characteristic of Stantonbury led on to success.

Sidney Stringer School and Community College opened in Coventry in

1972 to serve a multiracial district. Its story involves a stimulating approach to learning and teaching in a comprehensive school but also has much to say in the field of community education and community schools. Its first head, Geoffrey Holroyde, brought substantial experience of industrial management to the task and combined this with clear educational perspectives.[14]

Many other schools were well known to those actively working for the transmission of comprehensive principles into practice. Among those which gained early respect by their example were schools as varied as Settle High in a rural part of the West Riding of Yorkshire under the headship of Michael Tucker and Vauxhall Manor Girls' in an unfashionable district of London led by Miss E M Hoyle. Both these schools took a prominent part at a conference on non-streaming in comprehensive schools organised by *Forum* magazine as early as 1966.[15] In the late 1960s and early '70s, a number of large schools in different parts of the country made contributions to the development of good practice which became well known nationally. The Thomas Bennett School in Crawley, Sussex was an example; its head from 1966 to 1973, Pat Daunt, like colleagues in other forward looking schools, was much in demand at education conferences. In most regions there were schools which created interest in their localities where heads and staff were making conscious attempts to create a more common curriculum which had cohesion and relevance for all students.

This glimpse of the work of some of the schools which tackled the problem of internal selection shows that they achieved considerable success but often met with open and coordinated hostility from vested interests. Nevertheless, they collectively established a bridgehead of purpose and opportunity for the educational future of all young people and their experiences have lessons for today.

Teaching strategies

Teachers in these and many other schools helped their students to develop in self-confidence and capability using a variety of teaching methods. Meeting as a whole class representing a cross-section of the year group provided unique opportunities for teachers to stimulate and inspire young people; work in small groups helped them gain essential experience of collaborative activity towards a common purpose, whilst independent learning made it possible to adjust to the needs of individual students as their studies progressed. Similar principles have been applied from the primary stage (particularly since the demise of the eleven-plus) to adult education where successful lecturers have always aimed to adapt their methods to the needs of their students. Finally, at degree level, the notion that teaching method should be adapted to circumstance was highlighted by the arrival of the Open University in 1969 where personal study at home is supplemented by a week or more together with tutors and fellow students held normally during vacation time.

Terms like independent learning and team teaching have been used by schools and teachers committed to improving the effectiveness of the learning process and have therefore been associated with progressive educational methods and ideas. In the early days of comprehensive education, 'progressive' had its literal forward looking connotation but, as time went on, it became indistinguishable from words of abuse like 'trendy' and thus fell into disuse — sadly in many ways as its opposite 'regressive' is clearly undesirable. A third possibility — maintenance of the status quo — is hardly an inspiration for young people looking forward to contributing to, and benefiting from, a period of unparalleled technological advance. Yet the loss of 'progressive' need not be taken harshly if we define more precisely the aims and direction of educational developments and the means by which effective practice is to be assured. 'Progressive' was used to justify very different developments not all of which were for the better. Similarly, independent learning is not, in itself, an indicator of good practice though it will usually be an important part of a well conceived classroom strategy.

Team teaching

The early model of team teaching used by Hedley Walter School was described by David Warwick (1971) in *Team Teaching*, a book widely read at the time. It requires several classes, or even a whole year group, to be timetabled simultaneously for their lessons in a particular subject with the same group of teachers. This technique of block timetabling opens up various possibilities for teachers to work as a team. A characteristic of Warwick's model in its original form was the lead lesson at the start of a topic. A member of the team with specialist knowledge or interest prepared and introduced the topic to the whole group in a hall or lecture theatre to stimulate the initial interest of the students. This was followed with work in classrooms, workshops, laboratories, library and resource centres etc. as appropriate. All teachers in the team assisted and monitored the work of groups and individuals for the remainder of the topic which, typically, lasted a fortnight to three weeks.

Despite use of audio-visual aids such as film strips, slides and audio tapes (today, videos and computers) in both lead lessons and follow up, team teaching in itself did not guarantee effective learning. However, where the opportunity existed for team members to regularly monitor progress, pool their ideas and plan appropriately, team teaching could prove stimulating for the staff and lead to effective and interactive learning experiences for the students. Following approaches based on the lead lesson other, and perhaps more flexible, methods of organisation have developed. The example at Highgate Wood School involving choice in English Literature is an excellent one not least because of its in-built opportunities for planning and evaluation by members of the team.

Independent learning

Independent learning replaced earlier terms like 'resource based learning' and 'individualised learning' as representing more precisely what was intended. The encouragement and nurture of independence among even very young children can be most helpful to their mental and intellectual development, as observant parents soon discover. But it must not become a fetish. Used as the dominant means of classroom organisation, it demands immense time from teachers: before reaching the classroom they must prepare work sheets, guides to reference material and arrange to keep detailed records of individual progress. In the classroom, even the most active teacher is able to devote only a minute or two per lesson to the specific requirements of each member of the class. However, whilst cost/effectiveness in terms of time cannot justify independent learning as a dominant mode of teaching, we must pay tribute to the work of so many subject teachers in the 1960s and '70s who gave unstintingly of their time to make possible the teaching of non-selective groups based on independent learning: work and dedication which opened up a new range of pedagogical opportunities and insights in primary and comprehensive classrooms.

Apart from constraints of time, there are other reasons for avoiding a single route based on independent learning. First, there is the sense of satisfaction among any group of learners in joint achievement. This arises from their experience of interactive learning among themselves and with their teacher. Such experiences are closely allied to an important perspective in 'Why No Pedagogy in England?' Simon summarises the ideal of the Plowden Report *Children and their Primary Schools* (Department of Education and Science, 1967) as the 'complete individualisation of the teaching and learning process' and comments:

> To start from the standpoint of individual differences is to start from the wrong position. To develop effective pedagogic means involves starting from the opposite standpoint, from what children have in common as members of the human species; to establish the general principles of teaching and in the light of these, to determine what modifications of practice are necessary to meet specific individual needs. (p 99)

Once stated, this observation makes great practical as well as theoretical sense. Supported with related research, it could open out possibilities to capture the imagination and enthusiasm of practising teachers and re-awaken widespread interest in the full opportunities of comprehensive education. Pedagogical issues are discussed in detail by Galton, Simon and Croll in *Inside the Primary Classroom* which is a stimulating and practical report of the first observational study of primary classrooms in Britain (Galton *et al.*, 1980). This was a substantial and authoritative research project providing much food for thought to all involved in education no matter what the age of the students. The authors conclude that the debate on teaching methods and teaching styles 'should now be carried out in a more conciliatory and informed manner with less conviction on either side that they hold a monopoly of the truth'.[16]

Flexible learning

Flexible learning is a more recent addition to the educational vocabulary appearing in the late 1980s and closely associated with the Technical and Vocational Educational Initiative (TVEI) of the Department of Employment. 'New "How to Learn" Initiative Launched by Employment Department' is the heading of a January 1991 press release which continues: 'Flexible learning is a strategy for effective learning which confronts the traditional view of the teacher as 'the font of all knowledge' and encourages the student to become actively involved in their (sic) own education'. Whilst it is necessary to keep in mind the limitations, discussed in Chapter 4, of this type of approach interesting and significant work is being done in schools and further education under the aegis of flexible learning. For example, Don Amphlett (1990) in *Flexible Learning in Schools: The Oxfordshire Experience* notes (p 2) that Her Majesty's Inspectors stressed the advantages of flexible learning and teaching methods in their report *Secondary Schools: an Appraisal by HMI 1982-1986* (Department of Education and Science, 1988a). The inspectors state: 'If schools are to undertake successfully a consideration of some of the major cross-curricular developments which are being encouraged, senior management has to seek organisational structures and flexible arrangements which are likely to bring them about'(p 38, para 146). This comment is entirely consistent with every successful system based on non-selective grouping. *Flexible Learning in Schools* contains several case studies showing that many schools had full time librarians and/or flexible learning coordinators and used funds to establish computerised catalogues of resources. These developments are most desirable and lay some of the foundations for more effective pedagogical practice in school. I was interested to read a report in Amphlett's book of a history project at Henry Box School involving students in years 7 and 10. The methods used appear to be a modern and successful development of resource based learning and team teaching — including a lead lesson.

In *Flexible Learning: Evidence Examined* the author, Mike Hughes (1993), describes work at Balcarras School in Cheltenham preparing students for GCSE in geography. With the cooperation of colleagues he was able to compare results with those obtained through traditional methods. It is clear that the flexible approach led to significantly improved results for students of all levels of capability. Equally impressive are the detailed comments from students concerning their interest in learning by this method. In an associated interview with Mike Hughes, Maureen O'Connor (*The Times Educational Supplement*, 1993) noted his association with a £5 million Department of Employment Flexible Learning Development Project and reports his view that teaching methods are crucial to raising levels of achievement and that the teaching methods that do the trick are what the DE diplomatically calls 'flexible' but which many on the Right dismiss as 'progressive'.

Special needs

Every individual has special needs of one kind or another and a comprehensive system of education should try to meet them as far as possible. The Report of the Warnock Committee of Enquiry into the education of handicapped children and young people *Special Educational Needs* (Department of Education and Science, 1978b) was followed by the 1981 Education Act which put into effect some of the recommendations. From then onwards 'special educational needs' largely replaced the use of 'remedial' or 'slow learners' in the educational world as the most common way of referring to young people with above average learning difficulties. In this section we use a wider interpretation of the term and look at two very different types of special need: those arising from learning difficulties and those of young people who are able to learn rapidly and in depth — sometimes referred to as 'gifted children'.

Students with learning difficulties

When I taught at Riddings Secondary School in Scunthorpe in the early 1960s (Chapter 3), we had three sizes of class with a norm of forty, which sufficed for English, mathematics, science and so on. There were half classes for practical subjects such as woodwork, metalwork, domestic science and needlework and these were segregated strictly by gender, as was almost invariably the case at the time. I counted it a considerable step forward when I managed to persuade the headteacher to agree to half classes for most science classes once a week for practical work.[17] The third size of class was reserved for the junior and senior remedial groups, made up from years 1 and 2 and from 3 and 4, respectively. Each contained thirty students so that they could receive more individual attention; there were no half classes for science although we still provided practical work for the full groups. The remedial classes had all their lessons separately except for PE when several classes were timetabled together for the subject. Again, this was a typical arrangement for the time.

The policy for 'the remedials' was one of almost total segregation as far as the curriculum was concerned, supported in a paternalistic, if kindly, manner. The work and activities of individual students, and of the two classes in general, was often commended at morning assembly but there was no doubt that members of these classes were perceived as 'different'. Misuse of the word 'remedial' as a noun to label and classify students was always objectionable; the word is, of course, an adjective which can be used legitimately in many circumstances, for example 'I should have been glad of a remedial course of action to improve my handwriting'. Like other stereotyping expressions such as 'the secondary modern child' and 'D-stream material' much damage was done to the self-respect and aspirations of young people labelled 'remedials' in staffrooms, education offices and in casual talk amongst adults and children. The term 'slow learners' is equally negative and, in my experience, teachers who maintain that such terms are only used in the staffroom or out of earshot of students delude themselves. Indeed, on a wider issue, I believe it essential to encourage conversation among professionals in terms which would be acceptable to parents, students and the wider public. It is necessary to take active steps to reduce to a minimum all 'shorthand' expressions used between professionals which engender unhelpful thinking. For example, after I became a head, I asked teachers wishing to discuss a student with me always to use his or her first name (or both first and surname) as this was part of the school's policy of making students feel individually respected.

Many newly emerging comprehensive schools established separate remedial groups, not dissimilar to those described. For morning and afternoon registration, however, all students were normally allocated to tutor groups containing a cross-section of the year group. Gradually schools provided more lessons in the first year or two taught on a tutor group basis but many continued to maintain remedial *departments*. A department implies a small empire requiring its teachers to have responsibility for a sizeable and identifiable group of students to maintain it. Many teachers involved in this type of remedial work were committed to their students and went out of their way to see that they played as full a part as possible in the life of the school community. Nevertheless, segregation became increasingly to be seen as an indefensible position contrary to the best principles of comprehensive education.

In its place comprehensive schools committed to furthering non-selective teaching methods developed equitable and productive methods based on the concept of remedial specialists rather than departments.[18] Two basic organisational arrangements emerged which enabled flexibility for students to receive varying degrees of help according to their changing educational needs. The first of these was by withdrawal from normal classes at certain times with the cooperation of the class teachers concerned and, as far as possible, with the consent of the students themselves. Ryhope's experience was, I imagine, similar to that in other schools who used withdrawal for this purpose: the amount of specialist help received by students in the first year varied typically from an hour a week to a third or even a half of the normal programme in exceptional instances. In some cases all the lessons of a particular subject (eg the modern foreign language) were used. However, as much specialist teaching during withdrawal was directed towards the development of literacy and numeracy, lessons were frequently arranged during English and mathematics time but always allowing students some time with their normal class. Despite organisational and pedagogical problems, this arrangement can work very successfully. As individuals make progress, the number of withdrawals is reduced and finally, the specialist staff may withdraw students only once a month or so for a check on progress. The success of a scheme of withdrawal depends on an appropriate ethos in the school, the cooperation of all concerned and the involvement of parents in a meaningful way, for example by helping with home assignments such as listening to their children reading. Last, but not least, it opens out opportunities for older volunteer students to make a direct contribution to the intellectual and emotional development of younger students by assisting with similar tasks to those of parents and even by substituting for the parents' contribution when, for any reason, this is not available. In most schools adopting this method students help during registration periods, at lunch time and, occasionally, at mutually convenient times during the day. The involvement of older students contributes immensely to establishing withdrawal as a normal part of a school's organisation to be seen as a service without stigma to those participating.

The second method of organising specialist help, also used at Ryhope from time to time, is to provide an extra support teacher for all or most lessons while a group of classes is timetabled for, say, English. Here the specialist works alongside the class teacher giving particular attention to the work of students who are experiencing difficulties. Three or four classes may be timetabled together and the specialist will work with each group on a flexible rota system. Clearly, this is a form of team teaching and has the advantage that students and teachers do not suffer from problems of continuity. The method requires the cooperation of all involved and, with careful week by week planning, can produce good results. The main criticisms centre round whether sufficient individual teaching focused on the particular needs of a student can be provided as effectively as in a withdrawal situation.

The pros and cons of the two methods are summarised in two articles in the magazine *Support for Learning*. Ron Best writes from personal experience as a support teacher in a school which had 'pursued with considerable zeal a policy of minimal withdrawal and maximum integration' (Best, 1991: 27) whilst Trevor Payne lists the advantages and disadvantages of extraction and in-class support (as he describes the methods) and reports the results of a small scale research into students' views (Payne, 1991:61). There are no easy solutions to the best ways of providing for those with learning difficulties in comprehensive education but, without doubt, they are entitled to full access to our educational and cultural heritage. Teachers in comprehensive schools have made a major contribution to the subject and we must ensure there can be no return to some modern reincarnation of 'the remedials'.

Finally, there is the question of special versus comprehensive schools for those with more acute learning or behavioural difficulties. This is a difficult and on-going question to which those with experience of good practice in both special and comprehensive schools have a particular contribution to make. Whatever developments take place should be made within a framework which engenders self-respect for the young people concerned, both inside and outside their schools, and is consistent with the principles of a fully comprehensive system of education.

Gifted children

Comprehensive schools regularly enrol young people who have already shown considerable talent whilst more have the potential, under favourable circumstances, to demonstrate similar capability. The term 'gifted children' is often applied but it is a loose categorisation which can generate misconceptions. Nevertheless, the need for comprehensive schools to stimulate and extend their most capable members was recognised from the start, as was the ineffectiveness of many of the attempted solutions stemming from the days of selective schools.

In the 1950s and early '60s many of the larger grammar schools favoured what was known as an 'express stream' of 25 or 30 students who had achieved the highest scores in the selection process. They were taught together and entered for most subjects in GCE O-level after four years rather than the customary five. This was held to have advantages, particularly after GCE, when an earlier start could be made with A-levels and time made available for preparation for the entrance examinations for Oxford and Cambridge universities.[19] During this period I worked with a teacher who had an intelligent daughter who was receiving the 'benefits' of this system. Vast quantities of homework coupled with a tendency to cram information during lesson time were the most notable features observed by her mother. She was greatly concerned that her daughter was being left with far too little time and opportunity to enjoy and explore growing up through her period of early adolescence. Whilst in due course she obtained the expected exam results it seemed doubtful, to say the least, whether the price had been necessary. Other members of express streams, not necessarily as talented or conscientiously conforming, often did far less well than their peers who took the five year course. For economic reasons express streams had to be of near normal class size and, inevitably, many of their members were there to some extent as make-weights. This once again demonstrated a tendency in our education system to produce feelings of failure among some of our most able young people.[20]

Examples of students experiencing distress were found in an investigation in the 1960s into streaming in grammar schools. When looking at the experience of eleven boys in one express class who felt themselves to be unsuccessful at the end of their second year, Lacey (1966) notes:

> Two of these boys had been considerably emotionally disturbed. Crying in lessons, crying before school and refusing to come to school. A third went through a similar period and his father wrote to the school complaining that 'the boy is utterly demoralised'. (p 261)

This kind of evidence must cause concern. Nurture of those with exceptional talents is essential, but not necessarily, and certainly not continuously, within a hot house environment. Express streams are a special case of streaming and some of the criticisms apply to any top stream where teachers and class members will usually be under considerable pressure to produce the expected results, preferably exceeding last year's in quantity and quality.[21] From time to time, parents and teachers have said to me that they are confident that comprehensive schools have much to offer young people who do not have any very noticeable academic bent, but that they have serious reservations for those variously described as 'high fliers', 'bright', 'having a good head piece' and so on. Teachers and parents, intentionally or inadvertently, can powerfully reinforce each others' ideas along these lines, for example during a discussion between a parent and a head of year. Warwick (1971) recognises in *Team Teaching* that the methods he describes must cater for the education of the gifted child and makes the following point:

> It can be maintained that in a streamed situation that this child is going to be held back. Normally he will be reduced to the pace of the slowest, for it is the essence of class teaching that all shall progress at a uniform rate. (p 80)

Whilst we have seen that class teaching has an important role in a well-planned teaching strategy, it is true that very able students are frequently held back where it is the all-pervasive mode. However, I think it unlikely that the pace will be that of the slowest; in most such classes strugglers will have to get along as best they may. The author develops his argument for non-streaming for gifted children in what might be seen today as over optimistic terms but this in no way invalidates the point that non-selective teaching provides the opportunity for a range of challenging initiatives and assignments in the classroom for all students.

Professor Joan Freeman (1991), author of a research based study *Gifted Children Growing Up*, has expressed some pertinent views in an interview for *The Times Educational Supplement* (1991f). She reported that many gifted children were:

> offered only one target — university — and often then, only Oxford or Cambridge.

She went on to identify a danger for gifted children, noting that they are:

> channelled in a very restrictive system, with schools trying to eke out every ounce of academic achievement when they need a wide range of opportunities outside the academic curriculum.

Freeman reports that some students were accelerated[22] one, two or even three years beyond their own age groups 'sometimes with disastrous effects'. 'I feel as if I've lost my youth' commented one sixteen-year-old. Her findings also showed that, at grammar as well as at comprehensive schools, 'the brightest children were often bored by repetitive teaching aimed at the middle of the class' while:

> Others in the study talked well about learning strategies, where they latched onto principles, rather than amassing information.

At the core of the matter as far as comprehensive education is concerned, she states:

> What's good for gifted children is good for all children — but they need something more.

In her book Freeman expresses important reservations about the practice of comprehensive education *as experienced by some of her sample* [my emphasis]. Her constructive suggestions, however, seem fully compatible with the ideas of comprehensive education put forward in this book. For example, stressing the need for flexibility and referring to withdrawal, she notes that 'handled sensitively, it does not seem to have the effect of upsetting the others in the class', a sentiment with which I wholly concur. The special needs of all young people, gifted in any direction, need urgently addressing and the suggestions for enhanced educational experience for all, set out in Chapter 5, should help to create opportunities in this field.

Freeman also deals with the need for enrichment:

> Enrichment should be a natural, everyday part of the school-day for all the children there. It can take the part of school outings, experts coming in to school to teach, laboratories being left open at the weekend for keen physicists, time to spend trying novel ways of approaching a technical problem and much more. (p 215)

she commends vacation courses as:

> a very enriching opportunity for the gifted to be with other people like themselves, so that they can relax and drop the energy-consuming defences which they normally use for support. (p 215)

Taken together, Freeman's observations make thought provoking reading. They surely suggest that, given the will and resources, the needs of all students, including the most gifted, can be met within a non-selective and flexible system of comprehensive education. A parent of a former student showed me a report concerning his son from the chairman of the Board of Studies in English and American literature of a well known university. Describing Mr 'Y' as the most able student who has been on the course in eighteen years, he goes on to outline his academic gifts and achievements and adds that Mr 'Y' is 'a straightforward, friendly and unspoilt young man. He is very well balanced, has a sense of humour', and so on. This epitomises what the majority of parents will want for their gifted children: opportunity to develop their strengths, encouragement to widen horizons and the chance to grow and mature as individuals and members of society.

For want of essential resources in the early stages of comprehensive schools many teachers were thrown back on their own ingenuity involving countless hours of labour, willingly given and well beyond the call of duty. I have no doubt that this commitment, so noticeable at the time, was a vital factor in encouraging curriculum development not only within schools but also by external bodies who worked to provide essential support. Many teachers saw these developments as essential if they were to do their professional best for their students in an already rapidly changing world. In the next chapter we consider the impact of educational initiatives which encouraged teachers and, through their ideas and materials, made an important contribution to quality and good practice.

7

Resources for Teaching and Learning

Teachers in comprehensive schools with non-selective teaching groups soon found it necessary to review their textbooks and resources to see how they could be adapted to the new situation and to the new opportunities opening up. Curricula and examination syllabuses needed modernising and many schools welcomed and made extensive use of curricular initiatives from national and local sources.

Teaching materials

Textbooks and alternatives

Under the selective system of schooling most grammar-school classes had one set of textbooks for the whole class. This was also the norm in modern schools when such a luxury could be afforded; one textbook between two or three students was more common. Teachers quickly saw that this situation was totally inadequate in non-selective classes and, as a first step, began to assemble a range of books and reference material for classroom use. This was certainly an improvement on a single or shared textbook but required class teachers to prepare study plans to help students to use the references effectively and systematically. The plans often included tests and assessments on each section of the work which could be taken individually by students as they completed their assignments and teachers noted that problems of continuity resulting from absence were at least partially alleviated. In total, however, the preparation of support material for a single topic, let alone a complete course, represented a substantial undertaking for a teacher. The style and content of existing textbooks and reference material presented a further problem. Textbooks had not been written for use in these situations and most relied heavily on the teacher to give frequent explanations and clarifications in order to make them intelligible. Reference material was often taken from newspapers, magazines and articles in encyclopedias or other standard works. Again these were difficult for students to read and comprehend and many teachers decided that it would be better to start from scratch and write their own bank of worksheets and assessment tests. A commonly used format was to prepare a basic worksheet covering the essentials of the topic, together with additional sheets which extended those who had completed the work quickly and accurately or, alternatively, provided further examples and explanation for students experiencing difficulty.

Preparing material

Plain-paper photocopiers were beginning to replace wax stencil and spirit duplicators in school; they added considerably to the ease of preparing sheets and, equally important, to the replacement of any which, however well teachers managed their resources, looked less than their best after a term or two of intensive use. Schools began to use what seemed an immense proportion of their limited capitation allowances[1] on reprographic equipment. I remember the arrival of a salesman at Ryhope School in the early 1970s who, after listening to our requirements, recommended an offset duplicator: an unheard-of level of printing facility. We watched the demonstration with wonderment and asked the price; we blanched but it could have been worse and, a few weeks later, our first machine was installed. I cannot recall the precise number of sheets of paper it processed in the first year but I do remember that the figure on the automatic counter left us in total amazement. How could we have managed without such a device?

Despite these technological improvements in reprographic methods, the task of preparing materials for use by school students was still a daunting one involving immense time and commitment. Nevertheless many teachers and senior management teams accepted the challenge and, in doing so, learned much of immeasurable value about the learning process. They began to focus their thinking on the principles which should underlie the design, content and format of teaching and learning materials of all types. Sharing the work load between a departmental team of teachers was an obvious step and required detailed discussion and debate within departmental teams which, in itself, was often rewarding and insightful.

Naturally, some of the finished products were far from perfect and overall results varied. I joined a third year science team for a year, teaching an 8 or 9-week module on reproduction to successive groups. I found the teachers' notes, hand-outs for students, advice on experiments, recommended visual aids and specimen tests — all prepared by the head of department — of great help and in no way constraining as far as my personal input to the lessons was concerned. Sometimes, however, home-produced material lacked consistency of approach and over-reflected the particular teaching styles of its authors. This made some worksheets much less effective when used by other members of the team. Finally, as the rate of national curriculum development increased, even the most carefully and effectively produced material was found to have a short shelf life. With their new-found knowledge and enhanced insights into the learning process, teachers naturally asked themselves whether their efforts could not be more effectively directed.

Fortunately, the need for more appropriate published material was increasingly recognised. A significant break with the textbook tradition came with the Humanities Project (also known as the Humanities Curriculum Project or HCP), described below. In 1970 this project commenced publication of a wide range of worksheets and reference material to enable students to study issues in considerable depth. For a variety of reasons, the materials themselves did not have a lasting impact in the schools but the ideas did. HCP proved to be the forerunner of a major output of material stemming from projects in many subjects and designed to be used independently and cooperatively by students in non-selective classes.

Resources for Learning Development Unit

Teaching and learning materials for use by the teacher as a resource, rather than as part of a prescribed course of study, started to appear in most subjects. In an imaginative development in 1974, Avon County Council established the Resources for Learning Development Unit which produced a wide range of materials on a shoe-string budget. These were taken up by schools throughout Britain and also abroad. In 1981, Avon proposed to close the Unit as an economy measure in response to government spending limits. The senior management team and heads of department of Ryhope School responded to an appeal from the Unit and wrote a letter to Avon's Director of Education which included the following statement:

We feel that the Avon RLDU has already made an outstanding contribution in the preparation of materials and in tackling the problems of organisation — yet it is only the start. We believe that the Unit is poised to make a unique contribution to the improvement of classroom practice in schools. Certainly its work so far has given us, at this school, tremendous encouragement.

The letter also dealt in more detail with practical issues in the classroom:

The problem for the teacher wishing to provide more opportunities for supervised individual study in the classroom has been twofold: firstly, a lack of suitable teaching resources such as assignment and monitoring cards, reference material, progress and assessment records etc. all of which need specially preparing for the task in hand. Whilst this type of resource is certainly no more expensive than an adequate supply of text books, it needs to be prepared by experts in the field. Secondly the organisation and management of these resources needs to be considered in detail at the time of their preparation if the teacher is to feel confident in their use and the pupils is to obtain maximum benefit.

We received a reply from the English Editor of the Unit thanking us and giving news that 'support is pouring in from all quarters'. His letter went on:

Your statement runs to the heart of all the work we are engaged in, and we could not have expressed the issues better ourselves. It is immensely gratifying and reassuring to know that what we feel to be vitally important work is appreciated so warmly by teaching colleagues far away.

In the event a compromise was reached and some of the work of the Unit allowed to continue. However, the correspondence illustrates the conditions under which those who were working to further the practical realisation of the comprehensive ideal did so with such little coordinated support and appreciation of what they were trying to achieve. Early in 1991, I telephoned the RLDU for an update on its activities, only to learn that Avon had decided to close the Unit in April 1993. Some of its work was due to continue under the auspices of a new resource service to be set up but, as a member of staff told me, their most important work is centred around medium and longer term objectives based on observation of how young people learn and the production of materials which have been tested and modified under classroom conditions. Whilst the events at Avon occurred under Conservative governments, previous Labour governments did little to promote the development of good comprehensive school practice and failed to provide the necessary capital and resource injection including in-service training for teachers, which the move to comprehensive education required.

Mathematics projects

Mathematics was one of the subjects in which the development of flexible resources as an alternative to textbooks was particularly welcomed by forward looking teachers. This reflected both the status of the subject, as perceived by teachers, parents and students, and the quantity and diversity of the material needed to cater for individual levels of attainment. Two of the best known initiatives, The Kent Mathematics Project (KMP) and the Secondary Mathematics Independent Learning Experience (SMILE), stemmed from work originated by Bertram Banks at the Ridgewaye School, Tunbridge Wells in the early 1960s.

Kent Education Committee adopted and funded KMP in September 1970 but it was not until 1979 that the materials were first published nationally. These provided a complete five year course to CSE and O-level as well as work for students with learning difficulties. Today the scope of the project covers the range from the reception class in an infants school to grade A*, the highest grade at GCSE. Student tasks are provided mainly in sets of well produced workcards carefully coded in level and difficulty. Detailed concept networks enable teachers to provide individual routes through the material according to each student's prior attainment and current progress. There are opportunities for members of a class to work collaboratively with others at the same level and motivation is seen as a vital factor in success. The tasks, motivating in themselves, also include regular opportunities for independent choice of topic. The networks are fully integrated with the student materials and, as the originator Bertram Banks (1991), has described in *The KMP Way to Learn Maths* — his down-to-earth account of the early development of the project — they are based on research and extensive trials together with a systems approach to programmed learning.[2] Thus KMP found it relatively easy to adapt to the requirements of the national curriculum and the project had its own GCE and GCSE courses until 1997. However, government demands for conformity in GCSE syllabuses (not applicable at University degree level one notices) means that schools using the materials must now choose a standard syllabus from one of the boards. Despite this handicap, the project is confident that modified, but still effective and important, work will continue at Key Stage 4 (note 5). The flexibility of the approach was illustrated a few years after the start of the project when several students obtained the highest grades at O-level two and even three years earlier than normal.[3] In 1989 the project was runner-up in the prestigious Jerwood Foundation award for 'an individual or institution that has made an original and significant contribution to the theory and practice of education'.

In the school year 1969-1970, Banks was asked to introduce coursework into two girls' comprehensive schools in the former Inner London Education Authority.[4] Following this initiative, interested ILEA teachers started to develop their own materials and, from 1972, a small group of schools shared the task of producing workcards for non-selective teaching groups. This was the start of SMILE which later had its own centre and several full-time staff. Its materials, which include workcards, games, videos, computer activities and textbook references became available nationally and by the start of the 1990s the SMILE Centre, by then supported by the Royal Borough of Kensington and Chelsea, was coordinating the work of over 400 schools who were using the materials. There are conferences and writing groups for teachers, a half-termly news booklet and a guide for parents. The associated GCSE course, which included a high percentage of coursework, attracted over 14,000 entries in 1991.[5] As Pete Mulloy (1990), a teacher using SMILE materials, wrote 'To be more specific about the way we manage such a system, ensuring that students experience working individually, in small groups and as a class, is not easy on paper because of the complex interaction involved. Much better to visit us and see for yourselves'. SMILE's stated aims are 'to foster a greater understanding and enjoyment of mathematics; to encourage collaborative work; to promote pupils' individual strengths; and to encourage them to become self-reliant and responsible for their own mathematical learning'. Whilst KMP and SMILE have important differences in philosophy, method and approach, they share similar fundamental aims.[6] Regretfully for Ryhope and many other comprehensive schools seeking to apply independent methods of learning, both KMP and SMILE became available nationally long after initial setting-up grants had been spent on books. In the case of Ryhope in 1969, these were from an already well established initiative, the School Mathematics Project, which was forward looking as far as content was concerned but whose materials were only available in textbook format. Later the SMP brought out a card-based course designed for non-selective groups which was widely used particularly in the earlier secondary years. Since the late 1970s, therefore, there has been no lack of material and choice — and plenty of successful experience reported in the literature — for schools considering non-selective methods for mathematics throughout the age range.

Schools Council

There was one large-scale development that made an especially significant contribution to primary and secondary practice in most subjects. The Schools Council was established on 1st October 1964, two weeks before the general election which saw the return of Harold Wilson as head of a Labour government after thirteen years of Conservative rule. It consisted of representatives of the Department of Education and Science, Her Majesty's Inspectors, local education authorities and teachers' unions. According to Maurice Plaskow (1985), editor of *Life and Death of the Schools Council* it was 'conceived as a hopeful act of reconciliation between central and local government and teachers' (p 1). Certainly the Council was seen as a hopeful step forward by many teachers and schools seeking to improve their practice and adapt to the changing educational and social circumstances which they met daily in their work. According to Arnold Jennings (1985), acting chairman of the Council at the time of its demise, one of its most daring features was to state as part of its constitution that:

> Curriculum should come first, and examinations follow it, and not as normally happened, the other way round. (p 18)

Clyde Chitty (1989), senior lecturer in education at Birmingham University and co-editor of the magazine *Forum*, described the Council as 'potentially an important agent for curriculum planning and development' (p 46). Indeed it was more than that with its potential to develop into a major institution through which the teaching profession could exercise appropriate and democratic control over important aspects of the education process and its development. No doubt with such considerations in mind the Council was much criticised during its lifetime, not least by the Department of Education and Science.[7] In 1982, it was abolished by the Thatcher government which undoubtedly facilitated the passage of ill-conceived legislation, orders in council and decisions of government appointed quangos which were to follow. Although there were weaknesses in the work and output of the Council stemming from a variety of causes including inherent conflicts in its structure, many schools found stimulation and practical guidance from its work. There were regional information centres and full-time field officers who organised courses and visited schools and departments where promising curriculum developments were in hand. I met several and found them knowledgeable, committed and well respected by the teachers and advisers with whom they came into contact.

It was the Council's national projects, however, which widened the thinking of so many teachers and gave them inspiration in the classroom. There can be few comprehensive schools who were seeking syllabuses and teaching materials which more effectively matched the aspirations and expectations of students and their parents, who did not make use of at least one of the projects. Primary schools too could find much that was related to teaching for their age range. The Humanities Project, under the dynamic guidance of its director, Lawrence Stenhouse, proved to be a milestone. This pioneering and influential initiative emphasised the need for school students to discuss and study controversial moral, social and political issues. Its suggestions as to how this might best be achieved in the classroom opened out a new range of possibilities for teachers and students. Although not a course in itself, teachers could choose from topics which included the family (history, future, conflicts, social class ...); relations between the sexes; poverty; law and order (police, politics, juvenile delinquency, punishment, protest ...); war and society and even education itself. Here resources ranged from curriculum to discipline, indoctrination to peer group pressure and purpose to private education. Today, the need to study and discuss such matters in school is generally accepted. In 1970, when the first five packs of material were published, they seemed startling to some but provided starting points and ideas for many who had sensed the narrowness of traditional syllabuses in several areas of the curriculum.

Although only a few of the Schools Council projects were aimed specifically at non-selective teaching groups, material could usually be adapted for this purpose. Teachers who used the materials had their own favourites. For me, these included the Integrated Science Project, established in 1969, the Careers Education and Guidance Project (1971), Writing Across the Curriculum (1971) and the History 13-16 Project (1972). All of these broke new ground, as did others like the popular 'Geography for the Young School Leaver' and its derivatives such as the

Avery Hill Geography Project. Teaching materials were usually published three or four years after a project was set up following trials in volunteer pilot schools. The following examples are included to convey something of the excitement and challenge of curriculum development of this type for both teachers and students. Although describing past events they illustrate the scope and need for teacher-friendly inputs into the national curriculum which generate new thinking and actively involve teachers in their development without the stress and feeling of manipulation engendered by top-down decrees from government sources or their quangos.

Careers education

Ryhope's first involvement with the Schools Council was as a pilot school for careers education and guidance — a project which came as a surprise to many schools. Although careers guidance usually existed in school in some form or other, the less than expert knowledge of many who dispensed it was frequently rooted in past ideas rather than in the contemporary and rapidly changing situation which faced school leavers. The relationship of school guidance to that of the careers service whose officers visited schools and interviewed students in their final year was often tenuous and rarely organic and productive. Careers *education* as a subject of the curriculum was hardly known. Indeed, only a year or two earlier and immediately prior to the establishment of Ryhope School, I had been told by Sunderland's deputy director of education at the time that we should be allowed a head of careers 'over my dead body'. Fortunately reason prevailed and the person appointed became well known, locally and nationally, for his work with the School Council materials. The project raised the status of the subject in schools whether or not they adopted the scheme. It encouraged role play and discussion on issues such as equal opportunities, sex stereotyping of jobs, interviewing for posts and organisation of work in industry and business. It had its own newspaper, *Framework*, piloted from an early stage of the project and first published in 1976 (Schools Council, 1976a). This contained reference and activity material presented in an attractive and user-friendly way and was accompanied by a teacher's guide (Schools Council, 1977). Group and class discussion was at its most fruitful when the topics were studied in groups consisting of a wide range of attainments, career hopes and expectations.

Integrated science

Increasingly during the 1960s many considered that science took up too large a share of the curriculum for students who took physics, chemistry and biology as separate subjects and too little for others who took a single subject, general science. With the arrival of the Schools Council Integrated Science Project (SCISP) in the early 1970s, it became possible to provide a balanced and intellectually acceptable science course designed both for those who intended to go on to further study in science as well as for many taking science as part of their general education. The course covered principles in physics, chemistry, biology and earth sciences (geology, meteorology etc) and occupied 20 per cent of time in the later years of school, equivalent to two subjects. This, in itself, was an important step forward as it enabled schools to provide a better balanced curriculum for all in the later years of compulsory education. Most schools offered their students English, mathematics and six other subjects to examination level. If three of these were sciences plus, possibly, computer science and/or technology (now compulsory under the national curriculum) there was insufficient time for a satisfactory complement of subjects from humanities (history, geography, sociology), languages and the arts. A choice of two sciences, for example physics and chemistry or biology and chemistry, led to imbalance in the science course.

SCISP did much more than provide an opportunity to broaden the curriculum important as that was. Several of the skills and attitudes listed in the teachers' handbook (Schools Council, 1973) and defining the aims of the course were unique at the time:

Organising and formulating ideas in order to communicate them to others.

Understanding the significance, including the limitations, of science in relation to technical, social and economic development.

Be willing to work (a) individually and (b) as part of a group.

Be concerned for the application of scientific knowledge within the community.
(p 6)

Seventy eight patterns (or generalisations) involving nearly two hundred concepts were to be understood and applied. These covered a range of scientific phenomena in a rigorous manner based on reputable, if not undisputed, learning theory. The scheme also required study of economic, social, environmental and technological implications of science. Ideas on how to teach the course were illustrated in a sample scheme consisting of students' books, teachers' guides and a variety of reference material. Use of these examples was entirely a matter of choice for the teacher and, as a consequence, the O-level and CSE examinations were both innovative and interesting for the candidates. The scheme allowed great flexibility: for example, being near the sea, SCISP students at Ryhope obtained their introduction to wave motion armed with stop watches by the shore rather than in the laboratory with a ripple tank or other specialised piece of equipment. Teachers, using this flexibility, attracted almost equal numbers of girls and boys and there was favourable feedback from former students. In a report prepared for the Secondary Science Curriculum Review in 1982, the deputy head of science at Ryhope commented on a conversation with a former student in his third year of horticultural science at university:

> When he first arrived at University he was taken aback because he seemed short of knowledge compared with fellow students. A little later he was far ahead on experience in organising his work and setting about research. He felt that this was of immense value to him and easily outweighing any problems arising from shortage of facts. (p 18)

Schools which pioneered integrated science received a full share of brickbats but the national curriculum, as well as several highly respected scientific bodies, have since come out in support of balanced science courses as their preferred option.

Writing across the curriculum

As its title suggests, this project applied to all subjects although in most schools, English teachers took the initiative. It was a joint project between the Schools Council and London University Institute of Education and, unlike the others described here, did not aim to provide a course and did not, therefore, produce sets of materials for class use. Its way of working, described in the first of its published booklets *From Information to Understanding* (Schools Council/London University Institute of Education, 1973a) included:

> Collaboration with teachers in schools, in varying degrees of association, from shared teaching to postal communication.

> Discussion with teachers as widely as possible through meetings and conferences.

Publication of a variety of short working papers, discussion documents and bulletins.

This makes an interesting comparison with the rapid action, top-down methods of the national curriculum and, indeed, the project made major contributions to educational thought and practice. Firstly, it highlighted the importance of a sense of audience — how the writer pictures his reader. Describing this concept in Why Write? (Schools Council/London University Institute of Education, 1973b: 3-10), the authors use the following categories:

—Child (or adolescent) to Self

—Child (or adolescent) to Trusted Adult

—Pupil to Teacher as Partner in Dialogue

—Pupil to Teacher, Particular Relationship

—Pupil to Teacher seen as Examiner or Assessor

—Writer to his Readers (or his Public)

As soon as these are listed, one realises how different the style would be for each of the 'audiences' and how important it is for teachers to be aware of the learning possibilities opened up. The same booklet also identifies three functions of writing:

—Expressive:

> in which it is taken for granted that the writer himself is of interest to the reader; he feels free to jump from facts to speculations to personal anecdote to emotional outburst and none of it will be taken down and used against him — it is all part of being a person vis-à-vis another person. It is the means by which the new is tentatively explored, thoughts may be half-uttered, attitudes half-expressed, the rest being left to be picked up by a listener or reader who is willing to take the unexpressed on trust. (p 11)

—Transactional:

> in which it is taken for granted that the writer means what he says and can be challenged for its truthfulness to public knowledge, and its logicality; that it claims to be able to stand on its own and does not derive its validity from coming from a particular person. So it is the typical language of science and of intellectual inquiry, of technology, of trade, of planning, reporting, instructing,

informing, advising, persuading, arguing and theorising — and, of course, the language most used in school writing. (p 12)

—Poetic:

in which it is taken for granted that 'true or false?' is not a relevant question at the literal level. What is presented may or may not in fact be a representation of actual reality but the writer takes it for granted that his reader will experience what is presented rather in the way he experiences his own memories, and not use it like a guide-book or map in his dealings with the world — that is to say, the language is not being used instrumentally as a means of achieving something, but as an end in itself. (p 13)

I have included these descriptions in full to show how teachers could become excited about curriculum development. Work such as this provided both insight and inspiration and caused imaginative teachers to look in a new light at their own experiences as well as their work with students. Another pamphlet from the project *Keeping the Options Open: writing in the humanities* (Schools Council/London University Institute of Education, 1974), gave some interesting facts and figures: the audience for students' writing was, until the sixth form, almost invariably the teacher to whom 90% of writing in the first three years of secondary school was addressed (p 3). Fellow students and a wider public were, apparently, never included showing that many opportunities were being missed in school classrooms. Similarly, transactional writing was the dominant mode (approximately 90%) in history, geography and science, none of which produced any evidence of expressive writing (p 2). Yet the latter is the language 'by which the new is tentatively explored'. As a science teacher, I tried a few changes from the familiar 'the water was poured into the beaker and the cork placed carefully onto the surface ...' type of writing to more expressive forms in which students responded to their thoughts and observations in a much more down to earth manner. The results were more than promising, especially in the early stages of a new topic.

The title of this Schools Council project referred to 'Writing' but the team was also much concerned with the wider idea of 'Language' whose relationship to the learning process was a matter of deep discussion and inquiry at the time. Many teachers recognised that expressive talk plays an important part in the learning process and their experience links very closely with the theoretical work of Nina Talyzina (Chapters 2 and 6) as an essential stage in the assimilation of knowledge and the development of mental activities. It is also pertinent to Brian Simon's call for more research into pedagogy (Chapter 6). The further contribution of the project was in helping to prepare the way among teachers for the idea that each school should have a language policy across the whole curriculum so that the importance of language in the learning process could be coordinated and developed. However, despite the prominence given to the idea in the Bullock Report *A Language for Life* (Department of Education and Science, 1975), this aspect was only partially developed; it is more difficult than it looks but this should not be an excuse for neglect. All in all, Writing Across the Curriculum, a relatively small scale project, had a remarkable impact.

History 13 to 16

The History 13 to 16 Project, established in 1972, radically changed thinking about what could and should be taught in school. Like integrated science, this project enabled teachers to have considerable choice in the details of content and methods of teaching whilst maintaining a common philosophy and purpose. This philosophy, together with the framework and overall content of the course, are described in *A New Look at History* (Schools Council, 1976b) and summarised inside the front cover of each of the topic guides for teachers (Schools Council, 1976c):

> To suggest suitable objectives for history teachers, and to promote the use of appropriate materials and ideas for their realisation. This involved a reconsideration of the nature of history and its relevance in secondary schools; the design of a syllabus framework which shows the uses history may have in the education of adolescents; and the setting up of experimental O-level and CSE examinations.

The syllabus for the third year included an exploration of 'What is history?' in which students investigated historical mysteries such as what happened to Tollund Man, found in Denmark and dating from the first century BC. They examined evidence and learned to ask at least some of the right questions. In the following two years leading up to CSE and GCE, students undertook a 'Study in Development' tracing the history of medicine from early civilisations, through the public health arrangements of the Romans, to the increasing use of technology. This was linked to social, scientific, religious and political influences and proved an interesting and broadening experience for students. Other elements were 'An Inquiry in Depth' with several choices of topic ranging from Britain 1815-1851 to The American West 1840-1895. Two topics were required from 'Modern World Studies' which included the Arab-Israeli Conflict and The Irish Question and, finally, there was a choice of local history topics under the heading 'History Around Us'. The National Curriculum Working Party for history, responsible for drawing up the original proposals, appeared to ignore the existing scheme and did not, therefore, build on the direct experience of the teachers involved. Nevertheless, good sense has prevailed and a broadly similar course continues to be available for the GCSE.

Demise of the Council

These examples show why the work of the Schools Council seemed like a lifeline to many working in the schools. It generated excitement among teachers whose enthusiasm proved contagious with both students and colleagues. True, most of the projects were 'top-down' in the sense that a small group of teachers and other professionals formed closely knit teams which directed the projects under the ultimate control of committees of the Council. Nevertheless, all projects included trials of the material in volunteer schools and feedback was taken seriously by the central team before the final version was released. Critics point to the lower than expected take up of the majority of projects and attribute this to the lack of a sense of 'ownership' of the materials by classroom teachers. Whilst there is doubtless much truth in this, I believe that there were other factors operating. At the height of its output in the 1970s many comprehensive school heads and staffs were easily persuaded that they might be labelled trendy or worse if they departed far from traditional syllabuses. Others simply lacked the time, finance or vision to face the considerable demands when taking on a project.

Criticism of 'top-down' organisation must also take into account the situation at the time. There was a desperate lack of syllabuses and teaching materials appropriate for use in schools who wished to break down some of the barriers between the traditional 'academic' curricula for those deemed capable, and 'practical' programmes of study for others. Time was of the essence and, if Ryhope's experience was typical, teachers in many departments envied colleagues who had a good Schools Council project to work with. The problem with 'bottom-up' work is that it is very time-consuming and does not always lead to a coherent finished product. Despite the many advantages of involving a broad base of practical experience in development work, I believe that the School Council's method of working was largely justified in the contemporary educational environment. Although the Council did not sufficiently address the problem of curriculum planning as a whole — and certainly not in the context of the rapidly expanding comprehensive sector where the need became increasingly felt as the 1970s proceeded — there is no doubt that in its relatively short life the Council made major contributions to educational thinking. Together with the democratic involvement in its committee structure of local authorities, teacher unions and practising teachers this was seen as a threat to Conservative values in the 1980s leading to the Council's demise and loss of accumulated expertise.

Contribution from organisations

Mathematics projects, the Avon Resources for Learning Development Unit and the Schools Council were just a few of the organisations which provided practical help and encouragement for workers in the field.

Subject associations

Most subject associations for teachers encouraged their members to participate in curriculum development. The National Association of Teachers of English (1976), for example, was extremely active in promoting discussion and activities around 'Language Across the Curriculum'. In *Language across the curriculum: Guidelines for Schools* the Association highlights the language policy of a middle school.[8] It reveals the constructive and concerned feeling that often permeated discussions at the time, as the following extract shows:

1   That a non-stressful but secure atmosphere has been created which should encourage children to talk.

7   That the child is helped to use reading and writing to gain knowledge, understanding, pleasure, satisfaction, discrimination, a sense of values, control over inner feelings and enlargement of sympathy.

10 That he is helped to become more competent socially through learning how to express himself. (pp 13-14)

The Association for Science Education, whilst remaining neutral on matters of grouping by ability or non-selectively, produced two substantial and highly informative booklets in their Study Series *Non-Streamed Science — A Teacher's Guide* (Association for Science Education, 1975) and *Non-streamed Science: Organisation and Practice* (1976). The former was written by a member of the Association's sub-committee which had been set up to study the teaching of science to non-selective groups and the latter was a collection of writings of the personal experiences of practitioners. Ryhope School hosted a north east regional meeting of the Association in 1976 which revealed something of the atmosphere of the time. The title of the Saturday morning session was 'The Teaching of Science to Mixed Ability Classes'. Over 100 science teachers — two or three times the average — attended the talks, discussion and demonstration lessons with groups of students.

Goldsmiths College

It was becoming increasingly obvious that the normal school subjects were not providing all that a school curriculum should offer its students. The humanities and careers education projects made important contributions but there were many other matters requiring attention. The systematic study of issues concerning the environment, health, peace and war, and personal and social relationships did not fit easily within traditional subjects. How were these to be taught and where was the time to come from? Answers to these questions had to be found within a growing climate of opinion for all students to experience a balanced curriculum throughout their period of school attendance. In other words, there was increased wariness about 'dropping' subjects during the secondary stage. Integrated studies, also referred to as interdisciplinary or cross-curricular studies, offered possibilities and merited examination. Ideas ranged from the modest telescoping of three subjects into two of the Schools Council Integrated Science Project (with the addition of much new and relevant material) to utopian ideas of abandoning subject barriers. Organisations started to tackle the problem and an important step forward occurred with the formation of the Curriculum Laboratory at Goldsmiths College, University of London. In *Young Lives at Stake: A Reappraisal of Secondary Schools* Charity James (1968), director of the laboratory at the time, described how its work had focussed on four elements of the curriculum:

—Interdisciplinary studies

—Autonomous studies (ie subject teaching in those aspects where linear treatment is required)

—Remedial education (help for all pupils where, for any reason, they are being held back in their studies)

—Special interest studies (pp 126-132)

No doubt the totality of the operation involved in adopting such a programme in full would have daunted any school and I know of none that attempted it. But that is not the main point. The work and thinking of the staff of the laboratory over several years, augmented by the contribution of serving teachers and advisers on pilot courses or seconded to the college, addressed real issues in the schools with vision. Much of this thinking has long been assimilated by schools and it is interesting to note, for example, that James amplifies the reference to remedial education with the phrase 'education related to special needs'. As we have seen in Chapter 6 it was over a decade later before 'special needs' came into common use in the schools.

Examination boards

Public examination syllabuses may not immediately come to mind as a resource for teaching and learning but, in fact, many schools used them in this way. At the time when comprehensive schools were first coming to grips with curricular matters, there were eight GCE and twelve CSE boards. There was no compulsion for a school to use any particular board though assessment procedures made it almost essential to use the local one for CSE examinations. For GCE, however, it was possible to 'shop around' and enter candidates for different subjects with different boards. Despite a small extra cost and a need to check administrative details extra carefully with teachers and candidates, the system provided a worthwhile, if limited, degree of flexibility for schools concerned with curriculum development. The boards were not passive onlookers and, despite an educationally somewhat conservative image, facilitated curriculum development in several ways. They approved and moderated school based schemes, worked with national organisations such as the Schools Council and initiated schemes in traditional and new areas of the school curriculum often based on work at one or more of their examination centres in schools and colleges. In Chapter 6 we noted the opportunities provided in CSE mode 3 examinations for schools to submit their own syllabuses and assessment schemes for approval and moderation by the board. This process led to new subject titles some of which represented important steps forward in curricular provision. The best of these gained wider acceptance as ideas were disseminated in the regions via moderators who visited the schools to coordinate and harmonise assessment procedures and teachers who met at coordinating meetings and agreement trials. The latter were occasions where standards were compared and adjusted to the board's requirements.

The following example shows the kind of opportunity which was available. At first, as was customary at the time, the home economics department at Ryhope School offered only cookery and needlework for O-level and CSE. Under forward-looking heads of department and their staff, this programme was expanded on the CSE side to five subjects: the original two plus home management, child development and fabric design, the last in collaboration with the art department. Home management included school based activities such as convenience cookery and furniture restoration and featured a link course with a local college of further education for electrical work and painting and decorating. Child development appeared well before it became generally popular in schools and included a strong craft element of soft toy and garment-making. In fabric design, also distinctive at the time, students learned to apply appropriate techniques to the design of fabrics for a variety of uses in the home. The courses were popular with staff and students and the exhibitions, mounted as part of the assessment procedure at the end of the course, were widely admired for their variety and quality.

Ultimately, and not unreasonably, the CSE boards had to call a halt to new titles but the opportunities provided were an encouragement to purposeful thinking among teachers throughout the country. An important, if mundane, use of mode 3 was to match a CSE syllabus to a corresponding one in GCE so that students could be taught together for all or most of their time before final decisions about entry had to be made. Sometimes the GCE syllabus was far from ideal but comparison of alternatives on offer often produced an acceptable syllabus and assessment scheme. GCE boards also permitted school based syllabuses and assessments, similar to mode 3, but the administration involved in preparing a submission daunted all but a few schools and departments from availing themselves of the opportunity.

National developments for secondary education, including those of the Schools Council, often depended on cooperation between the project team and a GCE board. When the syllabus was complete, the participating board made it available nationally through all the other examination boards. Chris Little (1992), executive officer of the School Mathematics Project, has emphasised the close relationship of examination boards and national projects. Writing before the national curriculum became operational for years 10 and 11 (Key Stage 4) he commented on the relatively favourable situation current at the time:

> The structure leaves curriculum projects like SMP (which in maths have had a major influence on the development of GCSE) free to propose their own innovative syllabuses, supported by curriculum materials. Teachers like this arrangement. They can be reasonably sure that what they are teaching is appropriate for what their students will be tested on. They can select syllabuses which are properly piloted, and reflect how they want to teach mathematics, within a broad framework for GCSE.

Initiatives by the examination boards themselves seemed few and far between in the late 1960s and early '70s. Enthusiasts searched hopefully through prospectuses to see if any new syllabuses were on offer. Yes, subjects such as sociology and environmental studies were introduced at A-level and made an impact in some sixth forms whilst alternative syllabuses for O-level subjects appeared with more frequency and, in most cases, proved a little more challenging than the traditional format. At Ryhope, a breakthrough came in 1976 when the Joint Matriculation Board introduced a new subject 'integrated humanities' for examination at O-level starting from 1978. This fitted closely with our CSE mode 3 course in social studies taken by all fourth and fifth year students.[9] Despite its rather uninspiring title (which we used in preference to social studies only when examination entries were being made), this was a radical and exciting syllabus which originated in response to a proposal from Page Moss Comprehensive School in Huyton. Like Ryhope, they had established a similar scheme as a mode 3 CSE examination. The Joint Matriculation Board (1977) in its annual report for 1976-77 noted that 'as with many other JMB syllabuses, the integrated humanities syllabus had its origin in approaches made by individual centres'. It continued:

In this instance a great deal of interest was generated by the Humanities Curriculum Project sponsored by the Schools Council and the Nuffield Foundation and the conviction, on the part of those involved, that a study of some of the social and moral aspects of the modern world which concern the lives of individuals and the communities in which they live should form a specific part of the curriculum offered to their pupils.

In subsequent regulations and syllabuses (eg Joint Matriculation Board, 1983), the board made minor amendments to the wording of this aim and added the significant comment that 'Such a study should prepare the individual to take his place as a responsible member of society'. To directly link the aim of an O-level examination with personal responsibility was, in itself, a highly innovative action. The new syllabus was also among the first at O-level to be assessed entirely on course work and it was a relatively straightforward matter for a school to run a concurrent CSE mode 3 and enable the full range of students to study the issues together in a course which combined rigour with flexibility in content.[10]

The Joint Matriculation Board also came to the rescue of science as a single subject for those unlikely to specialise in the subject but requiring a broad educational experience. In 1979 the Board produced an O-level syllabus in environmental science for first examination in 1981. Although the title indicated some specialisation of content this was not found to be a serious reservation in practice; the prescribed topics provided the opportunity for good science to be applied to topics of importance.[11] The aim of the course (Joint Matriculation Board, 1981) was to give examination centres:

The opportunity of introducing pupils to an understanding of the impact of science upon the lives they lead and the society of which they will be a part through courses which consider the environment in which the pupils live their immediate lives and the wider environment upon which they are dependent.

This made environmental science a very satisfactory complement to integrated humanities.

In the 1980s all examination boards provided initiatives in the majority of subject areas and built up experience which was, in general, put to good effect for the introduction of the GCSE, first examined in 1988 by five new boards made up from the existing CSE and GCE boards. Their joint experience included, as we have seen, considerable emphasis on course work rather than final examinations, an approach which has proved highly motivating for many students. David Moore, general secretary of the Association for Science Education, quoted in a report 'Absurdly low ceilings' (*The Times Educational Supplement*, 1991h), has summarised the situation. He noted that 'a step-by-step measure of performance is immensely valuable to some young people' and added, significantly:

> Some of the coursework produced by the most able young people for GCSE is absolutely stunning.

Thus, with the arrival of GCSE, there was much more relevant experience to draw on than in the key period covering the early development of comprehensive education when parent, student and teacher judgments were being made about its efficacy. Then there was a dearth of readily available tools for the job in the form of syllabuses, methods of assessment and physical resources. Today the position is much more favourable in this respect.

Summary chart

In this and the previous chapter we have considered the exciting range of learning opportunities which stem from a policy of teaching students in non-selective, flexible and purposeful groupings. We have seen the need for resources designed for use with a full range of learning strategies; for back-up services for teachers and support staff, and curricular decisions based on the interaction between content, purpose and teaching method (Chapter 4). Figure 1, based on the assumption of a first class education for all (the crucial 'For whom?' question of Chapter 4), summarises the inter-relationship of the main elements discussed. The diagram indicates a common entitlement for all students within which further activities inside and outside the classroom — the enhanced educational experience of Chapter 5 — should be organised.

Note that Figure 1 shows the development of positive self-concepts arising from suitable curricula and appropriate pedagogy. Many other factors will be involved but the contribution of good teaching practice matched to stimulating content is crucial.

TEACHING IN NON-SELECTIVE GROUPS

requires:

| TEACHING METHODS | supported | RESOURCES, TIMETABLING |
| matched to learning objectives | by | STRATEGIES and initial and in-service TRAINING |

as a basis for providing for all students:

A FULL RANGE OF
CURRICULUM EXPERIENCE
with learning support and
opportunities for more advanced
study

&

FULL ACCESS TO
EDUCATIONAL
OPPORTUNITIES throughout
their school careers

This will help to develop:

POSITIVE SELF-CONCEPTS & HIGH EXPECTATIONS in every
student

and contribute to their entitlement to:

SUCCESSFUL ACCESS throughout life to the main areas
of human knowledge and experience

Figure 1

8

Care, Guidance and Strategic Planning

When large comprehensive schools first appeared on the educational agenda, many thought that they would be impersonal establishments and few could visualise the consequences of the headteacher not knowing the names of all the students. In the event, comprehensive school planners responded with purpose designed or adapted buildings and local education authorities appointed teachers with specific responsibilities for the care and guidance of students and liaison with their parents. 'Pastoral care' was the name given to the new arrangements brought in with comprehensive schools for the welfare and well-being of their students. Despite connotations of sheep and shepherds or pastors and priests (which led me to prefer 'care and guidance') this aspect of school life quickly came to be seen as a necessary and natural part of every school's provision. In most schools, parents still had direct access to the head but, for the majority of matters concerning their children's progress and well-being, they quickly adapted to asking for (or writing to) their group tutor, head of year, head of careers or other appropriate member of staff. In this chapter we examine ways of organising care and guidance and review local authority services, built up over the years which now urgently need defending. In the field of strategic planning, we note that, if schools are to marshall all their resources to educate their students in the widest sense of the term, it is essential for them to integrate their systems for care and guidance with those for curriculum development. The chapter concludes with an assessment of the comprehensive challenge based on the ideas developed in Chapters 6, 7 and 8.

Need and response

When schools were small and selective, each class had a form teacher who took them for five minutes for registration in the morning, led them to morning assembly which followed and saw them again, momentarily, for afternoon registration. Hopefully, but by no means always, the form teacher took the class for one of the subjects on its timetable; if, however, the school was of mixed sex and the teacher's subject woodwork, cookery or PE, he or she taught only boys or girls respectively. Classes were invariably streamed and, at the end of each term in all grammar schools and many moderns, the form teacher added a few remarks in the tiny space available at the foot of the report sheet which accompanied each student home on the last day of term. Despite this severely limited contact, a rapport often built up between the form teacher and class members. At Riddings Secondary school in Scunthorpe, in the early 1960s, I asked to be the form teacher of 4G. 'G' stood for 'general' in lieu of any more positive description as this group was the bottom stream apart from the remedial class (Chapter 6). Our form room was one of the science laboratories and, in the days before laboratory technicians, I used volunteers to help where possible. I lived on the estate served by the school and at lunchtime, one Easter weekend, there was a knock on the door and a group of a dozen lads, mainly from my class, were outside. They had brought a member on 4G's register to meet me whom I had not seen for a while; he was home on leave from a residential establishment following a juvenile court appearance. It was one of those incidents in a teacher's life which makes the job seem rather special.

Houses and years

The form teacher system was correctly seen as inadequate for comprehensive schools with numbers on roll up to two thousand compared with two to seven hundred in most grammar and modern schools. New arrangements for care and guidance fell into two broad categories based on houses or years.[1] In the former, students were sub-divided into a number of houses, usually four or six, each containing students from every year. The term 'house' originated in the public boarding schools where discrete buildings or sections of the main building acted as a base for eating, sleeping, homework etc. Most purpose built comprehensive schools designed for a house system also provided some geographical identity, usually a house room for assembly which doubled for teaching purposes, school meals or both. However, many comprehensive schools were formed by amalgamation of two or three existing schools or were based on a single school which was extended. In these cases, there was usually no special provision and house meetings were held in halls and gyms on a rota system during the week. A room for the head of house and his or her deputy, usually of the opposite sex in a mixed school, was a welcome innovation assuring teachers, parents and students of a degree of privacy for discussion previously unknown in state schools. Purpose built or otherwise, an even number of houses was generally preferred to facilitate the organisation of sports competitions. This activity seemed very important to many planners in the 1960s but, in the light of experience and changing social attitudes, gradually diminished in significance.

As time went on, more comprehensive schools preferred to base care and guidance on year groups where all the students in a year formed the unit, again with or without physical provision.[2] For schools wishing to provide opportunities for internal competition whether sporting, road safety quizzes, fun events or whatever, the year system presented no serious handicap. Year staff could arrange these activities either on a tutor group basis for maximum participation or by combining tutor groups into clusters for minority interests. Year groups have important advantages over houses which are discussed below but, in the day to day routine of school life, heads of year and heads of house share common responsibilities. With the establishment of house and year systems the terms 'group tutor' and 'tutor group' replaced 'form teacher' and 'class', the new names reflecting the extended and interactive roles envisaged for both teachers and students. In the most successful year systems, group tutors are actively involved in all aspects of the life of the year[3] but in practice this was difficult to achieve, particularly in the early development of comprehensive schools. Many tutors felt their role was to teach and not to act as social workers as they saw it whilst some heads of year jealously guarded their authority and were reluctant to consult their tutors, one or two of whom may have been senior heads of subject departments. However, the main reason for lack of full liaison between individual tutors and heads of year is still present and arises from constraints of time and availability. Most heads of year teach a reduced timetable and are often the only staff available to deal with a situation quickly and efficiently — if not always as effectively as might have been possible with wider consultation.

However efficient a system for care and guidance may be on paper, the work constantly involves human relationships. Here teachers' abilities vary considerably yet, from the start, they have received only minimal help through in-service training. It is no wonder, therefore, that there are still a few teachers who see pastoral work as an unnecessary intrusion on their time which could better be given to lesson preparation and marking. In contrast countless group tutors and heads of year make major contributions to the educational and social welfare of their students. Through unobtrusive guidance and support, teachers help their students to enjoy and get the most from their school experience and, in doing so, many become highly respected by both the students and their parents. Fortunately young people are able to adjust to a wide range of personalities among their teachers. I recall two excellent tutors of first and second year groups with very different personalities which they naturally reflected in their classroom organisation. However, they shared a vital attribute: the members of their groups knew that all their activities mattered to their tutors and that they were approachable, each in his or her own way, on the hundred and one problems which can arise among students of this age. Few difficulties arose from the groups of tutors like these.

Even with a totally committed and competent staff some teachers are more approachable on certain topics and by particular students than others. This is most noticeable with older age groups. For example, two enthusiastic and capable women colleagues both held posts of responsibility in the pastoral system. Each was well respected by students and parents but only one was consulted on fears of pregnancy. Teachers also differ in the efficacy and acceptability of the advice they are seen to give and such basic considerations, of human nature rather than professionalism, demonstrate that to set up a pastoral system, necessary as that may be, is in itself not sufficient. The ethos of the school as a whole must encourage an atmosphere in which students feel free to talk to teachers as the need arises, whilst accepting and respecting the established means of communication for everyday events. A team approach by the staff, both at year and school level, is an essential supplement to formally organised hierarchies which, however well planned and intended, do not cut much ice for a young person with a real problem. The matching of a formal structure to good sense and understanding is the key to every effective system of care and guidance. I have no doubt that the quality and quantity of personal attention possible in comprehensive schools with effective arrangements for care and guidance makes them seem more student-centred and less regimented than was the case in the smaller grammar and modern schools, usually run as single units, which they replaced.

Whole school possibilities

At one time, a few local authorities appointed qualified teachers, usually with further relevant experience or training, to act as counsellors who worked on a school basis and operated to some extent independently of the year or house system. Not surprisingly this well-intentioned initiative, which recognised the need to supplement formal systems of care and guidance, was less than totally satisfactory to the counsellors, year staffs or students themselves. A more lasting, but only partially exploited, development occurred where a local authority provided a youth wing on the school campus together with a teacher-youth worker or, where no accommodation could be provided, an unattached youth worker based at the school.[4] When the talents and professionalism of a competent youth worker are matched with understanding at school management level, exceptionally good work can develop both in school and outside. In other cases, youth workers have found it difficult to combine youth and school roles and are not always helped by management attitudes which identify any sign of informality as a threat to the authority structure of the school.[5]

Finally, for a short time in the early 1970s a few trained teacher-social workers were attached to comprehensive schools in some authorities. This arrangement had considerable potential. Working with year staffs, the teacher-social worker could support individual students and visit parents conveniently and, where necessary, speedily. With a small mainstream teaching commitment, the person had credibility with teacher colleagues whilst, as a social worker, he or she could offer specialist advice to adults and students individually or in groups. Financial considerations were, as far as I know, the main reason for the demise of teacher-social workers. Their work was presumably seen as expendable yet there remains an unfilled gap in many schools today.

Welfare

Protection and security

Name-calling, constant irritations, threats from older or stronger students, physical attack, racially motivated harassment ... all these are possible in school however alert and concerned a teaching staff may be. Young people whose development — physical, emotional or intellectual — is above or below average for their age may experience self-consciousness, feelings of insecurity or an inability to make lasting friendships. This can lead to deep unhappiness over a period of time and prevent the young person from getting the most from his or her education. Clearly it is the responsibility of every school to minimise these possibilities with supervision, observation and remedial action. Group tutors and heads of year have a key role and it is important that when anti-social behaviour occurs, as inevitably it will, that the response of the school is seen to be effective by all parents and students involved.[6] In this way, trust and cooperation are built up for the future. It is also important that students are helped to understand the need for personal responsibility and cooperative action in these circumstances. 'Never tell tales' is an admirable sentiment insofar as it concerns one's mates and some unimportant detail of school life but, in serious situations, it needs replacement by a message on the following lines: 'Don't hesitate to talk to your group tutor or another teacher if someone in your group is being got at; you can be assured of confidentiality and, as well as helping the person suffering the effects, you will be making a positive contribution to the well-being of the tutor group as a whole. The teacher will provide protection for the injured party but will also help those responsible for the unhappiness to recognise the upset and distress caused by their behaviour'.

I found that school students of all ages respond to this kind of approach and often supply vital information which would not be obtainable from any other source. As a practical and confidence building measure after an incident which had come to my notice had been dealt with, I often asked friends of the student who had been on the receiving end to give their group tutor a daily report of whether or not all was well and, for added authority, to report to me at the end of the week. I always took care that my request to act as a 'bodyguard' was made without pressure and it was almost always accepted. Despite understandable nervousness at first on behalf of the sufferer as to the likely effectiveness of this follow up, the real and practical responsibility undertaken by friends had an almost hundred per cent success rate. 'Never tell tales' is brief, simple and dangerous; the more considered statement requires a spirit of service on behalf of the students reporting a problem or incident, mutual trust between them and the teacher, and considerable skill and sensitivity by the teacher in following up the information so that there is a positive all-round outcome. The results of such a policy, applied consistently, are far-reaching and prove educative for all students in the school. The treatment of misdemeanours has a powerful influence on the hidden curriculum (Chapter 4) and the topic is further considered in Chapter 9.

Attendance

Many students insist on attending school despite illness, plaster-encased limbs, walking aids, or wheelchairs unsuited to multi-sited buildings without lifts or ramps. Despite these handicaps most manage one way or another. At the other extreme, there is school refusal which can be a major problem. One case, revealing the skill and patience of the staff from a local children's hospital, particularly impressed me. At the hospital's request, members of their staff started to bring a young lad to the school for an hour at a time, later increasing to half days, two or three times a week. Sometimes this proved too much and he ran out of school but as time went on his confidence slowly and fitfully returned until, eventually, he was back full time and without assistance. He was a capable student and successfully completed his school education. In the most critical period he was assisted by the understanding attitudes, not only of the teaching staff most concerned, but also of fellow members of his tutor group who understood the circumstances and offered him their support. In between these extremes there is truanting, absence condoned by one or both parents and 'dolling off' or 'bunking' from lessons after morning or afternoon registration. In these cases Educational Welfare Officers now more often referred to as Educational Social Workers play an increasingly important and professional part. No longer are they simply the 'school board man' (or 'lady') though this description, dating from the school boards set up under the 1870 Education Act, has remained remarkably persistent. The ESW can only hope to succeed, however, if the school makes adequate arrangements for his or her effective liaison with staff with pastoral responsibilities. Indeed, in all aspects of attendance during the period of compulsory schooling, cooperation between agencies is all-important.

The school psychological service

Educational psychologists should play an important role in the care and welfare of school students. In collaboration with teachers they have much to contribute to understanding the learning process (Chapter 6), to identifying causes of learning difficulty and in devising and monitoring appropriate programmes of study. Educational psychologists are also involved in the welfare of individual students following referral for learning or behavioural difficulties by a school or other agency. The more serious of these referrals require educational psychologists to undertake detailed assessment and to prepare statutory statements concerning the young person's needs. This leaves little time for work with young people in the context of their home and school environments. Many psychologists complain, not without reason, that their services are too often called for in 'fire-brigade' situations where there is already a major crisis. Indeed, the potential of the service remains largely unfulfilled because of the wholly insufficient number employed. Teachers often see school psychologists as people on the periphery of school life who make fleeting visits. Yet, even in these restricting circumstances, those who combine expertise and professional independence with an understanding of young people and of teachers show how much could be achieved.

The ideology of the school psychological service should be in harmony with that put forward for comprehensive education. One important aspect is discussed by David Smail (1991), District Psychologist of the Nottingham Health Authority and Special Professor of Clinical Psychology at Nottingham University, in a pamphlet *When I Was Little: The Experience of Power*. The author draws attention to issues concerning the influence of power in human relations and refers to the 'methods and precepts' of psychology:

> Psychology's ... isolation of the person from a social world and its 'therapeutic' emphasis on his or her own responsibility for personal shortcomings, all serve to provide us with a kind of sanitised technology of conduct which turns totally blind eyes to the crushing and rapacious machinations of power which envelop us as soon as we emerge from the womb. (p 2)

He goes on to outline the nature of the forces which surround a young person and concludes that:

> Because psychotherapists and counsellors are for the most part kind and well-disposed people, it's easy to overlook how punitively moralistic are the buried assumptions of many forms of so-called therapy which, when all is said and done, really do place tremendous pressure on people to *conform*, whether to the norms of the wider society or perhaps to the often rather ill thought-out ideals of 'personal growth' etc.
>
> Maybe it would be better to cast a more *appreciative* eye on our patients and clients, to learn what they have to tell us about the world, and to help them respect themselves for the characters that they are. (pp 22-23)

To follow through such ideas also needs time and resources. Indeed, a considerable injection of funding and a corresponding commitment on the part of national government is needed for the school psychological service to operate effectively in all its main aspects, not least in preventative work. The results would enhance the quality of life of many young people in education and that of their families.

Medical and dental services

School medical and dental services play an important part in the welfare of young people, particularly in the field of preventive medicine. Routine inspections, immunisation sessions and fitness checks before outdoor activities are all conveniently and effectively arranged on a school basis. The work of these services can be supported in a practical way through educational opportunities. For example, Ryhope, like many schools, had a near hundred per cent record for voluntary immunisation of first-year girls against rubella (German measles). The risk to a foetus of its mother catching rubella during pregnancy are well known and the school medical service issued small, attractive cards to congratulate each young person and provide a record of the event if she later forgot whether or not she had been immunised. Lessons for both girls and boys arise and I made a point of presenting the cards at a year assembly taking as a theme the history and value of preventative medicine. The school medical officer provided information on the discovery in Australia of the connection between rubella and the development of the foetus. The students were fascinated to learn the details of how a doctor, concerned with a larger than normal number of deformed children at birth, noticed from his detailed records that many of their mothers had caught rubella in a local outbreak of the disease. Indeed, health care is a subject for education as well as a service to students. Many opportunities arise in school where its importance can be stressed, for example when young people take part in fund raising activities which aim to improve health and prevent disease in third world countries. Their interest can be widened and their understanding deepened with simple scientific descriptions of how their efforts are being used. For example, the United Nations Children's Fund (UNICEF) organised annual sponsored walks in the Grisedale Forest in the Lake District. Illustrated information sheets showed how oral rehydration therapy can save the lives of millions of children and, as a reminder, each participant received a plastic spoon specially made to take just the correct quantities of sugar and salt to counteract diarrhoea and dehydration. Again I congratulated the participants at assemblies and used the materials to broaden the knowledge and political understanding of all present.

It is surprising how many school students need attention for illness and injuries of varying degrees of seriousness during the course of a week. Young people suffering from asthma may need urgent attention and there is an increasing number of prescriptions for tablets and other medication which need safe-keeping and administering under supervision. As a result, there is need for a nurse to be permanently attached to every large comprehensive school together with its nearby primary schools. Under existing circumstances schools usually have a teacher or a member of the support staff[7] qualified in first aid but emergencies happen at very inconvenient times — usually when the teacher has a class which cannot, or certainly should not, be left. To be fetched from teaching is far from ideal but has to be resorted to in some situations but this is only one of the problems facing anyone who takes on these voluntary responsibilities. The time taken to locate a parent or relative to accompany their child to hospital can be considerable whilst there are constant worries concerning possible misjudgment of the seriousness of an accident or illness when a mistake could, literally, be fatal.

Problems range from minor illness to serious accident and, as well as providing essential care, the teacher on the spot must exercise judgment concerning whether the student is making a meal out of very little or, alternatively, is putting a brave face on a more serious problem. A case involving the latter was brought forcibly to my attention at an open meeting for parents organised by the parent-teacher association. I had given a progress report concerning the school and asked for questions but was totally unprepared for one of them: 'Is it the policy of the school to send someone home on his own with a broken ankle?' It turned out that the student in question had fallen in PE; the teacher had asked him how he was at the end of the lesson and had offered to take him home. The young man had replied that it wasn't that bad and, as he didn't live far from the school, he would be quite OK on his own. In the rush of the moment, and with other commitments imminent, the teacher agreed adding that he must be sure to go to the doctor for a check. True, this incident revealed defects in school procedures which were rapidly reviewed and improved but the point remains 'that, under the circumstances of a busy school on a large site, errors of judgment are always a possibility and likely to be more serious without ready access to the expert knowledge of a resident nurse. Schools know how quickly confidence-building relationships, built up over time, can be impaired if an incident occurs which appears to parents to show a lack of care for their child in distressing circumstances.

Effective planning

Early misconceptions

Early approaches to care and guidance in comprehensive schools seemed to be based on an assumption that large schools, although necessary (Chapter 5), were inherently inferior to smaller ones. As we have seen, a common response was to try to adapt the concept of houses in independent boarding schools. This approach was poorly matched to the needs of comprehensive schools whose students did not live, let alone sleep, in separate buildings and where friendships matured in the home and in the community as well as at school. Allocation of students into houses often appeared arbitrary in ways which mattered to young people: friends who lived in the same street could not meet in house rooms at lunch or break time and were often barred from attending each other's house disco or trip. The house system which cut across the organisation of teaching and learning could lead to a sense of detachment by senior staff. Head of house job specifications, written or assumed, related only to pastoral and not curricular matters and teachers appointed were rarely seen as directly involved in the serious work of curriculum and academic attainment. At best, their contribution was accepted as valuable, particularly in dealing with 'trouble', but separate from the 'academic' side of the school; at worst it was regarded as little more than a way of rewarding experienced teachers who lacked the formal qualifications regarded as essential for any comparable post involving subject department responsibility. The role of care and guidance in school had not been adequately thought out in terms of the strengths and needs of comprehensive schools.

Coordination

As year groups became more popular as the basis for care and guidance the potential for more coordinated educational objectives as well as improved efficiency became clear. For example, matters such as option choice and careers guidance must be organised as a partnership involving appropriate members of the school's senior management team and the staff of the year group concerned. In a house system all houses are involved with each process every year leading to an excessive number of planning meetings, differences in interpretation of policy or to both. Working with a generously provided and purpose-built house system at

Wyndham School in Cumberland, it was noticeable that meetings were required for almost every activity planned on a school basis when the time could have been more profitably used for actions which directly benefited the students. This inherent inefficiency was the over-riding factor which influenced me, on appointment to Ryhope School, to choose a year system. It proved to have many beneficial consequences, not all of them foreseen when the decision was made. Care and guidance based on a year system does not remove the separation of curricular and pastoral functions but it can reduce the problem considerably; in practice, schools which chose year systems developed a greater homogeneity between care and guidance and the curriculum whether or not they had planned to do so. Year groups are natural entities of a school: members of a new entry come with friends from junior school and have the maximum opportunity of making new ones. At assemblies and similar occasions, teachers can tailor their remarks according to the age of the students knowing that the majority of what they have to say will be relevant to all present. When, very occasionally, transfer of a student from one tutor group to another is necessary, the head of year will have several choices for the student. With encouragement and patience, each tutor group can develop a corporate identity which forms the basis of a wider sense of community at year group and school level.

Attempts to break down the educative process into isolated compartments are counter-productive. For example, a curriculum for years 10 and 11, carefully designed to provide equal opportunities for girls and boys, will be sabotaged if guidance on choice of options is given along sex-stereotyped lines. Conversely, heads of year who appreciate the need for equal opportunities in all aspects of school life will find effective curriculum guidance a near impossibility if the timetable has been constructed on the assumption of traditional sex-roles. Year staff have direct experience to contribute to curriculum planning, including homework and assessment policies, based on their contacts with parents and students. Similarly, heads of subject departments and their staffs have much to contribute to the care and guidance of students arising from their contacts in the classroom. Subject teachers and group tutors are, of course, one and the same people emphasising different aspects of their role at different times of the day and mainly with different students. Other areas requiring joint activity include records of achievement, which aim to assist students both in the learning process and in their personal development, and problems concerning behaviour which are as often linked to inappropriate curricula and teaching methods as to home and social circumstances. Those responsible for care and guidance in school must, therefore, be directly involved in the curriculum programme of the school and *vice-versa*.

School policy making

Management structures and decision making processes vary from school to school but, with the introduction of systems for care and guidance, most established separate committees for heads of subject department and heads of year or house. The former planned and implemented policy concerning the curriculum and examinations. Regular items on the agenda included homework policy; assessment techniques; arrangements for internal school examinations; allocation of the school's capitation funds for books, stationary and equipment to each department; methods of acknowledging good work or exceptional effort; disciplinary concerns in the classroom; detentions or other means of ensuring that work was completed, and the promotion and demotion of students between streams and bands where these existed.[8] Head of department meetings were also the main forum for curricular initiatives especially if these involved more than one department in an inter-disciplinary or cross-curricular activity such as sex education or environmental studies. Heads of year planned and coordinated policy concerned with school routine, disciplinary matters and social events. Hardy annuals for the agenda included: attendance and punctuality; supervision at break and lunch time; operation of disciplinary procedures; differing interpretations of school policy; complaints from teachers over the work or attitude of particular students and classes; identifying students who are under-achieving; parental complaints over excess homework or lack of it; school reports; Christmas activities; community service; social events, and last, but certainly not least, achieving conformity in dress.

The functions of the two committees overlap and interact in the key areas of curriculum, assessment and teaching method, school routine and the maintenance of good order. Unfortunately, as can be inferred from the above, heads of year often saw themselves as a kind of emergency service which had to clear up the results of other people's errors and omissions with little opportunity to influence the policies which caused the problems. A deteriorating attitude to work in tutor group 9.5 (group 5 in year 9) may be improved with a pep talk from the head of year but, in all probability, the root cause is connected with the effectiveness of the teaching, perhaps resulting from the group having a disproportionate number of inexperienced or less competent teachers. In such cases guidance from heads of department to the teachers concerned are equally necessary. Heads of year are also in the front line for complaints by parents concerning any aspect of school policy. If they do a good job, which is usually the case within the parameters set, their contribution to the smooth running of the school is appreciated — but essentially as maintenance engineers rather than policy makers and planners. Heads of subject departments can also feel short-changed. In contrast to the immediacy of much head of year activity involving day-to-day working with the senior management team (head, deputies and other senior teachers), it is easy for heads of department to feel isolated. As long as examination results flow and their administration is up to scratch, they may feel that their opinions on wider school issues are regarded as marginal. One must be wary of stereotyping but, as far as many schools are concerned, I believe that these views contain sufficient truth to be a matter of real concern. Job satisfaction is a pre-requisite for effective teaching and guidance.

A joint school policy committee, representative of teachers with both year and curriculum responsibilities, is a first step towards the creation of an integrated policy. At Ryhope we found it helpful to retain regular, non-policy making, meetings of heads of year to deal with day-to-day routine, social events and so forth and less frequent meetings of heads of subject department to sort out the minutiae of examination arrangements and the like. Both groups were classified as sub-committees of the main policy committee and we involved other teachers through working parties on particular issues. Whilst details of organisation will depend on local circumstances, an arrangement such as this can do much to eliminate unnecessary divides between 'pastoral' and 'academic' matters and establishes the right of every member of staff, directly or through the head of department or head of year, to present their views on matters which they consider important. Thus the educational case for schools to integrate their systems of care and guidance with arrangements for curriculum planning and implementation is a very strong one.

Comprehensive challenge

We can now set the topics of Chapters 6, 7 and 8 collectively into a wider context. In the 1960's and early 1970's the role of education in influencing and changing values in society was a topic of debate not only among people directly involved in politics and education but also among many parents and members of local communities. People from all walks of life looked to comprehensive schools to increase opportunity and fairness in education; their hopes and expectations gave encouragement to those working for the new developments who hoped that, collectively, their efforts and commitment might contribute to the creation of a more just and caring society. Similar feelings, at times perhaps latent rather than active, are alive today and one of the purposes of this book is to suggest areas where action could open up educational and political understanding as a pre-requisite for the further advancement of state education.

The mismatch within the education system between the immediate requirements of capital and the longer term interests of the majority (Chapter 1) lead to a corresponding organisational conflict in schools which has to be resolved. The response of many, in one form or another, was to establish academic and 'non-academic' streams and thus produce a near replica of the selective system within a single institution. These schools paid minimal attention to the potential of comprehensive education but reduced (or, at least, postponed) some of the immediate conflict. A much smaller number of schools had a clearer vision of the scope of comprehensive education, if underestimating the major conflict in values likely to arise when the expectations of all students were raised to a higher level. These schools integrated their pastoral and curricular arrangements and organised their teaching around non-selective grouping and a more common curriculum. Observation suggests that when these three aspects of school organisation are promoted together with vigour and determination conditions are created which can release tremendous potential in the performance of staff and students both inside and outside the classroom. Naturally there are risks and dangers but there are also unique opportunities for intellectual and personal development.

Today, as a minimum response to the intrinsic conflicts arising from the struggle for true comprehensive education, every school development plan should aim to increase the awareness of parents, teachers and students concerning the potential of all the young people in the school as well as providing practical proposals to widen and deepen personal development irrespective of class, colour, gender and current level of attainment. Figure 2 aims to depict the challenge presented by comprehensive education; to summarise the opportunities latent within it, and to indicate why it is seen as such a threat by its more politically aware opponents.

THE CHALLENGE OF COMPREHENSIVE EDUCATION

A combination of:

| NON-SELECTIVE GROUPING | & | A FULL and EXTENSIVE CURRICULUM FOR ALL | & | INTEGRATED CURRICULAR and PASTORAL PROVISION |

Provides the basis for:

| EFFECTIVE TEACHING and LEARNING STRATEGIES | & | ACCESS to the MAIN BRANCHES of KNOWLEDGE | & | ENHANCED STAFF-STUDENT RELATIONSHIPS with more effective help and guidance |

Together, these have the potential to:

1 Broaden educational, social and political perspectives
2 Increase personal and collaborative aspirations

Resulting in:

Students, staff and parents thinking more deeply

and

Reactionaries asking: Where might that lead? **DANGER!**

Figure 2

9
Aiming for Maturity

Adolescence is a period of rapid growth in maturity providing schools with a unique opportunity for nurture and guidance. We must therefore aim at relationships between adults and young people, as well as among young people themselves, which are conducive to maturity of outlook. We commence this chapter looking at the needs and significance of parents as partners and the strong influences which young people experience from their peers. We look next at how values are transmitted through school organisation and ethos using the diverse examples of record keeping and the promotion of good order. We discuss ideological, legal and practical aspects of rules and customs concerning school wear and, finally, look at initiatives for student participation in aspects of school policy making — a neglected but fruitful area for development.

Parents and peers

Parents as partners

Notes, letters, telephone conversations, home visits and newsletters; progress reports, reply slips, individual appointments and parents' evenings to discuss work and progress; parent-teacher associations and parent governors — just a few of the ways in which schools communicate with parents and encourage response.[1] Yet however necessary and informative such activities may be, partnership has a deeper significance than communication alone. The extra vital ingredient is not easy to describe: it concerns the development of a reciprocal feeling between teachers and parents that the personal and intellectual development of each student is, in important respects, an outcome of their partnership. An organic relationship of this nature is not achieved overnight, nor is it helped by legislation which extols shopping around in place of community values. Nevertheless, it is a goal to strive towards and, when parents and members of the community talk naturally of 'our school' or use 'we' in reference to some of its activities, this is an indication of progress. Few parents want to take over the detailed running of a school or to interfere with the work of teachers whose commitment and competence they respect whilst senior staff should be able to deal with situations where the greater good of the majority of students may be at risk from special pleading on behalf of a few. What almost all parents appreciate, if they are to feel an integral part of what is happening to their child, is encouragement. It is so easy for even the best-intentioned schools to appear threatening and to induce feelings of inadequacy. Guidance and understanding are as necessary for parents as for school students and, in both cases, must be based on mutual respect.

First impressions are always important and school office staffs usually deal with initial requests from parents both on the telephone and in person. Despite improvements in recent years, they work under pressure stemming from inadequate staffing levels and salaries which fail to reflect the responsibilities and skills of the job. Professionals, students, parents and tradespersons require their assistance — sometimes all at once and not necessarily in the most cooperative of spirits. Yet, in my experience, visitors and callers were always met with courtesy and helpfulness — a commendable achievement in light of the range of circumstances met by the staff. Many parents make appointments with obvious advantages to school and home but none should be told to ring back or return later if this can possibly be avoided. The problem may be urgent or at least seem to be so; alternatively, it may simply be a matter of convenience when a parent is in the neighbourhood of the school. There should always be a teacher available who can take the call or meet the parent briefly and propose a constructive course of action. During nineteen years as head I only recall one occasion when a parent was turned away: a mother came to the office window and asked for me but was told I was out of school and to try again next day. The person who gave this information had only joined the staff that morning and was momentarily on her own. Mention of office windows is a reminder that, even today, many school entrances are less than welcoming places especially when compared with the importance and resources attached to the design of reception facilities where organisations depend on custom for their livelihood. Nowhere is the need to encourage access greater than in schools with a high proportion of families from deprived neighbourhoods or from ethnic minorities.

Peer group influence

Parents know about peer group influence on their offspring. They are familiar with plaintive pleas claiming that 'I shall be the only one in my class who hasn't been allowed to stay up to watch tonight's film on television' (or whatever); they know of the extraordinary status attached to certain 'designer' articles of clothing like expensive brands of trainer shoes. Pressures here stem from television advertising reinforced by friends and acquaintances and rise to a crescendo as Christmas approaches. And peer group influence is not something that we leave behind with childhood and adolescence; a moment's thought shows that our own behaviour is daily subject to these influences which, of course, may be positive or negative. Peer influence on the development of young people at school can be very strong. It affects attitudes to study; co-operation or otherwise in matters of discipline; choice of school; popularity of subject options, and participation in extra-curricular activities. In many respects girls and boys experience different influences: for example, girls may come to feel that, despite what their teachers say, science and technology are not for them whilst most boys experience pressure to maintain a macho image. Peer influences have their origin in the wider social and material environment of young people but they are closely related to the hidden curriculum, school ethos and the quality of relationships. Although it is never easy, it is almost always possible for parents and schools to at least partially combat the more harmful influences and strengthen the constructive. We shall see examples of this process in the remainder of this chapter.

Often the best way to help individual students gain in confidence, apply themselves more consistently or improve their sense of social responsibility will include the involvement of peers. As we have seen (Chapter 8) one reason why the tutor group is such an important unit in school concerns the opportunity for a group tutor to foster a corporate sense of identity and responsibility conducive to the well-being and development of all members of the group. (The argument also applies to year groups and comprehensive schools as a whole but the tutor group of 25 to 30 members provides special opportunities). A few years ago *The Times Educational Supplement* had a feature article on independent school brochures and prospectuses. More and more were including photographs of friendly-looking, happy, active and studious young people already at the school, implying that the particular institution had a head start as far as positive peer group influence was concerned. Whether or not glossy brochures would help in the state sector, primary schools and comprehensives both have a duty to provide opportunities for all their students to develop mutual understanding so that they can constructively support each other inside and outside school.

Records and relationships

School records have proved a growth industry in the educational world in recent years with most of the attention on progress in the classroom. Here, we look at aspects of record keeping which help directly in the care, guidance, growth and personal development of students. All schools need such records. Group tutors may know their groups extremely well and be mines of information when asked about particular students but this is no help when a tutor is absent, moves to another post or is teaching when the head of year receives a telephone call or unexpected visit. Records need to be in an agreed format but it is important that each tutor should have the opportunity to provide a personal and insightful input rather than just responding to headings on a printed form.

Priorities and values

The content and style of record keeping influences the priorities of teachers who provide and update the entries. Old style school reports allowed only one line for comment on each subject and thus induced such well known phrases as 'could do better'.[2] Records help to transmit values and, wittingly or unwittingly, reflect the hidden curriculum (Chapter 4). For example, at one time most mixed schools separated their registers and class lists into boys first, followed by the girls and the simple expedient of keeping all such records in alphabetical order was a first step towards fostering non-sexist attitudes. The personal touch is further enhanced by listing first names before surnames: 'Susan Thomas' followed by 'David Thompson' is so much more personal than 'King, Brian', 'Morgan, Frank' followed further down the list by 'Adams, Jennifer'. The cumulative influence of apparently minor procedures such as these is not to be underestimated. To support the personal approach tutor group lists can be designed to contain information about interests, activities and family matters. In 1975 Ryhope School introduced extended tutor group lists for use mainly by senior staff who met many different students and their parents in the course of their duties. Tutor group lists, as typed, looked as follows:

TUTOR GROUP 1.2　Ms Bewick　Room S2				
Information:	m			
	8	Mark Anderson	*Michelle 3*, Andrew F	16 Byrne Street
	9	*Tracey Bell*		18 Poplar Close

Ms Bewick (all names are fictitious) is tutor of group 1.2, the second (non-selective) group in the first year. Mark Anderson has a sister, Michelle, in the third year and a brother Andrew who is a former student of the school. Mark has a birthday in August (the 'm' column shows the month of birth) and is, therefore, one of the youngest students in the year whilst Tracey, born in September, is among the oldest.[3] With the aid of an electric typewriter and an italic golf ball — modern technology of the time — the sexes were easily distinguished when required. The information columns starting from the left are for the teacher to fill in. My copy could have looked like this:

TUTOR GROUP 1.2　Ms Bewick　Room S2									
Information:					m				
6 7 7	g			f	8	Mark Anderson	*Michelle 3*, Andrew F	16 Byrne Street
4 2 5		b	c		9	*Tracey Bell*		18 Poplar Close

The numbers on the left show the results of National Foundation of Educational Research tests designed to provide an estimate of verbal, numerical and perceptual ability respectively.[4] In the other information columns I recorded a variety of activities using a colour code for easy recognition. In the example, 'b' stood for learning a brass instrument, 'c' membership of the choir, 'f' for the first year football squad and 'g' reminded me that Mark had acted as a host during a visit of governors. The tutor lists were always to hand and proved extremely useful if a parent telephoned or a head of year wanted to discuss a problem. I always consulted them prior to visiting a tutor group to look at work they were doing or before occasionally taking a class when the normal teacher was absent. A quick reminder of who was who (at one time we had twenty-four Thompson's) and a look at the tutor group photograph was a great help and enabled me to demonstrate in a practical way the personal interest which I felt. I soon found that it was fully acceptable to students if I took the file (and the photographs) into the classroom to remind myself of details on the spot. A discussion of Mark's project might finish with an enquiry after Andrew, whilst Tracey would be glad to know that her musical activities were known about 'at the top'.

Harnessing the computer

Preparing extended tutor group lists had obvious limitations. An already over-stretched clerical staff had to type new lists from scratch each year whilst not forgetting to change the golf ball after nearly every entry! Changes during the course of the year had to be made by hand and there was no space for a record of current attainment to complement the information from standardised tests. Today, most schools have some form of computer based management information system with which to facilitate the production and analysis of routine information and thus provide a sounder basis for guidance to students and parents. For example, if up to the minute data on attendance is needed, information technology can save time spent previously in sending for attendance registers and avoid the hazards of trusting to memory.[5] With a little thought and ingenuity schools can now provide easy access to information specifically recorded to include the more informal and personal side of school life including background details which, sensitively used, can assist teachers in establishing and maintaining good relationships. Effective guidance is also dependent on easy access to correspondence, files and reference material of all kinds. Here the computer can be used to construct and update an index of what is available adding, from time to time, comments and amendments which transform the index into a personalised data base. Computers are well established in the sphere of educational and vocational guidance. Popular programs guide those considering higher education through the maze of courses and admission requirements whilst other interactive programs enable individuals to input a series of personal attributes and interests and to receive information on a range of career possibilities matched to this data. Programs such as these encourage users to widen their horizons and develop lateral thinking.

However, just as development work on computers in the learning process will only be clearly focussed when it is allied to research into more effective pedagogy (Chapter 6), so constructive and imaginative use of computers in the field of personal development depends on recognition that care and guidance, growth and development are inextricably related to the curriculum (Chapter 8).

Good order

Whilst nothing worthwhile can be achieved in school without the maintenance of good order,[6] the means applied to achieve it must be fully compatible with the duty of helping all students to reach the highest possible degree of self-discipline and responsibility, individually and collectively.

Abolition of corporal punishment

Widespread use of corporal punishment in British schools was a most serious impediment to the development of staff/student relations based on mutual respect. It was finally abolished in all state schools from August 1987 following a parliamentary debate won by a single vote on 22nd July 1986. This represented a tremendous victory for the pressure group STOPP (the Society of Teachers Opposed to Physical Punishment) who, for eighteen years, had publicised the issues and coordinated activities through a network of supporters including teachers, parents, local councillors and other wellwishers. From the start of the 1980s, Tom Scott, the newly appointed and highly resourceful full-time education secretary, extended the Society's information gathering activities to build up a widely based national picture. This formed the basis for an effective media campaign which included the use of case studies of victims named or anonymous according to parental wishes. The reports were scrupulously accurate as were descriptions of the adverse effects of corporal punishment in Britain compared with European countries where, starting with Poland in 1783, it had long been dispensed with. Four countries, including Greece and Italy had never used physical punishment.[7] With steadily increasing local and national authority, STOPP became a focus for all committed to abolition. The organisation was guided by a London based committee and supported by small groups of activists in the regions. Special credit must go to Tom Scott for the ultimate success. The society's annual reports had titles such as *Catalogue of Cruelty: a dossier of child-beating incidents reported to STOPP* (1984a) and were accompanied by national and regional press releases, the latter highlighting local incidents and punishment statistics together with the names of local contacts, thus assuring media interest at all levels. *Catalogue of Cruelty* documented 169 case studies grouped under headings such as 'European Court of Human Rights', 'Sexual and Psychological Damage', 'Illicit Violence', 'Trivial Offences' and 'Public Beatings'.

Stopp News (STOPP, 1986) brought the news of abolition to its subscribers as follows:

> The victory by just one vote — 231 to 230 — followed several weeks of intensive lobbying by STOPP of MP's of all parties. Thirty seven Tories including eight ministers joined the opposition parties in voting for an end to the British practice of beating pupils.

The vote came after a debate lasting over three and a half hours at the Report Stage of the Education Bill. The Bill already contained a section outlawing corporal punishment due to the House of Lords vote in April, and the vote was on an amendment to remove abolition from the Bill.

The bulletin went on to give extracts from speeches, a list of how MP's voted and an account of campaigning immediately prior to the debate. This had included ten-page briefing papers for MP's, letters to the thousand parents who had approached STOPP in the last three and a half years asking them to write to their MP, and last, but not least, an account of how a mother had contacted the STOPP office on the day before the debate and had been put in touch with the *London Evening Standard.* As a result, and with the full support of the parent, the paper published a photograph on the afternoon of the debate which 'showed appalling bruising on the buttocks of a thirteen-year-old boy five days after he had been caned'. The reason for this assault? 'For not doing well enough in an exam'. The photograph was referred to in several speeches and if one MP changed his or her intention as a result of the mother's action, then that was sufficient to carry the day. Much else had happened before the issue reached parliament. Throughout the country there were individual schools which abolished or never used corporal punishment. In 1979 the London Borough of Harringey became the first to abolish it in all its maintained schools and, by the time of the parliamentary debate, 34 local authorities out of 116 in England, Wales and Scotland had followed suit and seven more had fixed dates for abolition. STOPP was active in disseminating information and lobbying on all these developments. An excellent early account tracing the abolition campaign from its roots in the 17th century,

but concentrating on the contemporary situation, is given in *A Last Resort?*
Corporal punishment in schools edited by Peter Newell (1972) a founder
member of STOPP. Later, while Shirley Williams was Secretary of State in
the Labour government, he edited the *Abolition Handbook* (STOPP,
1978/79) which was, in effect, a campaigners' reference book. It provides
a convenient summary of facts and arguments.

STOPP's achievements were accomplished with a very small number of
paid-up subscribers. Until the last two or three years they were looked on
as cranky by many of their colleagues but, as the public became better
informed, opinion started to change inside and outside the schools; finally
the 'few' were imagined to be many and their ideas seen to be humane and
practical. For campaigners everywhere, the STOPP story has messages of
hope and encouragement; it still awaits a full account but in *Children are
People Too* (Newell, 1989) the author gives a very useful overview in a
chapter entitled 'The Long Struggle to End School Beating in the UK'.
Whilst the case against corporal punishment centred around its
inhumanity, there were many other objections. Some youngsters felt they
had to be involved in anti-social activities to show that they weren't
'chicken' about receiving a beating. 'Quickly over' was no help to the
inadequate or to those who needed guidance and support over a period of
time. 'An effective deterrent' was refuted in copy after copy of school
punishment books in which headteachers were required by law to record
instances of corporal punishment but which were rarely, if ever, inspected.
Multiple entries showed how often the same person was punished for the
same offence. Surveys revealed strong social class and racial correlations;
students whose parents were in the lower socio-economic groups and/or
of Afro-Caribbean origin accounted for a disproportionate number of
recorded punishments. 'A last resort' was given the lie by statistics from all
over the country although these often underestimated the frequency of
canings and slipperings because of widespread but unrecorded use, usually
by teachers other than the head and deputies.[8]

Constructive methods

Despite predictions of anarchy following abolition, the necessary changes
occurred smoothly and with minimal opposition even from previously
strong supporters. Nevertheless, we must remember that during the whole
period of state education, only in the last ten years have all schools had to
rely on humane and positive approaches for the achievement and

maintenance of good order. There remains much to learn and we must beware of other unacceptable practices such as the use of sarcasm or the setting of tasks like writing an essay or doing some mathematics which intermingle punishment with curricular objectives. There remains plenty of scope for constructive and effective action and, in general, methods employed should be the minimum necessary to achieve the desired effect. For example, students involved in some out-of-character or not too serious misdemeanour usually respond very favourably to an opportunity to demonstrate improved behaviour and avoid the need for the school to involve their parents. This is a matter of fine judgment because, if behaviour does not improve, parents may well feel that, had they known earlier, their influence would have been positive. On the other hand, when schools and heads of year go too quickly to parents, they remove an opportunity for the student to demonstrate personal responsibility — and may also induce a justified feeling in parents that the teaching staff ought to have been able to deal with the incident without undue fuss. A wise teacher will give school students in trouble an opportunity to express their point of view and take it seriously, as a basis for further inquiry. Whilst there is always a risk of being taken for a ride, this can be much reduced with experience; it frequently turns out that an apparently straightforward incident has more than one side to it and young people quickly feel resentment if they are not allowed to put their case.

The effectiveness of talking with young people whose behaviour has given offence is frequently underestimated. For a constructive outcome, teacher and student should both be seated or both standing rather than the teacher seated behind a desk and the 'culprit' (already condemned) standing on the other side. This sends the wrong messages from the start and, if there are mitigating circumstances, the student feels little confidence that they will be given credence assuming he or she gets a chance to explain them. It is also important to concentrate on the anti-social activity itself and what is to be done rather than the moral or personal standards of the offender. In this way both teacher and student can look at the problem in an objective rather than emotional manner and, responding to this kind of approach, many students are ready not only to accept that their behaviour has been anti-social but to suggest constructive ways of making amends. I vividly recall an incident involving three boys aged 11 or 12 who had gone into a nearby allotment at lunch time where a man kept a variety of animals mainly as pets. They had caught a chicken and wrung its neck. The owner of the allotment, whom we knew as a parent of students in the school, rang up. Recognising his specialist knowledge and constructive nature, we asked if he would come to school next day and speak to the boys personally concerning the incident. This he did and I asked if he would like me to be present. He preferred to be on his own so I vacated my room, sent the first lad in and waited outside. It was quite a long talk and a very quiet and thoughtful young man emerged to be replaced in turn by the other two. The parent obviously believed in the value of concrete situations as an aid to learning and had brought a sack with him. He placed this on the floor between the two chairs arranged for the occasion with the headless chicken laid on top. The young people grasped the point.

Not all problems have such effective solutions. When talking proves ineffective or is judged insufficient, there is a range of other options which can be considered each with an educative as well as preventative or restrictive purpose. One frequently used procedure is useful for students whose standard of work has dropped or who are causing disruption in class: the students are issued with daily report cards to monitor work and behaviour. They present the cards in each lesson for their teachers' comments and signature and take them home for perusal and comment by parents who, whenever possible, have been contacted and consulted beforehand. A typical response might be as follows: the cards show rather patchy improvement at first and are followed by a discussion at the end of the week with the head of year who stresses the need for consistency. Much improved comments follow during the second week and the student then requests to be kept 'on report' for a third and final week so that further credit can be gained and he or she can establish this improved pattern of work or behaviour with classmates. Once again, not every case has satisfactory outcomes and, going further along the scale of seriousness, arrangements can be made to separate the student from his or her normal teaching groups for a short period of set work under supervision in a room made available for the purpose. In other situations, short term exclusions of 24 or 48 hours provide a cooling-off period and time for reflection but the initial contact with parents in these situations is all important — letters are rarely successful. Parents will usually do all they can to assist and support especially if they see that their child has not been written off, however serious the offence. These and similar procedures give opportunities for the person involved to show that he or she has grasped the point and to gain credit for improved work or behaviour.

The 1986 (No. 2) Education Act was the first legislation to specify detailed procedures, including the right of parents to appeal, governing all types of exclusion. Long overdue, legal safeguards are particularly important in cases where it seems impossible to deal with a young person's behaviour under normal school conditions without the education or security of other students being seriously threatened. Then a permanent exclusion is usually necessary followed by transfer to a pupil referral unit established by the local authority. However serious the problem no young person should appear to be finally rejected and, at first, many authorities required students attending the units to remain on the roll of their previous comprehensive school with the intention of regular liaison between school and unit followed, where possible, by return after a period of time. Regrettably, this rarely happened and, since the 1993 Education Act, the units are now schools in their own right. Many of their staffs are dedicated and highly skilled at their work but the whole process of exclusion and its educational consequences needs careful monitoring to ensure that students are not prematurely manoeuvred out of their normal schools and have opportunities to return if attitude and behaviour improve. Transfer to a special unit should be a last resort: but that is an overworked phrase in the history of education.

Need for encouragement

Successful arrangements for promoting good order in a non-authoritarian manner are based on simple and acceptable means of encouragement. The majority of students are more than willing to cooperate in achieving an atmosphere in the school conducive to learning and mutual support, providing encouragement applies to all students, covers the full range of activities and occurs as a natural process.[9] Since my experience in secondary modern schools I have regarded contrived schemes, such as merit points and other rewards of that kind, as an administrative abomination for the staff which generates more negative tendencies among students than positive ones. I was interested to see a similar conclusion reached by primary school children. In 'Merit points provide no incentive' *The Times Educational Supplement* (1992a) reported research at Liverpool Polytechnic (now the Liverpool John Moores University). The children placed 'praise in front of other children' and 'merit points' at the bottom of a list of ten rewards. They valued 'having their parents told about good behaviour; good written comments; good marks, and having work on display'. The researchers found, however, that:

Teachers are far more willing to tell parents about bad behaviour than good behaviour. This is despite the fact that telling parents about positive things is ranked top of all incentives by the children ... Informing parents about bad behaviour is the second most common sanction; telling them about good behaviour is only the eighth most common reward.

They comment that these findings reveal 'a gross discrepancy ... which requires examination', a point brought home to me after a survey of letters sent home by heads of year at Ryhope during one particular period. There were a few letters giving or acknowledging information and making appointments; a large number complaining of lateness, forgetfulness and minor misdemeanours; a few on more serious matters, but discovery of a letter of praise was a rarity. I reached the conclusion that, for all practical purposes, parents opening a letter and seeing it was from school must say to themselves 'Trouble'. Encouragement of students should involve internal networks to facilitate communication between, say, a subject teacher and the student's group tutor or between a head of department and head of year with good news communicated to parents through message, letter, telephone and personal contact.

School wear

Distinctive school clothing originated in the public schools, who wished to stress their exclusiveness. It was later adopted by grammar schools for similar reasons, which are inappropriate for a comprehensive system of education.[10] As well as an ideological message, there are practical and educational considerations which cause pause for thought on this issue. School clothing needs to be adaptable: a student may have a drama lesson which involves sitting or lying on a hall floor, proceed to a workshop or laboratory and feel the need to dissipate surplus energy outdoors during break and lunch times. Clothing for school should therefore be working gear rather than a selection of items derived from ideas of 'Sunday best'. This does not imply that anything will do — school is neither a football match nor a disco. The *Handbook for Labour Governors* (Socialist Education Association, 1985) asked some pertinent questions in a section entitled 'Ethos':

Does the school prescribe a set of identical garments to be worn by all students? This is a very negative even though a traditional approach. On the other hand, does the school accept a positive duty to teach dress sense by encouraging young people to be individual while discouraging inappropriate wear or dangerous dress?

The requirement is for practical, everyday clothing suitable for the job in hand. Most school uniforms look dated and dowdy and deny students any meaningful choice of clothing.[11] Here the 'hidden curriculum' is in marked contrast to the official one: design is firmly established in the latter and, thanks to human achievement through technology (a national curriculum subject), good quality and relatively inexpensive clothing is readily available in the shops. Apparently our school students are to learn about these achievements but not participate in an aspect which affects them directly. Modern clothes are designed to make the best of a rich diversity of human shapes, colourings and personalities and to be suitable for a variety of jobs. Most adults like some opportunity to express themselves and their moods through the way they dress — and education is about feelings and emotions as well as facts and processes.[12] Uniformed schools deny this modest entitlement to their most important members, the students.

Agreed, there are differing views on the merits or otherwise of school uniform and every headteacher is subject to the decisions of the governors and education committee. One might argue, therefore, that policy concerning clothing is simply a matter of democratic decision. In Britain there is another factor to be considered. As G R Barrell (1963) in his well respected book *Teachers and the Law* said:

> It is not legally possible to compel pupils at a maintained school to wear school uniform, and the only pressure that can be brought to bear in this direction is through the medium of the school's esprit de corps. (pp 235-236)

Esprit de corps is an imprecise quality on which to base action and, should such appeals to students and their parents fail, then headteachers, whether or not acting under specific instruction from their governing bodies, must turn for their authority to the dubious area of case law, in particular the case of *Spiers v. Warrington Corporation* (1954). This concerned a girl who was excluded from school by her headmistress for wearing trousers. Her mother maintained that they were necessary on health grounds and continued to send her daughter to school each day. And each day she was refused admittance on the grounds that her presence would be prejudicial to school discipline. Warrington's action was successful and the mother found guilty of failing to ensure that her daughter attended school. However, as the solicitor to the National Union of Teachers, in a letter in 1971 to the director of education for Sunderland, contended:

> The case cannot, in my opinion, be regarded in any way as an authority for a Local Education Authority to make the purchase of a specific school uniform a condition precedent for admission to a maintained school.

Case law forms a very unsatisfactory basis for policy and, in the case of uniform, transforms the situation into a personal confrontation between head (and governing body) and the parent concerned. In practice, a strict uniform requirement can only be maintained through an authoritarian approach from the teaching staff which has an adverse day-to-day influence on staff-student relationships as well as a deeper ideological impact. The head must be prepared ultimately to exclude a student for wearing, shall we say, a blue jumper instead of a green one and, if challenged by the parents, he or she must be prepared to defend that action in a court of law as being essential for the discipline of the school.[13] If a teacher is trying to build an understanding, non-threatening relationship with his or her students, it does not help to have to start each morning and afternoon session by going round the class to check that everyone is dressed precisely according to arbitrarily stipulated requirements. The detrimental effect on staff-student relationships is not to be underestimated; failure to conform may lead to anything from turning a blind eye on the part of the teacher, through letters to parents, withdrawal from educational visits and team events, various forms of blackmail such as an 'invitation' to find another school and, ultimately, to exclusion — all for a highly questionable objective. I am happy to be counted amongst those who prefer to see young people dress informally. They feel more grown up and it is certainly part of the job of a school to assist in such development.[14] School uniform started to become more popular again a decade or so ago particularly in its extension to junior and infant schools.[15] Then, as the educational market took an increasing hold on events, there was a resurgence of emphasis in all sectors with, crucially, the apparent support of most parents under the changed circumstances. Nevertheless, it is noticeable from television that there are schools which have dispensed with uniform whilst maintaining just the sort of atmosphere which most parents would wish their sons and daughters to experience.[16] The time will surely come when school uniform and the authoritarian procedures it engenders will disappear without loss to educational standards but with an all-round enhancement of goodwill.

Student participation

Influence and responsibility

Students influence policy in a hundred-and-one ways but their contribution is not always recognised, let alone encouraged. Young people need to gain experience which will prepare them to take an active part in democratic society and a comprehensive school, especially one run on non-selective principles, provides favourable conditions. The students themselves are the starting point because they influence the quality and nature of their education through their everyday responses to the teacher in the classroom. Every teacher knows the feeling when a lesson has been less than successful and failed to motivate the class; he or she will undoubtedly reflect on the causes and make modifications for next time. Equally, teachers cannot fail to be influenced when students indicate, however subtly (and with due regard to peer group influences!), that they have enjoyed the lesson. Body language, contributing information, asking questions or staying behind to look at resources are just a few of the signs that the lesson has been well received. Extra-curricular activities such as sport, drama, music, outdoor activities, clubs, sponsored events and community service are all influenced by the attitudes of students. Students also contribute to perceptions of the school by fellow students, staff, parents and the local community not forgetting year 6 pupils in primary school whose decisions whether or not to attend the local comprehensive may be crucial for its continued prosperity and even its existence.[17]

There are occasions when students' opinions are sought directly, for example in choice of a friend to be in the same tutor group when transferring to the comprehensive school or when year 9 students make their choice of options. The latter, incidentally, affect the deployment of staff and resources. As well as opportunities to exercise personal responsibility, wider involvement of young people is important. Groups of students may suggest activities, perhaps for a good cause, and offer assistance; teachers may seek volunteers to assist them with the library, art displays and so forth or arrange duties on a rota basis so that as many as possible are involved. In some schools head boys and girls, prefects and monitors may be appointed to undertake supervisory and other duties but this practice is authoritarian, at odds with the aim of comprehensive education, creates more problems than it solves and restricts other forms of participation. Finally, students may elect tutor group representatives and delegates to year or school councils.

A school council

There are difficulties with democratic representation but also many potential benefits for the school itself as well as for its most active participants. In the early 1970s, Ryhope school had an elected sixth form council which later became the 'Upper School Council' including fifth year students. The constitution defined three functions for the council: the first two concerned finance and the organisation of social and cultural activities whilst the third provided for the council to:

> advise the headteacher on suggestions for the development of any aspect of the life of the school. From time to time the headteacher may ask the council to appoint representatives to discuss aspects of school policy with members of staff.

Elections for tutor group representatives, chairperson and other officers all worked well and three non-voting members of staff, including an honorary treasurer elected by the upper school tutorial staff, had an advisory role. The constitution included a mandatory requirement that all upper school tutor groups should have an opportunity to discuss resolutions with their representatives prior to meetings. Any upper school student could attend council meetings as a visitor and the constitution, as a whole, was designed to give a real opportunity to influence policy. The council had its successes and the minutes for the succeeding four years provide interesting and varied reading; nevertheless, it was unable to satisfy the expectations of the senior students as a whole. Motions concerning important aspects of school life, however constructively intended, often affected the welfare of students in other years and overlapped the spheres of interest of teaching and non-teaching staff, the parent-teacher association and the local education authority — all of whom were entitled to be consulted. Many of the ideas put forward were a response to real problems but motions and resolutions often led to understandable concerns and, as far as the students were concerned, to procrastination. By the end of 1973, I had become convinced that new thinking was necessary. During the next few years the upper school council continued, now dealing mainly with social affairs, whilst in the school as a whole we tried to create a climate which encouraged and helped students to express opinions. Elected tutor group representatives operated in some years and, from time to time, tutor groups were asked to consider and prepare reports on some specific matter of school planning. Occasionally, informal delegations of students asked to discuss an issue which concerned them; they were received with the same courtesy that adults would expect and I tried to give them a considered and constructive answer after consulting with others as necessary. But student participation was not seen as a priority by many teachers including, crucially, some heads of year. Several members of staff saw it as harmful so inevitably results were patchy. Nevertheless, initiatives by teachers at all levels helped students of Ryhope School to feel that their opinion mattered.

Participation

In 1974, staff and students from Ryhope and two other schools in the north east participated in a day conference organised by Durham University's Institute of Education with the title 'Pupil Influence in the Curriculum'. Lawrence Stenhouse, formerly director of the Humanities Curriculum Project (Chapter 7) and then director of the Centre for Applied Research in Education at the University of East Anglia, gave a stimulating opening address. This was followed by three simultaneous staff/student role plays on a theme centring on complaints at an open day following a drama presentation on aspects of teenage life by members of a general studies course. After lunch teachers and students (the latter with the help of a member of staff for guidance) discussed the issues separately and the conference concluded with a joint plenary session. One of Her Majesty's Inspectors was present and all agreed that it had been a stimulating and rewarding event. The conference demonstrated dramatically, in more senses than one, the potential for a direct student input into school decision making although it was to be several years before another really significant development occurred.

In 1979 a sub-committee of the Ryhope School Association (Chapter 11) involved school students when planning two events. This was a success and I subsequently raised the possibility of student representation on the RSA executive. Members received this suggestion favourably and, after details had been considered by a working party, the annual meeting of the Association agreed to co-opt two boys and two girls from the fourth year with full voting rights on a year's trial. Twelve months later, following success of the trial, the student composition was amended to two representatives each from the fourth and fifth years. Responsibility for the choice of delegates was in the hands of myself as president of the Association, the Association secretary and heads of year concerned. The agreed procedure was as follows: each fourth and fifth year tutor group elected representatives to a student committee who, in turn, elected a chairperson and secretary together with four delegates to the RSA executive. Student committee meetings were attended by a sympathetic head of year in an advisory, non-voting capacity and the agenda of each meeting included a report back by the RSA delegates together with consideration of the next month's RSA agenda. Tutor group representatives were asked to work with their group tutors so that they knew the views of their members but delegates to the RSA were not mandated and thus remained free to act and vote in the light of any new information or thinking which was put forward.

Towards effective representation

Whilst democratic responsibility deriving from independence had been the key idea in the early 1970s, emphasis was now on participation in the decision making process with more realistic possibilities for effective involvement. Principles established through the RSA were extended to school affairs generally and three class representative committees, as they were known by the members, were established for first and second; third and fourth, and fifth years respectively. Each committee worked with a supportive but unobtrusive head of year or a deputy head and items for the agenda could be submitted by tutor groups, heads of year or the senior management of the school. Matters concerned with year group activities could almost always be settled at the meeting but items with wider implications usually resulted in a request to a deputy head or the headteacher to meet a delegation. Such an arrangement could, of course, become paternalistic or mere window dressing but the opportunity for elected student representatives to work closely with two or three senior members of staff opened out many educative possibilities when the teachers concerned appreciate the value and significance of the experience for both school and students.

On one notable occasion in June 1985, when most fifth years had left, the third and fourth year committee, as the senior group, met entirely on their own initiative. On the previous evening, the local paper had published proposals for reorganisation of secondary education in Sunderland, naming Ryhope as one of the schools for closure. After morning break there was a knock on my door and the chairperson and secretary of the committee asked to see me. They had held a meeting and decided to form a campaign committee and sought my agreement. They already had a plan of action which included asking the local paper to meet them. 'Class of '85 to contest closure' was the subsequent headline in the Sunderland *Echo* (15 July) to an extensive report which explained:

> In an effort to save the school from closure third and fourth year pupils have set up their own campaign committee with elected officers. They are spending their lunch breaks planning tactics and sending off letters appealing for support ... The chairperson of the campaign committee, 14-year-old Clare Ashbridge, told the Echo: 'This kind of practical operation is one of the things we like about Ryhope. It's a part of learning. It tests our initiative because we are on our own.'

Regrettably, the efforts of the students, together with many others, were unsuccessful (Chapter 16) but their commitment and initiative emphasised again that one must never underestimate the potential of young people for initiative and responsibility. There was to be a final reminder of this truth in Ryhope School's last year. The staff had decided to put a special effort into producing an attractive and interesting record of achievement file for each fifth year student and involved the fifth year council at the planning stage. The council recommended follow up discussions for all fifth year students in careers education lessons (which were taken by the head of year). This resulted in general approval of the scheme together with some key recommendations one of which concerned the title of the document. The staff had suggested 'Personal Achievement', 'Record of Achievement' and so on — all good names from the educational in-phrases of the time. The students reacted with a distinct lack of enthusiasm and suggested something much more practical: 'Final Report'. They recognised that this title had currency value with employers, admissions tutors, parents and relatives. It was adopted.

IV

CREATING A NON-SELECTIVE ENVIRONMENT

10

Aims and Curriculum

In Part III we examined methods and organisational matters which support non-selective policies in important areas of school life. Now, in Part IV, we look at the task of establishing and maintaining such an approach across the whole range of a school's activity. Discussion is centred on the real situation of a particular school with due weight given to the influence of subjective factors such as personalities, social and political events and resources of every description. Nevertheless, its focus remains outward looking as we note how broad principles were developed and modified by the opportunities and constraints of specific circumstances. Chapter 10 is concerned with the formation of Ryhope School in Sunderland in 1969 together with key decisions and management implications concerning aims and the curriculum.

Preparation for opening

The school was formed when the education authority amalgamated two long established schools — one grammar and one modern — situated on opposite sides of a main road on the outskirts of the town (now city). The grammar school had opened in 1911 as a mixed secondary school in a building of some architectural distinction; it was one of the first secondary schools to be established by Durham County under legislation stemming from the Education Act of 1902. By the 1960s the school had expanded; major extensions included a three-story classroom block (known as the tower block) during the construction of which the local contractor who had put in the lowest tender was declared bankrupt. Neither the design nor the quality of construction came anywhere near the best standards for school building realised elsewhere at the time. Immediately prior to amalgamation, the school took students from the adjacent former mining villages of Ryhope and Silksworth and from two other districts of the town with a higher proportion of residents in professional and managerial occupations. In the older age groups, students included many from outlying districts in County Durham. There were 780 students on roll in its final year as a selective school including over 150 in the sixth form. A year previously the staff had petitioned the Secretary of State for Education and Science to retain its selective status. Ryhope Modern School was also provided by Durham County and built to a solid and functional design typical of the 1930s. It was a mainly single story, rectangular-shaped building surrounding two open grass areas; the classrooms were entered from covered ways which offered a little protection from the elements — they were later enclosed — whilst a central assembly and dining hall, also serving as a gym, linked the two longer sides of the building between the grass areas. By the late 1960s the school served all students of Ryhope (other than Roman Catholics) who had been unsuccessful in the 11plus examination for grammar school entry; it also had a late entry from other modern schools in the area for students who wished voluntarily to stay on beyond the leaving age of 15 and take public examinations. There were 500 on roll prior to amalgamation.

In 1969, Sunderland education authority arranged to place a footbridge over the road, build a new science laboratory on the modern school site, erect a pair of demountable classrooms there and arrange for the new comprehensive school to serve the neighbourhoods of Ryhope and Silksworth incorporated into the borough from County Durham two or three years previously. Ryhope School had an opening roll of 1300 including 270 first years who formed the first fully comprehensive intake from the new catchment area which in itself represented a considerable change over and above the change to a comprehensive system. Both school buildings had many classrooms with untreated wooden floors making cleaning difficult and doing nothing for the aesthetics whilst some of the desks looked as if they had survived from the opening dates of the respective schools. Coming for interview at half-term on a snowy February day from a purpose designed comprehensive and community school in Cumberland, the physical aspect provided a marked contrast. In the event, with gradual improvements and further extensions, the building proved reasonably functional educationally but presented an organisational and supervisory challenge to management at all levels.

Logistical problems stemmed from a 'trunk route' starting from the foot of the classroom block and adjoining hall in the grammar school extensions, proceeding along a corridor which linked the new buildings to the old, down the main corridor of the original grammar school building (planned for a roll of 200) through the main entrance, across the footbridge and into the modern school block. At the start of the morning and afternoon sessions up to a thousand young people could be on the move in either direction producing a high density on the bridge and a bottle neck in the main corridor where students joined the flow from classrooms and the upstairs science and art area of the main building. One-way systems, 'keep left', circular traffic flows, 'up' and 'down' staircases, were all tried with only partial success. There was also minimal indoor space for students to gather when not in lessons. Even the old coat hanging areas which had sufficed, at a pinch, in both schools for shelter in wet weather had disappeared and become the school office, medical room, heads of year offices and later rural science and mathematics laboratories. Nevertheless such problems as these were seen as relatively minor impediments to the job in hand.

I came to regard a decision made in the April before the school opened as one of my most important — minor though it may have seemed to many at the time. From the beginning we called the grammar and modern school buildings the north and south blocks respectively. The names themselves would win few prizes for imagination but they served a very useful purpose: no one had to refer to the grammar school and the modern school buildings and it quickly became accepted that life went on in the south block or the north block. In practice nearly all students had lessons in both blocks and that was important too. The first two years were to be based in the south block and the other years in the north block, reflecting the relative sizes of the buildings but every student in the first and second years had some lessons in the north block and nearly everyone based in the north block received some of their teaching in the south block.

Surprising experiences

Three incidents will help to set the scene and give a flavour of the time. In the April before the school opened I was finalising the staffing structure with the assistant director of education and visiting the two schools. I dictated a letter to the well-respected senior clerk of the grammar school and in due course she brought it to me for signature; I thanked her and added 'I may as well take the copy away with me'. Her face dropped: 'We don't usually do copies' she said. One can note, as an aside to management matters, that the period of education covered during the life of Ryhope School saw a massive increase in paperwork of all descriptions. It reached a situation, unknown in earlier times, where if a school hadn't every detail, aim and speculative thought down on paper (with copies for everyone who was anyone) it could not possibly be involved in worthwhile education.

Next came the affair of the head of department post for careers education and guidance. Whilst all my other recommendations for the staff structure of the new school were approved, some naturally with modifications, the deputy director of education at the time announced that the careers post would be established 'only over his dead body'. This was my first battle — and one which proved successful — the appointment finally being approved and the school becoming the first in Sunderland to have such a post. As the ultimate purpose of every secondary school is to prepare its students for leaving, the precedent set did not seem to offer too serious a threat to the future stability of education in Sunderland. Following a flash of imaginative thinking by a colleague, we constructed an office for the head of careers by dividing an art room store into two sections separated by a partition. Fears of setting a precedent surfaced again a few months later when an internal telephone system was being planned. With twelve extensions to cover the two buildings I naturally included the head of careers' office but apparently this was not acceptable as the proposals had to go before the School's Sub-committee (and presumably become public knowledge). After some 'off the record' soundings I re-submitted my recommendations a few days later with the careers extension replaced by an 'office on the science corridor' — which just happened to include an art room and its store. The list went through without further comment though the incident helped to make curriculum development at the time, at least as far as the establishment of careers education in Sunderland was concerned, seem somewhat akin to life on the frontier.

The third incident occurred during the summer term prior to opening. We held three Friday evening meetings for parents: one for new entrants and two for parents of students already in one of the existing schools. For the latter, I was determined to speak only to mixed groups from both schools and well remember the meeting for those whose children were in years 1 and 2 in their current schools. After outlining aims and organisation and including a number of reassurances to meet justifiable concerns of parents, I invited questions from the floor. A father rose to ask a question or, rather, to make a statement. 'My child passed the 11-plus last year and went to the grammar school but she is going to be based in the modern school building; she is being denied the right she has won.' The speaker turned out to be a Labour councillor for Ryhope.

Planning for the new school

Whilst there was naturally some opposition and lack of enthusiasm for change, comprehensive education was looked forward to by many in the district. This incident indicated that there could be problems. but the decision to treat the school as a unit gave status to all young people, who were now equal members. For older students, we established an upper school of fifth, sixth and seventh year members (today years 11, 12 and 13). Our nomenclature was unusual for the time, sixth and seventh years replacing the more common 'lower sixth' and 'upper sixth'. The arrangement seemed to appeal to the students and from an early stage, despite the accommodation constraints, we were able to establish an upper school common room and an elected upper school council. A pleasing number of the fifth year modern school students stayed on for at least the sixth year of the new comprehensive school. Whilst much of our curriculum development was understandably concentrated on the first year, in 1969 Ryhope became the first school in Sunderland to offer A-level sociology and, a little later, the first to offer engineering science at this level. At the same time the option system in the fourth and fifth years was improved to broaden the range of subjects. Much of the most important planning had to occur before I became an employee of Sunderland Education Committee as, although offered the appointment at the February interview, the commencing date was fixed for 1st September. The reason given was that, before then, 'both schools would still have their own headteachers'. I did not get the feeling that flexibility was a high priority in the administrative circles of the borough.

September 1st was a Bank Holiday and the school was to open on the following morning. I was granted permission to delay the arrival of the students until 10 am, making it possible for me to meet some of the new staff for the first time. Fortunately, during the summer term, I had been able to make visits at weekends including those for the parents' meetings. These were facilitated thanks to the cooperation of Cumberland Education Authority and the head of Wyndham School, where I was deputy, who agreed to me leaving about mid-day on the Friday. Even more fortunately the Cumberland term finished a week before Sunderland's, and I spent most of that week in the schools. At Wyndham School, incidentally, the head was appointed two terms in advance of opening and I was appointed one term in advance. There were unexpected problems at Ryhope such as no timetable prepared. Instead, each school had left its existing timetable in the hope that these would do for their own students who, by decision of the Education Committee, were to continue to be taught in their own classes.[1] Such details as compatibility, staff deployment, allocation of rooms and the requirements of the new comprehensive intake into the first year were all left to chance. Fortunately a young member of the former modern school staff accepted the job of timetabling in the absence of more experienced volunteers and achieved a commendably satisfactory coverage during the school holiday with only the most limited opportunity for staff consultation. His dedication to the job and the hours put in typified the commitment of many teachers to comprehensive education at that time. Despite these efforts there were, inevitably, amendments to be made throughout the autumn term as staffing was completed and adjustments made.

Aims and objectives

The 1988 Education Reform Act (Department of Education and Science, 1988b) established a common aim for all state schools to provide a 'balanced and broadly based curriculum' which:

(a) promotes the spiritual, moral, cultural, mental and physical development of pupils at the school and of society.

(b) prepares such pupils for the opportunities, responsibilities and experiences of adult life.

There was no previous national requirement for schools to adopt curricular aims, not even under the Labour governments of 1964-1969 which promoted the introduction of comprehensive education on a national scale.

Sunderland's overall objective

Some local education authorities, however, produced worthwhile documents and Sunderland adopted an excellent 'overall objective' in 1976. This went to the heart of what comprehensive education should be about:

> To provide all children and adults with equal opportunity of leading as full and satisfying a life as possible by encouraging and promoting:
>
> 1 The acquisition and use of basic skills (reading, writing, speech, linguistics, mathematics).
> 2 The development of creative and physical qualities.
> 3 The development of greater awareness and understanding of both individuals and society.
> 4 The eradication of notions of inferiority and superiority insofar as these may be created by selectivity both between and within schools.
> 5 To extend as far as possible the area of choice for parents and pupils.

In 1969, in common with the majority of schools at that time, Ryhope had no written aims and objectives though implicit aims were clarified and communicated through the actions and responses of staff, students and parents.[2] In 1977 I asked the staff to consider Sunderland's overall objective with a view to extending the ideas to cover some of the more important aspects of the work of the school up to that date. The final result, reproduced in the appendix, reflected the range of curricular and other initiatives that had occurred in the first eight years of the school. I added a postscript noting that it seems to cover:

> almost everything of importance which should go on in a school. We must remember, however, that a comprehensive school embraces the whole spectrum of human aspiration and activity and that no statement of aims, however detailed, can hope to cover every eventuality. Indeed there is a tendency when writing down a list of aims to be over specific in areas of current debate at the expense of equally important aspects now taken for granted. We have recently passed through a period in which all too often 'youth' has been portrayed in a negative light and now is the time to re-emphasise that the formative period of adolescence should be a challenging one for all young people. If a school is to play its part to the full then its community of adults and pupils must be caring and understanding: dynamic, creative, optimistic — and, above all, alive.

The director of education included the complete document as an appendix in a report to the governors in January 1978. He used an argument, fairly common at the time, claiming that 'it needs extension in order that the objectives are as far as possible assessable'. Developing this line of thought, he added 'Unless assessable criteria are formulated, judgment can only be entirely subjective and this is likely to lead to uncertainty and anxiety which in turn may in certain circumstances lead to a sort of 'crisis' situation in which every issue is doubtful, at risk, and there is little confidence anywhere about anything'. Such arguments reflect a behavioural approach to educational management and invite the response 'Are the only acceptable educational aims to be those which are quantifiable and thus assessable?'[3] Not according to the authors of the Education Reform Act who refer to spiritual, moral and cultural development and include 'society' in their remit. And would members of a local education authority, with a large Labour majority committed formally to the development of comprehensive education, really find the straightforward extensions discussed, amended and finally approved in a series of committee and full staff meetings likely to lead to 'uncertainty and anxiety' and thence to a 'crisis situation'? Of course not, unless there was an intention to obscure the issues by those who are alarmed by the implications of a fully comprehensive system.

Priorities for a comprehensive school

I came increasingly to recognise the importance of having a concise written statement of the aims and principles of the school on which to base and defend planning and action.[4] Perhaps the following example, which I have drawn up from contemporary Ryhope documents, could be adapted and incorporated into a 'mission statement',[5] to use the jargon of the moment, for a school aiming at a non-selective approach:

School students are entitled to learning and social experiences which are stimulating and demanding and which maximise their opportunities for future happiness and career development.[6] The nature and quality of their relationships, as well as curricular and extra-curricular provision, are major influences in this process as they grow up through the exciting period of adolescence. Hence, the school aims to:

- Provide an educative and challenging curriculum with open access for all students throughout their time at school.[7]

- Foster participation in the educational and learning process among and between students, teachers, parents and members of the community.[8]
- Supply informed and unbiased educational and vocational guidance for students and their parents.
- Embrace the concept of a neighbourhood and community school.[9]
- Respect and promote the individuality of each student within a context of collective activity, care and responsibility.
- Seek cooperation and understanding among students giving special emphasis to countering racist, sexist and other stereotyping attitudes.
- Promote a welcoming and unregimented ethos.
- Be alive and active.[10]

Setting and achieving objectives is now often placed under the heading of 'The School Development Plan' another expression with a reassuring ring and a strong business pedigree. Yet few, if any, books, articles or in-service courses on school management and school effectiveness adequately address the question of setting and achieving objectives which derive specifically from comprehensive principles. The situation during initial teacher training used to be a little better. The inclusion of philosophy of education and sociology of education courses for the Bachelor of Education degree and post-graduate Certificate in Education could not fail to address such principles. In the opinion of Maurice Levitas, former senior lecturer at a college of education, 'This and this alone constitutes the right-wing objection to educational theory and its championing of teacher apprenticeships'. Conservative governments soon reduced the input of colleges and universities to teacher training replacing time 'saved' with longer and safer 'on the job' training in schools. (The near demise of history of education courses was described in Chapter 1, note 3).

Currently, we have an abundance of handbooks, guidance materials and in-service courses, most of which assume that staff consensus exists or is readily achievable; in other words, they are based on a fairly straightforward bureaucratic model of management which does not adequately fit the facts of school life.[11] There is, of course, much to be gained by having a soundly based development plan and we shall return to the issue of consensus in subsequent chapters. As well as many obvious areas for scrutiny, any serious quest to achieve comprehensive objectives across all aspects of school life should include commitments to:

- Help adult and student members of the school community to maintain self-respect at all times.
- Plan the curriculum as a whole in the interests of all.
- Integrate curriculum planning with arrangements for care and guidance.
- Ensure that all decision making processes are consistent with fully comprehensive aims and objectives.
- Explain the reasoning for actions and decisions and provide time for students and adults to grow and adapt.
- Provide individuals with more than one chance.

Curriculum development

It is time to return to the young people in September 1969 awaiting their first experience of comprehensive education. There were no selective schools drawing students from the area and few, if any, attended independent schools. A population bulge meant that no secondary schools had vacancies and catchment areas were precisely drawn so that virtually all students attended their neighbourhood school. No measurements or indicators of social and educational background were available but the future careers of Ryhope students confirmed classroom observation that the intake covered a full range of academic attainment but with a reduced proportion in the range who might expect to go on to higher education. Study of previous grammar school examination records supported this view: students from Ryhope and Silksworth had produced an average number 'passing' the 11-plus but a smaller than average proportion obtaining the highest grades at GCE 'O' and A-level examinations. This was, I understand, the main factor on which the head and staff of the grammar school based their appeal to the Secretary of State for Education and Science against going comprehensive claiming, in particular, that there would be insufficient students to maintain a viable sixth form. Nearly all the 270 pupils due to transfer to the new comprehensive attended two large junior schools in Ryhope and Silksworth or a small Church of England school in Ryhope with about twenty pupils in each year. As was common practice pupils were taught in non-selective groups in the two Ryhope schools whilst Silksworth was the only junior school in the borough to stream its pupils by 'ability', a policy it retained well into the 1980s.

Grouping students in classes

The first task was to allocate new entrants to the nine tutor groups. Each junior school pupil was asked to chose a friend (possibly two) to be with and preferences were noted such as twins wishing to be together (or not)[12] and pupils best kept apart. The tutor groups were then made up with roughly equal numbers from the two larger junior schools; those from the church school were placed in only four or five of the groups to help them to feel more confident. The head of year used junior school records to make each tutor group reasonably balanced for attainment and thus a microcosm of the whole intake; in practice each group quickly developed a character and ethos of its own which, in turn, was influenced by the personality, commitment and philosophy of the group tutor.

A key policy decision was to determine the relationship of teaching groups to tutor groups. At Wyndham School we had gone some way towards widening the ability range in teaching groups but I was concerned that at Ryhope we lacked experience in this field. I said to the staff that I thought it would be best to prepare the first year timetable in three sections each containing three tutor groups who would have their lessons for each subject at the same time. This block timetabling would enable us to teach the more 'academic' subjects such as English and mathematics to two groups roughly parallel in attainment together with a third group for those with greater learning difficulties. By this means I hoped that we might be able to provide a little more help where it was most needed. That decision caused disappointment to a number of younger teachers several of whom told me (together with a few older hands with substantial experience of teaching 'bottom' groups) that they would like to see the full ability range in each class.[13]

Perhaps surprisingly, it was mathematics teachers at Ryhope who were in the vanguard of those calling for non-selective groups. I was impressed with the enthusiasm and the professionalism of the young teachers who put their views so strongly and I agreed to have non-selective groups up to the first half term because there had been time for only minimal liaison with the feeder junior schools and we did not have a sufficiently detailed knowledge of our young students' previous progress. 'We shall see how they get on and then go to my scheme after half term' I stated confidently, but I was not to be let off the hook; after about a week of the second half of the term the teachers came to me more determined than ever and said that morale was not what it had been among the students and some of them were already feeling themselves to be failures. They had a strong point — I had been much impressed by their work in the first half term — and we returned to non-selective grouping at the start of the spring term in January. When it came to timetable planning for the following year the teachers said 'We think we can continue without selection for the second year but, if mathematics is blocked in groups of three forms, should we at any point during the second year feel that we cannot continue, then we can re-group the classes according to attainment. Much the same happened in the third year whilst, in the fourth and fifth years, we were able to introduce team teaching and flexible grouping as described in Chapter 6.

Curriculum issues in years 7-9

The mathematics development involved an undogmatic but committed approach on behalf of many people. Creating a favourable organisational framework (in this case block timetabling) provided only the starting point; realisation of the potential in the situation had to be worked for assiduously and continuously. The process by which we established flexible teaching in mathematics throughout the school (Chapter 6) might be described in today's management language as a rolling development plan. True the steps and stages evolved from constant discussion rather than written statements of intent but this is both a natural and effective method if real progress is to be made in a period demanding widespread changes to meet new situations. Much discussion took place between the timetabler and one or two colleagues at a time standing in front of the timetable planning board.[14] The aim was to match teaching groups and subject departments in a way which allowed teachers as much flexibility as possible in planning the learning programme for their students whilst at the same time retaining opportunities in the timetabling process to respond to developments in other areas of the curriculum. For the many enthusiasts involved at all levels, the ideas and aspirations seemed to fit in well with their understanding of comprehensive principles which, incidentally, featured quite strongly in the media.[15] Nevertheless it was easy for those most directly concerned, myself very much included, to assume, at least sub-consciously, that once the purpose was understood its essential virtue would be automatically accepted.

Similar non-selective principles were applied throughout the curriculum and, whilst not neglecting the needs of older year groups, curricular developments were especially focused to meet the requirements of the first

comprehensive intake as it moved up through the school followed by
subsequent years with a similar composition. By September 1971, the start
of the third year for these students, integrated science had replaced
separate sciences; technical studies and home economics were being
taught to boys and girls in mixed groups;[16] careers education formed part
of the third-year curriculum; mathematics included several 'modern'
topics,[17] and English had an increased emphasis on oral and creative
activity. Remedial work was seen in terms of individual help for all
students with most effort naturally concentrated on those with the greatest
need (Chapter 6); a dilemma with modern languages is described in
Chapter 4.

Resistance to change

One planned development had not got off the ground at this stage as a
result of circumstances which, in one form or another, occurred in many
developing comprehensive schools. The initial staffing structure approved
by the local authority included a social studies department incorporating
history, geography, sociology and economics together with religious
education, the only statutory part of the curriculum. Social studies (like
science) had a single head of department rather than independent heads
for the separate subjects. This arrangement required the head of
department to 'encourage close links in the teaching of these subjects
particularly in the first few years'. The first head of social studies sadly
died during the first term of the school and the further particulars for his
replacement, prepared by myself and approved by the senior inspector on
behalf of the authority, stated explicitly that 'further developments in this
wide area of study depend very much on the guidance and encouragement
of the head of department'. The person appointed by the Education
Committee[18] was a longstanding ex-grammar school subject specialist who
was hard to persuade to look beyond subject boundaries. For three years,
albeit in the friendliest manner, he resisted proposals for a move towards
an integrated approach in the early years without putting forward
alternatives.

Eventually, I reached a decision that only one way remained if the ideas
of many members of staff were to be harnessed and our school students
were to benefit. I told him that integrated social studies would be
introduced into the first year in the following September and that, for this
group, history, geography and RE would no longer appear on the

timetable as separate subjects. Such methods of managing change are rarely listed in textbooks on school management yet it was a pragmatic and necessary response and released the energy and professional skills of several members of staff involved with the development. Naturally there were limitations as to what could be achieved but the foundations were laid for a social studies course throughout years 1 to 5. Over a period of years, the course became a feature of the curriculum at Ryhope. This experience, and many similar elsewhere, challenges a frequently emphasised aspect of school management, namely that consensus and 'ownership' are essential prerequisites of successful change. Attractive as such utopian conditions may seem, the theory needs modification if positive action is to occur in a real world in less than fully favourable circumstances. There is a danger of waiting for ever and thus restricting educational opportunity for current and future school students. Many comprehensive schools had inconsistent and fragmented curricular policies as a consequence of allowing heads of department and other key staff so much independence (including, in effect, a power of veto) that they were nick-named departmental barons among Her Majesty's Inspectors.

Managing for flexibility

The social studies and mathematics developments had very different characteristics but their outcomes provided an important element of flexibility for the teachers concerned which, as discussed in Chapter 6, is essential for successful teaching in non-selective groups. During the first two or three years at Ryhope we identified other conditions, related to flexibility, which proved helpful to all concerned:

- Lesson lengths should be sufficient for teachers to be with their groups for a substantial period at a time.

- Teachers should see their groups reasonably frequently during the week.

- Faculties and subject departments should have their teaching rooms close together so that groups of classes can be taught effectively by the staff team.

Such conditions as these encourage effective teacher-student and teacher-teacher relationships. In Chapter 4 we saw that content, method and purpose are closely inter-connected and part of the case for integrated programmes of study in subjects such as social studies and science is that they open up more positive and effective conditions for teaching and learning. In particular, all three of the conditions can be satisfied for subjects which, singly, would merit only two 35 minute periods or one 70 minute period each week.

I have vivid memories concerning lesson length at the commencement of the school. By the end of the last week in August 1969 the new timetable, arranged in eight 35 minute periods each day, was 80 to 90 per cent complete. During the weekend this relatively happy feeling was interrupted by a disturbing thought: with the considerable distance between parts of the two buildings, much time was going to be spent both by students and staff moving from one room to another several times a day. Demountable classrooms in the grounds of both the north and south blocks and the process of crossing the bridge ensured that much of this movement would be subject to the vagaries of the weather. Together with the usual end-effects at the start and finish of each lesson for settling everyone down, distributing equipment and materials and collecting books etc., effective lesson times looked more like 20 minutes even if our students would not lack for fresh air and exercise. What could be done? Too late to rearrange rooms and teaching schedules and undesirable anyway but the solution when it came — I forget who had the idea — was disarmingly simple. It derived from another category of decision-making process omitted in most textbooks, namely 'flash of inspiration under crisis conditions'. The proposal was to operate on a two-week timetable with four 70 minute periods each day; teach the odd-numbered lessons on the existing timetable during week 1 and the even-numbered on week 2. So from the start of the second week Ryhope operated with 70-minute lessons instead of the 35 or 40 minutes customary at the time in all types of secondary school.

Teaching staff quickly adapted their lesson organisation to meet the new circumstances and I believe that the majority welcomed the increased flexibility provided by these more substantial periods of time. With occasional exceptions of newly appointed members of staff in their first week or two as they adjusted their techniques, students at the start of the teaching practice who needed to convince their tutors that a change in lesson plan was necessary and some teachers of modern languages who believed that 'little and often' was the only way to progress.[19] I received few complaints during the succeeding years. Not, that is, until the issue was stirred up during the events described in Chapters 13 and 14. The arrangement provided two periods in the morning and two in the afternoon with the customary breaks separating the periods in each session. As well as reducing movement problems, except following morning and afternoon registration when all tutor groups moved to the start of lessons 1 and 3 respectively, the symmetrical nature of the timetable gave maximum flexibility to the timetabler enabling him or her to interchange morning and afternoon lessons during the planning stage. Significantly, it enabled staff requests for double periods (ie for complete morning or afternoon sessions) to be met so that field work, linked courses with local colleges of further education and project work such as that required for A-level engineering science could be undertaken under favourable circumstances.

Comprehensive curriculum for years 10-11

In 1972 the school-leaving age was raised to 16 and required all students in the third year at that time to stay at least until Easter of their fifth year. Thus, Ryhope's first comprehensive intake was also the first to have the benefit of the full period of schooling. As mentioned in Chapter 6, we received inspiration for curriculum development from a BBC broadcast for teachers which opened up the possibility of an unstreamed curriculum in the vital last two years of schooling. Some details of Ryhope's overall curriculum plan at that time are described in an article in the magazine *Ideas* (Copland, 1975).[20] All students took English, social studies and careers; mathematics; science; physical education, and one creative subject from a list of five. This provided the core of the curriculum and ensured balance whilst a choice of three further subjects from a list of 21, arranged in three groups, enabled students to complement the compulsory part of the curriculum to meet their personal interests and requirements. This initial pattern, proved remarkably durable. The term 'core' was less than inspiring and, in due course, core and options were referred to as 'essential and further studies'. A link between English, social studies and careers — described originally as an inter-related course — was intended to exploit common ground in matters such as role play, reporting and communication skills in order to make efficient use of both teachers' and students' time. This proved difficult to achieve in practice and, after two or three years' experience, the subjects were taught separately though still as part of the common curriculum.

At first, the science course within the common curriculum was based on Nuffield Secondary Science, a widely used and popular resource of ideas from which courses with different emphases could be selected or devised. It was taught on a team basis to all members of the fourth and fifth years thus keeping together, for a part of the curriculum, students wishing to specialise in science and their colleagues who had chosen other options. Those taking further science had additional lessons so that, building on their basic work, they could specialise in two separate sciences such as physical science and biology or physics and chemistry. In 1974, starting with the fourth year, the Schools Council Integrated Science Project (Chapter 7) replaced the further science choices greatly enhancing the cohesion of the science programme. Later, the head of department and I invested much hope and some effort in a project known as CESIS (Curriculum and Examination Systems in Integrated Science) which aimed to combine the excellent materials and ideas of Nuffield Secondary Science and SCISP so that a course drawing on both could be taught successfully to a wide range of students either as a single or double subject. Unfortunately CESIS failed in this aim partly because the two courses were based on different criteria being theme and concept based respectively. Also, by the time CESIS appeared in the mid-1970s, non-selective teaching, which had provided a special impetus for this project, was under national attack and teachers were wary of developing their work further in this direction. Finally and reluctantly it was agreed at Ryhope in 1977 that those choosing further science would have all their lessons together thus separating 'essential' and 'further science' groups.

Despite these difficulties the basic structure of the common curriculum and options was retained throughout the life of the school and built on and improved in the light of experience, advances in curriculum development and the availability of resources. In 1976, for instance, Ryhope became one of the first schools in the north east to introduce a pre-vocational City and Guilds Foundation Course. This was in construction followed a year or two later by commercial studies. The courses proved popular and fitted into the curricular framework by replacing two options. Students continued with the remainder of their studies in their normal groups thus avoiding the need for a separate pre-vocational stream — a great advantage in a comprehensive system.[21]

Choosing subjects

A '4th and 5th year courses' booklet, primarily addressed to students, provided the basis for educational guidance and choice for members of the third year and their parents. The booklet improved in content, layout and scope over the years but remained a single document and described a single set of arrangements for *all* students in the year — a characteristic of Ryhope's curriculum philosophy. In all its versions the booklet retained the advice contained in its first edition in 1972 that, after consulting parents, friends and teachers, 'You know yourself best so when you have considered all the facts you will be in the best position to make the final decision'. The combination of a substantial common curriculum with informative and non-authoritarian advice spread over about a month enabled students to exercise genuine personal responsibility without risk of too early specialisation. The forms which students completed to make their choices included a box for anyone to tick who wished to 'have an opportunity to improve my basic work ... with Mr B and his staff'. Mr B was the respected senior remedial specialist and the invitation to tick the box reinforced a point made frequently at meetings of parents and students that extra help could be requested directly as well as provided following teacher referral. Accompanied by the head of year and head of careers I spoke personally to all third year students at the start of the choice process. After a brief introduction to the arrangements for study in the next two years, the significance of the choices to be made and the dangers of sex-stereotyping, I recommended that everyone should chose at least one subject (out of a total of eight or nine) purely out of personal interest without regard to its usefulness for a career or other purpose. In our first comprehensive intake two friends who subsequently gained a first-class honours degree in chemistry and a second-class honours degree in mathematics respectively, chose rural science as one of their subjects and each obtained a CSE grade 1. I don't suppose there are many people with degrees of that kind who have a qualification in rural science but these two young men made their choices because they were interested in the practical study of living things. Long may our education system provide such opportunities.

Whilst we prepared students for both O-level and CSE examinations in the majority of subjects, some of the most popular choices in the further studies list including building studies, fabric design, home management, motor vehicle studies, rural science and typing were teacher designed courses examined under CSE mode 3 arrangements (Chapter 6, note 7). In the essential studies programme, science (as a single subject) and social studies were at first offered only for CSE because suitable O-levels were not available until the late 1970s (Chapter 7). This arrangement, though not ideal and not without its critics, was based on the opportunity to provide challenging CSE schemes of work (Chapter 6, note 7) and can be compared with the all-CSE policy of Sutton Centre (Chapter 6). In many subjects, CSE mode 3 syllabuses were matched to O-levels to help provide a fully comprehensive curriculum in the fourth and fifth years. Our active head of careers, who took all third to fifth year classes for a 70 minute lesson each fortnight,[22] was vigilant in taking up any report brought back by students who had been questioned about the worth of CSE qualifications. Often when employers and college tutors heard the reasoning behind the curriculum and examinations policy they responded most favourably.

Examination results

The interpretation of examination statistics is always a complex matter open to debate and argument. An attempt is necessary, however, and nowhere more so than in schools organised for non-selective teaching several of which received accusations of not caring about examination results — invariably the reverse of the real situation.[23] I kept a record of higher grade passes[24] from three years before the separate schools were amalgamated and then through Ryhope's time of becoming fully comprehensive in all years. I based the data on the results of all school students who were in the catchment area of the comprehensive school. All Ryhope and Silksworth students who were selected by the 11-plus went to Ryhope Grammar School and others took CSE and/or O-levels at Ryhope Modern School. However, many at the grammar school came from a wider area so their results were not included.

For the three years before the schools became comprehensive an average of 239 higher grade passes were obtained, almost exactly one per fifth year student.[25] The first comprehensive year took public examinations in 1974 with an increased number of students staying to the end of the fifth year as a result of the raising of the school leaving age. From 1974 to 1979 inclusive the average number of higher grade passes was 362 (or nearly 1.5 per student representing a 50 per cent increase). The highest number achieved was 427 (1.8 per student) in 1978, a year when the school was under considerable attack (Chapter 13). From 1980 reduced numbers in the fifth year and a smaller proportion of able students meant that results were not directly comparable. However, analysis of examination results is further discussed in Chapter 12.[26]

Statistics are only part of the story. A young man who had been a student in the modern school for four years just before the schools became comprehensive went into the fifth year of the comprehensive, worked very hard and obtained three higher grade passes. I don't recall the details but remember that he wanted to do science but had not obtained any higher grade passes in science subjects. He asked if he could still take science in the sixth form and was counselled as follows: it was explained that A-levels are a demanding course and that one could come out with nothing; it was a risk and it was a question of whether or not he wished to take that risk. We also gave information on alternative courses such as the ordinary national diploma (the forerunner of BTEC national certificates) that were available in a college of further education. He chose to enter the sixth form, worked very hard but, to everyone's consternation, missed all three of his A-level subjects by narrow margins. He was disappointed but not deterred and went on to Sunderland Polytechnic (now the University of Sunderland) to take a bridge course. A year later he qualified for entry to a degree course in one of the biological sciences and subsequently obtained an honours degree. Later he won prizes for science and obtained a master's degree.[27]

The destinations and careers of former students provide a good qualitative 'performance indicator' and one can note that Ryhope students in the fifth, sixth and seventh years went on to a very wide range of careers, not least in degree and diploma courses. In this connection a note in the prospectus of the faculty of materials at the University of Sheffield (1980) caught my eye. It offered a list of the present appointments of some of the graduates from the faculty, adding:

> the standard of a department being perhaps best judged from the careers of those who have passed through it.

We refer again to the interest shown in the career prospects of Ryhope students in Chapter 12.

Timescale for change

I was criticised in some quarters for the speed of curriculum development at Ryhope, especially in the early years of the comprehensive school. This was long before Conservative ministers resorted to curriculum development by Order in Council following the 1988 Act; anything done at Ryhope would have seemed pedestrian by those standards. Nevertheless, there was urgency. Our students deserved the best which we could provide and, with so much goodwill from parents, students and teachers, one wanted to see existing, as well as future, students benefit from the possibilities inherent within the comprehensive system. For example, in 1970 we started mixed craft lessons for boys and girls in the second comprehensive intake but the previous year group did not totally miss out as we were able to provide a building studies option for girls as well as boys in their third year. The BBC broadcast for teachers, described in Chapter 6 and referred to above, occurred on 22nd March leaving very little time to prepare a non-selective teaching programme for the fourth year to start in the following September. But suppose the developments were postponed for a year? The consequences looked uninviting: former pupils of the Ryhope junior schools would face selection for the first time in their school career and textbooks and equipment would have to be purchased for a very short working life. The timetabler would need to prepare 'one-off' selective timetables for the fourth year in 1972 and the fifth year in 1973 committing with them teachers, resources and specialist rooms. Compromises would certainly be necessary in 1973 when trying to match a fourth year comprehensive timetable with the fifth year selective one and, last but not least, having put their best efforts into the selective courses teachers might well be reluctant to change again. In all probability, postponement would have meant a continuation of selection for several years. Many well-intentioned schemes in comprehensive schools met such a fate.

There were other causes of urgency. As noted in Chapter 4, it is essential for the curriculum to be seen as a unity of inter-related components and fatal to plan and execute it as the sum of disparate parts. It follows that as soon as a step towards a comprehensive curriculum is taken in one area, its long-term success may be put at risk if the new development appears isolated in philosophy and practice from much of what is happening around it. Even when new developments form the majority of the curriculum, pieces left over from the past can act as rallying and growth areas for dissent. A hiatus in philosophy arises from partial development of non-selective teaching methods. Often these are applied only in the first year or two of secondary education (years 7 and 8) and, even then, there may be exceptions for high status subjects such as mathematics, science or modern languages. In these circumstances, non-selective teaching is seen, at best, merely as a pragmatic answer to disciplinary and other problems (Chapter 2, note 6) or as a gesture to equality before the serious business of teaching the later years in bands, streams and sets begins. In such circumstances we stand to lose the argument, not only in the specific matter of selectivity, but also in the wider acceptance of comprehensive schooling. We need the courage of our convictions if parents and students are to see the methods of teaching throughout our schools as both fair and effective.

APPENDIX

Sunderland's overall objective extended by Ryhope School

The objective is in capitals with each of its five parts followed by the extensions:

TO PROVIDE ALL CHILDREN AND ADULTS WITH EQUAL OPPORTUNITY OF LEADING AS FULL AND SATISFYING A LIFE AS POSSIBLE BY ENCOURAGING AND PROMOTING:

1 THE ACQUISITION OF BASIC SKILLS (READING, WRITING, SPEECH, LINGUISTICS, MATHEMATICS)
For full and satisfying membership of a modern society everybody has a need to be able to read and write, and to use mathematics. Other skills too are essential eg: practical skills like cookery and 'do it yourself' not forgetting that these may include the need to follow sets of practical instructions. Fact-finding skills: knowing what up-to-date information is needed and how to find it. Management skills which enable people to organise themselves and others. Social skills which enable people to live together. *Acquisition of basic skills need not imply a restricted curriculum as many of them will be taught as part of courses with broad objectives.*

2 THE DEVELOPMENT OF CREATIVE AND PHYSICAL QUALITIES
Nowadays this has come to mean not only art and PE but also the opportunity to experience and work at many activities some of which will lead to hobbies and lasting interests. Pupils often have or develop individual interests in which the resources and expertise available through the school can be of great help to them. *There is a very strong implication that the school organisation must be sufficiently flexible to allow for spontaneous as well as planned activity.*

3 THE DEVELOPMENT OF GREATER AWARENESS AND
   UNDERSTANDING OF BOTH INDIVIDUALS AND SOCIETY
   Awareness also of the physical environment and the way in which scientific
   knowledge has contributed to civilised life. We need a knowledge of the
   things around us and of societies of other lands and other times in order to
   understand our own society and our responsibilities within it. It is here that
   an individual develops the capacity to enquire, discover and think for
   himself — a capacity he needs if he is to critically appraise society and
   where necessary to take his part in changing it. *In addition there are skills
   and techniques of thinking and problem solving which should be taught in
   school and, wherever possible, this should include taking part in real life
   decisions.*

4 THE ERADICATION OF NOTIONS OF INFERIORITY AND
   SUPERIORITY INSOFAR AS THESE MAY BE CREATED BY
   SELECTIVITY BOTH BETWEEN AND WITHIN SCHOOLS
   Here the school especially considers cooperation as well as personal
   development. We must encourage the development of mutual respect,
   understanding and sympathy by, making provision for the growth of:
   self-awareness and development; group awareness and inter-dependability,
   and mutual support between individuals and groups *Research evidence
   shows that the fellow students with whom a pupil learns affect his
   aspirations, self-esteem, overall progress and last, but not least, the values
   which he acquires from his lessons. The composition of learning groups is,
   therefore, a crucial factor in the achievement of the aims of a school.*

5 TO EXTEND AS FAR AS POSSIBLE THE AREA OF CHOICE FOR
   PARENTS AND PUPILS
   We recognise that this is dependent on (a) the four areas above and (b) the
   opportunity for each individual to qualify himself in a manner which will
   enable him to choose his life style after he has left. *The word 'qualify' here
   means more than paper qualifications (including testimonials and
   references): it implies an outward-looking perspective on behalf of the
   school — so that a pupil's time at school is, indeed, a preparation to leave
   it.*

11

Activities and Quality of Life

The activities a school promotes and the relationships that develop make a vital contribution to the education of students. So this chapter is concerned with events, mainly outside the classroom, which provide opportunities for participation and initiative together with implications for school management. In most schools, and Ryhope was no exception, preliminary work is necessary if our young people are to derive maximum benefit; in particular, impediments to fully cooperative relationships need to be dispensed with.

Clearing the decks

My list included prefects, corporal punishment, gowns for teachers and, as I hoped, compulsory uniform. Boys were no longer to be addressed by their surnames while, in the classroom, there were to be no form orders or formal examinations in the first three years. Time was very short and, as these matters appeared fundamental, there seemed no point in pseudo-consultation for the sake of appearances which would be misleading and undertaken at a high cost in managerial integrity. With the exception of uniform, which required consultation with the local authority (Chapter 11), I therefore announced my decisions to the staff giving my reasons for them, mostly before the first term began.

No prefects, gowns or sexist forms of address

The values and assumptions underlying prefectorial systems have been discussed in Chapter 9 and, in a large school, there is the additional problem that prefects will often not know those to whom they are giving instructions — a challenging situation even for professionals. The process of selection of prefects may well, in the words of Sunderland's overall objective (Chapter 10) induce feelings of superiority by the selected and inferiority by those passed over. Finally, there is the question of privileges: distinctive badges, a prefects' common room, even piping on the school blazer — all setting students apart from one another.

Most of the grammar school staff had worn gowns at assemblies and some also in the classroom. This was divisive for teacher colleagues as only those with a degree were qualified to wear a gown.[1] The practice also established a psychological barrier between teaching staff on the one hand and students and support staff on the other and carried the hidden message that academic learning was paramount. My decision came as a shock to several ex-grammar school staff and one came to tell me that he felt that he had been deprived of his entitlement but that, nevertheless, he would accept the ruling. Whilst calls for the return of prefects and corporal punishment were voiced from time to time in subsequent years, gowns were never again an issue. No doubt this was partly as a consequence of the much higher percentage of non-graduate staff in the comprehensive school than in the grammar school with several non-graduates holding senior positions. Gowns were seen as an anachronism in the context of comprehensive education but even so, nearly thirty years later, there are headteachers who walk around their buildings and conduct assemblies and speech days in 'academic dress'. As they do so they make a significant contribution to the hidden curriculum (Chapter 4).

The archaic distinction in which girls were called by their first name (or both first and surname) but boys by their surname only was current in both schools. I thought it would be an easy job to humanise staff-student relationships in this respect and to remove what would now be seen as a sexist practice. Surely everyone would see that conversations such as 'Jean, what do you think the author was trying to convey at this point in the novel?' ... 'Do you agree with that, Brown?' were past their sell-by date. The majority of staff agreed and, after some understandable anxiety concerning how the boys in their classes might react to such a dramatic change — perhaps seeing it as a threat to a macho image and an 'us and them' approach to teachers; perhaps even leading to a total breakdown in discipline so carefully built up over the years — despite these fears, first names for students became the norm though the process was never quite complete. A few teachers found it extremely difficult to implement and a few had no intention of changing. I made sure that whenever the conduct or progress of a boy was being discussed in my presence, his first name was included but I estimate that it was seven or eight years before boys rarely heard themselves addressed by any member of staff with surname only. One by-product of this policy was a rumour which persisted throughout the lifetime of the school. This was that I had instructed all students to call me 'Dick'. Whilst I should not have felt that the fabric of society was about to collapse if my first name had been used, it was not in my nature to give out an instruction on how I was to be addressed. In fact no student, in my presence, called me other than 'Mr Copland' or more frequently by the title passed down over generations: 'Sir'.[2]

No corporal punishment

In the region, Ryhope School was soon noted for not having corporal punishment, being one of a tiny number of secondary schools which did not at least claim the right to use it 'as a last resort'. Both the existing schools at Ryhope had used corporal punishment but during my interview for the headship I had said that I was not prepared to have corporal punishment in the school.[3] I explained to the staff that the practice would be discontinued and that it wasn't a matter for debate because it involved striking somebody with a piece of wood or other object which was unacceptable on moral grounds. It carried the implication that, ultimately, force is correct, a message I certainly did not wish to see perpetuated; it was also unacceptable on practical grounds. We found with experience that rejection of corporal punishment helped in the successful detection of anti-social behaviour, for example if a student was involved in petty theft in the school. Fellow students were much more willing to tell a member of staff in confidence what was going on if physical chastisement was not to follow. It was made clear that successful detection was not only a first step in protecting the interests of fellow students but also helped the offender to develop a fuller sense of responsibility. Disciplinary procedures in school are not only preventative and protective but should help all young people to develop in maturity and personal responsibility. Our basic rule was that people and property should be treated with respect. Absence of corporal punishment made Ryhope a target for some who claimed that corporal punishment was essential for good discipline and that acceptable standards were impossible without it. This reaction was to reach its apogee in July 1982 when a local independent socialist councillor complained to Sir Keith Joseph, Secretary of State for Education and Science, concerning the lack of corporal punishment at Ryhope (Chapter 15).

No form orders — and no formal examinations before year 10
Actions in the classroom affect attitudes and perceptions in all aspects of school life. One practice, common in selective schools, often had a devastating effect on conscientious and sensitive students. This was to place all the members of a class or form in a rank order by totalling marks in each subject from tests, examinations and homework. The frequency of this administrative operation — it had few diagnostic properties — was usually termly but could occur as often as once a fortnight. Ranking of students is clearly inappropriate for a comprehensive school and teachers recognised that students with learning difficulties faced particular humiliation in such circumstances. Similarly, the majority of teachers appreciated that written examinations for a whole class or year would be equally unacceptable. My initial 'decree' on this matter was accompanied by stress on the urgent need to develop informative and appropriate techniques of assessment and communication with students and their parents (Chapter 12).

One may note that seventy teachers at the opening of the school had only six teacher-years of comprehensive experience between us, five of them from me. By the end of the first term (one third of a school year) that had grown to nearly thirty teacher-years representing an increase of 500 per cent. The benefit was clear both in confidence built up and the wealth of practical ideas forthcoming.

Extra-curricular activities

Activities outside the classroom rarely feature in books on school management except to suggest that they make a useful selling point to parents and students. This seriously underestimates their value and importance as a component of school life, albeit one which depends upon the willingness of teachers, often assisted by parents, to give their time and commitment.[4] True, it is less easy than previously to find teachers who will devote themselves to regular activities such as sports teams or drama groups. This arises partly from changing social habits and increased family commitments but also because there are many more demands on teachers' time and mental reserves as a result of continuous developments in curricula and teaching methods, in-service courses, administrative demands of the national curriculum and assessment procedures. In an earlier period curricula changed slowly and lessons were given largely according to a set pattern. Then an hour's coaching after school and a

Saturday fixture on a nearby sports field[5] could provide a pleasing break from the normal run of professional life and an opportunity to meet students in a more informal way than was possible in the classroom.

Scope and variety

Despite these considerations Ryhope, in common with a majority of schools, had its full share of activities both traditional and novel. Among the former, football teams were active and successful throughout the life of the school whilst the teacher in charge took parties on fifteen consecutive annual visits to London for 'teach-ins' organised by the Football Association. In the later years of the school he ran, almost single-handed, five teams each year giving a much appreciated service to players and parents. For many years there was also immense enthusiasm for rugby football under a head of physical education widely respected for his personal commitment as well as the remarkable success of his teams in all age groups. Parents assisted in coaching, transport, fund raising and a rugby tour to France.

Women PE teachers organised netball and hockey teams which provided no less enjoyment for players but whose work went otherwise unnoticed; unlike football and rugby there was rarely a 'gate' of parents, locals and members of the school at these matches. Teachers ran fencing and table tennis teams; gym, chess and computer clubs; visits to outdoor centres in Middleton-in-Teesdale, Keswick, Alston, Wooler and other locations; others arranged ski trips at home and abroad and language visits to Germany, France and Spain. Music specialists prepared superb brass bands, madrigal groups, ensembles of every description and choirs which filled the stage. One head of department arranged concert tours to Germany during consecutive summer holidays and gifted teachers of drama produced plays which varied from the spectacular *The Fire Raisers* (1970) to north-east playwright C P Taylor's *Operation Elvis* (1984). The latter concerned a disabled child in a wheel-chair and, on a memorable afternoon in Washington, Tyne and Wear, the play was presented to an audience from a centre for disabled people. The rapport and warmth of the relationship between the cast and the mainly adult audience was a credit to the producer and his cast. Over the years several students were accepted for the National Youth Theatre.

'Radio Ryhope' was an early example of a grass-roots project. In 1971 the producer of *The Fire Raisers* came to me saying he had offers of

sophisticated recording and transmitting equipment free of charge from
the BBC and local traders. Soon a willing team of helpers had transformed
a cellar into a recording studio and wired tutor rooms to receive both
school and off-air broadcasts. Student engineers and production teams
briefed presenters and disc jockeys for the first broadcasts in 1972.
Transmitting times were for 15 minutes before school and during break
and lunch times. Requests, suggestions and so on, assured identification
and participation by students whilst professionals took an active interest
and helped to establish a close relation between the school and the media.
My contribution, as head, was to resist the temptation to say 'No' and thus
reduce the potential for subsequent 'hassle' but at the expense of an
opportunity for creative activity. It was not to be my last such decision and
I regretted few.[6]

Good causes deserve a special word, not least because the contribution
made by teachers and school students is not widely known. We received
frequent requests for the school to help in both local and national
campaigns and we made a selection based on interest for our students
whilst avoiding overload. A summary for 1974/75, typical for the period,
showed that, excluding money collected for school purposes, the school
raised £782 — a splendid total. Students themselves suggested good
causes and devised and took part in sponsored events and other fund
raising activities. Their scale varied from small groups of friends raising a
few pounds for a local appeal to £525 sent towards the 'People's Boat to
Ethiopia' Appeal at the time of the famine in 1984. Older students were
often asked to help as collectors for flag days and house-to-house
collections and finally there were efforts in kind rather than cash such as
Christmas parties for elderly people. All charitable efforts were coordinated
by the senior mistress and, with so much money being handled and up to a
thousand sponsor forms circulating, great care was necessary in
administration and accounting. The wider implications of appeals were
taken up in year group assemblies and, whenever possible, we asked a
representative of the organisation to come into school to explain the work
done by the charity so that students could be better informed.

Tommy *and* Stardust

The director of Ryhope's two rock operas in the mid-1970s came to
Ryhope on teaching practice in his final year (1973) and then joined the
staff in September of that year.[7] During his first term, he came to me to

say that he would like to produce the rock opera *Tommy*, created by Pete Townshend, lead guitarist of 'The Who'. This ambitious project — the first ever stage performance — had the enthusiastic support of a music teacher who had also just started at Ryhope though with a year or two's teaching experience. The world of *Tommy* and its portrayal of the drug scene was definitely out of my ambit at the time but I asked a trusted senior colleague, experienced in performing, to read the script.[8] With a gleam in his eye, he recommended going ahead and a little later, one lunchtime, a dozen interested members of staff met to discuss with the young director how they could help in different ways. He said he was planning to run the show for four nights, Wednesday to Saturday, which caused us some surprise as most school productions struggled to last two or three public performances. There was more to follow: at that time a typical charge for a school play was 10 pence or, for a particularly prestigious effort, tickets might be 15 pence. One of those present asked the director how much he proposed to charge. '50 pence' he replied to stunned silence as we looked at each other. '50 pence?' 'Oh yes', he said 'that's about right' and, as he seemed confident, that became the charge. Shortly before the opening date, the school office staff informed me that they could do little work because of the constant stream of phone calls trying to obtain tickets which were changing hands at £2 or £3 each in the town. On the opening night a queue stretched from the hall entrance to the main road — a new experience for everyone. It was a superb show and on the last night I again witnessed something which I had never seen before in school: as the performance came to an end there was a spontaneous standing ovation.

This brilliant production used sophisticated amplification equipment to extend the pool of students who could be drawn on to play major parts. Indeed the large cast, not to mention the band and production team, were drawn from the widest cross-section of students and the whole affair captured the imagination of the school and helped to weld staff, students and parents in a sense of common achievement. A further surprise came during the following week. The front page of the *New Musical Express* (1974) — a prestigious publication in its field — headed 'Was school ever like this?' was entirely filled with photographs of the principals. Inside more than four pages were devoted to interviews and photographs with anyone and everyone followed by a detailed review which concluded 'I've never enjoyed a show so much in my life. That's how it seemed to me, anyway. It was tremendous.'

'Beat that!' seemed to be the general sentiment as far as thoughts for 1975 were concerned but planning had already started. *Stardust* was a different show altogether and even more ambitious; it ran for six nights, involved a massive cast, was adapted by the director from the original by Alan Connolly to give it a north-east setting, and featured on London Weekend Television's arts programme, Aquarius.[9] The production team were on location at Ryhope for three days to make a film about the school and its educational ideas as well as the performance itself. Russell Harty, the presenter, commenced an extensive article in the *Guardian* (1975): 'There are just a few things you come out of saying "Oh God, I wish I hadn't seen it" not because it's been awful, but because, perversely, you want the magnificence of it to wash over you again, the novelty to knock you down, the freshness of it to green up in front of your eyes'. He listed examples commencing with 'my first hearing of Belshazzar's Feast' and concluded 'to this distinguished list, I unashamedly add Stardust at Ryhope School, Sunderland'. Peter Mortimer, theatre critic of the Newcastle *Journal*, described it as 'probably the most ambitious venture ever attempted by a school in this country, a vast three-hour multi-media affair, a cast of more than 100, live and recorded music, movie films, slide projections and a complex stage arrangement split into four performing areas ... At times one had to be reminded that this was the creation of school children. Scenes such as the rock mass "Sanctus" are virtually magnificent, the stage a whole spectrum of white and shrouded figures bearing candles and the rendition of John Lennon's "Imagine" is beautifully performed, the flower "children" moving off stage into the audience to offer them their gifts.' The show included a five-minute film about a pop-star returning to Britain. The producer, after receiving the briefest of 'requests' from the director, hired a couple of coaches and took a group of first, second and third year students to Newcastle Airport one Sunday afternoon. He had persuaded the airport manager to let them take over the next plane that landed and, whilst the passengers remained inside, the actor pop-star emerged from the plane to cheering crowds of youngsters around the airport — with such realism that many on the plane were convinced it was for real.

The Aquarius programme ran for fifty minutes at peak viewing time: 10.45 pm on the Saturday before Christmas. Next morning I met many delighted students, parents and well-wishers in the locality, where the programme had revealed a previously unimagined breadth and depth of local talent. Obvious also was the extensive cooperation between performers, members of staff and a host of helpers from outside. As Derek Bailey, the editor of Aquarius, said in a letter to me after the filming: 'Our admiration for those behind 'Stardust' was confirmed in every way ... We hope [the programme] does Ryhope proud — you deserve it'. It did.

The musical director, whose flair included writing and adapting scores for his players even as he conducted rehearsals, had decided to move abroad at the end of the term. Thus he and the director who combined so productively, were only on the staff together for two years and the unique experience which they provided for students could only have occurred when it did. This emphasises once again that situations in schools change unexpectedly and that opportunities must be grasped when circumstances are favourable. Non-rigid organisational structures and flexible and imaginative approaches by school management, especially in matters involving the arts, are a necessary pre-requisite.

Added dimension

Extra-curricular activities provide a further dimension to school experience especially in bringing people together in common purpose. In this respect we should not underestimate relatively simple activities which strengthen the quality of life of a school. For example, the value of the school disco was strikingly demonstrated during the first term of the comprehensive school when mid-term discos enabled everyone, whether ex-grammar, ex-modern or comprehensive intake, to participate on an equal footing. Discos remained an enjoyable feature of school life until later years when their attraction to 'outsiders' made it increasingly difficult to undertake the essential supervision of the buildings and grounds. On the advice of older students, we made more use of facilities in the town which had single entrances, 'bouncers' and a credible image. In the later life of the school, creative activities continued to flourish and prove popular with young people and adults. One of the most successful started modestly and, like Topsy, just grew. The show involved miming to music and, after an initial success, it became known in consecutive years as The Euromime, The Worldmime and, finally, the Megamime with over twenty acts. Student entertainers such as 'Trendy Wendy' and 'Bill's Aces' presented items based on popular tracks of the time. The shows appealed to parents and relatives as well as fellow students and tickets were again hard to get. As the teachers in charge noted light-heartedly in a programme: 'There is nothing in the Mime that will ever be studied for

O-level or A-level but for pure energy and entertainment value it takes some beating. Certainly the young people from Ryhope and Silksworth have a great deal of natural talent when it comes to performing'. This relatively simple production required each act to rehearse separately and be responsible for its own costumes whilst demands on stage management and lighting were well within school resources. It was an example of the satisfaction to be gained by doing something simple, very well.

It was always a pleasure to see so much being created by staff and students as I visited activities, joined parents when school parties were setting off by coach, spent evenings with groups at outdoor centres and occasionally took part in staff-student matches of various kinds. I was even recruited for an early mime show by a persistent fifteen-year-old who showed remarkable skill and patience in bringing me up to an acceptable standard for her act. However, grass-roots ideas need more than initial approval from the top. Once an activity is operating, problems may arise and, as the original idea was approved by the head or senior management, there is a corresponding obligation to help to find solutions. These may also require imagination and initiative.

To complement existing good work, teachers would surely welcome a well resourced and staffed service within a programme of enhanced educational experience (Chapter 5) to support school initiatives, provide additional resources and, where necessary, to provide continuity following changes in circumstances of individual teachers and schools. Developments along these lines could provide all our young people with a valuable added dimension to their school experience.

Equal opportunities

Fawcett Society

In 1986 Ryhope entered for the 'Positive Action' awards of the Fawcett Society, which has campaigned for equality between the sexes since 1866, and received a commendation for its 'challenging attitudes and its long-term anti-sexist policy'. Our submission was entitled 'Attitudes and Expectations in the Ethos and Curriculum of a School'. In the introduction I noted an incident which I observed from my room when thinking about how best to present the report: 'I walked to the window and glanced at the bridge. The scene was unremarkable — or so I thought at first. A fourteen year old lad was walking up the steps and half a dozen girls were descending. All were involved with their own affairs and keeping to the left as is our custom. Life was normal ... yet, something caused me to look again. Ah, that was it! Ian was wearing a red cookery apron and carrying a bowl of tea towels — indeed, an uneventful scene in 1985 but one which provides some food for thought'. (I might have added 'not least in a former north-east colliery village'). Promoting anti-sexist and anti-racist attitudes is necessary in all aspects of school life and we have already seen some of the implications for curriculum and guidance.

The Fawcett Society required contributions from girl students, who wrote mainly about these aspects. One was from C in the fourth year who described her wish to be a designer and her option choices which included fabric design and engineering drawing. She concluded 'I am very glad that I am lucky enough to go to a school where children of both sexes are encouraged to break down the barriers which have stood for so long ... Teachers in our school teach a very broad range of subjects and openly encourage both boys and girls to take whatever subjects they fancy — so if a boy wants to do child development, cookery and needlework he can do it without being made to feel a cissy. Equally girls can do motor vehicle studies, building studies and engineering and technical drawing without being made to feel they are losing their femininity. They can still look as good in overalls and a safety helmet as in a skirt and apron.' J also referred to appearances: 'There are about twenty-five students in my cookery group of which only two are boys. The boys are as good as, if not better than, most of the girls. And don't they look "cute" in their red-checked aprons!'

A parent governor — a youth training officer and mother of a student who joined the technical branch of the Women's Royal Naval Service — widened the issues: 'Many girls leave school having low expectations of themselves in terms of employment and there is a strong tendency for girls to drift into early marriage and dependency on their husbands. At Ryhope School these issues are studied in great depth as part of the social studies course and in making both girls and boys aware of these trends the school has encouraged them to question whether this should be so and how the situation can be changed to allow girls to reach their full potential ... Another noticeable fact about Ryhope School pupils is that friendships seem to be based solely on common interest ... they are positively encouraged to cooperate rather than to compete. This attitude is carried on outside school resulting in friendships between young people regardless of their sex, a situation found only rarely in young people ...' This was a generous statement from someone who knew many students of the school and their parents. It again illustrates that in equal opportunities, as in every other branch of education, appropriate attitudes and relationships must accompany progressive policies and development plans.

Anti-racism

A school with only two or three students and one or two teachers from ethnic minority backgrounds must adapt its approach to anti-racism whilst striving for total commitment to such a policy throughout the school. Teachers of integrated humanities (Chapter 7) developed sensitive techniques for topics such as 'Persecution and Prejudice' which included giving time and opportunity for group members to respond if a racist view was expressed by one or two of their colleagues; this was often more effective than an immediate intervention from the teacher. Themes in our secular assemblies aimed to raise issues and awareness and most students from ethnic minorities got on well with fellow students, particularly those whom they knew well. However, the situation was never one for complacency and we were taken by surprise when a parent withdrew her son following harassment in the summer holiday; unknown to us, this was followed up after term began with threats at school. Staff-student relations also demonstrated that there is never room for complacency. One of our teachers originating from India spent fifteen respected years at Ryhope and, by example, helped his students to understand in a practical way the importance of mutual respect and understanding between races. Another, although also a conscientious and enthusiastic teacher, was regrettably harassed by name-calling, especially during one particular period. Although in situations like this there may be contributory causes these must never serve as an excuse. Nevertheless, despite a range of actions by myself and senior staff including day to day support by the head of department; exclusion of certain students pending contact with parents, and written guarantees concerning future behaviour, it proved very difficult to achieve a fully satisfactory outcome.

School ethos

Students need to enjoy school and to have high self-concepts if they are to fully benefit from their education.[10] An age range from 11 to 16 or 18 represents a huge span of physical, mental and social development — from late childhood to young adulthood — and the challenge for schools is to manage the situation so that students of all ages are treated as competent, thinking people with opportunities to learn self-responsibility. Schools which treat their members as 'children' do them a great disservice and, as part of a regular review procedure, it can be revealing to check whether details of everyday administration and organisation — often a cause of petty irritation for students and teachers alike — remain necessary and reasonable and provide a framework for personal and collaborative development. Informal contacts also affect the maturity of relationships among students themselves and with adults. Visitors often commented that our students seemed happy, communicative and mentally alert and it was not surprising to see a member of staff having a joke or gentle banter with a couple of students — or even a succession — as he or she walked down the corridor. Some may see such informality as encouraging lack of respect but the opposite is true because young people develop in self-confidence and responsibility if they experience relationships of this kind with adults. Informal contacts are particularly important for students with special needs and in this respect, the senior student volunteers who listened to individuals reading and helped with structured assignments (Chapter 6) played an important part in establishing an ethos in which support lessons were seen as a natural part of the educative process. I never heard of an incident in which students receiving additional support were ridiculed. Ryhope had many visitors including student teachers from home and overseas, especially during the formative period of the 1970s. On one occasion I counted twenty adults in a room with two teachers and about twenty young people with special needs. Both students and teachers seemed almost unaffected by this audience and continued with their work whilst taking time to involve the visitors — a reflection of the quality of relationships patiently built up inside and outside the classroom.

Many members of staff enjoyed the opportunities to develop and extend their professional skills but others, despite our promotion of such conventional values as hard work and consideration, saw the school as somewhat isolated from the main stream because of non-selective teaching, rock operas, lack of corporal punishment or whatever. Subsequent events were to affect all concerned. Up to the mid-1970s our students were often envied by those from other schools but when Ryhope started to receive hostile publicity — notably from 1977 — they began to be challenged on the streets, in buses and wherever young people meet. Many vigorously defended the school against all comers, even though as time went on and media coverage intensified, they were increasingly subjected to taunts and insults. I learned on many occasions from parents how strongly their sons and daughters — including those of a quiet disposition — had supported the school. Parents were also affected and met criticism at work and in their social contacts. Whilst the majority did not accept what was being said was necessarily accurate it was inevitable, over a period of several years, that many should wilt. For many others — parents, teachers, students and well-wishers — adversity strengthened their understanding and resolve. We shall examine details in later chapters.

Ryhope School Association

Ryhope Modern School had a flourishing parent-teacher association in 1969 and many parents and teachers welcomed a proposal to establish a corresponding body for the new school. At the time the Schools Sub-committee of Sunderland's Education Committee acted as the Governing Body for all primary, secondary and special schools in the borough, an arrangement with administrative and time saving advantages but with the handicap that there could be no close relationship between the governors and individual schools.[11] The role of a parent-teacher association was, therefore, particularly important and a steering committee was quickly formed. The new Association was to play an important part in the development of the school and, though its constitution underwent several amendments over the years, the spirit of the first which recognised the partnership of parents and teachers remained. The Association aimed to 'promote closer parent-teacher cooperation; to further the interests and welfare of the school and its neighbourhood; acquaint parents with the work of the school; organise and promote ... social contacts ... between parents and teachers, and act as a vehicle for the expression of the views of the members to the appropriate authority.' Of six original aims the traditional one of fund raising was number six and, even then, there was to be no one-way hand-over of money. The wording clearly stated 'for objectives determined by the Association'. The constitution established the headteacher as honorary president and the deputy as vice-president whilst two later amendments were specially significant. In 1973 the name was changed from a parent-teacher association to the 'Ryhope School Association' to reflect the interest and involvement of a small, but important, number of 'friends of the school' who were neither members of staff nor parents. In July 1980 membership of the executive was extended to include 'four pupil representatives, two each from the fourth and fifth years' (Chapter 9).

Activities

Activities varied as the school developed and included dinner dances; pie and pea suppers followed by 'Any Questions' on school affairs; meetings on modern mathematics, teaching English, careers, and resources for learning; visits to Sunderland Polytechnic (now the University of Sunderland) and to a local college of further education; a fashion show and a dog show and talks on education at working men's clubs chosen for easy accessibility in different parts of the catchment area. Educational events were particularly popular in the early years of the school when comprehensive education was new to the area. The Association hosted a BBC Radio 4 'Any Questions' broadcast in 1977, organised successful barn dances and parent-student games evenings in the school hall and, for twelve years, ran a Summer Fayre in aid of school funds each June.

The first Summer Fayre, in 1971, raised an undreamed of sum in excess of £900 which was spent on bright and cheerful curtains for the school hall and an electric duplicator. Each Summer Fayre had an extensive range of stalls, displays by students, popular afternoon teas and one or more 'star events' such as a presentation by the aptly named 'Chaos' team, and trials for motor cycles and horse drawn carriages (not on the same occasion!). The mayor of Sunderland opened the 1971 Fayre and was followed mostly by people with local connections such as a former student of the grammar school and member of Sunderland's FA Cup winning team (1973) and the school's recently retired and much respected senior clerk (1981). Associated with each Summer Fayre was the 'Headteacher's Giant Raffle' for which local traders provided up to ninety prizes each year. In 1971, the first prize was a weekend for two at a top Newcastle Hotel (which cost the Association £14.74 to include two nights and three main meals) while 1973 saw our first cash prize of £100. Novelties included 'lunch for two in the school cafeteria — coffee with the headteacher', a well-deserved tribute to the quality of the school meals service and the high local reputation of Ryhope School canteen staff. There was a variation in 1974 when the location switched to the home economics department and the prize became 'Be a guest of the head at a Cordon Bleu lunch — specially prepared by our pupil chefs (prize for two)'.

Allocation of Association funds was made on a democratic basis at extraordinary general meetings; these could be lengthy and sometimes fraught as members tried to whittle down a proliferation of educationally and socially desirable suggestions submitted by staff and parents. Requests for equipment and learning materials to help with special needs were assured of a sympathetic reception and showed how people react purposefully when in a position to take an overall view rather than individually as customers or consumers. An important item in 1973 was the purchase of the school's first video recorder heralding what was to prove a major resource in schools (Chapter 4, note 10). Over the years, money was provided for library books; clubs and societies; outings and team travel expenses; a grass cutter and a moped for the rural science and motor vehicle courses respectively; musical instruments; camping and sports equipment; fish tanks; a rain gauge; materials for members of the building studies course to construct an aviary, and a mobile disco. The RSA gave short shrift to proposals, however worthy, which they felt should be provided by the local authority as part of the basic requirements of a school. Thus textbooks, basic laboratory ware and kitchen utensils do not appear on any finally approved lists. There is a sharp contrast today when schools are almost forced into fund raising efforts to provide what would have been seen before the 1988 Act as essentials.

Committee work

The executive committee, elected at the annual meeting, applied itself to the aims of the Association through detailed work and action. In 1973 it undertook a major survey of the school buildings and prepared a report which, after listing many deficiencies, concluded 'With purpose built schools money is made available to provide a high standard of education both physical and academic whereas at Ryhope no such money was made available and all that we seem to have gained is a bridge.' The report was followed by a conducted tour for local councillors who recommended that a copy of the report be sent to the director of education, together with a list of priorities, and that local councillors be invited to executive committee meetings on a rota basis. The work of the RSA committee was undoubtedly an important factor in substantial improvements which took place in following years. The committee took an active role in the working party to plan uniform details after the parental vote in 1978 (see Chapter 13 for context). The committee prepared occasional newsletters for parents and provided volunteers for evening discos. As 'Silksworth Parent' writing to the local paper put it:

At 10pm I looked back on what had been a most rewarding evening. The music, lighting and sound were in the capable hands of the senior pupils, while volunteer mothers, assisted by pupils, sold soft drinks, crisps etc, and willing fathers kept a diplomatic eye on the proceedings ... For three hours 350 children of all ages had, to put it in their own words, 'a great time'.

'For all ages' is a reminder that events of this kind contributed directly to a sense of unity among students.

The committee was active in the National Confederation of Parent-Teacher Associations, whose local branch successfully campaigned for an elected parent representative on Sunderland's Education Committee. In 1976, the Association provided the main input for an evening session of a course run by the University of Durham for heads, deputies and assistant teachers on 'Parent Participation in the Secondary School'. At a crucial meeting for parents two years later called by the chairman of the Education Committee (Chapter 13) the RSA chair and vice-chair wrote to parents stressing its importance and offered a service: 'You may, however, be unable to attend, or too shy to ask a question — your Executive Committee would, therefore, be pleased to put your questions or comments to the Governing Body on your behalf. (Names of parents contributing in this way will not be made public)'. Three years later, the committee submitted a 'Report on the Life and Work of the Ryhope School Association' to Her Majesty's Inspectors on the occasion of a full inspection. The work of the committee inevitably reflected strains and divisions surrounding the school. During periods of peak publicity in spring 1978 and autumn 1982 the executive issued statements and letters to the press which were factual and fair and reflected a deep sense of responsibility on behalf of parents, staff, students and the community to 'further the interests and welfare of the school'.

Despite these achievements the RSA faced two problems common to many such organisations. Firstly, committee work appealed only to a small proportion of the many parents ready to help a school in practical ways and, consequently, executives were not fully representative. Secondly the time commitment for both staff and parent representatives was considerable and a 'time audit' (to use a topical management concept) might have raised questions about whether this was the most effective means of formal parent-teacher cooperation and representation. Nevertheless, the notable contribution of the Ryhope School Association in such a wide range of activities and policy initiatives is clear. Today's parent

governors, concerned with high powered decision making to balance the
budget, hire and fire staff and exercise responsibility for anything from
moral education to grass cutting, rarely have time to be involved in such
down-to-earth activities.[12]

Social amenities

Many excellent features have been incorporated in the design of schools
since the second world war and have made a significant contribution to the
quality of life for both students and staff. Nevertheless, as we have seen,
compulsory banishment to playgrounds in all but the most extreme of
weather conditions is not acceptable (Chapter 5). For several years at
Ryhope students were able to use tutor rooms before school and at break
and lunch times. However, a split site, rambling buildings and
demountable classrooms made effective supervision difficult and left scope
for misuse of rooms by a minority. In the spring of 1977 I therefore
agreed to recommendations that, during break and lunch-times, the
buildings would be cleared. It was an unhappy, if inevitable, decision and,
on the day the system came into operation, I heard the first raised staff
voice calling 'Get outside!' Soon 'passes' were necessary for students to
attend activities, team meetings and so on and, for those who remained
outside at lunchtime, women dinner supervisors went far beyond the call
of duty by organising games and generally befriending the students.
However, I doubt whether activities like Radio Ryhope, which flourished at
times when students could be in their tutor rooms, and large-scale events
such as the rock operas, whose preparation needed access for large
numbers at all times of the day, could have taken place if these procedures
had been in operation earlier.

School toilets often have a bad reputation among students and a
negative impact on the perceived values of a school. Official regulations
are concerned more with quantity than quality but this is only part of the
need. Small out-of-the-way toilets are an invitation to vandalism and
'take-overs' by groups of students whose presence is intimidating to
others. Much time is devoted to supervision whilst senior members of staff
such as heads of year and deputy heads have to deal retrospectively with
problems. Sometimes toilets are locked, except at specified hours, with a
staff member or the school office acting as key-holders for emergencies.
Obtaining the key not only causes inconvenience to the holder but
embarrassment to many students, especially younger ones, who may prefer

to wait desperately until they reach home. Far better to think positively and prevent the majority of these problems at source; the time has arrived for the ideas of total quality management (Chapter 17, note 3) to be applied to this important aspect of school life! Toilets should be viewed as an amenity as well as a necessity and designed to the highest standards. Every sizeable school needs a central toilet block with easy access, plenty of space, cheerful tiling, extensive mirrors and full-time, well-paid male and female attendants who would liaise with a designated member of staff. A five-star facility would include lockers for valuables and equipment and I am confident that developments on these lines could make a very practical contribution to the quality of life for students and the job satisfaction of staff — and all at modest expense.

Facilities which are taken for granted in everyday life may be lacking in school. During the 1980s Sunderland Borough Council dispensed with window cleaning in all its public buildings as a response to economic cuts — a ban which lasted for at least four years for the schools. Window cleaning is unlikely to come high on a list of priorities for comprehensive education yet when windows get dusty a building becomes dull; inevitably, this has a depressing, if subliminal, effect on the spirit and morale of those who work there and is not acceptable for the young people of an advanced economic society. Now such decisions are matters for local management but governors are still left with agonising decisions between desirable amenities which should be seen as essential.

APPENDIX: Clothing and uniform issues

What to wear for school (Chapter 9) proved a long-running issue at Ryhope and revealed sharp differences of opinion. My views were well known locally and, in particular, I was not prepared to exclude a student over uniform. The possibility of having to face a judge but to be unable to say on oath that I held uniformity in dress to be a pre-requisite for effective discipline, was not one to relish (Chapter 9, note 13). At different periods during the lifetime of the school, the Education Committee took a greater or lesser interest in the subject and for several years in the mid-1970s we were allowed to operate without uniform, a factor appreciated by many young people at the time and also by many staff and visitors, not least those with interests in the creative side of education. The annual group photographs show students dressed in a practical manner with little or no sign of ostentation or 'one upmanship'. The 'Welcome to Ryhope School' booklets for parents of new entrants had a simple statement on clothing: 'We hope that all pupils will come to school neat and tidy wearing suitable clothes of their own choice. We find this is more practical in this day and age and also saves expense'. Not having to enforce conformity did much for staff-student relationships. However, just as there were some who could not envisage discipline without corporal punishment (and serious work without selection) so, there were those who considered that *esprit de corps* — I prefer 'comradeship and identity' — was impossible without distinctive clothing and insignia. In response one can note that during occasions as varied as the national networking on TV of *Stardust* to the response to the school closure proposals, members of the school fiercely identified themselves with both its successes and struggles. One teacher after joining the staff from London described Ryhope as more like a village school in terms of community — a compliment to staff, parents and students.

In the spring of 1978 the chairman of the Education Committee announced a parental ballot on uniform (Chapter 13). This achieved a greater than 2:1 majority in favour, a result hardly surprising as the letter to parents containing the voting forms not only commenced 'The Governors of Ryhope School believe it will be very helpful to the school if pupils wear school uniform' but also included a sheet, dated the same month, giving details of a much enhanced scheme of financial assistance towards the costs of uniforms. The result was to apply immediately to younger students so we established a joint working party with parents, teachers from the art and home economics departments and students from the years affected. Our annual 'Clothing leaflet' for parents of new entrants commenced: 'The Governors have approved the following clothing recommendations prepared after discussion between parents, pupils and teachers in 1979. The aim is to make the clothing acceptable to all pupils, at home and at school...' Despite grants and efforts to keep costs to a minimum, we were conscious that parents had spent substantial sums on uniform. I was anxious not to let them down whilst continuing to reject exclusion and its consequences as an ultimate sanction. For anyone not wearing the approved clothing the head of year wrote a personal letter to the parents based on an agreed outline. The example shows in italics where the standard wording is personalised; an actual letter would have been prepared in normal type throughout:

Dear *Mr and Mrs Smith,*

I am enclosing a copy of our school clothing leaflet which was agreed by the Governing Body after consultation with pupils, parents and teachers of Ryhope School. As there is a considerable choice of clothing we believe that all our school students would be able to dress attractively and economically within the approved requirements.

I have spoken with *Steven* concerning his *trousers* and, from our conversation, I understand that it will only be a matter of days before normal school clothing will be worn. However, in order to be fair to all pupils, we ask for a brief note from parents to cover the period when permission can be given for a variation of school clothing.

Could you please complete the slip below and return it to the group tutor tomorrow evening. Thank you for your cooperation.

> Yours sincerely,
> *John Brown*
> Head of Year

A typical reply slip might read:

Dear Miss *Bewick,*

Would it be possible for Steven to wear denim trousers because his school trousers are torn and I am getting him a new pair at the weekend.

> Signed *(Mrs) Jean Smith*

If there was no response in a day or two, a follow-up letter added a note of urgency and, if still to no avail, a third letter offered an appointment 'as we do not seem to be making progress on this matter'. It concluded 'As the requirements of school clothing are determined by the Governing Body, it is necessary for the school to inform the Director of Education in the case of non-compliance. Naturally we only wish to do so as a last resort and I hope that we can agree satisfactory arrangements after discussion'. This approach was costly in time even with the help of the school-based Education Welfare Officer (Chapter 8) but it was reasonably successful for two or three years and longer with younger age groups. But as time went on there was an increasing problem of maintaining the broad support on which a non-authoritarian approach ultimately depends. Enthusiasm for wearing uniform reduced with experience and as a fifth year student said to me in June 1982 'Most of the year voted for uniform as first years; most regret it now and think it is daft'.

12

Records and Assessment

Evaluation and assessment are essential to the educative process and exercise great influence. Nevertheless, they must always remain ancillary to the curriculum and not determiners of it. In this chapter we look at means, including records of personal achievement, used to monitor and acknowledge the progress of students at Ryhope. The emphasis is on the opportunities and requirements of a non-selective system.

Internal records

Name, address, date of birth and attendance appear on all school record cards. In earlier days many also included unsubstantiated comments concerning family background and other highly subjective opinions but, thankfully, this is now unacceptable and, to an increasing extent, illegal. There remains much that can be helpful to students' progress. In this complex and rapidly advancing field record-keeping must be responsive to national and local developments and should give opportunities for teachers to contribute their own ideas and specialist knowledge. At Ryhope, record keeping and assessment were based on the principle that they should positively assist the educative process of all students and support a non-selective organisation and ethos. As time went on the opportunities and advantages of making records as open as possible to both parents and students became increasingly apparent.[1]

Progress in subjects

Assessing and recording progress in subjects as diverse as English, art, mathematics and physical education is a skilled operation and it is essential that each subject department should be able to choose appropriate methods. The topic was a high priority from the first weeks of the comprehensive school and constantly developed by subject departments. Methods for each subject were influenced by developments in the assessment techniques used in public examinations and received a boost at Ryhope during the early 1980s as a result of the interest and specialist knowledge of several teachers including a new deputy head who, shortly before taking up his appointment, had been seconded for two years to study for a degree in Educational Technology.[2] These teachers were specially interested in improving assessments and records as part of a diagnostic process to guide colleagues in arranging programmes of study for more effective learning and teaching. The details are matters for specialists and we shall concentrate on the question of guiding the *overall* progress of students. This may vary over periods of time and also from subject to subject. If, for example, a particular student's performance is about average in history the teacher may assume that this is his or her norm whilst, in fact, the person may be working significantly below or above the standard attained in other subjects. Similarly a sharp falling off or acceleration of work in science may be confined to that subject or, alternatively, be part of a more general change. Teachers need to know such information if they are to respond constructively but there is a problem. A mark of 60 per cent in subject A may be among the best in the group while the same mark in subject B may be about average. A group tutor or head of year cannot be expected to keep track of the detailed assessments in every subject.

Standardising assessments

To overcome this difficulty we adopted a common format for comparison of results on a school basis whilst retaining considerable flexibility for the assessment of each subject. A senior teacher used a statistical procedure to convert the scores and grades for each tutor group into a standard nine-point (or stannine) scale in which a score of 5 indicates average and 1 and 9 represent the lowest and highest attaining respectively.[3] A staff booklet outlined the advantages:

> Comparison between attainment in different subjects is facilitated: eg a stannine 7 for English indicates that the pupil has a significantly better performance relative to other members of his group than a stannine 5 for maths. Comparison between performance in different groups is facilitated: eg a stannine 6 for a social studies group of thirty pupils can be compared with the same pupil's

stannine 4 for technical studies in a group of twenty (assuming both groups have a similar distribution of attainment).

The booklet included some actual second year stannine scores with comments from the head of year. The following table and comments are based on the original:

Student	English	Maths	Science	Hist	Art	Home Econ	Tech Studies
A	7	7	8	4	5	5	8
B	5	5	6	6	5	5	6
C	8	8	7	8	8	7	8
D	5	3	3	4	8	1	5

Student A: Interviewed about inconsistency in history

    B: Average student working consistently

    C: Very good — sixth form potential?

    D: Below average but generally consistent; congratulated on good art work. Problem in home economics to be resolved.

In a period before key stage tests, stannine scores were useful when transfer of schools occurred. The contributory junior schools had different systems of assessment which we transposed into stannines and, conversely, when a student transferred from Ryhope to another school, we sent stannine scores from subject assessments accompanied by an explanatory sheet. Nevertheless, the staff booklet also included some words of caution:

> Stannines cannot mitigate the effects of different bases of assessment by teachers even within the same subject, eg a pupil's first year science teacher may emphasise neatness of work and calmness of manner whilst in the second year a different teacher assesses signs of scientific insight and problem solving ability.[4] Under these circumstances very different stannines could be obtained although the pupil's general effort was similar in each case. Nor do stannines on a class basis show how well or poorly the group as a whole is making progress, eg tutor groups 1.1 and 1.2 may have a similar range of stannine scores for English but these show progress *relative to other members of the group*. If the overall progress of one of the groups has been retarded for some reason this will not be shown.

There were other limitations including the assumption of a normal distribution (note 3) which is by no means applicable to all learning situations. For example in the driving test candidates either do or do not meet the criteria for a licence — there is no range of achievement indicated — and there are many corresponding situations in school. Also the stannine scale measures progress relative to others. This means that a conscientious student in a consistent group will remain with the same score for a long period — hardly the greatest of incentives and least of all for those with special needs. This made stannine scores generally unsuitable for discussing directly with parents and students. Despite these limitations, the system served an important purpose and, as the booklet concluded: 'Stannine scores are no panacea but, thoughtfully used, they can assist a teacher in the guidance of his pupils'. Today, computer programmes open up other possibilities for the standardisation of assessments[5] but the topic as a whole remains a complex field. This is especially so if the aim is to facilitate individual progress rather than to label students (and their schools) in rank order as a basis of selection in which those from the highest social classes have a massive in-built advantage (Chapter 2).

Tests of general ability

There were several tests available which purported to measure general ability. All such tests have affinities with intelligence tests and the results must be treated with extreme caution (Chapter 9, note 4). From 1971 we regularly used tests of this type and later, when they became available, adopted the so-called AH2 and AH3 tests from the National Foundation for Educational Research. These claimed to measure verbal, numerical and perceptual abilities. Each school could compare its results with those of a national sample with which the tests had been standardised and our motive was to try to get some more or less objective picture of the intellectual range and ability of our intakes. We gave the test twice in the career of each student: a few weeks after arrival and during the third year. Teachers supervising the tests had to be appointed as registered administrators by the NFER who held the copyright. The results showed that we had a full range of scores but with fewer than the national average among the highest achievers on the tests and proportionately more at the lower end of the range. Whilst this was scarcely news, it was interesting to note confirmation of our personal observations. Although the tests were classified as relevant to groups rather than individuals, we made some use of individual results. After converting them to the stannine scale they were useful as a guide to action rather than as a precision measurement. For example, teachers responsible for special educational needs scanned the first year results to see whether any students, not already coming to them, should have more specific tests to assess whether they needed specialised help. Also (as described in Chapter 9) I included the results on my copy of our extended tutor group lists using them, together with other information on the list, as a broad indicator before visiting a lesson with a tutor group, talking to parents or consulting colleagues.

Record cards and tutor files

In 1969 most schools had a record card for each student containing a variety of information including assessments. Many less than productive hours went into planning and agreeing the design of the cards by a committee representing the schools in an authority — usually with little all-round satisfaction. Re-design was again on the agenda in Sunderland when I arrived and likely to take at least a year or two. So to avoid delay and frustration we prepared our own version: a loose leaf system with cards indexed for easy access in a file for each tutor group. Information recorded included a photograph, family and medical details, records of school progress and space for comments. The system proved to be rather inflexible and although the cards continued for several years, they were later transferred to a folder for each student which also included correspondence, notes, copies of school reports and of reports for the Juvenile Court and so on. Whilst this was a worthwhile improvement it was still too centralised as, for a variety of reasons, the folders were kept in a filing cabinet in the head of year's office. This meant that the group tutor 'responsible for the educational and social guidance of his pupils'[6] did not have continuous access to them. We therefore sought to supplement what existed by recording less formal, but educationally significant, information.

Tutor files were the responsibility of the group tutor. They consisted of ring binders with sheets for a 'Diary of Events in the Tutor Group', a list of tutor group members and A4 sheets for each student. As well as the usual personal information such as address and siblings, group tutors recorded the names of teachers for each subject; school and out of school activities, and comments on general matters and on work. The tutor was free to add any further material such as photographs of activities, programmes of events participated in and so on. The main purpose, however, was to enhance the insight that group tutors could give concerning the young people in their charge. In this respect many showed a flair for understanding and communication. The following examples of entries by a first year tutor with their interesting details of activities and depth of general comment show what could be done:

Activities:

Enjoys running, cricket and cycling (also builds bikes) ...

Raised £10 in £2 scheme [a fund raising activity by the group]; entered her dog in the school dog show.

Keen member of the First Year rugby team. Member of team that won the Town Championship. Regular position — winger ...

General comments:

D's obvious maturity has been much in evidence this year and she maintains a quiet reflective view of school and social relationships. Such maturity would appear to be partially the result of living with numerous older siblings who must set important models of behaviour ...

G has transferred from tutor group 1.1 partly because of his 'membership' of a group/gang of boys who were causing problems inside and outside the classroom ... Although speculation, I believe that he feels that he must live up to his brother's reputation although he is physically and psychologically different... (*The tutor continued with specific suggestions for help*).

These constructive comments are in sharp contrast with one noted from another tutor file which describes facts but omits understanding: 'P just does not make any attempt to fit into school, is continually late, very poor at handing in homework and does not get on well with other pupils'. Fortunately there were few entries of the latter type and, whilst not everyone had a flair for such work, the majority provided an informative picture of each member of the group's personality, interests and school progress. I received the files to read on a rota basis, often combining this with a visit to the tutor group. The need to get as full information as possible to group tutors concerning activities of their students caused some administrative problems and there was a little duplication with other records. Nevertheless the files were a positive development, not least in enabling the professional skills of teachers to be acknowledged and used more widely. As well as for day to day contacts, the files provided a useful source of information for references and testimonials and for reports for the Juvenile Court.[7]

An extended debate among a number of committed tutors centred on the question of confidentiality versus openness in the files. Some felt they could contribute most by fully involving their students in recording and discussing their entries whilst others felt equally strongly that they could analyse situations more constructively if the files were confidential. We stuck with confidentiality at first, moved to a period of leaving the decision to group tutors so that we could gain wider experience and ultimately decided to transfer confidential records to folders leaving tutors free to involve their students as fully as they wished. A joint memorandum in 1985 from a group tutor and her head of year shows the possibilities:

> Tutors to enter comments in consultation with the pupil involved; pupils to be encouraged to make comments, pin point their own strengths and weaknesses, set themselves goals and to consider how these can be achieved and how areas of weakness can be improved upon. Pupils to countersign any comments made by the tutor and/or add their own comments.

Such an approach seemed closer to the spirit of student participation which we were promoting elsewhere in the school (Chapter 9). Joint entries implied joint ownership but, of course, an individual's records were never made available to other members of the tutor group unless specifically authorised by both tutor and student. Several routine forms also had a personal aspect. One provided an immediate opportunity for a busy teacher to commend a student who had done well. It simply said 'I have been pleased with the work of ... ' and the group tutor or head of year to whom it was sent could add their own word of encouragement. We had daily report cards (Chapter 9) for students whose work and behaviour were below standard and, in some cases we arranged 'customised' versions in consultation with individual students. In rare cases where collective tutor group action and responsibility needed emphasising, a report involving the whole tutor group was customised to be fully relevant to the particular problem. All forms of recording and assessing must be supported by personal contact from senior management; regular visits to classes and tutor groups provided essential feedback from teachers and students concerning how policies are working out where it really mattered: in the classroom.

Reporting to parents

Whilst school reports are usually addressed to parents, in reality they are also for students and both are entitled to an honest and balanced statement. This should include assessments compared with previous performance and estimates of grades which may be achieved in any forthcoming public examinations. I am far from convinced, however, of the necessity and value of assessments in which the grade awarded produces a rank order and depends, not only on the quality of the students' own performance, but also on that of others.[8]

Progress reports

We used the term 'progress report' as an alternative to 'school report' with its rather negative connotations and chose a loose leaf format to avoid the 'halo' effect (Chapter 9, note 2). We also obtained permission from a somewhat surprised officer of Sunderland Education Authority to go to professional designers for high quality folders and insert sheets. These were of A4 width and slightly under one-third A4 height making an aesthetically pleasing and handy-sized booklet.[9] Teachers completed sheets independently for each subject and sent them to group tutors and heads of year for their summaries. Finally they were collated with information and reply sheets and attached to the cover with a brass paper fastener. The information sheet explained that 'the reports are designed to show how much effort each pupil is putting into his/her work' and, to help both writers and readers in this early period of comprehensive education, each subject sheet had a printed list of items relevant to successful learning:

Interest and Enthusiasm	Practical/Drama
Written Work	Homework
Creative ideas	Tests/Exams
Discussion/Questions	

There was a box after each item for the teacher to indicate that 'his/her best efforts are in these aspects of the work (tick); an exceptionally good effort (two ticks); more attention needed (circle); much more attention needed (two circles)'. A blank or dash indicated 'working satisfactorily' but teachers were asked to see that every student received at least one tick for each subject.[10] There was also an item for overall progress with a choice of three indicators: I — definite improvement; S — quite satisfactory; N — definitely not so good. These printed items took only a small amount of space, leaving room for written comments by subject teachers.[11] The reports served a useful purpose at the time, providing a simple assessment including reference to previous performance. Later, as experience grew, we moved to sheets which were blank except for subject title, name of student and date. These were welcomed and provided scope for the best report writers to produce exceptionally constructive and illuminating comments. For most, the art of report writing needs study and training; vague or negative remarks and the use of jargon need eliminating and many of us need guidance in the art of effective communication using an economy of words.

Books to parents

Progress reports are only one of several means by which parents can receive information on school progress. For several years we asked students to take home all their books and files for a weekend each term. This proved popular with parents and the majority of students. An accompanying letter told parents that:

> Each pupil has been asked to explain the books and files to you and also to tell you of other important work which is not written down, for example subjects with a strong practical emphasis such as art, technical studies ... If you can spend half an hour or so with your son or daughter letting them tell you about their school work, we are sure that it will encourage them in their studies ...

Comments on reply slips were collated and typed for each tutor group and sent to all teachers concerned. The operation certainly helped to promote communication between parents and their children concerning school work and we realised from both written and verbal comments that parents were often surprised by the breadth, depth and quantity of study undertaken by school students.

Records of achievement

Three years after the 1944 Education Act, a brief report by the Secondary Schools Examination Council (1947) led to the introduction of GCE to replace the School and Higher School Certificates. The first of the Council's eight recommendations was as follows:

Every pupil on leaving a secondary school should be provided with a comprehensive school report containing the fullest possible positive information about him and his abilities and potentialities. (p 4)

For many years this recommendation was largely ignored and many school students completed their secondary education often with no documentation at all. At most they received a school testimonial (usually inadequate) and an examination certificate of limited currency to all but the academically talented — a hopelessly inadequate record of school life. So, in 1974 with the raising of the leaving age to 16 effective for the first time and our first comprehensive intake approaching the end of the compulsory part of their education, we investigated the situation. By then a record of personal achievement (RPA), operating in Swindon from 1969 under the direction of Don Stansbury, had paved the way (Swales, 1979).[12] On a visit there, I was impressed with two basic principles which had been established:

- The need to distinguish between a record, which describes what has been done, and an assessment. Swindon illustrated the distinction by contrasting an application form for a job (record) with a reference for the job (assessment). Both have an important role but in schools we have concentrated almost exclusively on the latter.
- Ultimately it should be each student's own decision as to what goes into the record.

Although our own work diverged from Swindon's RPA in important respects the significance of these two principles played a central part in our thinking.[13]

Personal achievement files

We chose 'Personal Achievement File' as a descriptive title for an A4 loose-leaf document and received a £400 setting up grant from the local authority. Unlike Swindon, where the record of personal achievement formed the focus of a significant proportion of the timetable for fourth and fifth year students not taking examinations, Ryhope's was intended for all students as an 'end of course' record prepared in the final weeks of the fifth year.[14] There was a free choice whether or not to complete a file and a further option, resulting from the loose-leaf arrangement, enabled students to choose which sheets to finally include. In practice, a full

cross-section of each year participated. An attractive design for the cover
and inserts was, as with progress reports, a first priority. Each file had an
information sheet followed by separate sheets for each subject studied.
These were colour coded for humanities; science and technology, and
creative studies and each subject had an individually designed logo
together with a short printed summary of the nature and aims of the
course. The aim of English, for example, was:

> to encourage each student to develop to the full his or her ability in written and
> spoken English; to understand and assimilate written communication of many
> kinds; and to read, enjoy and appreciate critically novels, poetry, drama and
> media.

Art teachers described their course as:

> progressing from the delightful child art of the first year to the more mature
> work of the teenager. In the fourth and fifth years the opportunity is given for
> individual study of a wide range of specialised crafts.[15]

Subject sheets had plenty of space for students to comment and many
used the opportunity to produce lively and insightful contributions. Here,
for instance, is C describing her drama course 'This option is great; it
brings you to think more about the way other people think ... We make
different people out of ourselves and put them into a different situation.
The lessons are very enjoyable and I look forward to being part of them. I
always seem to end up in a daft mood after doing drama, as it takes away
my shyness and helps me feel more friendly towards the people around
me. I find that if I feel tense when I go into a drama lesson the group all
try to make each other feel less tense ... Some drama should have been
done in English lessons in the fourth and fifth years ... I would have
missed out on something if I hadn't taken drama as an option'. This
account, so obviously the student's own work,[16] provides plenty of
openings for an interviewer as well as valuable feedback for English
teachers and curriculum planners. Entries which drew on personal
knowledge always added interest. W, for instance, wrote in his metalwork
report 'Metalwork is my father's life as he works as a blacksmith. I hope to
make metalwork my life. I enjoy starting with bright drawn mild steel and
ending up with a sprocket remover or other useful tools which I made
during the course'.

The overwhelming majority of students asked their teachers to add their
comments in a space provided on the subject sheets. Many of the

responses showed a warmth and dialogue with the student reflecting the mutual respect on which their relationships were based. Other sheets covered hobbies and activities; courses linked with local colleges of further education, and social and community work. Photocopies and originals of newspaper and magazine items often found a place while certificates went into a plastic folder. The school provided a service entitling each student to two mounted photographs for inclusion in the file. These were usually requested in a craft room, laboratory or other specialised area to feature the individual with a project or activity. Finally there was a very special sheet, coloured but otherwise blank, for messages from friends and teachers producing a range of witticisms and good wishes to complete the file in a pleasing, informal way.[17] The results of this project, planned with the dual purpose of providing an interesting record for family and friends and to be of value at interview, emphasised the importance of the original recommendation by the Secondary Schools Examination Council. The files proved very popular with students while jobs were readily available but, as youth training schemes and unemployment increased from the end of the 1970's, their practical value appeared to the students to diminish. Eventually, with much regret, we had to suspend the scheme. Nevertheless, the school continued its interest in profiling and, just before it closed, came up with a thoroughly revised and popular version known as 'Final Report'. We consider this development below within the wider sphere of certificates and testimonials.

Certificates and testimonials

So far, we have concentrated on recording rather than assessment although there may be a thin dividing line between the two. For example, students placed certificates and their school testimonial, both involving assessment, in their personal achievement files which were a record. Students gained certificates, in and out of school, for a wide variety of activities: first aid and dancing, proficiency in musical instruments, sports awards of all descriptions and on linked courses at colleges of further education. Certificates marking success in Sunderland's modern language proficiency tests became very popular among Ryhope students in the mid-1980s. The Department of Education and Science, as well as other bodies, had called for a widening of the language base from the traditional French and German and the school had responded by making Spanish the language to be studied by all students in the first three years. As the first school in the local authority to take this step, our staff, in consultation with the modern language adviser, were closely involved in establishing the content of the three levels of the Spanish versions of the tests. Level 1 was described as providing 'an introduction to the language' whilst at level 3 'candidates have acquired a good working knowledge of the language and are well prepared for further studies'. The certificates contained information on the tests and details of the student's performance. This was shown as pass or credit in reading, listening, speaking and writing in contexts such as 'express likes and dislikes' (level 1) or 'read, understand and enjoy a story or letter' (level 2).[18] All levels required a knowledge of life and customs starting with Spanish people themselves at level 1 and including Argentinian, Colombian, Cuban, Puerto Rican and Venezulan by level 3.[19] Level 1 tests were available from the end of the first year and the others at any time up to the fifth year. Students arranged with their teacher when to take a test and they could resit at a later date if unsuccessful in one or more parts.[20]

A school-produced PE certificate (note 9) was awarded to students who successfully completed the course in Further PE Studies as an option in the fourth and fifth years. Although we were not able to make this a CSE course as planned, it attracted a range of interested students. The course description on the certificate included coaching as an aspect of service to others:

> Students are encouraged to improve their own personal standards of performance, to understand complex skills and teach those skills to younger children.

The certificates included a detailed comment by the head of department who signed them jointly with myself. They were highly valued and, by no means confined to more gifted athletes.

Attendance certificates — also school-produced — became popular with the majority of students in the 1980s. They certified the percentage attendance in the fifth year with a space for special circumstances and comments where appropriate. With much time spent in schools following up absentees it was always a reassuring experience, when signing the certificates, to note how many had attended very well.

Testimonials could be used separately or included in personal achievement files or the Final Report.[21] The bulk of the preparatory work, involving up to 240 students, was completed by heads of fifth year who showed commendable dedication. The drafts were sent to me for any observations and then typed on suitably headed sheets which showed all subjects taken by the student. As with school reports, testimonial writing proved highly specialised and while doubtless our testimonials contained imperfections,[22] they were appreciated by both students and parents. Here is an example from 1986:

> C is a most helpful and cheerful student who has at all times shown himself to be honest, reliable and trustworthy. He is popular with both staff and students who appreciate his loyalty and enthusiasm. C can at all times be relied upon to carry out tasks without the need for supervision. He has worked steadily at his course of studies and in the majority of subjects he has done well. C is an able conversationalist and is prepared to express his views clearly and in a mature manner. He has made full use of his time outside the classroom being an active member of both the school and local drama clubs. He enjoys music and squash and has been a source of positive motivation within the school's student council. On several occasions he has instituted and organised successful events of a social or charitable nature and should be commended for this. We are confident that as C matures further he will add to his many positive qualities and attributes.
>
> We wish him every success for the future.

For most students the attendance certificate and school testimonial represented a practical record and assessment to complement examination results. Indeed many obtained jobs and training places before the latter were known taking these two school documents to interview in support of their applications.

Final Report

In the last year of the school (1987/88) we produced a record of achievement for fifth year students as one of two major projects which helped to make the year an active and stimulating one.[23] Although very different from the original personal achievement file, the Final Report retained several of its features. It was an A4, end-of-course, attractively designed document with a range of subject and other sheets; it had a wallet for certificates and a 'special friends and best wishes' sheet now in the form of a jigsaw pattern and described as 'a lovely idea' by Mary James, research fellow with PRAISE, the Pilot Record of Achievement in Schools Evaluation.[24] The photographic service took an unexpected turn. Planning a similar arrangement to previously we enlisted the services of our senior science technician who was also a gifted photographer. Finding difficulty in getting potential subjects to the right place at the right time and with the project to be photographed he suggested, as an alternative, a black and white portrait of each student. Initially it was difficult to find volunteers but as soon as the first results were available he had problems of a different kind. The photographs were of such quality that requests for delays flooded in: 'Can it wait until after the weekend when I'm getting my hair done?' was a typical comment from boys and girls naturally wishing to appear at their best for the sitting. After mounting, the portraits had pride of place at the front of every file.

In a report on the project I referred to student participation in the choice of 'Final Report' as the title (Chapter 9):

> The practical nature of this decision placed the document firmly in the mainstream of school-home-career communication. Students recognised that their recommendations had implications for the content and style of the final document and this, in turn, affected staff interpretation of its role and scope.

The main implication, reflecting the requirements of the time, was a greater emphasis on assessment in the subject sheets. These had a common format for title, logo and course description creating an effective overall design but departments were free to use the area allocated for text as they thought best. For example, computer studies and social studies described the ability of students to undertake 'satisfactorily', 'well' or 'very well' tasks such as 'analyse problems and suggest methods of solution' (computer studies) or 'interpret arguments' (social studies). English and science assembled computer banks of positive statements which noted, for example, a student's ability to 'speak and write sensitively in a manner appropriate to the audience and circumstances' (English) or to 'devise a possible solution to a technological problem' (science).

Each student received a printed selection of these statements representing the breadth and depth of his or her achievements on the course. Whatever system was adopted, all subjects provided space for personal comments from teachers. These were valued and contributed much to the interest of the finished documents. Students expressed ideas on other aspects. According to my report they:

> saw the value of an input into the document by themselves but wished it to be brief. This was partly because of time commitments with GCSE in mind and partly because of some lack of confidence in their ability to communicate as effectively as they would wish through the written word.

To solve this problem we abandoned ideas of student comments on each subject; instead we provided two sheets each divided into three sections. These were labelled Works Experience, Interests and Part-time Work respectively on one sheet whilst the second had only a page title 'My thoughts on:' Here, students used two or three sections to write about themselves, individual subjects, school in general, career intentions or special interests. Additional sheets were available if required. Throughout the operation members of staff reported a favourable response from students:

> Personal comment sheets were completed very willingly. Many took time to repeat and improve their efforts until satisfied that they were of an adequate standard ...

> On leaving day I noted the special care with which students removed the reports from the envelopes and opened them to read ...

> Despite the short period of direct involvement students have felt a sense of ownership ...

Students reported favourable receptions at interview and the pages of the Final Report were arranged in a convenient order for such occasions. The testimonial and attendance certificate (when used) followed the photograph; subject sheets came next and the student's personal contribution and certificates completed the document. With time at interview usually at a premium, teachers' written comments on subject sheets provided a useful summary of attitude and performance and it was therefore easy for interviewers to gain a quick general impression and then follow up any point of particular interest. Feedback from parents at a parents' evening generated a thought on the validity of such a document which I described in my report:

> This problem, which occupies much thinking and debate when profiles[25] are considered, appears to have been at least partially resolved in the current project. Readers and users of a Final Report would expect comments to carry the validation of the teachers who sign them and the school which issues the report.

This is exactly what happens with a routine progress report to parents and it may not be too simple an idea to apply the same principal to profiles. The need for evolution in subsequent years is also important:

If the personal involvement of staff and students is to be maintained, there must be opportunities for meaningful development. Yesterday's forms with tomorrow's people is a recipe for constraint rather than vitality.

The positive results of our project would not have been possible without a tremendous team effort from the teaching and technician staff and the LEA's art adviser, all of whom freely and generously gave their time and pooled their expertise. With this in mind it is interesting to note that each Final Report cost a total of 90 pence inclusive of photograph; the 1988 entry fee for GCSE was £11.25 per subject.

National record of achievement

From the summer of 1993, all state secondary schools were required to issue their year 11 students with a National Record of Achievement though, as a survey of records of achievement by Sunderland's inspectors and advisers commented, 'Central government support ... seems to some to have waned'. In fact, a few months before the 1997 election, Conservative government ministers were planning a rename and relaunch following the failure of the original scheme to catch on with either employers or further and higher education. The NRA did not draw on experience and expertise gained over more than two decades and ignored the recommendations of the Pilot Record of Achievement in Schools Evaluation. According to a report ' "Passport to life" issued' (*The Times Educational Supplement*, 1992c) the NRA was 'introduced largely ... at the instigation of the Department of Employment'. The report noted that its 'glossy leatherette folder will contain details of a pupil's exam successes, national curriculum assessments, vocational qualifications and non-academic achievements in sports, arts, music, outdoor pursuits or community work'. The emphasis was overwhelmingly on assessment, which would inevitably enhance feelings of rejection among students whose strengths lie elsewhere than in examination and test results. Don Stansbury (1992) in a Forum article 'A Loss to Comprehensive Education' puts it as follows: 'An idea of considerable importance to comprehensive education has been lost. It is the idea of personally compiled records which began as a response to the Newsom Report in 1963'.[26] It is important that we do not judge the progress of the NRA at least in its present form, as reflecting on the ideas first put forward by the Secondary Schools Examination Council in 1947 and explored and developed through many initiatives from the 1960s to the '80s.

Monitoring examination results

Unlike the records and assessments so far discussed, examination results arrive up to two or three months after students have completed their courses. We have already noted some results (Chapter 10) and here we look at more detailed methods to monitor performance within a school and provide the staff with pointers for future action. Comparison of performance in different subjects is a topic of interest to all schools but valid comparisons are not easy as, in the later years of school, choice of subject leads to groups of varied size and attainment. One subject may attract mainly able students who achieve better grades than those taking a less academic alternative yet, if one could take into account the general level of attainment of each group of students at the start of the courses, the results of the former might represent only a moderate achievement and of the latter a minor miracle by the teachers concerned. Sometimes this is referred to as 'value added' though it is a difficult measure to quantify and was rarely attempted until recently. Nevertheless, at Ryhope we had a system for comparison which, though simple in concept, provided useful pointers for follow-up.

Each subject received a quota of higher grade passes based on the total number obtained by students taking that subject.[27] Comparing actual results with the quota provided informative and sometimes surprising feedback on which to base future action. Results as varied as 20 per cent of quota and 200 per cent were not unknown though a range between 70 and 130 per cent was more common. The results were discussed with the head of department concerned and occasionally with advisers but were not made generally available. Above and below quota results occurred in all areas of the curriculum and several subjects had substantial variations over a period of time. The method also provided information on the relative performance within subjects of higher and lower attainers. The following table gives the actual results for students taking environmental science in 1982:

Total HGPs per student	1	2	3	4	5	6	7	8	9	Total
Env Science students gaining one or more HGPs in any subject	33	12	8	12	3	11	2	1	-	82
Env Science students gaining an HGP in env science	7	4	3	10	-	10	2	1	-	37

82 students of environmental science obtained at least one higher grade pass overall and achieved a total in all subjects of 232 HGPs (1x33 +

2x12 + 3x8 ...). Assuming that each student took 8 subjects (note 27) the quota was $232 \div 8 = 29$. The results for the subject were good as the percentage of quota (or performance indicator) was $37 \div 29 = 128$ per cent.

The table gives further information. 33 of the group obtained only a single higher grade pass in total but seven of them achieved this in environmental science. On average, only four of the 33 (1 in 8) would be expected in each subject entered. Those achieving 5 or more higher grade passes there are 17 (3+11+2+1) in total and thirteen of these (10+2+1) were successful in environmental science. Thus the department achieved good results both for its borderline and more capable students.

A note on value added

We should expect some correlation between the results of the tests of general ability, described above, with the examination results for the same age group at the end of their fifth year. In preparation for this section I analysed results for the period 1978-1988 for which full records were available. I compared the proportion of Ryhope students with AH3 scores representing the highest 23 per cent nationally (stannines 7, 8 and 9) with the total higher grade passes gained per hundred students. The correlation coefficient was 0.76 representing a significant relationship.[28] A similar result (0.75) was obtained for the percentage gaining five or more higher grade passes. In other words, the greater the proportion of high attainers on entry, the larger the number of higher grade passes in the fifth year!

Not perhaps the most surprising of results but of interest at a time when 'value added' is a popular field of educational research and seen as an antidote to the divisive publication of examination league tables. In fact, there are also many dangers in value added comparisons — for example they can be used to confirm low expectations. Drawing useful conclusions is a difficult task and much depends on the validity of the measures. The AH2/3 tests, for example, were probably the best available at the time but retained many of the deficiencies of intelligence tests including a class-based content biased in favour of students from the higher socio-economic groups.

The main purpose of statistical analysis should be to add insight to strengths and weaknesses of curriculum organisation and teaching method. Subsequent modifications should be based on sound pedagogical principles designed to increase opportunities within a non-selective framework (Chapter 6). Nevertheless some value added information is useful — perhaps essential — if only to defend individual schools from invalid and unfair comparisons from whatever source they may arise.

In the 1970s there were other influences at work which affected examination policy. As comprehensive education expanded a number of schools started to view the system as a hierarchy: GCE for the ablest, traditional CSE examinations for the next best and school-based CSE mode 3 for the 'also-rans'. CSE boards unwittingly assisted this thinking by accepting some reduced content mode 3 schemes in which students could obtain no more than a grade 3 or 4. This made it increasingly difficult for schools such as Sutton Centre, Wyndham (Chapter 6 especially note 7) and Ryhope to use the range of examinations in the most constructive manner; it was always necessary to counter feelings that mode 3, in particular, was less demanding. A second and more serious problem for Ryhope concerned 'spin-off' from widely publicised attacks on the school. Over a period of several years this inevitably affected the expectations of some teachers, students and parents with a consequent effect on school performance. Whilst our results were 'mid-table' for schools in Sunderland according to the director of education's annual statistical analysis,[29] this did less than justice to the effort and application of so many of the staff at all levels.

Feedback from careers

The head of careers kept detailed records of students' post-school destinations with data from the careers service and from former students who came to see him and report progress and prospects. This provided up-to-date feedback on many aspects of work and further study which was put to good effect in careers lessons and in guidance for individual students. In October 1979 I was able to report to parents:

> I have just heard that 92 per cent of last year's fifth year have so far got jobs or are continuing in full time education at colleges or in the sixth form. It keeps up Ryhope's splendid record and is a credit to the joint efforts of teachers, pupils and parents. Thank you for your continuing support.

The figures for students with jobs included those who were on youth training schemes but later, with access to improved information, we were able to distinguish the categories more easily.[30] Former students also went on to a wide variety of degree courses ranging from freshwater biology to psychology and from history of art, film and design to quantity surveying. Others took diplomas in travel and fine art; in clothing management, in civil engineering ...

The annual work experience week was carefully monitored by the careers staff who visited many of the participating firms and organisations and helped to sort out any problems which arose. This played an important part in building up good relationships with commerce and industry. The following letter from a systems manager mentions qualities which are always important:

> It is not common practice for me to write to schools on the subject of pupils who have spent time in my Department on Work Experience Schemes. As an 'old boy' [*the writer was female*] of Ryhope School, however, it is with some pride that I am able to write to you today about DH. D was with the Company for only one week but during that time he was a worthy ambassador of your school. He was polite, of smart appearance, and punctual, but above all he was interested in what we had to show him. He was not afraid to ask questions and those he asked demonstrated some insight into the nature of the work ...

Indeed when Ryhope students were involved outside the school environment they were noted for their interest, alertness and willingness to speak, show initiative and take responsibility. Such qualities were fostered by many of the staff, not least by members of the careers department.

Chapters 10 to 12 have given a glimpse of the aims and work of the school. In the formative years of comprehensive education, there was a steady demand for our staff to speak or run workshops at meetings and conferences whilst, throughout the life of the school, teachers, lecturers and students from local schools and colleges made regular visits. The director of education referred to the liveliness, educational awareness and involvement of Ryhope's teachers many of whom were promoted not only for their personal and professional qualities but also for their knowledge and involvement with educational issues of importance.[31] However, we must now turn to the sustained pressure under which the school operated and to the broad-based efforts to defend the gains achieved.

V

POWERFUL FORCES:
extraordinary happenings

13

Defending Gains

Ideals, ideas and methodology are essential ingredients for creating anything worthwhile. So also is the ability (ie the power) to implement them. Such power is as necessary for constructive action as it is obvious in destructive situations. The period of rapid comprehensive development starting in the late 1960s was characterised nationally by widespread public support but also by a sustained campaign of opposition led by vested interests. Even the most modest developments in the interests of all students met forceful opposition deliberately generated or arising as a result of ignorance, disinformation and uncertainty. The national controversy was mirrored at Ryhope and, throughout Part V, we discuss matters which generated strong emotions both favourable and otherwise. We consider a period of sustained pressure under which the school operated and the extraordinary means by which power was exercised and responded to. At a time of direct local authority involvement in the day to day affairs of schools and, in a borough in which the Schools Sub-committee of the Council acted as the Governing Body for all schools, many of the circumstances described are outwardly different from situations which might arise today under local management. Nevertheless, the nature of the underlying forces which came into play when an attempt was made by a school to introduce and maintain a system of non-selective education has changed little.

Maintaining momentum
During my time at Ryhope I noticed that several of the heads of schools which could properly be described as progressive only stayed in their posts

for about seven years. They moved on to other schools, to lecturing, inspecting, writing and so on and I wondered if seven years might mark a significant stage. Rates of progress in school development plans will have slowed down; vested interests regrouped, and problems of introducing further necessary developments multiplied. The heads, themselves, possibly thought that elsewhere provided greater opportunities to contribute to the cause. Put another way: the committed people I am thinking of wanted to achieve something and felt it was getting increasingly difficult to create what they wanted to in their present circumstances. True or false, it remained an interesting thought especially as, after seven years at Ryhope, the intensity of activity surrounding the school increased markedly. The precise reasons were doubtless complex and debatable but we can gain some insight from contemporary attitudes. By the late 1960s some saw comprehensive education as the great leap forward which was going to solve all our social and educational problems. That was certainly over-optimistic — indeed utopian — but at least it was optimistic. By the mid-1970s the press, at the instigation of its backers, was implying that comprehensive education was the root of all our difficulties and problems. This was nonsense; the strength of the attack on comprehensive education was because of its success and potential. Schools which had developed comprehensive principles furthest were the most likely to be attacked and there were several notable examples (Chapter 6). Each of the schools had its own particular circumstances, its own history, its own mode of development but each was challenging accepted values of the time.

Secret report

In the autumn of 1976, soon after the arrival of a new director of education, Sunderland's senior inspector got in touch with me and said he would be bringing a team of advisers to the school to acquaint themselves more fully with what went on; it was the director's view that not enough was known at the Civic Centre about how schools really operated so all schools were going to be visited in the course of time; it just happened that ours was first. I should have reacted with caution; in fact, I welcomed the initiative and thought it could do nothing but good for the senior administrative staff of the authority to know more about what went on in the schools. So in late November we had a four-day visitation as it was called. All seemed to go off quite well as such affairs normally did: advisers and inspectors went to different classes and talked to members of staff; they spoke to me and I gave them statistics and policy documents and answered questions and philosophised a little about aims and plans — and that seemed to be that. Then in the following February, the director rang to say the report was ready and that it contained serious indictments of the school. He wished to come with some colleagues and discuss it with me that day and hold a staff meeting on the following afternoon. I received the document, labelled 'Strictly confidential', and read it that evening with amazement. Although it ran to 57 pages — and was written in a readable, in parts almost racy, style — I found the statements of 'fact' and analysis incredible. It was a dangerous document indeed.

There were inexcusable errors: the report on the business studies department suggested that it was somewhat lacking. This seemed scarcely surprising as we didn't have a business studies department. Our policy was against early specialisation, feeling that students interested in business and commerce were best served with a broad general education with economics, geography, sociology and typing all available as options in further studies. Then there was the report on music which stated 'The Headmaster professes support and interest but gives little or no clear directive as to the role of the subject in the life of the school'. Following an immediate complaint on this travesty of the truth, a final version of the subject reports came through with the comment replaced by 'The status and ethos of the subject within the school does not reflect the interest, considerable support and keenness shown by the Headmaster to promote a flourishing music department.' I was happy to concur as far as my part was concerned — we had staffing difficulties in music at the time — but the incident showed how easy it was for advisers, whose work I had respected, to get caught up in the 'hidden curriculum' surrounding the visit.

Errors were not confined to subject reports. A miscalculation by the mathematics adviser had our staff teaching much longer than the national average, leaving less time for preparation. After a challenge I received a revised figure well within national norms. More importantly, the report contained serious mis-representations not least in its 'analysis' of examination results. There was no clear distinction between results associated with the selective entry and those with the comprehensive intake; a prominent table concerning O-level results noted a 'decline' in several subjects including separate sciences without linking the change to the introduction of integrated science as the preferred and, eventually, only science option. Reduced numbers in history were highlighted without mention that we had widened the choice for students by introducing economics and sociology. Wider choice, popular at the time, obviously implied fewer results per subject but the total for the three subjects was almost exactly the same as the earlier figure for history alone. The report treated O-level results in all subjects separately from CSEs rather than in combination. It failed to even mention higher grade passes (Chapter 10, note 24) which provided an important basis for comparison in a curriculum where both examinations were used constructively to achieve well-defined aims. Many of the report's criticisms concerned curricular matters which had been discussed and approved with advisers at the time of their introduction whilst, throughout the report, the comprehensive approach inherent in the overall objective of the local authority was ignored.

Philosophy of the inspectorate

Unusually for an inspector's report, this one revealed some of its underlying philosophy. It expressed criticism of 'the extent of the school's common core curriculum' (a concept central to the national curriculum) and recommended us to reconsider the place of social studies in it (the vital role of this subject is discussed in Chapter 7). The science report questioned the place of integrated science (highly recommended on introduction of the national curriculum) whilst the main report noted 'a comparative lack of academic competition' Rank orders of students perhaps? Bands and streams? The sixth form was said to suffer from 'a lack of separate identity' (exclusiveness?) and half a page was allocated to the case for prefects (Chapter 11) involving sixth form students. The report added 'academic achievement is not apparently stressed, or targets set, as requirements for entry'. In other words we operated an open access non-selective policy for all who wished to stay on in the sixth form and for whom we could provide suitable courses. We also encouraged students to explore alternatives such as courses at colleges of further education and make informed choices. On discipline I was correctly quoted as believing that, when in trouble, students need guidance and a strategy for improvement and that punishment, as such, is often a counter-productive activity. With revealing imagery the report went on to claim for punishment that 'intelligently applied it can purge the guilt of the transgressor, and reinforce the self-esteem of the innocent'. Equally revealing imagery occurred in the statement commencing 'A child in school uniform tends to behave as a school child ...' (reproduced in full in Chapter 9, note 14).

Management methods were criticised. The report summarises the headteacher's role as 'to find the right staff for the right job, to make clear what the job is, and to leave them to get on with it. This does not appear to have happened at Ryhope School'. Such a *laissez-faire* approach is certainly not a democratic one. In fact applicants for posts received substantial written details of the aims and organisation of the school and the requirements of the post at a time when this was by no means universal practice. Extensive interviews added clarification and I talked personally to successful applicants in detail concerning their role. The inspectorate's simplistic approach (one notices the absence of any mention of accountability) may be fine as long as all goes smoothly. When it does not, it is the duty of the head to intervene and this, perhaps, accounts for a further comment: 'His style of leadership appears to have owed more to autocracy than democracy.' There are two replies to this charge: firstly, a certain minimum acceptance of comprehensive principles and methods is a pre-requisite for all members of staff; in the overwhelming majority of traditionally orientated schools, freedom for individual initiative is dependent on rigid adherence to the dominant philosophy of the institution. Secondly, as we have seen, so many of the best ideas at Ryhope came from members of staff including those in the first years of their teaching careers demonstrating that there was a high degree of flexibility especially for those willing to be flexible themselves.

Methods used by the inspection team were dubious despite a claim that 'If the Inspectorate feel that they have had to express extreme views in this report they have done so according to professional standards'. Throughout the report there was evidence of a pre-agreed line as advisers, consciously or otherwise, made similar comments in widely different circumstances — a clear case of the 'halo' effect (Chapter 9, note 2). Anecdotal evidence suggests that several members of the team asked teachers leading questions such as 'What do you think is wrong with this school?' whilst at least one meeting took place with a small group of teachers including some committee members of the staff council, set up a few years previously, who came out convinced that I was on my way out.[1] The report had quotes from unnamed teachers including one, described as a 'senior member of staff', referring to his 'abdication from curriculum because I don't agree with it'. This statement was apparently received without remonstrance from the interviewer who was himself or herself a senior officer of the local authority. There is a place for anonymous observations in an inspection but there is a corresponding duty to meticulously check out the facts. Here we had the technique of denunciation. Naturally the report contained valid criticisms and observations but, in the light of the very different educational and ideological starting points of the writer of the report and the concept of comprehensive education as set out in earlier chapters of this book, it was impossible to enter into profitable discussion as widely as one would have wished: a tremendous effort had gone into creating the school and it was not to be abandoned on biased evidence.

Immediate reactions

The director of education declared the report confidential and it was never shown to the staff; instead he told them that it contained areas of serious criticism concerning the quality of education at Ryhope and (by implication) that this was no fault of theirs. This naturally increased uncertainties in the minds of the staff whatever their view on educational developments at the school. In his talk the director grouped criticisms into four areas: divisions within the staff; usage of the premises; examination results, and organisation — the last including a need for clearly stated aims and objectives. We shall consider them in reverse order.

The importance of a clear written statement is fully acknowledged (Chapter 10) though the fact that Sunderland's overall objective was virtually disowned by all who tried to reverse the direction of the school is another matter. The basis for allegations of inadequacy of the organisation were never clear to me. My policy, especially in the formative years of the school, was to allow flexibility within a managed framework, so that middle management, as well as individual teachers, could exercise their skills in ways which drew on their personal and professional strengths. This policy was, perhaps, insufficiently defined in places and, as our experience grew and best practice developed, some of the flexibility became unnecessary and even counter-productive. One must aim for an optimum balance between uniformity and flexibility in any school organisation so that teachers can do a good job and students and parents feel that the school is effective but not inflexible. In 1977, many teachers thought this was about right but, in retrospect, it may be that the balance was rather too much towards flexibility.

Examination results have been discussed in Chapters 10 and 12. The inspectorate might legitimately have commented on policy concerning the ratio of CSE to GCE O-level entries but it was highly disingenuous to present their report in a manner which implied a level of overall performance below the true position.

The school had problems in usage of the premises and in March, eight months before the visitation, the chairman of the Education Committee had written to me concerning high maintenance costs and vandalism. My reply expressed concern together with an analysis of the situation as a preliminary to further action. The perimeter of the school site was well over a mile with open access along much of its length while the caretaker's house was out of sight of the most easily accessible areas but it was not until much later in the school's history that security services were employed.[2] Nevertheless I accepted that internal damage during school hours certainly could not all be put down to wear and tear and saw the fundamental problem arising from 'the extensive use made of the building ... in the interests of the overwhelming majority of responsible and conscientious pupils'. I made several suggestions but did not, at that stage, consider putting all students out of the building at break and lunch time. I concluded my response 'As we know from discussion that the majority of pupils are as concerned as staff about unnecessary damage and are anxious not to lose their privileges I intend to involve them directly in the planning stage'. I sent a copy to the acting director of education at the time (the new director took up his appointment in the summer) and received a reply saying he found it 'most useful and illuminating' and offering to help in any way. He later proposed a working party of senior school staff and local authority officers and a preliminary meeting was held in mid-September. Among several proposals, Sunderland's senior and assistant inspectors agreed to visit the school on frequent occasions to observe the situation at first hand and to discuss the question of access and supervision with me.

Three weeks later, the staff council committee commenced an independent survey into vandalism which included questionnaires to staff and a sample of students. Their report was ready in mid-November, shortly before the inspectors' visitation. It contained emotive language reflecting an approach not shared by several teachers who spoke to me and, at a meeting with the officers, I 'regretted the tone of the staff council's report' but agreed that 'our present level of supervision and proper use and care of the building have proved inadequate'. Visits by the local inspectors to view the situation at first hand did not materialise and my response was to establish an internal working party consisting of three senior teachers and two senior heads of department. The work of this group was overtaken by the inspector's report and followed by the exclusion of students from the building at break and lunch times. In use of the building, as with organisation and examination policy, constructive improvements could have been achieved through cooperation between school and local authority but day-to-day management becomes very difficult if this process is used as an instrument for ideological change. The 'secret dossier' treatment of the report heightened anxieties and gave impetus to any existing feelings of a division between head and local authority.

The final category of the director's criticisms was of a different type. Divisions within the staff did exist and one must neither underestimate nor exaggerate their importance. Many schools have quite sharp differences among their staffs concerning philosophy and method. In the more formally organised establishments in the 1960s and '70s opposition manifested itself in criticisms of rigidities and restrictions, corporal punishment, selection into streams and bands, over-formality and so on. None of this prevented the schools functioning normally within the Articles of Government and their local authorities' procedures. There were three differences at Ryhope. Firstly, pioneer work was being done so that comprehensive education could be a reality for the students already in the school as well as laying foundations for future generations. This required educational development on a wide front supported by continuous servicing and monitoring; inevitably there were problems and imperfections as well as outstanding opportunities taken up within and beyond the classroom by many teachers. In these circumstances, opposition centred around calls for greater conformity in all aspects of school life, linking academic achievement with more formal and selective teaching methods and less flexibility in disciplinary procedures — in other words a retreat from the principles of comprehensive education established in earlier chapters. Secondly and crucially, it appeared that a small group of teachers felt they had the tacit support of some officers of the authority (and members of the Education Committee?) to act as a brake on more general developments at the school. It was possible to persuade some teachers that the head's policy was responsible for most problems which arose whether in teaching method or in disciplinary matters. With the latter there was an additional factor resulting from the vigour with which the National Association of Schoolmasters and Union of Women Teachers (NAS/UWT) campaigned in the region for the right of their members to administer corporal punishment. New arrivals to the staff were particularly vulnerable to indoctrination because all had to modify their methods to a certain extent, depending on their previous experience, and naturally needed time to adjust.[3] Despite these problems the staff as a whole continued to work collaboratively to meet the requirements and challenges of a modern comprehensive school.

However, another factor, surely unique to Ryhope, was about to emerge. This involved an attempt, over and above any unofficial liaisons, to establish an alternative decision making process by an extension of the role of the teaching staff and, in particular, that of middle and senior management. Its aim was to change the direction of the school.

Working party or Trojan Horse?

In March 1977, a month after the arrival of the inspector's report, I was called to a meeting with the director and chairman of the Education Committee to review progress. We discussed various developments and I accepted the director's suggestion of a staff working party to consist of heads of department, heads of year and other senior staff with a remit to examine all aspects of the school's development. Almost as an after-thought he asked if I would also agree to a mutually acceptable member of his staff attending meetings of the working party as a facilitator. Again I agreed and he suggested the authority's area inspector with whom I had a good relationship. I left the meeting thinking this was all a little unusual and the numbers very large for a working party (over twenty five in all) but, nonetheless, an arrangement that could bring a number of benefits. The first meeting was to be two days later at 4.30pm following a short meeting of heads of department and heads of year to complete existing business. I had asked the facilitator if he would come to the school at 3.30pm so that we could discuss a general plan of action. He was delayed — to receive a briefing from the director, as it later emerged — and we commenced the first meeting of the working party without prior consultation. A head of year asked if the head was to be chairman and a considerable discussion followed. I was agreeable that others might take the chair on specific issues but insisted on remaining the resident chairman in accordance with the duties and responsibilities of a head under the Articles of Government.[4] Shortly after this I withdrew from the meeting, considering it unconstitutional and not wishing to compromise my position in the future. The minutes record the subsequent discussion and a decision that the facilitator 'would go to Mr Copland with the advice that the meeting would go better and would make more progress with himself in the chair ...' So the director's representative had agreed to become chairman — a course of action, as I learned later, proposed by the director at the briefing earlier in the afternoon. A remarkable interpretation of my agreement to accept a facilitator.

This happened on a Thursday and the next working party meeting was scheduled for the following Monday. There was much to be done. After consulting the regional official of the National Union of Teachers I requested an urgent meeting with the director. After my representations he agreed that, in view of the Articles of Government, the working party could only be advisory, not executive and that he would put this in writing in a letter to me. With this vital clarification and despite other concerns including the lack of written terms of reference, standing orders and even a voting procedure I agreed to resume membership of the working party under the chairmanship of the facilitator.

The staff working party lasted for just over two months. It held thirteen often fraught and lengthy meetings and there were several associated full staff meetings (at which the facilitator was not present). Some positive developments emerged[5] but working party discussions often led to frustration on all sides. On several occasions the chairman allowed discussion on papers distributed by members at the start of a meeting leaving no time for perusal. Corporal punishment and length of lessons proved to be key topics in terms of time taken and attempts to make radical changes. On 25th April, 16 working party members voted for corporal punishment with 1 against (myself) and 1 abstention. Seven members had sent apologies and two left before the vote. At least two of those voting for corporal punishment were against it personally but, in a highly charged atmosphere, were persuaded of the rights of colleagues to make their own choices in the matter — a sentiment held strongly by teachers on a variety of issues.[6] A full staff meeting was arranged for 28th of April and a ballot agreed with the single question 'Do you want corporal punishment to be available within the school?' — wording which again appealed to the 'right to choose' aspect. The result: Yes 51, No 13, with 2 absent. Several teachers had issued discussion papers on the topic and one, reflecting another strong influence on the staff, finished: 'Sorry to attack your principles, Mr Copland. I'd be quite happy to keep things as they are, but not with that report on the boss's desk and those inspector chaps demanding changes'. I repeated to the director my unwillingness to permit corporal punishment and left the matter at that. According to the minutes of what proved to be the last meeting of the working party (26th May), the facilitator 'recalled that, on corporal punishment, there had been "an expression of feeling", as a result of which he had reported back to the director that there seemed to be an area of disagreement between most of the staff and the headmaster. The director had discussed this with Mr Copland, and we were still awaiting a decision'.

A discussion on length of lesson, a topic known to have the director's support, also went on for several meetings.[7] Fundamental changes to the structure of the timetable, built up over several years to meet a wide range of curricular objectives, had massive implications and by May delays were endangering the planning and construction of the timetable for the following September. It came as no surprise, therefore, that at the 26th May meeting the facilitator also reported that 'the director had made a decision on the matter of length of periods. It was that the school should keep its present four lesson day ... because of the short time available to make changes'. The facilitator had still further news, this time concerning a person with widely acknowledged legal and political acumen 'Now there was a new chairman of the Education Committee ... he might not favour the idea of a staff working party and might therefore suggest something different for Ryhope'. This occurred on a Thursday and, on the following Monday, I held a normal head of department and head of year meeting which dealt with routine and planning items. Except for a subsequent report to the staff by the director, the working party did not figure again in the life of the school; and corporal punishment was never permitted. So ended the first of a series of attempts to make fundamental changes which were to cover a period of seven years until, in April 1984, the local paper had a news item 'Ryhope School gets "Full Marks" ' concerning a letter from the Secretary of State to Sunderland's director of education.

Publicity and policy

It is scarcely surprising that rumours had abounded from soon after the arrival of the inspector's report. Teachers were asked by their students 'Is Mr Copland getting the sack?' while people whom I knew in the locality asked 'Is everything all right at school?' Whilst such circumstances tend to weaken the basis of authority in any school, the majority of our students

— even the youngest — quickly developed a remarkably mature outlook. It was to be further tested.

Press and governors

In the sixth months following the end of the staff working party in May records show that the staff put commendable effort into educational and organisational development and continued to provide a wide range of activities for students. In November a small team of HMIs made a helpful three-day visit to the school.[8] However, on the morning following their visit (18th November) the Newcastle *Journal* newspaper had a full page spread with selected extracts from the local inspector's report; it turned out that my copy had been taken from a cupboard in my room during the half term break, photocopied and given to the press at a time chosen to make maximum impact. Under a headline 'School under microscope' there was no shortage of quotations including comments on examination results in an article which commenced 'Inspectors called for a complete rethink about the running of the school, after looking at the headmaster's progressive methods.' Naturally, publication of these extracts was damaging to staff and parent morale. The governors met on 28th November 1977 to consider the situation and received two reports from me. One was entitled 'Summary of action since the working party finished at Whitsun' and the second 'A few thoughts on the successes of Ryhope School' with the latter confined to conventional academic successes and designed to set the published material in context.

The governors adopted a 7-point plan for the school which included a second deputy head and an additional teacher for special needs. Both of these were very welcome and soon afterwards all schools were allocated second deputies. Two other proposals created major problems. Despite earlier acknowledgment of the time scale involved, the 70 minute lesson module was to be changed to 35 minutes from the beginning of the spring term involving a major rewrite of the timetable within 15 working days.[9] Another of the points in its original form stated 'The headmaster is recommended to discuss sympathetically with the heads of department of the school the arrangements for mixed ability teaching with a view to permitting alternative arrangements such as setting to operate in *the year group that the teachers concerned consider appropriate*' (my italics). In other words, decisions on selective and non-selective teaching were to pass on a piecemeal basis to individual teachers — a recipe for curriculum anarchy. There was no mention of Sunderland's commitment to non-selective methods in their overall objective and certainly no parallel arrangement was envisaged for other schools in the borough in which the head favoured selection and some heads of department might have preferred non-selective groups. Discussions were to be completed in time for the new arrangements to operate from the start of the spring term. The governors accepted my amendment to change the wording in italics to 'the year group considered most appropriate' thus returning operational responsibility to the head under the Articles of Government. The remainder of the seven points included reviews of policies for the curriculum, examinations and student responsibility.

A day or two later the chairman of the Education Committee (also leader of the Labour Council and chair of the Schools Sub-committee which acted as the Governing Body) addressed the staff in the presence of myself and the director. I recorded my impressions of this and other events a few weeks later in a letter to the NUT regional official. I referred to a 'hectoring tone' taken by the chairman, possibly arising from annoyance that I had responded to the publicity about the school through a local television interview (he preferred to handle such matters himself). 'He left the staff in no doubt that the Governing Body would sort the head out if he didn't conform and indicated that his views on education were very different to mine'. I concluded by saying that attempts to embarrass a head before his staff cannot be in the interests of the profession and that the chairman's remarks 'left some members demoralised and others buoyant that my position was becoming untenable'.

With the approval of the local authority, who provided a supply teacher, I took the curriculum coordinator off his important teaching commitments immediately after the governors' meeting as the only way to meet the deadline for timetable changes; even so, he was unable to finish alterations until after the spring term started. Most subjects preferred to stay with 70-minute lessons, some had a mixture of 70 and 35 minutes and, if I remember correctly, only music and modern languages went for 35 minutes only. The teaching areas for these subjects were on opposite sides of the main road and as, logistically, most 35 minute lessons had to follow each other on the timetable it was often a case of languages in the south block followed by music in the north or vice-versa. This led to considerable loss of teaching time and is typical of problems likely to arise when attempts are made to prescribe the detail of a school's organisation from outside. I held discussions with all heads of department regarding grouping of students based on a questionnaire which I prepared for the purpose. This covered policy on allocation of both staff and students to teaching groups, monitoring of student progress, curricula and schemes of work. The results were more promising than expected under the circumstances. Several subjects including English, social studies and all creative subjects remained non-selective throughout the year groups. Except in modern languages there was no setting before the third year and only a little then.[10] The integrated science option maintained non-selective groups up to the end of the fourth year.

Chairman and parents

The spring term of 1978 was a notable one. We were without a deputy head as the previous holder had been promoted to a headship too late for the school to obtain a replacement.[11] Working parties on examinations and responsibilities met regularly under the terms of the 7-point plan and a governors' meeting was held at the end of January. Following his own assessment as well as my criticisms, the director of education withdrew the local inspector's report replacing it with one of his own. Though too late to avert the worst of the damage, this was nonetheless a welcome step. A governors' meeting was held at the end of January and its proceedings were largely based on the director's report.[12] It was decided that the working parties were to report by the end of the term and the governors would meet again at the start of the summer term to receive the results. The chairman announced that he would hold a meeting for parents in March after agreeing a date with the Ryhope School Association. Later in the term teacher unions commenced industrial action in support of claims for improved pay and conditions of service and I agreed arrangements with union representatives for sending students home when supervision could not be provided.[13]

On the evening of Wednesday 8th March 1978 the chairman, accompanied on the stage by the director, one or two governors and myself, addressed a packed, all-ticket meeting in the school hall. Industrial action reduced teacher attendance but at least one union left it to members' discretion. My letter to the NUT regional officer gave my viewpoint at the time: 'The chairman gives an impression that parents can rely on the governors to sort things out and, by implication, that the head will have to be forced against his will.' He failed to indicate my cooperation expressed at the two governors meetings and 'as a result, staff morale hit rock bottom ... Teachers working for my removal are greatly encouraged and once again my authority is publicly undermined.' The effect on parents was not exactly confidence-building either. One, a member of the local Conservative Party, gained applause from those around him, as well as the next day's headlines, by calling for my resignation. However, the chairman knew the rules and referred to contracts of service and so on. Others alleging lack of standards had clearly been influenced by rumour. After a while, a parent in a different part of the hall, almost certainly making her first-ever speech in public, spoke up in favour — not an easy thing to do in the charged circumstances. She also gained applause and others, including a member of the Education Committee who had had two children at the school, then spoke in support. Welcome as this was, it was still a very difficult meeting and, finally, having received permission from the chairman, I said a few words on aims and methods in an endeavour to send people home on a more positive note.[14]

Union input

Two days later, I saw the director and said, in effect that the parents' meeting, following eighteen months of publicity and lack of local authority support, was the last straw. I told him that I had learned just before setting out to see him that members of the NAS/UWT had passed a resolution of no confidence in my leadership. In my opinion, the only honourable course for the authority was public support or dismissal proceedings. In fact, the authority did not intend the former, whilst there were political ramifications with the latter which they also wished to avoid; Ryhope School had a reputation in the region for decency and hope far beyond its immediate environs. The vote had an undeniable personal impact but it was necessary to assess the situation in the whole political and social context of associated actions and events which had led up to it. In particular, lack of support from the authority caused many teachers to fear for their professional development and even their job security.

The chairman requested a meeting with me on the following Monday at which the director was also present. This was more productive than expected as we both accepted that things could not go on as at present and agreed the main line of a policy to put before the governors. I noted at the time, however, that 'the director appears to have reservations especially on the work side where he seems determined to continue to intervene directly on curriculum and teaching organisation'. The NAS/UWT, with 30 members, sent a copy of their resolution 'with the very best interests of Ryhope School, its pupils and parents, at heart' to the governors and to the press (!) 'to redress the balance of public criticism'. The Assistant Masters Association/Association of Assistant Mistresses (AMA/AAM), with 11 members, passed an identically worded motion next day[15] but sent it only to the governors whilst the NUT's 27 members, at a meeting which I decided not to attend in order not to inhibit discussion, prepared a statement for the governors which deplored 'the failure of the governors and director in not supporting the teaching staff position in public meetings and after publicity' and to request 'a statement of confidence and support for teaching staff to be made public by the chairman'. The director was requested to 'take early measures to end uncertainty, and effect such changes as are deemed necessary by him to create in Ryhope a satisfactory and stable working situation'.

Thus the chairman's meeting with parents had already had major consequences and more were to follow. On receipt of the first two resolutions the director met the union representatives; he requested the NAS/UWT not to publish but this was declined. The unions asked permission to present their case to the governors which was agreed, the presentation to be made through their regional officials with written supporting statements covering specific complaints. I understand that this engendered much activity in the last days of the spring term spreading over to the holiday. Perhaps it was not so easy to obtain precise complaints on specific actions of the head.

Easter came early in 1978 and the governors met on the first afternoon of the new term, Monday 3rd April. In the morning I welcomed the new deputy head and said I must leave shortly to meet the regional officers of the NAS/UWT and Joint Four (an umbrella organisation which included the AMA/AAM), each in the presence of the director, to receive their detailed complaints. I also had an appointment after lunch with the regional official of the NUT who was to accompany me at the governors' meeting. Naturally there was more than a little speculation by the staff on the likely outcome particularly as it affected my future. The deputy head, who was to exert a major steadying influence in the weeks and months ahead, often referred in his inimitable manner to the spectacular initiation to his duties and responsibilities which awaited him on that first day. I received a letter during the morning from the secretary of the Sunderland Local Joint Four with four points set out in general terms. The first claimed 'lack of support to the staff on matters of discipline, especially concerned with security of buildings, treatment of disruptive pupils and sanctions to enforce rules'.[16] Others referred to 'lack of progress from the working parties set up in January 1978' (which had been affected by industrial action); 'inadequacy of systems of reporting pupil progress and assessment' (hardly consistent with the developments recorded in Chapter 12), and 'lack of consultation and forward planning with regard to fourth year options ... also the same kind of complaint with respect to sixth form minority time' (The curriculum development recorded in Chapter 10 would have been impossible without consultation and forward planning — indeed I believe our record in this field was second to none and that the 'charges' were based on hearsay and/or personal disagreements with particular decisions). The letter, however, concluded by stressing that 'Our Association is giving support to our members' specific complaints and not to matters which could be seen as conflict of principle or ideology'. This was a clear indication that the local Joint Four recognised that there were deeper issues below the surface of specific complaints.

The NAS/UWT had no written report available but my notes show that their verbal statement covered similar issues to those in the letter from the Joint Four. The NAS/UWT added that standards of achievement had been an issue because of mixed ability classes too far up the school (although all heads of department had been consulted only four months previously under the Governors' 7-point plan). One specific complaint claimed that a fourth year integrated science course had been put on without proper consultation and with the minimum of preparation time. In fact the suitability of the course for our needs was assessed during a year and half of study, discussion and attendance at meetings by the head of department, deputy head (also a scientist) and myself; I was the last to be persuaded. Neither the teacher who had submitted the 'complaint' nor the union representative could have consulted the head of science. Another complaint followed an addition to the staff at mid-term which also involved the internal transfer of a young and well respected teacher from one teaching department to another for which he was equally qualified. Consultation showed that the proposed transfer met the teacher's career development wishes and had the support of his existing head of department and the local authority adviser. During these exploratory discussions, the transfer was confirmed with the teacher. Only afterwards was my attention drawn to the fact that the head of the receiving department, which was to gain an additional member of staff, had not been consulted. This was entirely unintentional and I immediately went to the person concerned and gave an unreserved apology. The omission and implied professional discourtesy were reported in the union submission but not my apology. This was a further case of accusation by dossier.

At the governors meeting itself, officials of the NAS/UWT and Joint Four presented their reports followed by the NUT who spoke on their statement. In my response, prepared at very short notice, I endeavoured to correct some of the inaccuracies, set more generalised complaints in context and emphasise that I had never knowingly acted unprofessionally towards a member of staff. (I attached high importance to correct practice and procedure both as a professional and as a trade unionist.) I added that I had always come to the support of any member of staff who had sought help, for example in cases involving disruptive behaviour. With questions and observations by governors this took up the whole meeting which was then adjourned to the next day to discuss the reports of the working parties on examinations and pupil responsibility. The adjourned session proved to be useful and generally constructive although the reports were not fully in the form originally intended as industrial action had prevented staff involvement and ratification of the final stages. As a result the governors resolved to meet again on 18th April requiring intensive action at school to complete the reports in time for the governors to receive them a few days in advance of the meeting.

Governors' plan

The final versions of the working party reports were received favourably though with reservations on one or two points. The governors voted 7-3 against corporal punishment and then presented a 10-point plan which had been read out to me on the telephone by the director two hours before the meeting. The chairman noted that the governors might go beyond their powers under the Articles of Government but asserted that they had a moral duty to spell out what they wanted to see done. He was therefore asking me to implement them, not threatening. If the governors' wishes were not carried out they would take legal advice; I ought to carry them out and the governors hoped they would be carried out. He would prepare and issue a statement to the press in the morning.

Point 1 of the Governors' Plan expressed the belief that 'Performance can be improved by regular yearly examinations throughout the school ...

and by extending setting'. Point 2 asked for further consideration to be given to student responsibilities and point 3 announced their intention to conduct a referendum of parents on uniform (Chapter 11). The school's proposals for more flexible lengths of lesson and for clarification of disciplinary procedures were supported in points 4 and 5 whilst point 6 stressed the importance of school assemblies (without referring to religious worship).

Point 7 required an organisational change to make the south block, the former modern school building, a lower school for years 1 and 2. (This instruction was deceptively straightforward but had logistic and educational ramifications likely to negate any advantages). Point 8 supported a school proposal to formulate job specifications for staff[17] and point 9 stated that 'the Governors will review the progress of the school each term on the basis of a report presented by the head after full consultation with his colleagues'. Finally point 10 noted that 'the Governors expect that, in future, significant changes in the conduct and curriculum of the school will not be implemented without full consultation with the staff and without the Governors' approval'.

Again there was no mention of Sunderland's overall objective; indeed point 1 indicated movement in the opposite direction while points 9 and 10 were clearly designed to prevent further non-selective developments. Some of the points directly involved the organisation and management of the school rather than its general conduct and curriculum (the sphere of responsibility of the governors set out in the Articles of Government). I therefore gave formal notice, as previously advised, that I intended to consult my union on the proposals. My return to school on the following morning occasioned surprise among some members of staff who had predicted my demise and, I understand, some loss of wagers made with colleagues. Most welcomed what seemed to be the end of a period of high profile and mentally draining experiences. The NUT advised a low key acceptance of the 10 points together with an expectation that 'in applying the recommendations in matters of internal organisation, management and discipline of the school, clauses 8c(i) and 8c(iv) of the Articles of Government will be fully implemented'.[18]

My thinking at the time was summed up in a memorandum to staff near the end of term as the second deputy head was about to take up his duties. Referring to a meeting between the chairman, director and myself in May, I stated 'Following clarification on some matters, I accepted the 10 points ... as a satisfactory basis for future development. The single most important matter for clarification concerned the reference to increased setting in point 1. It was accepted that this had already taken place under the 7-point programme. Staff will be aware that pupil grouping is a matter of particular concern to me and I expect to be involved directly (or through the second deputy head) in any future discussions and developments'. The summer term saw the re-establishment of more normal and thus productive relationships among all concerned.

14

Politics, Inspections and Parental Preference

A day or two after the governors' meeting of 18th April 1978 there was a knock on my door and in came a young teacher who had taken a full part in keeping the pot boiling through previous months. Though retaining a low profile at all times, he had been particularly busy helping to assemble the 'complaints' submitted by two of the unions. He arrived with a friendly and purposeful smile and a recommendation concerning curriculum development which could make a useful addition to our option choices in the fourth and fifth years and for which he was qualified to take a leading part. Like several of his similarly-minded colleagues he had considerable professional skill and I welcomed the proposal which was implemented in due course. On his departure from the room I was left with mixed feelings but smiled as I noted the change of relationship following the degree of support for school policy implied in the decision of the governors.

School and community

With the re-establishment of a more workable relationship between school and local authority, the majority of Ryhope's teachers, retaining their reputation for knowledge and experience, continued to be active in curriculum development and teaching method as well as in other aspects of school life. Whilst staff critics remained, so also did teachers who identified closely, though never uncritically or sycophantically, with the general aims and direction of the school. Other teachers, whilst not holding strong views on philosophy, wanted to do a good job without overt hassle and many who must have voted for the no-confidence motions joined their colleagues in making significant contributions to the development of the school. However, there were still external influences with which to contend.

On 26th April the Sunderland *Echo* again carried a front page headline, this time with ' "Tories" move to oust Ryhope headmaster', which described an attempt to bring a no-confidence motion to the Borough Council meeting that night. The Labour leader of the Council replied vigorously and the issue remained prominent for a few days. The leader appealed 'once again to all those concerned to allow the school to have a period of calm'.[1] Nevertheless the reluctance of the authority to identify with the aims of the school continued. The director addressed a staff meeting on 2nd May and wrote to me next day saying 'how disappointed' he had felt with my answer to one of the questions and I responded expressing 'acute concern at the unbalanced picture of Ryhope School' which had been accepted and annoyance that 'my total cooperation at all times over the 7-point plan has been consistently ignored at meetings of governors, staff and public'. Under the Articles of Government I requested a meeting with the chairman of governors, who was accompanied by the vice-chair, director and deputy director, to clarify remaining misunderstandings. It was reasonably successful. All this had a continuing effect in the community at a time when spare school places in secondary schools continued to increase. It was no surprise, therefore, that our intake fell leading to further anxieties but it was important not to be distracted from concentration on the education of those in the school.[2] The following school year was relatively free of extraneous hassle and, acting as a constant encouragement, many parents and students remained highly supportive of the school and recognised the contribution and commitment of the staff. Press reports were concerned with sporting events, good works and an item on the first students in Sunderland to take the City and Guilds Foundation Course in construction.

In October 1979, local Conservatives leafleted students outside the school gates as they were leaving for home. Several returned immediately to let me know what was happening. The hand-out from 'Silksworth Conservative Ward Committee' was brief. It read:

Dear Parent,

You will have recently received a letter from Dick Copland, headmaster of Ryhope School. He omits to give details of actual results for the examinations. Gordon Bagier MP refuses to accept any responsibility for the school. Your own Labour councillors are strangely silent. Do you ever wonder why?[3]

The press had been alerted and a photographer was present at the scene. A couple of days later the Conservative spokesperson on Sunderland Council was interviewed on local radio. In answer to a question she gave the startling information that 'I do not see this as a political leaflet at all' and the less surprising information that she had written to the junior education minister Rhodes Boyson concerning the school.

One afternoon during the autumn half-term the Newcastle *Journal* rang to say they had received a complaint from 'a Conservative councillor'[4] who was complaining that the Gideon Society had been refused entry to Ryhope School to issue New Testaments to pupils. The councillor was concerned for the moral welfare of the pupils. The *Journal* had telephoned a contact at the Gideons who told them this had happened eight years ago and it was their policy not to ask again. I told the reporter that I had no recollection of the matter or the circumstances but could see no objection to the issue of New Testaments *to pupils whose parents wish them to receive one*. I pointed out that some parents would not want religious material given out at school. I telephoned a businessman connected with the Gideons and gained the impression that he was somewhat embarrassed by the affair. Later that afternoon I learned that the Conservative education spokesperson on Sunderland Council had been in touch with the Journal, declared herself greatly concerned that pupils from the school had not had an opportunity to receive the New Testaments and was considering submitting an emergency resolution to Sunderland Council at its meeting that evening. In fact the matter was not taken further either by the press or the Conservatives but shows how assiduously ways were sought to disparage the school. This particular affair had apparently been sparked off that morning by an item about the Gideons on local radio.

There were other matters which also received a somewhat over-the-top treatment. For example shortly after the Gideons affair the area administrator at a nearby hospital wrote to me asking assistance in dealing with a problem at lunchtimes when a few young people had started going up to the hospital causing some disturbance. Despite lack of specific information I assured him of all possible assistance and asked a senior colleague to investigate. A day or two later the affair figured in a press statement from the area health authority with mention that a 'Ryhope headmaster' had already been written to. A relatively minor incident but indicative of the diverse ways in which public confidence in a school is put under pressure.

Inspections and visitations

Full inspection

A week's full inspection by nineteen of Her Majesty's Inspectors occurred during the last week in February 1980. Despite limitations of such operations arising from the ideological stance of the inspectorate (Chapter 1),[5] most of the staff were quite encouraged by the general tone of the verbal reports given to departments and senior management at the end of the visit. As was customary at the time four of the team presented an oral report to the governors a fortnight later and I was able to confirm to the staff that it was in similar terms to that given to subject departments, the deputy head and myself. The written report was received in October and, as other schools had found, it stressed limitations and deficiencies.[6] Despite aspects of the work of the school selected for praise, it failed to respond constructively to the needs and aspirations involved in a non-selective approach. On the contrary, the report gave strength to teachers and local authority officers who wished to see an erosion of non-selective teaching. For example in the conclusions it is stated as a 'serious weakness' that 'the needs of all-ability teaching have not been fully realised and met, nor are the arguments for it accepted by all involved'.[7] In curricular matters 'Innovation and experimentation; some of it with inadequate planning' was contrasted with the need for 'consolidation and firmly-based development'.[8] Nevertheless the inspectors added their weight to the call for a period of consolidation and peace 'with all parties cooperating for the good of the students.'

The governors considered the findings at a meeting in November and the director invited me to submit a report outlining action taken or proposed and listed some 'general issues that HM Inspectorate appear to consider critical'. He concluded that 'apart from certain general issues, notably premises and adequacy of resources, the detailed follow up to the report is essentially a matter for departmental review within the school with the assistance of the Committee's inspectorate'. My report described the visit itself as stimulating with many useful suggestions from HMIs which the teaching staff were busy working on. As well as work in subject departments follow-up had included an anti-litter campaign and a graffiti clear up tackled on a whole school basis.[9] Imperfections in timetable design — a direct result of the intervention of the governors four years previously in their 10-point plan — were eased by returning to mainly 70 minute lessons; criticisms of staff communication led to amendments to the committee structure and, coinciding with the arrival of a new teacher as senior remedial specialist, we completely re-appraised the system of communication between remedial specialists and the staff.

Criticisms concerning lack of pace in the first two years gave us a deeper insight into a problem we had raised with the team at the start of their visit.[10] We increased the number of experienced teachers and resources for these years and gave a senior teacher overall responsibility for seeing that methods of assessment, homework policies etc. were fully effective.[11] As well as dealing in detail with specific criticisms my report examined the relationship of the inspection to Sunderland's overall objective noting that the inspectors had not clearly identified several major initiatives taken at the school in support of one or more sections of the objective. My report also noted that our non-selective approach opened up the possibility that all pupils should have *'throughout their school life* the opportunity to develop their talents to the full in the main areas of knowledge, culture, science and practical skills'; Ryhope was 'one of the few schools in the country in which all options are open to all pupils'. The basis on which the HMI report had been written made it difficult to 'adequately assess the success of some important features of Ryhope School especially those which bear most closely on the implications of comprehensive education.' With the conclusion of the governors' meeting, which was generally supportive, we looked forward to an extended period of normality and progress.[12]

Local visitation

Every school had a designated HMI but it was not until June 1981 that the one for Ryhope, who had led the team of inspectors, returned for a routine visit. He talked to me on arrival about progress since the inspection sixteen months previously and then went on to see various members of staff; there was no report or discussion at the end of the visit so I presumed he had found matters in order. In October, to the amazement of myself and members of staff, the director of education decided on a local mini-inspection of the school. At 10.15 one Friday morning, just as I was about to leave for an engagement, Sunderland's senior inspector called unexpectedly and informed me that he and two colleagues wished to look at the progress we had made in following up the recommendations of the HMI inspection with special reference to increasing the pace of work in the first two years. This was to be in no way an inspection and would take place during the following week from Monday to Thursday. Not surprisingly, the initial reaction of senior colleagues was that this was, indeed, another inspection of their work to add to those by the same local inspector (the ill-fated one of November 1976), by the four HMIs a year later, and the full inspection in 1980. With insufficient notice to prepare documentation I presumed that the first item on the visitors' agenda for Monday would be to receive an oral report from me outlining action since the HMI inspection. I was informed, however, that they first wished to talk to heads of department individually and then to visit classes. As the day proceeded I became increasingly concerned that no overall picture and framework was being sought and at 5pm I was telephoned by a headteacher colleague and asked 'How is the inspection going?' Feedback from staff revealed a series of questions, far wider than the terms of reference I had been given, reinforcing their feeling of being inspected. On the Wednesday I learned that, without my knowledge, heads of ·department were being asked to rate the academic and social performance not only of their departments but of the school as a whole on a 5-point scale ranging from 'the school is doing a first class job ...' to 'the school positively damages pupils'. The whole operation led to deep concerns among many teachers and doubtless gave renewed hope to those opposed to the direction of the school.

I let the director know that I was not pleased and that the net result was likely to be a further erosion of confidence in the catchment area. The questionnaire was withdrawn and, in the event, the final result proved more constructive than had earlier seemed likely. Consultations followed and, in a letter to me in the following month summarising a joint discussion, the director wrote 'I am very pleased to learn from the senior inspector that progress had been made in response to the comments by HM inspectors about years 1 and 2'. He referred to the 'improvement that has taken place' in special needs and had news of a possible minor works programme to upgrade craft facilities in home economics, art, and CDT (craft, design and technology). The only contentious, though important, area concerned the director's insistence on further discussions with teachers and inspectors with a view to 'reaching agreement on the teaching organisation' of certain subjects in the older year groups. The context indicated that he expected that this would lead to an extension of selective teaching groups agreed under the 7-point programme of the governors in 1977 (Chapter 13). I nevertheless welcomed the director's concluding comments that 'close and continuous cooperation between members of the inspectorate and you and your colleagues, notably in the areas indicated above, should produce further progress quietly and effectively, *building on what the school is doing*' [my emphasis]. Overall the staff had responded to a full inspection and to mini check-ups with a feeling that they had positive things to offer even though it seemed to them, not unreasonably, that they were being subjected to a level of accountability far beyond that expected of staffs of other schools.

Issue of confidence

The year 1982 commenced positively with a welcome and unexpected bonus in January when the school branch of the National Association of Teachers/Union Women Teachers informed me that 'We the members of the NAS/UWT at Ryhope School accept that school discipline can be maintained without recourse to corporal punishment and we believe that our efforts should continue to be directed towards developing alternative systems of effective control'.[13] Local papers reported teaching developments, sporting achievements and news of various activities and individual performances. However, in May a group of parents from Silksworth (including two prominent Labour Party members) organised a meeting for those who did not wish their junior school children to transfer to Ryhope.[14] Apparently feelings ran high. Two days before this meeting I was asked to meet the deputy director (the director was away for a week or two) with one or two other officers of the authority to discuss parental preferences for other schools. I formed the opinion that the ground was being prepared for my early retirement (I was aged 55 at the time). Two of the authority's officers attended the parents' meeting and both the NUT and AMMA (Assistant Masters and Mistresses Association) wrote to the director expressing concern that 'remarks could possibly be made which place their professional competence in doubt'. On the second working day after the meeting I was asked to meet the chairman of the Education Committee with the deputy director.[15] The deputy reported that the Silksworth parents had formed an action committee and that the Authority's officers present felt that they would seek publicity which would further reduce confidence. I was asked to consider retirement either at the end of the current term or after a possible three year secondment to the Open University. The deputy had prepared figures with pension entitlements.

Retirement declined

A fortnight later I gave my reply in a letter to the chairman. It linked educational developments at the school with the practical politics of building confidence. Referring to the common curriculum, by then seen as desirable by both the Department of Education and Science and Her Majesty's Inspectors, I commented:

> No one has officially stood up and said that Ryhope was and is on the right lines. What a boost this would be to the confidence of staff, parents and pupils.

In matters of discipline, where 'Ryhope is second to none in the commitment and work of the staff in this area', I noted that Sunderland was by then committed to the abolition of corporal punishment and that governors should be concerned that:

> one of their schools is singled out for a determined attempt to undermine public confidence because it is carrying out a policy already agreed to in principle by the LEA.

I anticipated that the provisions of the 1980 Education Act would mean that more parents will seek alternatives for their children through the machinery of parental preference:

> An obvious tactic will be to denigrate the local school ... and aim to gain the support of other parents at a time of natural anxiety as their children transfer from junior to comprehensive school. There will be other instances where a "run" on a school takes place ... If comprehensive education is to be a reality, a stand must be taken when such action occurs.

My letter expressed concern that a non-elected and self-selected group of parents should be seen to affect the course of education in a school of the local education authority (LEA) and noted that the leader of the Council, in another context, had pointed out the need to:

> oppose undemocratic pressure as an important principle.[16]

The right of parents to appeal was without question but there was no such right to:

> denigrate the school or myself in a manner likely to be detrimental to the education of other pupils whose parents do not share their opinions. Many a parent has told me in the past that because of what they had heard about the school they had doubts before their children started. The majority were quickly

reassured and some have gone on to be among our strongest supporters as their children have proceeded up the school ... We too have a "silent majority". I believe that they recognise and appreciate that Ryhope's aims (identical with those of the LEA) are in the best interests of their children. I submit that the Authority has a duty to these parents.

I said that if I acquiesced in the proposal made to me, my agreement would be:

widely and effectively used to discredit and destroy all that has been built up so carefully and thoroughly over 13 years and thus set back the cause of comprehensive education in the borough.

My letter concluded:

I have decided that I cannot agree to the request made. I can, however, assure you that I and my staff will spare no effort to work with the Authority in a joint effort to promote a more informed appreciation of the aims, purposes and achievements of Ryhope School ...

Mainly politics

Following this episode members of local Labour parties, the Sunderland Trades Council and trade union branches intensified their support. They included several councillors and the prospective parliamentary candidate for Sunderland North. As early as December 1977, following the leak of the local inspector's report, well wishers in the labour movement had been active raising issues concerning Ryhope School at meetings and strengthening the considerable support at grass roots. In November 1980 Sunderland South Constituency Labour Party (CLP) which included the Ryhope and Silksworth wards had organised a very successful day school for the northern region on abolition of corporal punishment in schools. It was opened by the local Labour MP and concluded with a resolution which called on all Labour councils which had not yet done so (Sunderland being among them) to take immediate action to abolish corporal punishment. In the summer of 1982 I was asked to address meetings of trade union and party branches whilst councillors raised questions with the director concerning admissions procedures, corporal punishment, streaming and banding in the borough. Sunderland South CLP passed supportive resolutions on Ryhope School which were passed on to the Sunderland District Labour Party and to the Labour group of councillors whilst Ryhope Ward Labour Party — a long-standing branch based on a strong mining tradition — wrote directly to the leader of the Labour group telling him that 'ward members strongly support the achievements of Ryhope School'.

None of these activities (including the meeting of parents in Silksworth) appeared in the media but, just before I declined early retirement, the Sunderland *Echo* (5 June) published a short letter claiming that 'many parents are unhappy' about Ryhope School. I decided to reply and a brisk correspondence followed during the next few weeks with 11 correspondents writing in support of the school to 3 against. The latter included two Liberal councillors from other parts of the borough without direct knowledge of the school and a local resident, 'One of the Old School'. Support came from individual parents (former, present and prospective), a Labour councillor, an advice worker and Labour Party member, students at the school, a students' year committee and other well-wishers. This open encouragement had an invigorating effect on staff, parents and students as did a full page feature by the *Echo* (8 July) with a prominent heading 'At Ryhope they do a G.C.E. in it!' This linked the school's approach to discipline and responsibility with the social studies course in the fourth and fifth years which included a term's unit on law and order (Chapter 7, Note 10).

At the beginning of July, a few days after a meeting of the District Labour Party, the leader of the Council wrote a personal letter saying he was 'directly concerned at this stage about one problem and that is the dramatic fall in the number entering your school ... and the possibility that this fall will continue and increase. On that basis the expressions of support etc. whilst they might be comforting to you, will not alter the fact that the school would become a candidate for closure ... [parents] have this choice, and the increasing availability of places in other schools is going to multiply the choice for them'. He requested a short paper giving my observations on how I thought 'the decline in entry could be arrested'. Certainly, after all that had happened, this was our most intractable problem; Ryhope's approach had been planned and developed in an era when schools served all young people in local communities and catchment areas (Chapter 5). Now, in addition to the effects of publicity, a market was rapidly developing among comprehensive schools. Those with a relatively large proportion of students from higher socio-economic groups proved an attractive prospect for many parents. Also, schools which make a favourable allocation of experienced teachers and resources to the higher bands and streams, in effect, offer incentives to the most capable students to transfer to them.

For September 1982 Ryhope had an intake of 160 and a total roll of 900 (totally viable numbers for a comprehensive school) but the intake represented a reduction of thirty per cent of those provisionally allocated by the local authority. This 'loss' had increased a little each year for several years and was gaining a momentum of its own as younger siblings followed older ones, estate agents recommended other schools and parents and children made early decisions to go elsewhere, influencing others in a snowball effect.

In my paper I accepted that a build-up in:

> anti-Ryhope activity ... especially in some parts of the community ... has affected pupil and parent expectations in some cases and so has worked to counteract the effectiveness of our positive work in teaching and discipline.

Both the school and the Ryhope School Association had increased community activities following the Silksworth parents' meeting 'when the full extent of this uninformed but damaging activity became clear' and the positive statements in the press had led to a boost in morale of the students. An enthusiastic and exceptionally well attended meeting for new entrants and their parents was encouraging but:

> changes in attitude take time and we recognise that our efforts now are directed more to the future than the present.

My paper emphasised, once again, the need to constantly campaign for comprehensive education; for implementation of Sunderland's aims, and for action on the abolition of corporal punishment which:

> would not only be an important step forward in the borough but also, in itself, a public demonstration of support for all schools who have already dispensed with this unsavoury and unnecessary practice.

Similarly a clear indication was needed that:

> schools are expected to move towards a realisation of Aim 4 [eradicating selectivity] ... teachers in schools which are concerned about the effects of selectivity would know that their efforts were appreciated.

I also reminded him that the borough had a specific objective supporting community schools and recommended that the local authority should:

carefully consider its policy on school size in all parts of the borough with the aim of insuring, as far as possible, the continuation of comprehensive schools for communities (Chapter 5).

I contended that a range of four- to eight-form entry[17] was practical and viable for the age range 11-16 and my report called for the establishment of a community project in Ryhope and Silksworth as in several other parts of the borough. This would provide opportunities for developing productive links between the school and the community with understanding enhanced:

in the most effective way — by active participation.

Finally my paper expressed concern over a reduction in facilities including the imminent closure of the school kitchen which had maintained the highest reputation for the quality of its meals since it was established in 1940. Removal of demountable craft rooms seemed based on the expectation of an increasing short fall of numbers which could become a self-fulfilling prophesy whilst engineering doubts about the viability of the south block had suddenly emerged. Here I commented that, nevertheless, a smaller school on a single site in the north block could have many advantages and would receive our full cooperation — providing the plans were 'comprehensive (in both senses of the word) rather than makeshift'. In the current circumstances, however, these actions gave an impression that the school was being dismantled around us 'without any clear and viable overall policy'. I did not receive an acknowledgment or any direct follow up to my paper but the situation concerning craft rooms was, at least partially, met by a subsequent upgrading of facilities.

The remainder of the term was busy with normal work up to the last day plus a varied range of activities including trips out, a parents' evening, participation in Durham University science department's sixth form project week and fun sports afternoons for first and second year students. These last brought back some old favourites like the sack race, three-legged race and throwing the wellie, and attracted many parents. Despite the problem of admission numbers, the school year finished in a positive and generally optimistic manner.

15

Sustained Attack

Councillor's complaint

One week after the end of the summer term the front page headline of the Sunderland *Echo* (30 July 1982) read 'Ryhope School Probe Sought' and reported the intention of the independent socialist councillor for Silksworth to ask Sir Keith Joseph, Secretary of State for Education and Science, to make a full investigation into discipline at Ryhope School as a result of complaints from parents in his ward who did not wish their children to attend the school. Earlier in the school year the councillor had been escorted from the council chamber during a debate on corporal punishment. The Newcastle *Journal* (26 November 1981) stated that 'he began shouting about Ryhope Comprehensive School ... and that his electors in Silksworth wanted the cane restored there' — an assumption that would certainly have been challenged by many whose children and relatives attended the school. He was present at the meeting of Silksworth parents in May (Chapter 14) where he read out a letter from a parent to the director of education complaining about incidents at the school.[1] His latest action set in train a series of events which was to affect all involved with the school and soon he received, as it became known later, a handwritten reply from the Secretary of State which said 'I share your concern at the continuing difficulties and problems of this school'.[2]

Remarkable developments

Between 30th July and 29th December at least seventy-six items about Ryhope School were to appear in the Sunderland *Echo*.[3] A few concerned normal activities and the remainder ranged from letters to the editor to two-page feature articles and from news reports (fourteen on the front page including ten main headlines) to editorials. Whilst the thrust of the

publicity centred around the issues of corporal punishment and my
personal position ('Cane-row head won't give in' — *Journal* 18 October;
'School head's job is in jeopardy' — *Journal* 17 November), the media
also highlighted wider matters during the five month period. These
included approaches to good order; maturity of students; curriculum and
teaching methods; the role of governors, and the aims of education
('Ryhope School aims to fulfil ideals' — letter from 'friend of Ryhope
School' *Echo* 14 October; 'The Battle for Ryhope School' — letter from
'Cicero' *Echo* 29th December). The concerns of teaching staff were
reported and political perspectives appeared. We shall discuss relations
with the media in the final chapter whilst here we note the widespread
interest, understanding and involvement in the affairs of the school which
resulted from media attention.

Following their report of the referral to Sir Keith Joseph, the *Echo* (3
August) offered me space to reply. There was a little more correspondence
during August and a group of Labour Party supporters, including
councillors and the prospective parliamentary candidate for Sunderland
North, formed a support group for Ryhope School.[4] By the start of term in
the first week of September everyone was busy with affairs for the new
school year and there were many greater priorities than thinking about a
complaint — even one to the 'top' — concerning lack of caning; indeed I
expected that little more would be heard of the matter. However, I was
soon to receive an indication that the school was under special scrutiny.
On 13th September two parents called about an incident involving sniffing
lighter fuel — the first such incident for at least two years. It was dealt
with effectively by the staff concerned according to recommended
guidelines neither to under-estimate its seriousness nor to over-react. A
senior member of staff made a full but discreet investigation and other
parents were counselled. Staff were asked to be vigilant and heads of year
explained the dangers in assemblies; the deputy head visited a local shop
selling lighter fuel. While this was going on the parents, who were
naturally worried and did not yet know of all the action taken, mentioned
the matter to the Labour councillor who had claimed a loss of rights at a
meeting for parents before the opening of the school (Chapter 10). He
recommended the parents to get in touch with the director of education
and I was asked for a report by the deputy director a day or two later.
Whilst the request was routine it contained a condescending comment no
doubt influenced by recent events: 'I think I need hardly point out that the
abuse of solvents and other volatile liquids by young people is a matter of

very great concern and the Committee will naturally be anxious to ensure that the practice is discouraged in its schools.' Did he really think that I should do otherwise?[5]

On 15th September an under-secretary of the DES 'directed by the Secretary of State' wrote to the director for Sunderland referring to the 1980 HMI report following the full inspection. He stated that 'HM Inspectorate have observed in subsequent visits to the school that some changes have been made' but claimed that 'many of the aspects of the school that gave cause for concern in 1980 remain'. No such thoughts had been passed to me. Excluding a visit in March 1982 in connection with a survey on sixth forms in the region, the only follow up by an HMI to the full inspection had been by our designated inspector in June 1981 which, as mentioned in Chapter 14, was concluded without comment or discussion. The writer from the DES went on to say 'I am to ask that the local education authority should as a matter of urgency consider what steps might be taken to improve the quality of education and management of the school in the light of the recommendations contained in the 1980 HMI inspection report'.

On learning of the letter from a helpful parent member of the Ryhope School Association (no doubt via the Silksworth councillor who had been sent a copy) it became clear that the councillor's complaint was to be used as a springboard for further attempts to erode distinctive aspects of the school. The director visited the DES on 24th with Ryhope School included on the agenda and, on 30th September, I wrote to Sir Keith Joseph asking for the precise nature of the complaints and detailing my concerns at the assumptions apparently being made about the school. I received a reply, dated 6th October, from a DES official which restated several points from what he referred to as 'the Department's letter' of 15th adding that 'the Authority will no doubt wish to consider carefully and in detail your own assessment of the position in relation to the educational objectives of the School'. He stated that the letter 'neither repeated nor drew upon comments made by Councillor N'. So whilst the public were correct in thinking that the developments were a direct result of the councillor's intervention, inquiries were to be based on a joint DES and local authority agenda.

Marathon meeting of the governors

The governors (ie the Schools Sub-committee sitting as the Governors of Ryhope School) were to meet on 5th October and copies of the letter from

the under secretary and the HMI report of 1980 were circulated. Because
of uncertainty at the intended course of events I declined an offer to
circulate material at that stage. The *Echo* (30 September) greeted the
forthcoming meeting with the headline 'Ryhope School Row Set to Break'
and correctly quoted me as 'amazed' at the way the DES had handled the
councillor's complaints. I hoped that the governors' meeting would be
'fact-finding and constructive' but I was also consulting my trade union
and writing to Sir Keith as 'it seems to me that there is a risk of
considerable injustice here'. Whenever interviewed I always tried to have a
message for parents, students and staff; on this occasion I said that 'we
shall be continuing with the educational work for which Ryhope School is
noted, and which has been recognised by the many parents who wrote to
the *Echo* in our support'.

At the start of the meeting the chairman of governors (also of the
Education Committee), referring to the under secretary's letter, said that
'the seriousness of the situation cannot be over-stated', and mentioned
the reduction in admissions. The director said that 'public confidence
needed to be restored' and then gave his interpretation of the HMI
report speaking, as it seemed to me, almost as if it was a new document
rather than one which had been discussed by the governors two years
previously and followed up by local inspectors. He referred to twenty six
paragraphs on which I was asked to comment. Despite lack of notice,
and without access to files and other sources of information, I stressed
the substantial progress made in almost all areas but was told by the
chairman that my suggestion that the sudden urgency of the situation
might have been at the instigation of the director and authority's
inspectorate 'could not be accepted'. The secondary schools'
representative, elected by teachers of the borough and currently a
member of the NAS/UWT, raised the question of staff disunity which
the director made full use of in his summing up. He concluded 'Any
reply to the Secretary of State must be specific and if that course of
action was to be taken it must be coupled with a public statement of
confidence in the school.'

The meeting then adjourned until 15th October with a press statement
confined to this information. Two days later the Sunderland District
Labour Party passed two resolutions submitted a few days earlier by
Sunderland South Constituency Labour Party (CLP). The first urged the
Labour group and Education Committee to 'implement and publicise the
aims of the Sunderland Education Committee's policy'. The second called

on the group 'to take urgent and decisive action to counteract once and for all the unremitting attack by certain individuals upon Ryhope School' adding that 'an unequivocal statement that Ryhope School is pursuing the aims of the Authority and thus has the full support of the Authority is required. This would immediately reassure parents and consequently assist staff and pupils of the school in their work.' An active and supportive Labour councillor for Ryhope wrote to the Secretary of State on 6th October and, next day, the chair of the Ryhope School Association sent him a copy of her letter soon to be published in the *Echo*. This finished 'Let the very competent staff get on with the job ... We all want the best for our children. I am one of the many who are quite sure that we have settled for nothing less'.[6]

On the 9th it was the turn of Neil Kinnock, at the time shadow education spokesman. He had been approached at the Labour Party conference in September by the prospective candidate for Sunderland North and had also consulted with the MP for Sunderland South (which included Ryhope and Silksworth). His letter to the Secretary of State was wide-ranging and made several important points. He concluded that 'you have acted with surprising irresponsibility and insufficient thought for the effect of your action on the welfare of the pupils at Ryhope School.' He sent a copy to Sunderland's director of education while Sunderland South's MP also wrote to the Secretary of State reinforcing the views of Ryhope's supportive councillor 'which outlines in an excellent way the complete case'.

I submitted a thirty-six-page document entitled 'Progress at Ryhope School' for the adjourned meeting of the governors. This had an entry corresponding to each paragraph of the HMI report showing the response of the school and further plans where appropriate. At lunchtime on the 15th, shortly before I left for the governors' meeting at the Civic Centre, I was handed a copy of a joint resolution from the NAS/UWT and AMMA. After expressing concern that recent adverse publicity had 'put in doubt the professional competence and integrity of the staff' and was 'causing a general breakdown in the community's confidence and support for the school' it went on to claim that, since 1980, 'the standards of behaviour have not improved significantly', 'lines of communication ... remain inadequate' and 'conflict within the school, ie staff v the Head, has not been significantly reduced'. I learned that the chairman had received a copy on the previous day. At the meeting I introduced my report and replied to questions and comments. The leader asked me about the HMIs recommendation for more homogeneous grouping (ie more selection) which I had not accepted and about records of maintenance and repair. (There was a standard procedure for all schools). The NAS/UWT and AMMA resolution was then introduced and I said that I agreed that adverse publicity had affected morale; that the school had been inspected enough, and that the matter had to be settled quickly. On the other hand I disagreed with most of the remainder[7] and did not believe that the statement represented the real view of the staff.

Questioning, none of which could be called friendly or supportive, continued and the director gave his comments. The governors decided on a further adjournment so that the director could visit the school and then give the governors advice. With the union resolution in mind, they also agreed not to consider anything at the next meeting which was simply 'dropped in their laps ... They needed time to read papers for themselves and things should not be read out to them'. Again no press statement was made apart from giving notice that the meeting would be reconvened. The *Echo* had 'Ryhope School scrutinised again' on the day before the meeting and 'Secret talks on Ryhope's discipline' on the day after. On 21st October the executive of the District Labour Party sent a statement to the Labour group who considered it on 25th October. The leader had also received a personal letter from the prospective candidate for Sunderland North in which he described something of his depth of feeling over the Ryhope issue, experienced also by many others with and without direct connections with the school. However, most of the group agreed with the leader's recommendation that 'governors who were members of the Labour group ought not to be subjected to any direction' and that it was necessary 'to keep the independence of the group'. A week or so later, on 9th November, Sunderland North CLP passed a short but highly supportive motion which again went to the Labour group and other parties.

On 12th November the governors continued their adjourned meeting with nineteen governors and several officers present. The director introduced a report which he had written commenting on 'Progress at Ryhope School'. I was invited to reply but was refused permission to circulate a folder for each governor containing examples of learning materials for first year students. Almost all the items had been prepared by teachers since the HMI inspection and included a science experiment sheet, mathematics contract sheet, a student's booklet for integrated studies and homework topic booklets. 'The governors were not qualified to make a judgment on their professional quality' was the reason given and supported by an intervention from the representative of the director of administration who sat with the governors to give legal advice. At least they could have observed the high quality of design and presentation and their user-friendly nature. The folders, intended to illustrate some of my remarks, also came under the ban on submitting material at meetings but this had not prevented the leader of the Council asking for maintenance costs which the deputy director just happened to have among his papers. He read out some figures which purported to show that costs for Ryhope were much higher than at four 'comparable' schools. Further questions led to more statistics being produced but it was impossible for me to make a constructive comment without seeing and evaluating the figures and checking to what extent like was being compared with like. Intensive questioning continued, some of it on comparatively minor details of school life. I hope that I responded vigorously although it was essentially a 'no win' situation. I managed to communicate that many members of the teacher unions who had sent the resolution before the previous meeting had gone out of their way to wish me success today.

The leader questioned me closely concerning my views on confidentiality of the proceedings — a subject which I realised might prove critical. Eventually I said that if the outcome was favourable I should confine myself to saying how delighted I was; if unfavourable I would say that I thought the governors were wrong but that what individuals had said at the meeting would not be relevant. This was acceptable to the leader. At this point I asked the chair whether I could, through him, ask the secondary schools representative whether he had discussed the proceedings of 5th October with anyone else. I had good reason for my question but it was ruled 'improper'. Soon afterwards I was asked to leave together with the director and his colleagues. On our return we were informed that the governors had reached a unanimous decision that 'satisfactory progress in meeting the criticisms of the HMI report ... has not been achieved'; that they had 'reservations about the management of the school', and would meet again 'to consider the position of the headmaster and the measures needed to deal with the criticisms of the Secretary of State and restore public confidence in the school'.

Despite the intensity of the proceedings I managed to make some notes as I dealt with queries and comments during the three-session meeting. The official minutes occupy sixty pages.

Activity, debate and demonstration

For the next three weeks, events came thick and fast whether in school, outside or in the media:

Saturday 13th November

This was the morning following the governors' meeting . I went canvassing for a by-election in another ward of the constituency; It was a fresh morning, there were plenty of canvassers and it did wonders for brain fatigue left over from the previous day.

Tuesday 16th

Many students had already asked their teachers about the situation so the school's morning circular[8] had the following entry in the staff section: 'When asked by pupils about my future I am replying politely on the following lines: "That will be decided in due course. At present I am your headteacher and together with the staff our one concern is your education". Colleagues may find it helpful to know this when making their own replies.'

Wednesday 17th

Today the morning circular contained information and advice for students following release of the press statement from the governors giving their decisions at the previous meeting.[9] The *Journal* and *Northern Echo* gave prominence to the news and also quoted from a statement which I had prepared.[10] Local radio and television arrived to interview me and the *Echo* had a front page headline 'Ryhope head's future in balance.' It reported that 'Governors will be ordering changes in the way the school is run and will make a final decision on the position of the headmaster, Mr Dick Copland, in the next few weeks.' Inside, the *Echo* carried a feature article which described positive aspects as well as a short interview with the independent socialist councillor. 'Cane is the great debate' was one of the headings.

Thursday 18th

The role of the governors was today's media theme with the *Echo*'s front page headline 'Governors at Ryhope attacked — They failed to visit crisis school'. A Labour member of the Education Committee (but not of the Schools Sub-committee and thus not a governor) was quoted: 'It staggers me that with one honourable exception none of the governors who have felt fit to pass judgment on the school have bothered to spend any time in visiting the school in recent years to assess its life and work.'[11] She herself had visited the school at her own request and had been 'very impressed indeed.' The *Echo* report, noting that I hadn't even been introduced to some of the governors, had a considerable influence on public opinion.

Friday 19th
At morning break the staff and I were taken completely by surprise. Outside the window of my room on the front field at least three hundred students gathered and called for me to come out. I considered that their obvious concern should be treated with respect and went out to meet them. The scene was quite emotional; the students had made up a song in my support to the tune of a popular hit of the moment — Grandad![12] It was a kind and thoughtful gesture but also one intended to influence decisions. When the bell went for the end of break teachers brought the students in and all lessons had resumed normally within ten minutes.[13] The staff were naturally anxious about their authority and we held special year assemblies where I thanked the students for their demonstration of support but also made it clear that there must be no recurrence and explained that this would be counter-productive. At lunch time three fifteen-year-old girls who had been the main organisers collected several hundred signatures from fellow students for a petition, and members of their tutor group wrote me a letter of support.[14] That evening the *Echo* had a brief account of the demonstration as some parents had contacted the paper after hearing lunchtime reports from their sons and daughters. The paper also reported Neil Kinnock's support for the head and staff at the school.

Saturday 20th
The *Echo* carried another strong letter from the Labour Party advice worker (Chapter 14). 'What we are witnessing is the acquiescence of weak and indecisive governors in the face of a sustained and irresponsible campaign against Ryhope School that has been waged over many years'.

Monday 22nd
A journalist from *The Times Educational Supplement* visited the school at her request. She was made welcome and readily accepted the one proviso, agreed with union representatives, that before visiting classes the approval of the teachers concerned should be sought and that questions to them would be concerned directly with work and activities in the room. As well

as class visits and walking round the school, she interviewed me and talked with several teachers about more general matters.

In the evening, as a guest of Sunderland AFC at Roker Park, I enjoyed watching Sunderland Boys (with two from Ryhope in the team) play Bradford Boys.

Tuesday 23rd

The regional officer of The NAS/UWT issued a lengthy press statement which went over much previous ground including a recap from 1978 stating that 'the majority of our members are not fully in accord with the headteacher'. The NAS/UWT statement was in time for distribution on the following day with the notices for the next governors meeting fixed for 3rd December. In the evening we held a meeting for parents and their first year students to discuss progress with group tutors and other teachers.[15] For the first time this annual event, coordinated by the head of first year, included a session with a panel of teachers, chaired by the school's deputy head, to answer questions and discuss the curriculum, teaching methods and 'ways in which you can help your child at home'. Before setting out for this very successful evening, many parents would have seen the *Echo's* informative two page feature on the school which included supportive letters with headings such as 'Society must care and share', 'School is oasis' and 'Gran found nice people' (identified as head and staff!).

Wednesday 24th

The NAS/UWT press statement was picked up particularly by the *Journal* and, understandably, caused concern among members of the Ryhope School Association and parents who had based their support on the considerable achievements of staff and head working together.[16] Sunderland District Labour Party issued a detailed statement following an emergency meeting on the previous evening. The *Echo* gave it almost complete coverage under the headline 'Ryhope crisis splits Labour'. The chairman told the paper that the District Party was dismayed at 'continuing and worsening attacks on Ryhope School and its headmaster. We have held our silence until now in the hope that Sunderland Council Labour group would intervene to halt the course of events ... The views of the District Labour Party have to be made public ... The motivation of those attacking the school is not a genuine concern for educational standards in the school, but a desire for a return to corporal punishment and grammar school-oriented streaming of pupils, all of which is opposed to Labour Party policy nationally and locally and the latter of which is contrary to the aims and objectives of Sunderland local education authority'.

In the early evening about three hundred people from Ryhope and Silksworth, half of them school students, demonstrated in an orderly — indeed exemplary — fashion inside the Civic Centre.[17] The Ryhope School support group had organised the event including transport and the demonstrators assembled outside the entrance to the council chamber where councillors and officers had to pass on their way to a full council meeting. There were short speeches, attentively listened to, but when the independent councillor for Silksworth appeared the students sang their song which made a considerable impression in the relatively confined space; apparently more than one councillor and officer looked distinctly pale. As the council meeting commenced Ryhope's supportive councillor took in the petition which had been collected and signed by students and the demonstrators left quietly. As Ryhope School was not on the agenda, the Council agreed to pass the petition to the Education Committee.

Thursday 25th

I received the agenda for the governors' meeting. It was accompanied by copies of various documents that had been considered previously together with a statement from the director of education consisting of twenty eight paragraphs and an appendix containing several pages of details of repairs going back to 1972. The statement covered familiar ground but was much more explicit in identifying me as responsible for alleged deficiencies as, for example, in this comment concerned with curriculum development: 'The changes instituted by the Headmaster at Ryhope are not unusual in principle. What is unusual at Ryhope is the Headmaster's authoritarian and ad hoc management of change.' (I refer readers to earlier chapters to make their own assessment). The purpose of the meeting was to 'consider the headmaster's position' and I was formally notified that I could be accompanied by a friend 'at any meeting of the Governing Body which may consider the question of your dismissal'.

Friday 26th

'Ryhope School in Sunderland doesn't seem like a school in crisis ... Critics say that discipline is part of the problem. But the day I was there the corridors ... were noisy but basically orderly and classes were at work.' These were the opening sentences of the journalist's report in *The Times*

Educational Supplement (1982). The writer assessed the school as 'nevertheless a difficult one to teach in' and quoted 'one seasoned member of staff' as saying 'The kids are working class kids and physically tough with it — although that doesn't mean they go around kicking people's heads in'.[18] The article described the history of the school, gave a summary of my views, interviewed several teachers and reported on class visits which the reporter clearly found interesting. In the evening, the Echo had a front page headline 'D-Day set at Ryhope' to announce that my future would be decided by the governors on the following Friday. It also had the views of the deputy leader of the Council who was a Labour councillor for Silksworth. He said that he had been happy to send his own son and daughter to the school and still had a niece and nephew there; however, he felt that the governors 'are the only people with all the relevant information'. He thought that there was an impression that the governors had already made up their mind but his information was that 'they were still considering all the evidence before them and would be considering further next Friday when the headmaster attended their meeting'.

On an inside page there was a feature article headed 'Background' with the main heading picking up the NAS/UWT resolution 'Ryhope staff "not in accord" '. The article also reproduced an anonymous letter sent to the independent councillor for Silksworth which, according to the *Echo*, started his campaign. The letter was on headed notepaper with the street name blacked-out but it was clear that it did not originate from Ryhope or Silksworth. On another page, letters of support received prominent coverage; they included letters from a group of older school students and a pair of younger ones.

Monday 29th

I travelled to London with the northern regional officer of the NUT to consult the Union's solicitor. As a result the regional officer wrote next day to the director asking for details and evidence to substantiate several of the sections in the director's statement and for clarification of procedures at the forthcoming meeting.

Tuesday 30th

I was informed by the NAS/UWT representative that his members were increasingly concerned by the political orientation of affairs, in particular a pamphlet prepared by the Ryhope School support group. This was a substantial document, well produced, informative and, in all but one respect, excellent campaigning material. The problem occurred after a summary of the principles under which the school operated and a comment that the school 'has many enemies who reject these principles'. Those identified included the Conservative government; ill informed local politicians, and unsympathetic officials of the Council. Heading the list was the National Association of Schoolmasters/Union of Women Teachers whose regional office had played an essentially negative part in the affairs of the school. However, it was a tactical disaster to leave open to interpretation that all Ryhope's NAS/UWT teachers could be so described.[19]

The *Echo* that night printed an excellent supportive letter from the owner of a local fish-and-chip shop who organised football teams consisting almost entirely of Ryhope School students.

Wednesday 1st December

'Unions fury on Ryhope School affair' — the *Echo*'s front page headline — concerned a Sunderland Trades Council statement which it described as 'a blistering broadside on the handling of the Ryhope School affair'. The statement noted that 'the majority of Labour councillors, by being mute on the subject, have allowed the issue to balloon. It is clear that a handful of individuals hostile to Ryhope School have resorted to any and every means to bring the school and its headteacher into discredit'. The resolution was sent on to a very successful public rally in Ryhope Community Centre again organised by the support group and chaired by the supportive councillor for Ryhope. Over three hundred people heard messages of support followed by a truly rallying speech from the prospective candidate for Sunderland North. A former student, making a surprise visit, was cheered when he made a short speech of appreciation. He had played a major role in the two rock operas and, by then, was working as a television presenter and interviewer on youth affairs. There were questions and discussion and, with one vote against, the meeting supported a message to the governors prepared by parents. I said a few words to thank all concerned for their support and encouragement and was more than taken by surprise when this received a standing ovation.

Thursday 2nd

This was the eve of the governors' meeting and an uneventful day at school. As usual friends of the school awaited the arrival of the *Echo* with mixed feelings. On this evening it gave a good report of the rally but also

gave prominence to a motion by NAS/UWT teachers sent to the chairman
of governors in which they confirmed their support for the recent 'not in
accord' press statement from their regional officer. There was a letter from
an Education Committee member (but not a governor) headed 'Defending
Principles' and a short editorial saying that the governors 'will face what
will be one of the most difficult meetings any governors have had to attend
either in this or any other school in the borough'. There wasn't much time
to study the details as we had an open evening for parents and pupils in
the last year of junior school starting at 7.30pm. Teachers, assisted by
volunteer students, put a tremendous amount into this event preparing
attractive displays and explaining and demonstrating teaching methods in
various subjects. The evening was well supported and had a friendly
atmosphere.

Arriving home about 9.30pm I started a final check in preparation for
the morning. As the proceedings would in many ways be like a court of
law I had realised that there was no need to rush my reply. I expected to
spend two or three hours answering the director's analyses, conclusions
and indictments and was to be accompanied by the regional officer of the
NUT. I planned to largely conduct my own defence as I was familiar with
the details and, about midnight, decided that I had made all reasonable
preparations. To some extent I was able to mentally stand aside from
events and view them almost as an observer so I felt quite relaxed.

Decisive events

As I tidied up my papers and my wife made a cup of coffee, Friday 3rd
December arrived and the doorbell rang. The supportive councillor for
Ryhope was there to say he had just finished collecting a petition with
1200 signatures (in twenty-four hours) and would be presenting it to the
chairman of governors at the Civic Centre prior to the start of the meeting
together with copies of resolutions and a selection of the letters of support
he had received from parents. Naturally this was a great boost.

Unexpected programme

I went into school for a few minutes in the morning and left a message for
the morning circular thanking staff and students for their efforts at the
parents' evening. Then on to the Civic Centre where the governor's
meeting was due to commence at 9.30am. The chairman received the
petition but it was nearly half an hour before the NUT regional officer and

I were asked in. After the normal courtesies the chairman said that the leader of the Council would ask me a question. Immediately I sensed that the agenda had changed and this was confirmed by the question itself which said, in effect, 'Will you carry out the instructions of the education authority? Don't answer immediately, retire for half an hour and return with your answer.'[20] I realised that the intention to remove me had been called off but was thrown somewhat off balance after mentally preparing myself for the role of counsel for the defence as well as prisoner at the bar. Leaving the meeting within a few minutes to face a new and unexpected situation left me in a state of some mental disorganisation. Fortunately this was not total; when the regional officer and I reached the room we had been allocated I explained that I certainly did not wish to answer 'No' to the question as that would be the end but nor did I want to answer 'Yes' in a way that would throw away so much that had been done at Ryhope School over many years. I asked if he could produce a suitable answer though I feared that I had set him an impossible task. As he worked at the job a messenger arrived to say that the governors would not be asking me to introduce corporal punishment (in retrospect, an indication that they were hoping for a satisfactory outcome).

The regional officer did extremely well. We went back to the governors and he gave our reply: 'Yes, with safeguards.'[21] I was asked a supplementary question and replied that if there was any proposal I could not carry out I would make this clear to the governors. The director, deputy, NUT regional officer and I were then asked to leave the meeting while the governors considered my replies. On our return I was asked again about action if I could not carry out a proposal and was given a copy of this question in writing. Again the meeting was adjourned so that we could consider a reply.[22] After bringing that back we were asked to leave for the third time that morning while the governors considered this second response. On our return, we were informed that it was accepted and they had resolved to draw up a programme whose implementation would be 'the subject of consultation between the headteacher and the chairman of governors in accordance with the Articles of Government.' The meeting then adjourned until later in the afternoon.

On resumption of the meeting we received typed sheets of instructions later to become the Governors' Programme, commonly referred to as the 18-point programme. It was implied that the governors had come up with these points during the recess but it was clear that considerable preparatory work had been done by officers before the meeting — my draft had 19 points with one crossed out. The first point was a set of aims for the school later identified (after considerable searching) as stemming from the Department of Education and Science in 1976.[23] After time to skim through the list we were told 'You may withdraw for twenty minutes to decide whether you will accept the programme.' At first glance I thought that the governors were demanding setting and streaming as well as separate classes for those with special educational needs (Chapter 6). There were other matters with far-reaching implications and we had twenty minutes to consider them.[24] Some of the points called on me to establish practices which were already an essential part of the organisation of the school and, in the absence of any clarification, could only be seen as professionally insulting.[25] However, when I re-read the list I saw that, although the governors clearly wished for certain policies, they had not felt able to specifically demand them. The programme laid down consultation and referral procedures designed to produce the 'right' decisions but I realised that, in practice, the procedures could also lead to more acceptable policies which would then carry widely based authority. For the second time in the day I was in a quandary. I said to the regional officer 'I can't accept this yet I don't want to reject it and effectively resign'. Again he produced a simple and impressive solution. We went back to the governors and he said:

> The 18 points involve very important matters and require detailed study. I request a fortnight for Mr Copland to consider them.

'That seems a reasonable request' said the chairman (or was it the leader of the Council?) and the governors agreed. The period for consideration had increased from twenty minutes to two weeks (nearer three in the event).

All that remained was for the governors to agree a press statement which included the first question asked at the meeting and a comment that 'If Mr Copland refuses to carry out any of their directions after consultation the Governors would immediately reconvene to discuss his future.' They added: 'The Governors trust that, given co-operation by all concerned such a situation should not arise and that the future of Ryhope School should be assured'. The 18 points were to be published after the school staff had seen them. Press and radio were waiting as the meeting ended and, on arriving home, the *Echo* had news of the petition and a letter of appreciation from a grandparent. Next day the front page headline reporting the governors' decision was 'Change — or Go.'

Framework agreed

The remainder of the term was not easy for anyone, myself included, although outwardly life appeared normal. The annual carol concert was its usual success for participants, parents and visitors while students enjoyed the Christmas parties and discos. We welcomed a visiting party of governors (established under one of the eighteen points): members of the music club sang for them; young people whom they met on the footbridge and in the corridors were friendly and polite; students with special educational needs involved them in their learning activities; first year groups discussed their work in maths and second year volunteers looked after them at lunchtime. On the Monday after the governors' meeting I had spoken to the teaching staff before school to report the result but apparently gave the impression of attributing responsibility for the current situation to them. Whatever I had intended to say, this was an unfortunate start, to put it mildly. I also gave a message for students through the morning circular which thanked them and their parents for their support, good wishes and cards I had received and took a positive view of the future of the school. During the day copies of the eighteen points arrived for display to the staff and, at a scheduled meeting, the school policy committee decided to invite the director to speak to a full staff meeting arranged for 15th December. On the day before the meeting the staff council met to discuss questions for the director.[26] Deep concerns over prospects for the school were expressed and an additional item, not on the agenda, was introduced. This was another 'no confidence' motion this time in the 'headmaster's ability to bring about the improvements that the authority has requested'. Forty-one teachers out of forty-five present (and fifty-five in total) voted for the motion which was then sent, as a resolution, to the chairman of governors and to the director.[27]

At the staff meeting, to which the chairman as well as the director came, the secretary of the staff council described the voting and added that 'this was not a motion produced easily or passed happily. It is a measure almost of desperation ... Of course we worry about our own jobs ... but more than this we worry that we may be failing, as professionals, the children in our charge. The school has been criticised, inspected, advised ...' The director pointed out that the resolution had no official status but that it would be dealt with confidentially and reported to the next meeting of the governors. He also assured the meeting that there would be a definite settlement this time and a commitment to the programme. At the end of the meeting the chairman wished everyone a Merry Christmas pointing out that life was not all problems. This was well received and led to an informal and surprisingly cheerful finish.

The *Echo* published the Governors' Programme in full and continued to give prominence on both the front and inside pages to Ryhope School affairs (twenty-six items from 6th December to the end of the year including news of the staff council resolution which, in due course, was passed to the media). Sunderland South CLP adopted a strong resolution which called for a review of the role of the governors in all Sunderland schools; expressed criticism of the Governors' Programme for Ryhope, and called for an examination into practices in other schools. The District Party held a special meeting.

A national officer of the NUT described four or five of the eighteen points as 'outrageous' whilst the union solicitor considered that several were matters of internal organisation. Whatever their legal status most were very loosely drafted revealing many ambiguities. I therefore prepared a detailed response for each of the points for my meeting with the chairman on 22nd December, the day following the end of term. He was accompanied by the director of education and deputy for a session which lasted more than three hours. The discussion was constructive and I received verbal assurances on many of my concerns. Nevertheless it was clear that, under the circumstances, both chairman and director were committed to the minimum of changes in wording and only two modifications were agreed. However, both were at the head of my list and the first concerned teaching groups. One item of the programme commenced:

> There is to be no automatic provision of mixed ability teaching.

When amended it read:

> There is to be no automatic provision of mixed ability teaching, setting or any other form of teaching group.

The effect was that whilst the case for non-selective methods had to be made out (no objection there) so also did the case for any other system. The amendment thus forestalled any possible attempt to summarily abandon non-selective teaching.[28] The second change was to clarify the composition of the proposed senior staff council and to establish my own membership of it. Also, following the experience of the staff working party (Chapter 13), it was agreed verbally that the head would chair the council.

Before the meeting commenced I had started to appreciate — and this became clearer during the following months — that, imperfect as they were, the eighteen points fulfilled one vital requirement: governors, officers, staff and myself would all be bound by the decisions. The tone of the meeting was generally positive and I signed a brief press statement with the chairman reporting my acceptance and stating:

> We trust that this marks a new departure. The developments looked for provide a framework within which all concerned may have confidence in the future.

On Christmas Eve an *Echo* report revealed that Conservative councillors had rejected this reasonable position by calling for the governors to be reconvened; they cited the length of the discussion between the chairman and myself as an indication that I must have 'argued every inch of the way'. Their demand was rejected and a meeting of the governors on 4th January 1983 accepted the amendments and approved a report by the chairman of his meeting with the school staff on 15th December. He stated that events had somewhat overtaken the staff meeting and the resolution of the staff council. With the governors' approval he would seek a further meeting with the staff. [29]

16

Final Phase

In this chapter we follow briefly the working-out of the Governors' Programme and how the process itself helped to improve the cohesion of the school. Two years later, Sunderland's proposals for the reorganisation of secondary education involved the closure of the school; this generated campaigning initiatives and educational developments with implications beyond the life of a particular school.

Governors' Programme

The Governors' Programme of eighteen points proved to be something of a watershed in the affairs of the school although this was scarcely apparent as the 1983 spring term commenced. Some teachers and parents were demoralised thinking that the school could not recover from the situation with the affairs of 1977 and 1978 still in mind and the negative effect which the publicity must have had on the confidence of parents with children in the junior schools. Several teachers including myself found it difficult to resume a normal professional relationship when the involvement had been so personal. The following months were certainly difficult but the task was clear and, slowly but surely, school life began to regain its full vitality. Working through the eighteen points proved a time consuming process. Data and opinions needed collecting; inspectors and advisers consulting, and papers drafting for consideration by the senior staff council and/or full staff meetings. Final versions needed to be typed for submission a week in advance of the meeting of the governors at which they were to be discussed. We submitted three full and one interim report for the first meeting of the term with four working weeks available before the reports were to be sent.

However, advised by the director who continued his close involvement in every detail of school life, the governors referred two of the reports for additional action and required a further report on one item.[1] After this experience a further stage in the preparation process became established: after approval by the senior staff council I sent a copy to the director for comment and discussion prior to its submission to the governors.[2] This greatly increased the chance of success. Some of the reports, like the constitution of the senior staff council, were fairly straightforward; two or three, including an analysis of the timetable and aspects of special educational needs, required major reworking of material by one or two members of staff to update and extend their practice and prepare reports in a form matched to the requirements of the programme. Other reports, including those on teaching groups and discipline, required extensive collaborative work in a very short space of time.

The governors met on ten occasions during 1983. There were also two visits by Her Majesty's Inspectors (two inspectors for one day in June and three for two days in November)[3] and a series of visits by local inspectors and advisers in October who produced a substantial and supportive report 'Review of Progress at Ryhope School'. Finally, on 20th December, the governors considered their reply to the Secretary of State on the basis of a report prepared by the director of education. This concluded 'In short, the Governors (and the head) believe that significant progress has been made in meeting the criticisms made by HMI in 1980. They also believe that the continued support the school will receive will bring further improvements in the immediate future in certain areas identified for further attention.' The report was approved by the governors and sent to the Department of Education and Science next day.

The Secretary of State replied favourably in February saying that he 'welcomes the progress made and hopes the school can now look forward to a period of consolidation'.[4] We had to wait a further two months, at a time when many parents made up their minds on choice of school, for the next meeting of the governors before, apparently, a public statement could be made but on 26th April the *Echo* had a news item 'Ryhope School Gets Full Marks'. True this was inside page news but nonetheless very welcome. The *Journal* and *Northern Echo* followed with similar reports and the former quoted me as saying 'It has never been fully understood how much of a strain all this has been to our 900 pupils but I think the majority of them have always believed they had a good school. There is no doubt that we have made significant improvements but we have not had to do a U-turn. Our discipline procedures now have more consistency about them and this has been achieved through the cooperation of parents and teachers. Morale is high once again.'

Professional relationships

Despite the intensity of work involved in the response to the Governors' Programme there were important advantages. Once each report was adopted then it became the policy of the school and incumbent on all to work to promote its objectives. In my view, this did more to solve problems of staff division than any other strategy.[5] Policies concerned with curriculum, good order and organisation and management were now legitimised as part of the democratic chain of responsibility rather than stemming from individuals or as a result of some pseudo-democratic arrangement such as the short-lived staff working party (Chapter 13). There was improved understanding between teachers and governors as a result of regular visits to the school by a sub-committee of the governors. Also, from November, some governors' meetings were held at the school during school sessions rather than at the Civic Centre. This helped to engender a sense of realism and the governors certainly appreciated the refreshments kindly prepared by the home economics department and personally served by students.[6] Several of the reports led to substantial improvements. For example, for special educational needs the school received extra resources including more modern diagnostic tests and also expert advice and support in the classroom.[7]

Other reports enabled definitive statements to be made on such matters as curriculum, discipline and on the composition of teaching groups. The last of these examined the principles involved together with the results of extensive discussions with subject teachers, heads of department and advisers and inspectors. In a 21-page report, subsequently approved by the governors, the first recommendation was that 'Ryhope School should work towards the full implementation of an effective non-selective policy of grouping'. This was followed by details of what was proposed in each key subject area. Years 1 to 3 were to be non-selective in all subjects from September 1983 and, by and large, existing arrangements were to continue in years 4 and 5. Teachers had expressed concerns about the adverse effects of disruptive behaviour in non-selective groups from a small number of students. This matter was addressed in both the discipline and grouping documents and the final recommendation of the latter provided an important safeguard that 'the Governors receive reports at each of their meetings concerning progress towards the establishment and maintenance of a working atmosphere in all classrooms conducive to the highest standards of learning. Such reports to be prepared by the headteacher and submitted first to the senior staff council for observations and comments'. Thus important principles concerning non-selective methods were approved together with a termly appraisal of progress.

Closure proposed

In August 1983 the Education Committee published a second discussion document prepared by the director entitled 'Falling Rolls and Re-Organisation of Secondary Schools'. This again set out four broad possibilities but, compared with the 1981 document (Chapter 14, note 12), it was more specific. Ryhope might close only if the present system (a mixture of 11-16 and 11-18 comprehensive schools) was retained; this seemed unlikely. A series of public meetings took place and at Ryhope, in October, parents present favoured sixth form colleges or, as second choice, tertiary colleges, the system eventually selected. In January 1985 a further document 'Falling Rolls and Reorganisation of Secondary Education' reported on the public meetings and went into more details. Again Ryhope was a possibility for closure under the existing scheme but not, apparently, if tertiary colleges were established. Nevertheless, parents had now twice seen Ryhope named for possible closure and this tended to confirm conclusions that many had already reached; namely that the authority would like to close the school. This naturally affected the projected admission numbers for September 1985[8] and, at a special meeting of the Education Committee four months later (30th May 1985), a report from the director recommended a tertiary system involving an expansion in size of two or three schools and the closure of Ryhope.

Grass-roots campaigning

Next morning the student council commenced their campaign described in Chapter 9. A little later parents of the Ryhope School Association issued a statement 'deploring the loss of the only secondary school in our community' and calling for the retention of the school on the north block site. On 3rd July the governors discussed a report from me together with attached submissions from the teachers' unions and student committees. I made specific proposals to enable Ryhope to be retained without the need for alternative closures emphasising the importance of schools and their communities and the viability of four and five form entry 11-16 schools (Chapter 5). The director was asked to prepare a detailed response to my proposals for consideration by the Education Committee. In answer to a question from the chairman concerning spare capacity I put forward suggestions, expanded in a subsequent letter to the director, involving what I have referred to in Chapter 5 as 'enhanced educational experience'.

Next day, at a public meeting in the school, parents made their views clear and afterwards several of them formed the 'Ryhope School Action Group', whose dynamic chairperson was soon to become a parent governor.[9] The summer holiday was imminent and the action group active. As a result of visiting parents at home — a task undertaken almost entirely by the chairperson — 700 letters of complaint went to the Secretary of State. Other members of the group contributed in a variety of ways and one managed an extended discussion with the Secretary of State on a 'Tuesday Call' phone-in on Radio 4. It was so effective that we asked for a transcript.[10] A working party from the Sunderland District Labour Party submitted detailed proposals to the Labour group supporting the general principles of the reorganisation plans but suggesting a number of improvements including the retention of Ryhope School. Later in the year four members of the action group sent in statutory objections with the main one receiving over 300 signatures, again following home visiting.

From September 1985, as a result of legislation under the 1980 Education Act, each school was required to have its own governing body. Two members of the action group were returned unopposed as parent governors and, at its first meeting in October, the supportive Labour councillor for Ryhope was elected chairman and proved a capable and respected holder of the office until the closure of the school in 1988.[11] A purposeful atmosphere led to lively educational debates and increased opportunities. In July 1986 a delegation of parents, led by the chairperson of the Parents' Action Group and accompanied by the chairman of governors in a personal capacity, was received by Bob Dunn, Under Secretary of State for Education and Science. The delegation, also accompanied by the MP for Sunderland South who had made the necessary arrangements, had prepared their case on a study of government policy: Ryhope School offered something that other schools in Sunderland did not; the government was committed to parental choice, yet they were planning to reduce it. They were well received by the minister and thought that they might have succeeded. Unfortunately Sir Keith Joseph had been replaced two months earlier and the new Secretary of State, Kenneth Baker, was much into efficiency and reducing school places rather than philosophy. The announcement that the appeal had been turned down came with approval of Sunderland's plans. The director received the news early on the morning of 4th November, informed the chairman of the Education Committee and gave it to the press for release that evening. He took no further action and I learned of the decision from the chairperson of the action group about 2pm shortly before I was due to attend a meeting with the director and secondary headteachers on an unrelated matter. I immediately called a staff meeting for afternoon break and prepared a short statement for students to be read to them afterwards by their teachers. As I recall, this thanked them for their support, appreciated their concerns and assured them that their school careers would be the top priority of all concerned.[12]

Involving parents

While the chairperson of the action group was making her rounds during the summer of 1985 she met me one day and said bluntly: 'I'll tell you something that I don't think you understand. Your pupils know much more about the school, what it stands for and why it does things than do their parents.' She was right. In school everything that teachers say, the formal and hidden curriculum, how disciplinary matters are dealt with, what happens about small things — all carry their messages to young people. From day one, the comprehensive school had a morning circular which went to each tutor group and year assembly. This contained factual information such as 'the chess club will meet today' but it also had guidance on how things should be done. This might refer to work, relationships or respect for others and enabled group tutors and heads of year to use items as starting points for discussion and guidance.

Student magazines appeared from time to time, including an impressive and popular magazine, *Why Not?*, edited and produced by four students entirely on their own initiative and, later, a wall newspaper 'Just for Starters'. In such formal and informal ways, young people become aware of what a school is about. Parents, on the other hand, are less well catered for. The local press is useful for some facts and ideas but is limited to what is newsworthy while, as we have seen in Chapter 11, the Ryhope School Association affected a relatively small number of parents directly. Like most schools we occasionally sent out newsletters and information sheets for parents but these were mainly confined to information concerning some forthcoming event. Parents' evenings and progress reports (Chapter 12) are useful but intermittent so, in practice, parents gain most of their information about school from their own children. Some keep their parents relatively well informed but others are unforthcoming on school matters whilst a few make a practice of winding their parents up with lurid accounts of alleged incidents. The action group chairperson asked me what I could do to improve the situation; she clearly expected a positive reply.

Weekly Newsletter

We hit on a simple idea — a weekly newsletter — which was to exceed all expectations. At first I thought that a weekly edition was more than was needed and might prove difficult to maintain. I doubted whether we should have enough worthwhile information every week as well as time to collect, edit, type and prepare material for duplicating and distribution with consequent demands on the services of teaching, clerical and technician staff.[13] However, we were won over by the advantages of regularity. 'Every Thursday' could build up expectations in the readership. At first we could not contemplate anything technically complex as this was before desktop publishing became affordable for schools; so the *Ryhope School Weekly Newsletter* was two sides of A4. Tinted paper and illustrations soon followed and it ran for three years and a hundred and two issues from the start of the new term to the week the school closed.

An effective editorial policy was crucial in order to develop a distinctive style and establish a committed, but not restrictive, policy in support of the aims of the school. In the early stages many contributions needed substantial editing to reduce length[14] and emphasise a sense of audience (Chapter 7) but soon members of staff revealed unsuspected journalistic talent and were much in demand for reports, interviews and so on. Final editing was done by a senior colleague and myself who collectively identified ourselves in the newsletter as 'The Editor'. Later our media and resources technician took over responsibility for type setting and made increasing use of technology as it became available. By arrangement with the teacher concerned he recruited students on a keyboarding course for word processing and other assistance. Getting a newsletter taken home is usually difficult in secondary schools. Many find their way into the litter bin (from the more considerate) or are dropped on the bus floor, street or wherever. It was in about the third week of operation that I knew we had succeeded when a group of fifth years were up in arms: they had not received their newsletter that week.

The *Weekly Newsletter* contained news, features and reasons for doing things and soon added examples of students' work including art, poetry and writing. School students, as well as adults, acted as reporters or contributors — a two-part 'Parents' Guide to Computers' by a fourth year student in the run up to Christmas comes to mind — and, on two occasions, a tutor group took responsibility for the whole edition. There were reports from student committees and by parent governors, and accurate explanations of issues involved during industrial action by teachers. A long running series 'Introducing ...' in which a member of staff or other person associated with the school was interviewed proved very popular[15] whilst another series tackled the complexities of assessment, examinations and qualifications explaining the school's policy in these matters. An appeal in issue No 5 on behalf of the child development course for a baby to bath produced a welcome offer from a former midwife from another part of the town. The *Newsletter* was already gaining a wider circulation! Above all it benefited from an advantage shared with the morning circular: it was possible to return to themes on different occasions and in different circumstances. This not only enabled a theme to be developed over a period of time but also made full use of topical events. I am certain that it helped many parents (not to mention students, teachers, headteacher ...) to a better understanding about the school.

Finishing strongly

After the closure of the school was confirmed the governors took action to bring forward the date in the interests of both staff and students. Third year students transferred to other schools at the end of the school year to enable them to have an uninterrupted two years before GCSE and there was no first year entry for the last year at Ryhope (1987-88). This left small second and third year groups and a substantial fifth year — 250 students in all. Corresponding transfers of staff took place with emphasis on staff development, an operation in which the role of the local authority was widely commended. By now the school was on one site and, in the final year with no forward planning and preparation to be undertaken, a little extra time was available for the staff to attend to the job in hand. This extra scope made a great difference. At the start of the year I had said, in effect: 'This is the final year of the school but the only education our students get; it has to be absolutely first class — there must be no feeling that the school is running down or that it is not worth doing something worthwhile. It must be a full programme in every respect'. Staff, students and parents all responded, for example in the 'Final Report' and Time Capsule projects described in Chapter 12.

Many subject departments were now under acting heads of department, some appointed to the school only in September, and several new to the responsibilities involved. It was the first year of GCSE entries and also the first year in which contracts of service for teachers included time for planning and school-based training at times when students were not in school. Though part of the legislation setting up these changes was ill-conceived and impractical, the need for such opportunities is a prerequisite for efficiency and effectiveness and was long overdue.[16] Several members of staff told me that the experiences of the final year helped their professional development and many students felt that they had gained something extra from their education. One fifth year student certainly felt it had been worthwhile. He or she finished a letter to the *Echo* at the start of the summer term 'I hope that when the school closes the teachers and the school will be remembered as both a place of work and fun. What a great school.' The two parent governors also had generous comments in a letter in the penultimate issue of the *Weekly Newsletter* of which the following is an extract:

> Many of us feel very saddened by the closure of Ryhope School; not only because of the loss of our community school but also of Mr Copland and his staff and the kind of education offered at the school. We are thankful that so many pupils have had the opportunity of experiencing this kind of 'learning for life'. There has been a long tradition of positive attitudes in the school, encouraging students to think for themselves, to acquire self-confidence and self-respect and to respect others ... The progressive methods at Ryhope have helped pupils to fact find and problem solve for themselves, to understand principles and processes rather than simply recall factual information, thus preparing them for life after school. To the end Ryhope School has continued to give its pupils the education that all children deserve. This is its legacy and its victory.

Education is a unique experience for every individual and, hopefully, these sentiments reflect the feelings of many former students.

VI

COMPREHENSIVE EDUCATION:
key to the future

17
Current Issues and Campaigning Strategies

Despite the ravages of the 1980s and '90s comprehensive education remains the key to the future. Its principle of an education of equal value for all school students needs to be re-established in the light of ever changing circumstances. Action in the defence and advancement of state education in general, and comprehensive schools in particular, is urgent and, in this concluding chapter, we examine how the ideas and experiences so far considered relate to current issues.

Legacy of the Education Reform Act

Legislation by Conservative governments after 1979 was based on the principle that the market is the most appropriate way of distributing services as well as goods. The Education Reform Act of 1988 was a major item embodying this principle but, before and after, there were other Acts, ministerial decrees and decisions of quangos furthering the process.

Diversification of schools

The legacy of Conservative legislation includes various schemes, starting with the ill-fated City Technical Colleges, for which private finance was sought though not very successfully (note 14 below). Following that experience the government started a new venture inviting schools to apply for designation as colleges of technology, languages, sport, music or arts. To qualify for this status, and benefit from finance and resources well above the level of their neighbours, schools had to find private sector backers to match funds from central sources. There is no evidence that dangers associated with such an early choice for young people, made while they are still in primary school, were ever seriously considered. Yet one of the basic considerations underlying a national curriculum is to avoid early specialisation so that each young person's interests and capabilities can develop in the light of growing maturity and new educational and social experiences.[1] The last scheme established by the previous government involves use of the Private Finance Initiative, with its customary financial and commercial strings, to fund the building of a few prestigious new schools.[2]

However, the most divisive scheme for diversification did not depend on external financing and thus appealed to many more schools both primary and secondary. Grant maintained status enabled schools previously maintained by democratically elected local authorities to become independent of such 'control' in exchange for central direction through a quango known as the Funding Agency for Schools. Apart from a much hyped 'freedom and independence' issue which carried with it connotations of higher status, the bait to go grant maintained included more generous funding than the government allowed local authorities to spend on comparable schools. Also grant maintained schools were allowed considerable freedom in their admissions procedures. At many but, in fairness, not all of these schools, abler applicants received preference while those likely to present difficulties of any sort could easily be turned away no doubt to swell the ranks of some local authority school with a sufficient number of problems already. Almost from the start grant maintained schools, previously non-selective, were permitted to select a proportion of their entrants for proficiency in fields such as music, drama and sport without this counting as 'a significant change of character' which would require the approval of the Secretary of State. In 1993 grant maintained schools, soon to be followed by schools from local authorities, were invited to apply for technology college or similar status. Finally in a White Paper *Self-government for Schools* published in June 1996 the government announced plans to permit selection on 'general ability' by both grant maintained and local authority schools — up to fifty per cent for the former, thirty percent for the specialist colleges and twenty per cent for local authority schools — a clear return to selective education. Before the proposals could be implemented the general election of 1997 intervened.

Eighteen years of Conservative rule saw the introduction of a national curriculum, local management, open enrolment, semi-privatised inspection teams and renewed emphasis on religious worship. We have glanced at religious issues in Chapter 4 and noted the role and significance of school inspectors in various situations. These 'reforms', which occurred with unprecedented speed, are well documented in the literature. Here we look more closely at a few aspects of the legislation particularly relevant to the theme of this book emphasising that, collectively, the developments formed part of a policy to downgrade the status of local authorities and the primary and comprehensive schools maintained by them.

Office for Standards in Education (Ofsted)

Revised style inspections through the Office for Standards in Education are creating unjustified anxieties for teachers and governors. Teachers in both primary and secondary schools feel under pressure to give undue emphasis to teaching methods and classroom organisation favoured by Ofsted. Many schools have re-introduced streaming and setting even from the earliest ages thus re-creating precisely the circumstances which Douglas warned about over thirty years ago in *The Home and the School.* (Chapter 2). Overall, the largely unaccountable Ofsted teams (Who inspects the inspectors?) seem unlikely to solve many of the problems noted in previous chapters.

Schools must be accountable and inspectors have an important role in this process. However, it does not follow that their function is best discharged through high profile visits to schools by teams of inspectors every few years. 'Snapshot' is an appropriate description of the Ofsted process where the business enterprise which has won the contract (naturally 'team' is the preferred description) liaises with the school only for the few days of the inspection together with an information collecting preparatory phase and a short period afterwards while the report is prepared. In due course a new round of bids will probably produce a new consortium for the next inspection. At least Her Majesty's Inspectors retained a continuous, if tenuous, responsibility for each individual school. Not too surprisingly Ofsted appears to equate community with local business interests rather than with the broadly based ideas discussed in Chapter 5.The whole process needs urgent review with emphasis on regular monitoring, advice, discussion and action.[3]

National curriculum

We have seen (Chapter 4) that the concept of a national curriculum is to be welcomed. Indeed it should be the centrepiece of the education service but the version introduced by the Conservatives does not fulfil this role despite features welcomed by teachers. It is one of the few items of educational legislation which caused any dissension in government ranks. For market enthusiasts a national curriculum presents a dilemma: if it is insufficiently prescriptive scope is given to the professionals; if over-prescriptive it reduces opportunities for schools to compete. In practice the national curriculum leant heavily towards the latter but was developed in a piecemeal fashion with each subject panel drawing up its syllabus independently and producing, overall, far more than could be taught in the time available. Changes in content and assessment procedures were essential but, in the meantime, only countless hours of voluntary and dedicated work by teachers avoided disaster.[4] On the positive side, the original version of the national curriculum had a welcome emphasis on the common entitlement of school students but some of the ideas put forward, especially at Key Stages 3 and 4, lead back to a two-track curriculum in which the higher educational levels are reserved for the more gifted and for those from privileged social backgrounds whilst the remainder are offered a utilitarian mixture of literacy, numeracy and 'relevant' vocational skills for those deemed 'unacademic'. We have noted the importance of jointly considering the needs of all students when planning the curriculum (Chapter 4). Now we consider how some of the changes actually encourage schools to adopt divisive practices.

Key Stage 4 (years 10 and 11) provides a good example. Here the national curriculum was soon reduced to a core of English, mathematics, science and physical education together with at least a short course in design and technology and in a modern foreign language. The status of information technology is still ill-defined and schools make their own decisions on how to complete the curriculum in these years. A two-track ethos can develop in several ways. Firstly, schools may be tempted to use their freedom of choice to offer outwardly attractive but inferior status courses to some of their students (Chapter 4). Next, in almost all GCSE subjects, assessments are arranged in so-called tiers, each tier covering either higher or lower grades with a small overlap. Students are often selected for a tier up to two years before the examination with consequent restrictions on access to a full curriculum for those designated for the lower tiers. Finally, there are various ideas involving hybrid courses between schools and further education and even talk of allowing some students to finish their schooling at age 14 at the end of Key Stage 3 and transfer to a college of further education or training provider.

In planning the national curriculum the first step should have been to make an audit of existing strengths and weaknesses; then, taking account of the time available for teachers and students, the primary need was to produce an outline plan or framework within which new ideas could be developed into practical, well-focussed and dynamic policies using the professional skills of teachers to the full. Broadly based and extensive consultation should have occurred at all stages. In the absence of these basic procedures the task of reforming the national curriculum without further upheavals, using some of the ideas described in Chapter 4, is unnecessarily complex — but none the less vital.

Local management

Local management of schools (LMS) has received undeserved acclaim. For example, in their Green Paper *Opening Doors to a Learning Society* the Labour Party (1993) suggested that only relatively minor amendments were needed to the government's legislation to make it more widely acceptable. Two policy statements *Diversity and Excellence* and *Excellence for Everyone* published, respectively, before and after the 1995 Party Conference emphasised Labour's commitment to this deeply flawed system. In government, the White Paper *Excellence in Schools* (Department for Education and Employment, 1997) strongly continued this theme.[5]

Although schools have welcomed opportunities to respond rapidly to perceived needs — and we have seen some of the consequences of remote governors with no real understanding of the schools for which they are responsible (Chapters 13 to 15) — the current arrangements for local management are a very important instrument towards the vision of a market determined education service and must be recognised as such. There was no dissension on this policy in Conservative ranks where strategies to divide and conquer are well understood. Major concerns in local management include:

- Role of local education authorities. Since their inception under the Education Act of 1902, the key function of these authorities has been to work for the highest standards of education in *all* schools for which

they are responsible. To attain this target they must be able to plan
necessary provision both in the mid- and long-term with access to
adequate resources of staff and materials. Under LMS this became
progressively more difficult as higher and higher percentages of
education budgets had to be devolved to individual schools operating as
cost centres. Nor should we underestimate the value of fair and
efficient local authority administration in fields as diverse as payment of
wages, contracting and monitoring the effects of educational policy.
Much of this work has been curtailed or set aside.

- Teaching staff. The largest item in a school budget is teachers' salaries
  so the temptation to casualise employment and to replace experienced
  staff with inexperienced teachers lower down the salary scale is very
  strong.
- Maintenance. As a cost cutting exercise painting and decorating, for
  example, may be done by volunteers or odd job firms. Where
  compulsory competitive tendering is required contracts are likely to go
  to bids dependent on low wages and poor working conditions. (True
  the latter situation applies to local authority contracts but at least the
  authorities are knowledgeable in a field where experience counts).
- Trade unions. LMS makes trade union organisation more difficult.
  With schools being relatively small units, cohesion is more difficult to
  maintain among members in a district or region. Indeed, where
  governing bodies and headteachers are hostile to trade unions,
  individual members, particularly school representatives, may need to
  keep a low profile lest their name appears on the next list of
  redundancies. Day to day work by trade union officials in support of
  members is also more complex as negotiations over similar problems
  (for example, redundancy) have to take place with many individual
  schools.[6]
- Competition and selective entry. Almost every aspect of LMS
  encourages competition between schools not least because their prime
  source of income is based on student numbers and ages. Young people
  with special educational needs, difficult social backgrounds,
  behavioural problems and/or from ethnic minorities may be seen as
  expensive in terms of staffing and resources. Indeed, their presence
  may be considered off-putting to parents who may be considering the
  school and there is widespread evidence that such young people are
  frequently refused places whilst others from more favoured
  backgrounds, are admitted. Although the Labour government is to

preclude overt forms of selection it is extremely difficult, under LMS, to eliminate covert selection. A school may denigrate the work of its neighbours to persuade 'approved' parents to enrol their sons and daughters whilst applying pressure on the 'less suitable' to seek alternative schools where their offspring will be 'happier' or 'find the work less demanding'.

- School governors. Governing bodies vary greatly in the expertise of their members especially in financial matters. A void in experience increases power for the professionals, especially the headteacher, at the expense of democratic cooperation. Alternatively, a financially 'expert' chair of governors may exert excessive personal influence. Under LMS, each governing body considers policies for one particular school even though decisions may have important consequences for others nearby. This antithesis of the role of local education authorities makes effective and equitable planning almost an impossibility.
- Professional leadership. Whilst schools should certainly account for their costs — and teachers need professional administrative support in this field — LMS in its present form puts a premium on business acumen rather than on educational understanding and pedagogical skill especially at senior staff level. As we have seen, managing the learning process is a demanding and full-time occupation; it must be restored as the key requirement of professional educators.
- Enterprise culture. Day to day decisions as a result of LMS will have their effect on students, staff, parents and governors as the values of the enterprise culture become part of the hidden curriculum (Chapter 4).

The above points represent just a few of the considerations which need to be addressed in any exhaustive treatment of local management. Before LMS, local authorities were certainly seen to have limitations and weaknesses as well as strengths but what is needed today is a concept of joint management of schools — JMS perhaps? — linking full democratic responsibility and accountability with effective management procedures.

Open enrolment

Legislation on open enrolment extended existing law on parental preference and enables parents who are in a position to transport their children or to pay for travel to enrol them in schools at a distance from their neighbourhood. In some cases, residents in a local authority with a comprehensive system are able to apply for places in a neighbouring authority with a selective system. Legislation also placed a duty on local authorities to provide facilities for extra admission numbers where schools were over-subscribed but pressure from the Treasury caused re-thinking on that matter. 'This school is over-subscribed' has become a significant selling point to attract both parents and teachers but, together with LMS and the grant maintained sector, open enrolment has made a planned system of educational provision almost an impossibility in some authorities. In an article in *The Times Educational Supplement* (1992d) Susan Young described the findings of a report *The Scottish Experience of Parental Choice of Schools* which showed that:

> The principal effect of parents' right to choose, has been to increase segregation between working-class and middle-class pupils. The impact on children's academic results was minimal.

In a second article (*The Times Educational Supplement*, 1994) Young reported on 'an influential new report' from the Organisation for Economic Co-operation and Development (OECD) entitled *School a matter of choice*. This study found that:

> Allowing parents to choose their child's school does not appear to improve performance in any of the countries where this has become the norm.

The report also found that parental choice:

> potentially makes it difficult to pursue some system-wide education policies, especially those associated with provision of one kind of secondary school for all pupils.

Solutions to problems arising from parental preference are not easy but policy on enrolment must take account of consequential effects on comprehensive education. Some of the issues (which affect both primary and secondary schools) were examined in Chapter 5.

From the arrival of the Great Educational Reform Bill (GERBIL) on which the Education Reform Act was based, trade unions and other organisations have produced information packs and offered advice and support for campaigning on specific issues. Information and support from Local Schools Information — an independent body funded by almost every local education authority — was decisive in many local campaigns which successfully resisted proposals for schools to opt out of local authority control, ie become grant maintained. LSI recognised that bewilderment and anxiety were the great dangers and offered, often in conjunction with the local authority, information, advice and speakers to ensure that parents, teachers, governors and the wider public were fully and accurately informed. With grant maintained status in its final stages, LSI is continuing its work and has put forward a simple non-divisive alternative to the government's proposals for new categories of comprehensive school (Note 5 above). Access to key information is, indeed, vital, if we are to re-establish the primacy of comprehensive education.

Re-establishing comprehensive education

In 1965 the Labour government issued its famous circular which requested, but as a circular could not compel, local authorities to prepare plans for comprehensive education in their areas.[7] Unfortunately Labour did not recognise the need to define the aims of state education in terms which would encourage and support the comprehensive development of the new schools.[8] Partly as a result of this void, comprehensive education lost ground under the impact of free market ideology.

Theory and practice

The fight back must be well-founded. Supporters of every description — teachers, educators, parents, school students — all need to be well informed. Historical and political perspectives are necessary as well as knowledge of more immediate educational issues so that no one goes empty handed to their work. We need to regenerate our educational processes through the advancement of pedagogy in the interests of all students including the gifted and those with learning difficulties (Chapters 6 and 7). Horizons need to extend beyond the school gate (Chapter 5) and both theory and practice should address the social and personal development of young people (Chapters 8 and 9). We must keep in mind that cultural activities in the curriculum can make a special contribution in this last respect and, above all, we must promulgate, as a central tenet, the entitlement of all young people to the prospect of a satisfying career. Once comprehensive education is re-established and again provides the framework for decision making, schools will need continuing support. The battle is never won (Chapter 3) so we need to constantly campaign within the profession, in trade unions and supportive organisations, and especially among the wider public with the object of deepening understanding and broadening support on important issues. These may be 'theoretical' such as the concept of intelligence and fitness for learning (Chapter 2) or 'practical', for example in providing opportunities for all who wish to learn a musical instrument.[9] Whilst every effort is needed to reduce unnecessary antagonisms in schools, we should neither expect nor aim for consensus on all issues because basic class interests ensure residual conflicts of educational concern (Chapter 1). For example, we have seen that, in the 1970s and '80s, schools in very different circumstances met with attack if they were perceived to overstep an imaginary line into the field of actively promoting education of equal value for all their young people (Chapter 6).

Issues such as these remain urgent and the arrival of a Labour government, with its declared concern for education, does not reduce the need for continuing pressure from many sources. 'What type of education is envisaged?' remains the key question.

Equal value for all young people

If progress is to be made towards an education which is intrinsically of equal value for all, then active promotion of means towards such entitlement is required and lies at the core of the process of creating and maintaining comprehensive education. Such a vital task must not be left, as has been almost entirely the case so far, to a few individual schools and the efforts of individual teachers. Situations, such as the following, illustrate why active and collaborative support at national, local and school levels is so essential:

- Raised expectations. These arise among parents and students as a result of comprehensive education but are difficult to fulfil in total given the resources available and limited training and job opportunities for many young people.
- School policy and organisation. As in any forward looking institution, policy and organisation need to be constantly renewed, advanced and 're-owned' by members of staff, students and parents.
- Appointment of staff. It is not always possible to find staff who combine the necessary professional expertise with a personal philosophy of

education consistent with promoting the concept of equal value. Under these circumstances (which need addressing through initial and in-service training) disproportionate demands may be made on the goodwill of the most committed staff.

- Non-selective teaching. However well conceived and implemented, a flexible non-selective approach to teaching may not, in itself, have an immediate appeal to all parents. Some, whose children would have been in the A-stream, may think they are missing out while others whose sons and daughters would have been in lower groups may consider that being educated with the ablest is too demanding. Support is needed in actively explaining and demonstrating the purpose and scope of non-selective methods to parents, school students and the wider community.
- Behavioural problems. Students with behavioural problems can generate great anxieties and absorb excessive amounts of time. However, many are helped towards a more responsible approach by staff and fellow students working together. A comprehensive school has access to rich resources of human talent within its community, including teachers who are brilliant in this field. More could be achieved with the help of enhanced support services on a local authority basis (Chapter 8).
- Deep-seated cases. For persistent and serious behavioural problems adequately staffed and resourced pupil referral units should keep open opportunities for rehabilitation of students through partnership with their original schools (Chapter 9). Totally unacceptable is the situation in which popular schools can, through permanent exclusions or their threat, export problems to neighbouring schools in less favourable situations.

Problems such as these remain largely unresolved and, even if some are submerged under the weight of more immediate considerations, they constrain the development of comprehensive education. Today, schools must contend with the effects of market values such as the scramble for admission numbers and competitive financing. Yet one of the most basic requirements for a system of comprehensive education is for a cooperative and supportive environment in which schools can operate and develop. Conditions of service and career prospects for staff need to attract recruits into the schools who believe that the service they are entering is not only worthwhile and challenging but also one where working conditions support the achievement of enlightened aims and objectives. Initial and in-service training relevant to these aims are both essential as is a new role for inspectors as an integral part of the support process. Currently they attach scant importance to key policies and initiatives because their terms of reference do not incorporate comprehensive aims. As we have seen above, the role of the inspectorate needs comprehensive (in both senses of the word) re-examination as does their experience, recruitment and training.

At all levels, there is an urgent need for active and practical support for teachers in the classroom; for research into pedagogy, the science of teaching; for resources of all descriptions, and for pilot studies into the possibilities of enhanced educational experience (Chapter 5). Appropriate statements of aims and objectives — even a mission statement or two — taken seriously, would be a source of encouragement to the many who want to see education of equal value become reality. Whilst all this may seem, at first sight, to be a distant possibility, situations change rapidly — for good or ill. Few in the mid-1970s foresaw the speed with which comprehensive education was to come under such serious threat in the next decade or two.

Subjective factors

Personal experiences are naturally much influenced by subjective factors (personalities, environment and the particular social, political and educational climate of the time) but such experiences often reflect objective considerations with more general applicability. Whilst subjective factors affect the way in which situations develop, objective factors, concerned with the nature of social and political forces, are also at work. Situations, outwardly diverse will, on closer examination, be seen to have common characteristics. For example, some claimed that Ryhope School proceeded too rapidly towards non-selective teaching methods pointing to schools which started with more limited objectives in this field. Certainly it was a common practice at the time to have non-selective groups in the first year or two while retaining setting for one or more of mathematics, science and modern languages. However, as attacks on comprehensive education gained momentum during the 1970s many of these schools abandoned further development and reduced and even eliminated steps already taken.[10] A second example concerns the wider significance of the events at Ryhope described in Chapters 13 to 16. These were clearly influenced by the subjective factor of a single governing body covering all schools. Had there been separate bodies for each school then events would have unfolded differently but key issues would still have come to the fore although we cannot say in what manner and with what results.

When under pressure at Ryhope and at the height of media activity I was fortunate to be physically fit, accompanied by a close family who were extremely supportive (unless I showed signs of wilting when they made their views firmly known), able to relax when the opportunity arose and, above all, able to view the nature of unfolding events as essentially political rather than personal. Letters and messages of support were a great source of strength as were conversations with parents, students, teachers and people from all walks of life who recognised the essentials of what was being attempted. In retrospect I probably under-estimated the way in which the school was perceived as different from others; at the time the procedures which we introduced and the attitudes encouraged seemed essential, but relatively minor, developments to facilitate study and personal development in a comprehensive context. No doubt I assumed too readily that everyone would understand the values underlying organisational and curricular development — at least after a little experience. The strength of the NASUWT (both in the school and in the region) was considerable. It was politically effective in certain respects, for example in the timing of resolutions, whilst its essentially conservative approach to educational matters had influence, not least in the professional development of a number of young teachers. The influence of the leader of Sunderland Council, the director of education and the senior inspector was also notable. Not only were they powerful individuals in their own right but had complementary approaches and expertise which made them a considerable force. The director, for example, had a prodigious capacity to produce detailed letters and reports, many at short notice. All appeared to want the school to continue, albeit for different reasons and on their own terms and there was a distinct if unspoken feeling that, if I would accept that I was in error and agree with what was being suggested, then all would be well.

Decision-making processes

Had the local authority wanted Ryhope School to succeed along the lines of Sunderland's own objective (Chapter 10) then the situation would have immediately been more favourable. One could have tackled problems familiar in most schools (under-achieving students, disruptive behaviour and so on) much more effectively. As it was there were easy opportunities to seek out, aggravate and manufacture deficiencies and to use all problems, large or small, as opportunities for fundamental change.[11]

Books and articles on school management have been a growth industry in recent years with much discussion of management structures, leadership styles, management of change and so forth. Less emphasis has been given to what several authors, including Eric Hoyle (1986) and Stephen Ball (1987), refer to as the micro-politics of school life, ie the informal networks and actions by which people seek to influence the course of events so familiar in another context to readers of politicians' memoirs. Hoyle notes that all organisations are characterised by micro-politics and schools are no exception. As he says 'the loosely coupled structure of the school invites micro-political activity' (p 171). The theme is an important one and I offer the following contribution based on personal observation and involvement: locally and temporarily, power belongs to those who seize it.

In this connection I became aware of a danger not always identified: the wider the distribution of decision-making, the more easily power can be assumed by reactionary groups and individuals. The open discussions, formal and informal, which characterised Ryhope's earlier years (and led to many fruitful — sometimes inspirational — developments) had, to some extent, to be curtailed in the light of experience for just this reason. It was too easy for some to genuinely or wilfully confuse exploration of possibilities with actual decisions and to use partial information for their own purposes. As Hoyle explains:

> How information is acquired, distributed, presented, doctored or withheld is
> micro-political ... Those teachers who have, or make it their business to have,
> access to information are in the stronger micro-political position.

And not only teachers. Access to information helps to determine the actions, positively or otherwise, of education officers, governors, inspectors, parents and many others. At Ryhope, lack of local authority support for the overall direction of the school undermined the confidence of some members of staff, appeared to threaten job security and influenced public opinion. Yet the achievements of the school were there to be built on — rather than attacked and reduced in effectiveness and in some cases made inoperable.

Legislation is necessary if aims are to be taken seriously but it must be effectively followed up. It is noteworthy that Conservative governments backed up the introduction of GCSE and key aspects of the 1988 Education Reform Act with in-service training for teachers and a massive public relations exercise for everyone else. Their lack of success in so many areas, though not in general for GCSE, derives from the inequalities and inadequacies of much of the legislation which proved unacceptable to professionals and parents alike. Obeying the law is a powerful incentive for most people and, if fully comprehensive education is to be re-established, then appropriate legislation and support is needed to provide a legal and practical basis for effective involvement by all concerned.

Campaigning issues

For significant improvements to state schooling, campaigning remains essential and the old socialist slogan 'agitate, educate and organise' is as relevant today as when it first appeared. Forming a support group, canvassing parents, producing newsletters and arranging a delegation may all be necessary in particular situations whilst, in any form of campaigning, the support and opinions of former students can be invaluable. Within the trade union movement the NUT has mounted a long running campaign for a single TUC-affiliated teachers' union seeking amalgamation with the NASUWT, also TUC affiliated, as a first step. This campaign to create a truly effective and powerful union needs widespread support.[12]

Use of the media, especially at local level, is not to be despised or rejected out of hand. Local journalists need to establish reliable sources based on mutual trust and, whilst headlines and truncation of reports may be at the mercy of anonymous sub-editors, I found that the majority of journalists took a professional pride in achieving accurate copy. All were willing to give me time to collect my thoughts and, if telephoned when my mind was on other matters, I always received cooperation if I requested a ring back after a short delay. Requests to journalists to read back sensitive wording were never refused but on the other hand 'No comment' asks for what it will get: virtually all the space allocated for the report given to the opposition. I found a similar wish for honest reporting among local radio and television reporters who would normally have an informal discussion to clarify background information before interviewing.

Campaign successes show what can be done and point the way forward. A Conservative government intention to recruit under-trained and low-paid additions to the teaching force (aptly nicknamed 'Mums' Army') was withdrawn under pressure. Parents saw through attempts to justify increases in class size especially when their attention was drawn to the different standards which applied for the children of government ministers in private education.[13] They were equally unimpressed with efforts to gloss over the rapidly deteriorating fabric of school buildings drawn to their attention by governing bodies, inspectors, trade unions, university professors and action groups. The boycott of standard assessment tasks (SATs) in 1993 and 1994, led exclusively by the NUT in the latter year, attracted much public support, proved highly successful and highlighted the government's real objective to increase competition between schools through the publication of league tables of results.

Whilst the growth in selective schools remains of great concern, the policy to establish business-supported City Technical Colleges ground to a halt two or three years after its inception.[14] Similarly the massive Conservative-led campaign of financial incentives and disinformation failed to generate a bandwagon of schools opting out of local authority control for grant maintained status. Grassroots campaigning supported by up-to-date, accurate information proved decisive. In the face of similar resistance, direct attempts to replace comprehensive systems by the creation of grammar schools has been a non-runner since the affair of Solihull in 1983 (Chapter 1). Indeed, Conservative policy for a grammar school in every town was a non-starter at the general election of 1997.

Fairness and common justice have a wide appeal so campaigning for public education must centre around the true priorities of the majority of parents: first-class schools — nursery, primary and comprehensive — easily accessible, serving every neighbourhood and district.

Notes and further information

Chapter 1. Role of Public Education

1 In 1870 the concept of elementary education had three facets: it was for the children of the labouring poor; it consisted of reading, writing and arithmetic, and it was not restricted to any age group (many adults attended night classes for elementary education). By 1944 the concept of 'secondary education for all' had been around in one form or another for over twenty years; its implementation following the Act had both positive and negative features which are discussed in Chapter 3.

2 Similar views to those expressed by Forster had been put forward much earlier by Adam Smith in *The Wealth of Nations* (1776).

3 The demise of the study of the history of education in initial teacher· training courses is highlighted in a report by Richard Aldrich (1989), senior lecturer in the history of education at the University of London Institute of Education and president of the United Kingdom History of Education Society. His report gives the results of a survey into history of education courses provided by tutors in charge of one-year courses for the post-graduate certificate in education (PGCE). 78 education departments replied representing an 85% response but there were only 6 where students took a separate course in the history of education. In one of these all students took the course but it lasted for a mere 1 to 5 hours whilst in the others, out of a total of 925 students, only 68 (including 38 from one institution) opted to take the course. Even then the historical content was often confined to short background notes relevant to the contemporary scene eg the introduction of comprehensive schooling or developments in the teaching a particular subject. Comments from tutors included 'with ever increasing initiatives there is no time for more' and 'the changes which have taken place in the last decade or more have almost eliminated the history of education at core and option levels'. This is in sharp contrast to the widespread belief in government circles that too much history of education and other theoretical irrelevancies are taught on initial courses of teacher education. The author draws two conclusions:

- In Post-graduate Certificate in Education courses in England and Wales at the present time there is virtually no history of education being taught as a separate discipline, and precious little in general education or other courses.

- Claims that teacher education via the PGCE route can be improved by the reduction or elimination of history of education courses are fraudulent ... A significant number of tutors believed that, even in a short one year course of initial teacher training, time should now be devoted to the subject.

4 Section 11 of the 1966 Local Government Act was originally designed to help local authorities pay for extra staff to assist with problems arising from immigration. Later it became the main source of money with which authorities endeavour to meet their obligations under the Race Relations Act. The Act places a moral duty on them to eliminate unlawful discrimination and promote equal opportunities but provided no money for this purpose.

5 The abolition of corporal punishment was an absolutely basic reform: it was abolished in the mines and factories in the 1830s, in the forces in the 1950s and in borstals in the 1960s. By the 1970s Switzerland and the German Federal Republic had joined all other European Countries from the Soviet Union to Portugal in abolishing it in the schools. All, that is, except Britain and the Irish Republic — and Britain had elected six Labour governments for a total of seventeen years following the second world war.

6 The Danish government introduced a national code of conduct into its schools on 1 August 1967. It set out the responsibilities and rights of teachers, students and parents in a cooperative, firm, sympathetic and understanding manner — in sharp contrast to the semi-legalistic language of Citizen's and Consumer's Charters in Britain and the United States. A statement preceding the legislation (14 June 1967) set the tone with its title: 'The Promotion of Good Order in Schools'. The statement is included as an appendix to the Society of Teachers Opposed to Physical Punishment report 'The European Example: The Abolition of Corporal Punishment in Schools' (STOPP, 1980).

7 The authority for a headteacher's decision on matters concerning school clothing is based solely on case law relying, in practice, on an individual judge's personal opinion concerning what is reasonable. No legislation empowers governors, heads or local authorities to prescribe specific clothing though obviously it should be practical for the job in hand and comply with the Health and Safety Act. Many school uniforms are impracticable for the varied nature of the job to be done which may include sitting on the floor during drama or working in laboratories and workshops. Many contravene the spirit, if not the letter, of the Sex Discrimination Act and there have been many cases of dispute and disaffection involving children of non-Christian faiths. Denmark, France, Germany including the former Democratic Republic, and the United States are just a few of the countries which operate successfully without them.

8 *Half our Future* was the title of a report by the Central Advisory Council for Education (England) and known after its chairman as the Newsom Report (Ministry of Education, 1963a). It was unfortunately based on old and negative ideas of intelligence and ability which have led to widespread educational injustice and whose significance is discussed in Chapter 2. Nevertheless, I remember

reading the report at the time and thinking that many of the ideas about curriculum and method were excellent but applied equally to all students.

9   At its 1989 conference, the NUT's weekly newspaper *The Teacher* was replaced by a journal of the same name sent to all members three or four times a term. The financial savings were considerable but, regrettably, many opportunities for topical and educative reporting, as well as the up to date exchange of information, were lost.

10   The comments of the Northern Region Education Alliance also stated 'The omission of any reference to the development and influence of trade unions is astounding'.

11   Help for teachers was sparse and there was no national programme of in-service education and training specifically designed to assist them to achieve comprehensive objectives. True there were optional courses — usually a day or a series of evenings — aimed mainly at heads of department and senior management of large schools but nowhere did in-service training match the extensive input under Conservative governments for the fulfilment of its own objectives such as the Technical and Vocational Education Initiative (TVEI) of the 1980s and Standard Assessment Tasks (SATs) following introduction of the national curriculum.

Chapter 2. Human Abilities and the School System

1   In 1953 Brian Simon of Leicester University School of Education published a short book *Intelligence and the Comprehensive School*. This included several examples revealing the class, rather than intellectual, basis of many of the questions used in selection tests. In one case working class pupils had to know that a parlourmaid is not expected to do the sewing in a house! The book was reprinted as part of *Intelligence, Psychology and Education* (Simon, 1971). The example quoted is on page 63.

2   One anomaly in testing had to be faced by all local education authorities: as girls mature earlier than boys, their scores on average were higher. Most authorities, therefore, required a higher score for girls to gain admission to grammar school than for boys.

3   'The Burt Scandal' *Radio 4*, 13 June 1982. The affair is also described in a chapter entitled 'The IQ Controversy: The Case of Cyril Burt' in Simon (1985).

4   Significantly, internal selection procedures were not within the scope of an HMI booklet *Mixed Ability Work in Comprehensive Schools* in the series 'Matters for Discussion' (Department of Education and Science, 1978a). However, mixed-ability grouping, banding, setting and streaming were described and compared in *Secondary Schools: an Appraisal by HMI* which covered the period 1982-1986 (Department of Education and Science, 1988a: 50-52). Referring to the formation of streams from primary records or internal tests the inspectors commented 'This practice was rarely satisfactory, and insufficient or inappropriate evidence was used to place pupils in streams in most of these schools ... The teaching in only one of the 10 streamed schools extended the more-able pupils.

Elsewhere, this form of grouping was associated with low expectations of those in the lower streams'. These comments certainly represented a step forward from an earlier report *Aspects of Secondary Education in England: a survey by HM Inspectors of Schools* (Department of Education and Science 1979) where observations on streaming are much less condemnatory. Unfortunately, the inspectors do not appear to have recognised that precisely the same arguments apply to banding and very similar ones to setting. Here their reservations are milder: 'Where a year group was divided into two equal-size bands, with the point of division approximating to the middle of the distribution curve of ability, students on either side of the dividing line, with very similar abilities, were often treated very differently in terms of teachers' expectation and, in some instances, curriculum opportunity'. Again, this observation is more than justified but it remains an observation only as HM Inspectors had no more to say. Yet the practice is horrendously unfair by any criteria. Nor do the inspectors appear to have seen the relevance of their observations to the seminal 1960s research in two stream primary schools which is discussed later in this chapter.

There is evidence in the HMI appraisal that non-streamed work is viewed as a divergence from the norm. For example, the inspectors comment: 'Teaching mixed-ability groups is a difficult undertaking and skill, calling for detailed preparation on the part of teachers and school before this pattern of organisation is adopted'. No one could question this statement as it stands but, as teaching itself is a difficult undertaking and skill, exactly the same requirements must apply to any other grouping. Marginalising of issues resulting from internal selection by local and national authorities has had further implications. As Joan Gregory (1987), Director of the Centre for the Study of the Comprehensive School, pointed out in 'Comprehensive comrades', a review of *Defend Comprehensive Schools*, a booklet prepared by Brian Simon for the Communist Party of Great Britain:

> Twenty years of officially recognised comprehensive education has failed to produce strong definitive statements about the criteria and values upon which the genuinely comprehensive school should be based. HMI reports do not include any attempt to evaluate the extent to which a secondary school may be genuinely comprehensive.

5 *Education and Environment* (Wiseman, 1964) was an influential book concerning secondary education. It was based on research at Manchester University into the effect of social factors on scholastic performance.
6 The dominance of pragmatic reasons for decision making in some comprehensive schools is illustrated in a comparative survey of comprehensive and selective schools in Triliw in Wales undertaken by Reynolds and Sullivan (1987).

Chapter 3. Arrival of Comprehensive Education

1 Excellent examples of scholarly but highly readable educational history involving comprehensive education include *Education and the Social Order (1940-1990)*

(Simon, 1991) and *Towards a New Education System, The Victory of the New Right?* (Chitty, 1989). Reynolds and Sullivan (1987) give a revealing insight into Labour Party attitudes to comprehensives after the war in the introductory chapter 'Comprehensive Schooling — A Historical Account and Explanation' to their book *The Comprehensive Experiment*. They note that Hugh Gaitskell, Roy Jenkins and Mannie Shinwell were all against replacing the grammar schools. (The no less important aim of replacing the public and independent schools was side-tracked by the Labour leadership).

2   It is instructive to note that John Major's government tried to reintroduce the term 'council school' to distinguish local authority schools from opted out grant maintained schools. Many, no doubt, still remembered the pejorative use of the term by the middle and upper classes in pre-war days.

3   Further information about Wyndham School is given in Chapter 5.

4   Observation suggests that New Labour sees internal selection in comprehensive schools as appealing to the voters of 'middle England'. It avoids the risk of not being selected for a grammar school yet provides many of its perceived advantages.

5   *The Alternative in Eastern Europe* is open to question concerning its overall political analysis but it has important things to say concerning education which are applicable to situations in many parts of the world.

Chapter 4. Attitudes and Ideology Behind the Curriculum

1   Home Economics is another subject which has diminished in status since the 1988 Act despite the opportunities it provides for boys and girls to experience together a wide range of creative, practical and management activities associated with the home (Chapter 7) and, through these, to make an effective contribution to breaking down sex stereotyping.

2   In the 1990s, the value of learning languages in school is more widely accepted even though the enthusiasm of many people from other countries to learn English still outweighs the commitment of the majority of our young people to learn French, German, Spanish, Russian, Japanese ... Learning a language to a reasonable degree of fluency in a range of contexts is a long and testing task requiring great commitment. Which foreign language to learn is always a debatable issue with the most popular choices depending mainly on economic and historical circumstances. Esperanto, the international second language, was included in the curriculum early in Ryhope's history and an option group took the subject to CSE level. Only problems of staffing continuity precluded longer involvement. The language has proved its worth for over a hundred years, is pleasant to speak and listen to and combines relative ease of learning with flexibility and adaptability to enable delicate shades of human feeling to be expressed. It has developed a rich and extensive literature of its own and presents no threat to any national language but enables people to communicate on an equal footing whatever the cultural 'standing' of their native tongue.

3   Practical examples involving the compatibility of content, method and purpose for

all students are discussed in chapters 6 and 7.

4   Means of providing for minority needs through increased flexibility are discussed in chapters 5 and 6.

5   *The Crest of the Peacock: Non-European Roots of Mathematics* by George Gheverghese Joseph (1994) was described by the New Scientist as 'invaluable for mathematics teachers at all levels'.

6   The national curriculum was intended to provide 75 per cent of the curriculum of each school, the remaining time being left to individual schools.

7   Materialist is used in its true meaning of a scientific explanation of the universe. As Georges Politzer (1976) says in *Elementary Principles of Philosophy*, originally published in France in the 1930s: 'Commonly we consider a materialist to be someone who only wishes to enjoy material pleasures. Playing on the word "materialism" which includes the word "matter", people have given it a completely false meaning.'

8   Events at Prestolee under its headteacher, Teddy O'Neill, are recorded by Gerard Holmes (1977) in *The Idiot Teacher*, a book which describes a piece of unusual educational and social history. The preface is by John Watts who was principal of Countesthorpe College, a comprehensive school in Leicestershire, and one of the leading schools in the 1970s in devising successful methods and organisation for corporate and independent study by school students. Referring to changes which O'Neill introduced to eliminate rote learning in favour of the teacher 'leading and facilitating', Watts comments:

> The teacher was a liberator, that most dangerous of agents, stimulating the ability to find out and the desire to do' rather than being the imparter of knowledge ... The children were 'to be allowed to work together, to discuss their work one with another, and to learn by helping each other'. Even today, this most common and effective way by which man has developed from his forebears, corporately identifying problems, devising strategies for resolving them and carrying those strategies out, is not only neglected in schools, but actively stamped out. Outside schools men and women have known that only united can they thrive, whilst inside the order of the day is still cut-throat competition and individual attainment. (p x)

The consequences are familiar today:

> The press obviously relished the local conflict that ensued. Their readiness to print hostile letters encouraged the prejudiced and self opinionated to vent their spleen. Easy misrepresentation distorted O'Neill's inspired 'happy as you do' into the insidious terms 'go-as-you-please. and 'do-as-you-like'. Parents who had been pleased to find their children learning and happy (that rare and often mistrusted combination) had their confidence undermined by these attacks. (p xii)

9   This was Risinghill School in Islington, then part of the Inner London Education Authority. There are differing views on the philosophy and organisation of this school but, whatever one's judgment on the matter, Leila Berg (1968) in *Risinghill: Death of a Comprehensive School* has given a graphic and detailed account of the

activities of inspectors, administrators, the local press, teachers, parents and school students. The school was closed in 1965 after only five years of existence.

10 Resources include books and magazine articles, information and work sheets prepared by the teacher, educational videos, audio cassettes for language learning, films and slides etc. The teacher may use resources for demonstration purposes to a whole class or make them available to the students on an individual or small group basis. The computer has helped to reactivate interest in these methods and given rise to several notable additions to the educational vocabulary, such as 'user friendly' and 'interactive learning'. The video recorder, nevertheless, has retained its position as the most popular and widely used resource in many areas of the curriculum.

11 'Flexible learning', also stemming from TVEI, is discussed in Chapter 6.

12 For a summary of my objections to enterprise activities of this kind, see Copland (1986).

13 GCSE boards offered optional syllabuses with 100 per cent course work in English, mathematics and integrated humanities as well as in more practical subjects. In 1992, Kenneth Clarke, the Secretary of State for Education and Science, limited the proportion of course work which could be included.

14 Fortunately, the selective aspect of Young's plan largely failed. The aims of the TVEI underwent considerable modification as a result of pressure from teachers and others and many schools obtained TVEI funding for use by all their students rather than named individuals undergoing specific courses as originally intended.

15 Maurice Levitas (1986) has given a concise but authoritative analysis of Gramsci's educational ideas which show how much of his thinking is relevant to issues in Britain today including the concept of the common (ie comprehensive) school.

Chapter 5. Enhancing Educational Experience: A Plan for Advance

1 John Sharp (1973), Wyndham's first head, described the philosophy and early development of the school in his book Open School.

2 Up to the mid-1970s most local authorities had only just sufficient school places to cater for their needs and most primary and secondary schools drew all their students from geographically defined catchment areas. In some cases secondary intakes were determined by the junior schools attended (known as feeder schools) but in practice the systems were almost identical. Liaison between primary and secondary stages, especially at the time of transfer, was a straightforward operation in principle as even the largest comprehensive schools had only a relatively small number of primaries with which to make arrangements. The arrival of the national curriculum, which could have led to deeper and more effective liaison, coincided with open enrolment one of whose results was the need for every primary school to prepare its pupils to go on to several different comprehensives. In the days of catchment areas, the majority of young members of a local community shared their educational experiences providing junior and comprehensive schools with a unique

opportunity to develop caring and supportive roles and to contribute directly to the quality of life in the locality. Although this opportunity was rarely fully exploited the basic idea contributed to many people's perceptions of the purpose of comprehensive education.

3   In the 1978 edition of *Intelligence, Psychology and Education* the epilogue has been replaced by an alternative chapter.

4   Tertiary colleges combine all post-16 work previously undertaken in schools, sixth form colleges and colleges of further education.

5   Although choice was popular among school students and their parents, it usually entailed sophisticated procedures to try to ensure that each student's final programme of work retained balance and left open career options. In practice many arrangements left the field clear for vested interests: subject teachers and heads of department with strong personalities gave 'encouragement' to the able and well behaved to choose their subject and equally strong 'advice', strictly neutral of course (!), to the remainder to choose something else. Students and their parents often felt unable to resist the recommendations of a head of year or group tutor who may have had rigid ideas on fitting students into an academic hierarchy of subjects and, in any case, was unlikely to be trained in educational and careers guidance. In schools which streamed or banded their students certain options were available only to particular bands. Students in the lowest bands chose from mainly 'practical' options which were missing from the choice offered the top band students. The latter, in turn, had exclusive choice of so-called academic subjects such as separate sciences and modern languages.

6   Stantonbury Campus is referred to further in Chapter 6.

7   Under local management and competition for students many schools have sought to improve appearances. Money has come from a variety of sources including generous funding for early grant maintained schools; savings on teaching staff at the expense of experience and/or increases in class size; employing people to work at substantially less than trade union rates, and fund raising activities which prove most fruitful in the more affluent areas and where the governors of a school have inherited marketable assets which can be hired out. Whatever the merits and necessity of improvements in school, we clearly need more equitable methods of achieving them.

8   Reservations concerning activities in enterprise centres are discussed in Chapter 4.

9   For an account of youth aspects of this study tour see 'Britain-GDR Youth Exchange: Background and Opportunities' in *Youth and Policy* (Copland, 1989). For an earlier view of the GDR education system see 'A Visit to the German Democratic Republic' King (1964) and Edward Blishen's follow-up '*Forum* Visits the German Democratic Republic' (Blishen, 1965). High standards of educational achievement were widely acknowledged and, in the late 1970s and early '80s, the GDR progressed to seventh position in the world ranking of industrial output despite a population of only 16 million. There was also a high participation rate in cultural and sporting activities by people in all age groups.

10   The booklet *Education in the GDR* is one of a series published by Panorama in the

GDR. They are not now easily available.

11 Pressures to copy educational experiences in related but different circumstances are a recipe for disaster; as a student, I remember a lecturer in teaching method alerting us not to make the mistake of teaching last year's class when faced with the one in front of you. However successful a previous lesson may have been, it could not be slavishly repeated as if nothing had changed; new students, a different classroom and a hundred and one other variables would affect the outcome. Good advice indeed.

12 Non-selective teaching in years 1 to 9 is long established whilst, more recently, TVEI and flexible learning initiatives, together with impressive independent work by teachers, is extending experience into years 10 and 11. Methods and opportunities are dealt with more fully in Chapter 6.

13 In the spring of 1993 the headteacher designate of a new independent day school appeared on television explaining that his establishment would be open from 8 am to 8 pm and provide a range of activities including meals and supervised homework. Many young people, whose parents can afford the fees, no doubt appreciate the opportunities provided in this further example of privately led 'enhanced educational experience'.

Chapter 6. Initiatives in the Classroom

1 School students' misconceptions and misunderstandings in mathematics are an important topic of research. Birmingham University published *Understanding in Mathematics* (L.G. Saad, 1957) reporting the results of tests for school students designed to provide information on their way of thinking. It revealed the conceptual complexity of supposedly 'elementary' work on fractions, decimals and other topics which made up the core of so much school mathematics at the time and gave a glimpse of gaps and misunderstandings among a majority of learners which, if not corrected, could only play havoc with their future prospects for more advanced study.

Surprisingly, this pioneer work received only limited acknowledgment in the educational world although there were several current projects to improve mathematics teaching in schools. It was not until the publication of a series of research studies by the Assessment of Performance Unit (APU), set up under the Labour government of 1974, that the issues received wider coverage. Also from 1974, a major research programme 'Concepts in Secondary Mathematics and Science' was based at Chelsea College, University of London. The mathematics team published their clearly recorded findings in *Children's Understanding of Mathematics: 11-16* (Hart, 1981). The results are both sobering and educationally challenging.

In 1988, I attended a half-day conference organised by Sunderland Polytechnic's Centre for Mathematics Education. Conference members participated in a range of activities prepared and led by Bill Brookes of Southampton University

School of Education under the title 'Language and Mathematics'. He set tasks for us to do which revealed staggeringly different thought processes even among mathematics specialists — a reminder, indeed, against complacency in thinking that we may have precise pedagogical answers for all our students.

2 This initiative, now followed by CAME for mathematics, is a good example of how teaching methods can be advanced through a partnership of specialists in an area of pedagogy with teachers in the classroom.

3 Since 1988, under local management of schools and financial constraint, the number of pupils per teacher is steadily increasing.

4 I refer to 'support staff' rather than 'non-teaching staff' as this is the term now used by the TUC and trades unions such as UNISON with members in schools. ('Associate staff' is an alternative suggested in a 1992 report from London University's Institute of Education). Context should avoid confusion with teachers, also known as support staff, who are based centrally in an advisory or similar centre and visit schools to work alongside school based colleagues in a variety of subjects. Teachers who work in special needs may also be known as 'learning support staff'. (note 18)

5 An explanation of examination grades is included in the section 'Terminology Explained'. With much smaller numbers gaining equivalent grades than today, this compares with an average of twenty two higher grade passes by students from the same area during the last three years of the selective system of grammar and modern schools.

6 The nature and limitations of express streams are discussed later in the chapter under gifted children.

7 Mode 1 was for syllabuses and examinations set and marked by the examination board, and mode 2 for those provided by small groups of schools.

8 Despite such a strong pedigree, mode 3 received many unjustified attacks which, together with the lunacy of a dual examination system, restricted its effectiveness

9 It was ironic to read in a report 'Opt-out floodgates open' in *The Times Educational Supplement* (1992b), one week after the general election of 1992, the current head of Hedley Walter School quoted as saying that the school would now be heading down the 'fast and furious' path to grant maintained status. 'We do not wish to be left behind as the "council school" ' he said.

10 Books about Countesthorpe include *The Countesthorpe Experience: The First Five Years* (Watts ed., 1977) and *Towards the Open School* (Watts, 1980). The first contains contributions from several authors including students closely associated with the college; topics range from teaching method to political reaction. Although the second book contains only one chapter specifically about Countesthorpe this sets the activities of the school in a wider post-war framework of education as seen by the author who was the college's principal at the time. As well as publications about the college as a whole there have also been contributions on the teaching of individual subjects. The latter include a book edited by Eric Green (1976), head of physical science at the time, entitled *Towards Independent Learning in Science* which contains articles from Britain and the USA covering the whole range of

school science up to and including physics and chemistry at A-level (Green, 1976). If successful methods of independent learning are possible at this level, then teachers of other subjects may look with confidence to see how similar principles — perhaps as part of a course — can be applied in their own circumstances.

11 When the need arose CSE mode 3 syllabuses could be made as intellectually demanding as any GCE O-level. At Wyndham School (Chapter 5), the head of craft and design prepared a successful and demanding CSE mode 3 syllabus emphasising a design approach; this was in the late 1960s before any comparable syllabus was available at O-level. A survey into headteachers' attitudes to CSE as an alternative to GCE was undertaken by Caroline Benn and Brian Simon (1972) for their review of progress towards comprehensive education *Half Way There*. The results (pp 268, 516 and 573) show that seventeen heads out of 128 replying in one sample stressed the need to replace two exams by one, most recommending CSE. In a larger sample of 521 replies, 199 (38%) of heads replied that the curriculum of their schools included subjects in which all students entered for CSE. 42% of these schools had CSE as the sole examination for music, 32% English, 27% maths and 18% physics and chemistry. 'CSE should replace O-level in all subjects in the comprehensive school' is a typical comment reported by the authors.

12 For a detailed account of Sutton Centre see the final report of the Sutton Centre Research Project by its senior research officer, Colin Fletcher (1983). For the core of the story see *Schools on Trial: The Trials of Democratic Comprehensives* (Fletcher et al., 1985).

13 A fuller account is given by a former member of staff, Bob Moon (1983), now Professor of Education at the Open University.

14 An informative account of Sidney Stringer School and Community College is provided by Royston Mchugh of the Open University 'Management in Education' course team (Open University, 1976). The author concentrates on management techniques and includes primary source material such as internal memoranda and letters to parents which give a realistic flavour of life and issues in a forward looking school of the early 1970s.

15 For a report of the *Forum* conference see the account for the magazine by Ray Pinder (1966). Follow up events are reported in the next two issues (*Forum*, 1967).

16 In a subsequent book *Crisis in the Primary Classroom* Galton (1994) claims that educational reforms are taking place in a pedagogic vacuum and that more needs to be done to learn about the process of teaching.

17 This was a novelty in the borough where science teachers in many schools settled for demonstration experiments only. Furthermore, the half classes were mixed groups under a timetable arrangement in which they alternated with art. This, too, was a gratifying development and a notable improvement on a previous school where, on arrival, I was told 'the boys do science, the girls biology'. As a keen young science teacher, I found almost incredible the classification of biology as a subject apparently separate from science and the policy itself a shattering commentary on the level of some curricular 'thinking' thirteen years after secondary education for all had been heralded in the 1944 Education Act.

18 At Ryhope School the teacher in charge of remedial work became known as the 'senior remedial specialist' with equivalent status to a head of department. After the 1981 Education Act, the title became 'senior specialist for special educational needs' — rather lengthy, it is true, but descriptive. More recently, many schools have adopted the title 'learning support department' which succinctly encapsulates the idea of offering a service to all students whilst maintaining the status of the work and the staff in the school as a whole.

19 The number of students in an express stream who might eventually go on to take the Oxford and Cambridge entrance examinations would be small indeed. Entry for most candidates at state schools was especially difficult because of the selection procedures at the time. Rather than making offers based on A-level performance, the colleges of these universities set entrance examinations to be taken in the autumn term following A-levels. Without an express stream this entailed staying on at school for at least part of a third year in the sixth — an arrangement which suited the public schools where a candidate's additional prowess, for example at rugby football, could enhance the reputation of the school. It was a considerable handicap for most students in state schools and, today, as with other universities, entry is based mainly on A-level results.

20 A-level grades are another example of manufacturing failure out of success: a pass in GCE at A-level represents a considerable achievement involving knowledge and understanding far in advance of that required for GCSE. Success, however, comes in five grades, A to E, with grades D and E accounting for 45% of all passes. Predictably, on results day, one meets students with, say, a D and two Es feeling as if they are failures — public conceptions surrounding these two letters is sufficient for that. Yet such a student has been successful in three subjects when a pass in two is the basic requirement for entry to a degree course. Supply and demand, however, leads to requirements of three or more grade A's in over-subscribed subjects at universities enjoying high status. The root of the problem is that grade A, achieved by outstanding candidates, is seen as the base-line with anything below as relative failure. It would help if results were notified in ascending order as for many other qualifications either as pass, credit and distinction or as grade/level 1, 2 and so on.

Naturally, if you fail to satisfy the entry requirements for the course of your choice, nothing will cheer you up as the news is received. However, your achievement stands and, hopefully, can be built on in an acceptable way. A comprehensive system of education must be about achievement at all stages with networks of opportunity to provide routes for personal progression. Incidentally, there should be nothing but contempt for a practice among some admissions tutors in higher education who, rather than rejecting an unwanted candidate, offer a conditional entry based on A-level grades which the applicant is unlikely to obtain. A grade 'B' and two 'C's may sound achievable but, as we have seen, it requires an above average performance. The disappointment of a conscientious student, likely to achieve passes at lower grades, can only be compounded.

21 Better education is not synonymous with ever more GCSEs although governments act as if this were so. Fortunately there are educationists, parents and thoughtful

people from all walks of life who recognise that a diet of too many subjects leads to cramming for written examinations, skimped coursework and associated stress on both students and teachers. Far better for students to have a manageable number of subjects which allows them time to enjoy their work, to investigate and explore ideas, to go beyond the bare requirements of the examination syllabus and to develop a thirst for further study. Examination passes provide too handy a performance indicator with which to satisfy inspectors and project the image of a school.

22 To accelerate students is to place them in classes one or more years ahead of their chronological year group.

Chapter 7. Resources for Teaching and Learning

1 Capitation allowances were for the purchase and replacement of books, stationary, office supplies, scientific apparatus, tools, equipment for sports, art, music, home economics — and consumable materials of all kinds. Sunderland's capitation allowances were typical for local authorities and, in the financial year 1988/9 immediately prior to the introduction of local management of schools, amounted to £27-80p for secondary school students up to age 16. Put another way, the allowance came to just over 3 pence per hour of lesson time per school student — a sum which puts into perspective the skill and resourcefulness of teachers who achieve their results with such tiny budgets at their disposal.

Schools occasionally received items of major equipment, such as lathes or new cookers, direct from the local authority whilst local advisers held small sums to assist school projects in their subject areas. With the arrival of desktop computers in the 1980s, some of these were provided directly by education authorities. Nevertheless, the total amount available for schools to adapt to new circumstances was very small indeed and this was especially true during the major development of comprehensive education in the 1960s and '70s. Heads of department were often unable to purchase newly published books and materials, which could have made all the difference to the teaching effectiveness of their teams, because they had already spent their allocation on replenishing older stock which was all that had been available at the time of purchase. When a new school opened, the setting up allowance was usually quite generous but its effectiveness was determined by the availability of suitable materials and equipment combined with up-to-date knowledge among those responsible for ordering.

It is no surprise, therefore, that the arrival in the mid-1980s of the Technical and Vocational Education Initiative (Chapter 4), with its offers of undreamed of sums of money for relatively sophisticated computer systems, electronics and a host of other equipment, received a ready response from schools. In accepting the money, many must have felt that a more detailed inquiry into the content and implications of the packages that went with it could wait a while.

2 Programmed learning, and its association with crude and expensive teaching

machines, had a brief period in the limelight in the educational world in Britain in the 1950s and early '60s. However, as Banks says in his book 'Programmed learning as a new dynamic teaching style in schools, was doomed from the start because it was in the wrong hands' (p 17). These hands were mainly those of the manufacturers of teaching machines but the essence of programmed learning involves 'systematic concept building rather than maths in bits and pieces' (p 24). There is much experience and research evidence to indicate that the understanding of concepts in mathematics and science is a much more extensive and complex operation than just a matter of choosing a few examples to illustrate ideas when the concept is first met. When students meet the same concept in a different situation they are all too likely to be baffled (and discouraged) if it is assumed that they fully understand it. Banks quotes the steps drawn up by the National Council for Educational Technology for a systems approach to solving complex problems in education — the procedure he used for developing programmes of study (p 84). It is interesting that the work of Talyzina and her colleagues (chapters 2 and 6). draws heavily on programmed learning and cybernetics, the latter also implying a systems approach. Her book *The Psychology of Learning* is subtitled 'Theories of Learning and Programmed Instruction'.

3   These early GCE successes are an indication of the immense range of mathematical understanding which has to be addressed no matter how students are grouped. I gained my first real insight into this matter when trying out an idea with a fourth year A-class of 40 secondary modern school students in 1961. The topic was substitution of numerical values in algebraic expressions, a notoriously confusing topic for many students. I prepared graded examples from the very simplest substitutions to those involving negative numbers, brackets, squares and cubes. To assist them, and to insure against repetition of error, each student received an answer sheet which also revealed intermediate stages in the substitution process. Students were asked to slide a sheet of paper down the answer sheet and reveal the answer. If correct, they were to slide the paper further and compare their method with the intermediate stage(s) shown. If incorrect they were to try to find their error before consulting the intermediate stage but, if still baffled, they could consult me. The purpose of the exercise had been fully explained so the necessary element of trust was accepted by all. The questions were, in fact, a simplified type of programmed learning but with the teacher available for general instructions and individual assistance. The paper sliding operation substituted for the function of a teaching machine in revealing steps and answers at appropriate points.

The results surprised me: I had allocated an 80 minute lesson for the activity and the first student finished very successfully at about the half way mark whilst there were several, at the end of the lesson, who had only completed about a third of the assignment. I reported this activity in a letter to *The Listener* (Copland, 1962a) noting that the approach described 'does seem applicable to those parts of any subject which must be mastered if further worthwhile progress is to be made but which are continual stumbling blocks to all but the most gifted students'. Certainly that lesson increased my understanding of the range of individual differences among students together with the advantages of programmed learning in aspects of school work. Similar processes, taught in a traditional way to the whole class, undoubtedly waste the time of the knowledgeable, frustrate the least confident and have only patchy success with 'middle of the range' students to whom such lessons are supposedly addressed. Two 'average' students sitting next to each other will bring to the same task very different mental banks of knowledge as well as different mental processes of learning.

4   The ILEA was the largest and only directly elected education authority in Britain until abolished in 1989.

5   Conservative government requirements concerning uniformity in the GCSE meant that SMILE's distinctive syllabus, with its 70 per cent course work component, was last examined in 1994. They are adapting to the new situation but this is not easy.

6   SMILE materials have more levels of difficulty than KMP but are not ordered within a level. The material is mostly written by teachers and published through SMILE; it is also replaced and changed more frequently. The KMP materials, being designed from the start as parts of a whole, are more structured. Both approaches have many adherents.

7   A powerful reply to criticisms of the Schools Council from the Department of Education and Science is provided in Plaskow's fascinating account in which each chapter represents a personal view written by an individual involved with the Council in a senior position. Referring to a document from the DES, Sir Alex Smith (1985), chairman of the Council from 1975 to 1978 comments 'The paper was generous in its criticisms of others, but had no word, no hint, of self-criticism of the DES' (p 106). He communicated these views to the Prime Minister, James Callaghan in October 1976 (p 108) without noticeable effect.

8   Middle schools were introduced in several parts of the country partly on educational grounds and partly to gain flexibility in the use of school premises for schemes of comprehensive reorganisation. An age range of 9 to 13 was typical though there were variations at both ends (Chapter 5).

9   The inclusion of social studies in the common curriculum for all students provided a more balanced and less specialised curriculum (Chapter 10). This was possible because of the time released by the double subject integrated science rather than three separate sciences. Ryhope entered its first candidates for the integrated humanities O-level in 1979.

10 The subject matter of the integrated humanities syllabus enabled schools to chose five topics from a list of ten each requiring a term's study. Examples included people and work, poverty, persecution and prejudice, the family, education, the mass media, law and order and war. The syllabus stated the main aim of each topic and specified sections for study which were a far cry from a list of 'facts' to be learned. For example, war had the following sections: roots of war; manifestations (ideological, economic, guerrilla, conventional military); effects; portrayal, and prevention — in total making it as much a unit on peace as one on war.

11 As well as a central theme concerned with ecosystems the environmental science syllabus included a strong technological element. This arose partly from topics

such as water treatment, extraction of metals and the supply of electricity but also as a result of a general theme of 'management'. The syllabus referred to the application of science in the interests of 'fundamental needs of man for the achievement of a healthy and satisfying life' — an excellent description of the purpose of technology.

Chapter 8. Care, Guidance and Strategic Planning

1 Schools on split sites were usually organised in lower and upper or lower, middle and upper age groupings. Care and guidance systems were adapted accordingly.

2 By early 1994 less than 22 per cent of comprehensive schools retained houses either solely or in conjunction with other forms of grouping. In contrast nearly 72 per cent used a year system alone or in conjunction with lower, middle and upper school grouping. The figures come from the survey of 1500 comprehensive schools by Caroline Benn and Clyde Chitty (1996) *Thirty Years On: Is Comprehensive Education Alive and Well, or Struggling to Survive?* (p 235)

3 From now on I shall refer to years rather than houses but, unless indicated to the contrary, comments apply equally to house systems.

4 'Unattached' referred to work undertaken by youth and community workers outside a specific centre or club.

5 A national youth service was established in 1939 and, under the 1944 Education Act, it became the duty of every local education authority to provide adequate facilities for:

> leisure-time occupation, in such organised cultural training and recreative activities as are suited to their requirements, for any persons over compulsory school age who are able and willing to profit by the facilities provided for that purpose.

As H C Dent (1968), a well-respected educationist and commentator of the time, noted in *The Education Act 1944*:

> The possibilities inherent in the above are limitless (p 35).

The youth service, being intended for those who had left school, was originally for young people aged between 14 and 20. This was amended to 15 to 20 on the raising of the school leaving age in 1947. Activities were largely based in youth centres but, today, few centres are able to meet the diverse and sophisticated needs of these older age groups. In recent years, therefore, there has been an increase in detached youth work, 'detached' being one of the terms now preferred to 'unattached'. The youth service has had a chequered career. Whilst its potential was recognised in the 1944 Education Act, the youth provisions of the Act were never fully resourced and implemented despite an optimistic pamphlet *Youth's Opportunity* (Ministry of Education, 1945) and the report of the Albermarle Committee *The Youth Service in England and Wales* (Ministry of Education, 1960). The latter stated that:

A properly supported Youth Service can help many more individuals to find their own way better personally and socially (para. 138).

The Albermarle Committee calculated that, in 1957-58, of every £ spent by the Ministry of Education and local authorities on education only about one old penny went on the Youth Service (para. 26). There is no sign that the situation improved during following years nor is there the slightest indication in the 1988 Education Reform Act that its compilers had any concept of the needs of young people and of the opportunities that exist outside formal educational and training environments. As a voluntary youth leader in Birmingham and Rotherham whilst working in industry early in my career, I found many opportunities for young people to take on genuine responsibility for organising the affairs of their clubs. On returning to teaching I noticed that opportunities for real initiative and non-authoritarian responsibility among school students were much less. Whilst there are fundamental differences between schools and youth work — the compulsory nature of schooling having wide ramifications — it is important that schools should encourage their students to seek and accept responsibilities of this type. There are no easy solutions but the best practice of the youth service provides useful starting points for consideration.

6 Most disciplinary situations are not to be viewed solely in black and white terms. Teachers who gain the widest respect allow all students involved in an incident to have a say however black the situation may look for some. Often this provides pointers to the most appropriate long term solution.

7 The term 'support staff' is preferred to non-teaching or ancillary staff for the reasons given in Chapter 6, note 4.

8 Illusions about the supposed ease of moving students between streams are discussed in Chapter 2.

Chapter 9. Aiming for Maturity

1 Strengths and weaknesses of parent teacher associations are discussed in Chapter 11.

2 The inadequacy of many school reports interested me from an early stage in my career and, following work at Riddings and Wyndham schools, I put forward some alternatives to traditional reports in an article for Educational Research (Copland, 1966). Those were days of strict streaming and some topics discussed no longer apply but others have still to be fully addressed. Many current school reports and records of achievement do their best to support my 1966 contention that 'the average report is distinguished by its unaesthetic dreariness' while there are still plenty of examples where the halo effect and stereotyping are present (p 200). The 'halo effect' describes situations in which teachers' observations reinforce each other, positively or negatively, if each contributor to the report is able to see what colleagues have written previously. However aware of the danger, it is easy to be influenced, perhaps sub-consciously, by the information before you; the only sure way is for each teacher to prepare his or her comments independently and for the

records to be collated when they are complete. A concluding overview by a head of year or group tutor is, of course, a different matter and is likely to be more valid if based on independent data. Attempts to assess effort (persistence is a more precise word) are also problematic. Under school conditions it is difficult to distinguish effort and achievement and research shows a close correlation in teachers' estimates.

3 Problems often arise in school because a person is more mature, or immature, than his or her colleagues. Girls, in general, mature earlier than boys in the early secondary years so there can be considerable differences in physical and social maturity between an older girl and a younger boy in the same tutor group. Pupils transfer from primary to secondary education in September if they are age eleven on 31st August; some will have just had their eleventh birthday while others are twelve or nearly so. Birthday information, therefore, may provide a source of guidance.

4 The use of the NFER's AH2 and AH3 tests at Ryhope, as well as the so-called stannine 9-point scale, are further discussed in Chapter 12. The results of the tests were standardised from the performance of a national sample of school students but need interpreting with extreme care for reasons set out in Chapter 2. The tests were given to all students in the first and third years and provided an indication of overall ability *as demonstrated by the student so far*. Information such as this can easily lead to stereotyping of students but it can also prove helpful if the information is used as a starting point for further observation and enquiry. When scores suggest that a student is capable of more than is being achieved, his or her work may need careful monitoring for a time. In another case the scores may suggest that a student who seemed to be under-achieving may, in fact, be trying harder than imagined and would benefit by encouragement rather than exhortation.

5 Possibilities for registration using computers include optical mark readers to transfer data from the class register and direct registration with each student inserting a personal swipe card into a reader on arrival at school. In either case the data can be analysed and searched for patterns of attendance such as regular absence with another student.

6 I prefer 'good order' to 'discipline' as the latter so often carries with it connotations of regimentation and passivity.

7 The Irish Republic and Britain were the only European countries at the time which still permitted corporal punishment in schools.

8 A typical STOPP press release based on statistics, on this occasion relating to Cleveland, was headed 'County's Horrendous Child-beating Statistics' (STOPP, 1984b). It revealed that 12,369 beatings had occurred in secondary schools in less than 3 years with a national 'record' of 5,326 canings in one year. Also in one year, one school in the county administered corporal punishment 1300 times and two children in the authority's schools were beaten 25 times each.

9 Encouragement is not a soft option and its role as a key to good practice in no way precludes the use of unequivocal comments concerning unacceptable standards of work or behaviour. So many disciplinary systems, however, seem to be based on

negative expectations to the detriment of the majority of well intentioned students.

10 School uniform, as a marketing symbol, fits neatly into a system of state education in which schools compete with each other for students. Where parents can afford higher quality wear and regular replacement the image will be more impressive than in schools where the majority rely on local authority grants towards a basic quality blazer, badge, tie and trousers or skirt — the latter often compulsory for girls and thus contrary to the spirit, if not the letter, of equal opportunities legislation.

11 Uniforms based on sweat shirts with the name of the school are an improvement being more cheerful and suitable. However, school students are still denied choice and there are problems as fashions change and a popular choice of a year or two ago, in its turn, looks dated.

12 Feelings and emotions on the one hand and knowledge on the other are often referred to in educational writing as the affective and cognitive domains respectively.

13 A court appearance was a real possibility. In 1976 I was subpoenaed to Durham Crown Court as an expert witness — i.e. a person not directly connected with a case but there to offer advice and give background information. The parent of a girl at a recently established comprehensive school in Sunderland was appealing against a magistrates' decision to uphold the action of the local authority who had brought a prosecution for non-attendance. She had been excluded from school for wearing sleeper earrings even though her parents had signed the authority's indemnity statement at her previous school prior to its incorporation into the comprehensive. For my first (and only) appearance in a witness box I answered barristers' questions on clothing policy at Ryhope School and my opinion concerning its relevance to discipline. The judge then turned to me and said 'What you are saying is that the action of your colleague was entirely unreasonable'? This seemed like the classic leading question and I asked politely if I had to answer it. I learnt that no such stricture concerning questioning applied to judges. 'You most certainly do' he said but at that moment a legal point arose among the barristers and I was asked to step down. At the end of the proceedings there was little disagreement on either the facts or the points of law so all hung on the personal opinion of the judge as to whether or not the action of the head had indeed been 'reasonable'. The judge found in favour of Sunderland and the affair left a lasting impression concerning case law in general and the powers of headteachers in matters of dress in particular.

14 The senior inspector for Sunderland took a different view on clothing. In a report on Ryhope School, later withdrawn on the instruction of the director of education (Chapter 13), he commented as follows:

> A child in school uniform tends to behave as a school child most of the time. That is, he or she adopts a certain role and with it concomitant attitudes and behaviour patterns; instruction is accepted from authority, pranks are played, work is done or not and consequently accepted. Members of the Inspectorate were struck by the fact that Ryhope School children (sic) were prematurely aged ...

A striking illustration of how clothing can be linked to ideology — and from a report which contributed to a sustained attack on comprehensive principles.

15 In the 1970s few junior schools or sixth form colleges and no colleges of further education required uniform, so one wondered what quirk in human development made it apparently indispensable for discipline and morale during the compulsory secondary ages of 11 to 16.

16 In the year 1993-94, 10 per cent of comprehensive schools in Britain were providing education for their students without a uniform requirement according to the survey by Benn and Chitty (1996) *Thirty Years On: Is Comprehensive Education Alive and Well, or Struggling to Survive?* A further 9 per cent did not require older students to wear it (p 237). Many countries have operated for years, if not centuries, without school uniform and national history, rather than educational criteria, appears to be the determining factor.

17 Parents may exercise less influence on choice of secondary school than is imagined. A small scale research project at Newcastle University by Bill Dennison and Alan Thomas found, in a sample of 72 primary children, that 60% said that they made the choice of secondary school and only 1 in 7 said they had no say. 'Once a sufficient number of children decide they want to go to a certain school there is a snowball effect and nearly everyone wants to go' said Dr Dennison (*The Times Educational Supplement*, 1991g). This research finding will come as no surprise to teachers in both primary and secondary schools.

Chapter 10. Aims and Curriculum

1 The policy concerning separate classes for past members of the two schools was maintained as a general principle although, during the first two years, a number of students from the modern school were transferred into classes that had originated from the grammar school.

2 The public schools of the last century saw no need to provide written aims. What the schools stood for was crystal clear to the upper class parents who patronised them. The purpose of state schooling needs to be no less clear to today's parents whose children have all to gain from a truly comprehensive system.

3 In contrast to subjective criteria, behaviourism in psychology emphasises the importance of an objective study of actual responses. It has been applied to various aspects of education including the learning process and schemes to improve behaviour. In general, it has proved very limiting.

4 I set out a 10-point list of principles and priorities which expressed my philosophy of comprehensive education in an article in the magazine *Ideas* (Copland, 1975). The list stressed the importance of cooperation rather than competition and the need for time for young people to develop in social responsibility as well as in intellectual capacity. It noted that school students have much to contribute to the planning and running of school life and that 'pupils and parents should not be hoodwinked, blinded with science or just plain deliberately misled'. The editor of the magazine was head of the curriculum laboratory at Goldsmiths College (now part of the University of London) and the majority of the readership were no doubt

enthusiasts for the main thrusts of comprehensive education at all age levels. My list seemed to me, at the time, to be unexceptional and reasonably explicit but it was not prepared or intended as an operational document for a particular school; consequently it was never used directly at Ryhope. I was to learn two years after publication of the article that the ten points were not drawn up in a sufficiently water-tight manner (Chapter 13). Rather as the computer programmer 'error traps' a program so that misuse induces a corrective response, so it is necessary to disseminate progressive educational ideas in a form as resistant as possible to misconception whether intentional or otherwise. Looking back I stand by the spirit of each of the items but would augment and clarify my meaning in several places. For example, one of the points referred to the need for 'a relaxed, enquiring and learning atmosphere' in the classroom. I assumed (wrongly as events were to show) that 'relaxed' would be interpreted in a college or university sense in comparison with the often rigid — even regimented — atmosphere existing in many schools.

5   When a term such as 'mission statement' is incorporated from the business world into the vocabulary of educational management, one must beware of substituting imposing sounding expressions, derived from very different circumstances, for incisive educational thinking.

6   John Hayes and Barrie Hopson (1971), in their seminal book *Careers Guidance: the role of the school in vocational development*, defined career in a broad sense as 'a person's total life pattern, which will include both work and non-work factors' (p 28).

7   The elements of the curriculum will change with time in the light of experience and in response to changing pedagogical, political and social developments.

8   I prefer 'participation' here rather than the currently popular concept of 'ownership'. Over-emphasis on ownership of the learning process by students may lead to limited horizons as we saw in connection with the work of Gramsci (Chapter 4).

9   'Community school' is used in the sense that the school sees its role as an organic part of the community rather than as an island within it.

10 Too many schools are essentially passive institutions, mentally and emotionally, as far as their students are concerned.

11 Without some bureaucratic structure few organisations could operate efficiently but schools do not fit into simple categories. Among books which describe and investigate a range of management models, including those recognising that conflicts of interest and ideas will inevitably arise in school situations, is *Managing Education: Theory and Practice* edited by Tony Bush (1989) of the Open University, an institution which has played a leading role in constructively applying management principles to educational situations. Other books containing relevant material include *The Politics of School Management* by Eric Hoyle (1986) and *The Micro-politics of the School: Towards a Theory of School Organisation* by Stephen Ball (1987).

12 A R Luria and colleagues produced remarkable improvement in a pair of five- year old identical twins with impaired speech production after separating them for

lessons. They found that, together, the twins had developed a means of inter-communication which bypassed the normal channels of learning thus restricting their chances of progress. Although this research deals only with one special case, it did much to emphasise the extent to which, for all children, language exercises a formative influence on mental processes. Had I been aware of the work at the time I should have ensured that parents were informed and consulted before allocating twins to classes. *Speech and the Mental Development of the Child* (Luria and Yudovich, 1971) describes the work. It was published in the USSR in 1956, in an English edition in 1959, and by Penguin in 1971.

13 In the late 1960s and early '70s many young teachers were recruited in response to increasing school rolls. A relatively high proportion were attracted and inspired by developments in primary and comprehensive education and strongly welcomed moves towards more adult relationships between teachers and young people. They supported good order and discipline based on self-and mutual-respect; shared a widespread feeling that education was very important, and felt that they could offer something to broaden the horizons and opportunities for young people. A few years earlier the Robbins Report into higher education (Ministry of Education, 1963b) had rejected ideas of a fixed 'pool of ability' from which students could be drawn and recommended greatly increased opportunities in higher education. One result was the introduction of three and four year Bachelor of Education degree courses (the latter with honours) — a development of tremendous significance in raising the sights of intending teachers. It was clear to us in the schools that colleges and departments of education in polytechnics and universities were providing more relevant and intellectually challenging courses with many lecturers going out of their way to offer encouragement and support to their students.

14 The 'Prograph' timetable board cost what seemed at the time like a small fortune from our capitation allowance but proved its worth over many years. A range of coloured and numbered pegs representing teachers, subjects and rooms slotted into a lattice divided up to represent years, forms and periods. The timetabler started by placing pegs for each teacher (one for each period of the week) into a side panel. As a teacher was allocated to a class and lesson, the appropriate peg was transferred to the main board. Remaining pegs indicated when the teacher was free to be allocated to another class or was entitled to a period without class contact. Colleagues, including myself, recommending changes could practise on sheets of paper; only the timetabler was allowed to move a peg! Obviously the person involved had great power over curriculum development but heads of department who learned how the system operated and understood the constraints arising from the requirements of other subjects could achieve much. Often a head of department had to be told that his or her initial proposals would not fit and the reason explained with reference to the board. Supplied with this information, many were able to return with revised proposals retaining much of what they hoped for and with a greatly enhanced chance of acceptance. With computer-assisted timetabling and a committed and resourceful attitude by the timetabler similar principles apply. We were fortunate, in this repect, throughout the lifetime of the school where the

first timetabler set an excellent example: he saw his job in terms of achieving overall objectives of comprehensive education and supported this with patience, imagination and a willingness to put time beyond the call of duty into this key task.

15 The school opened at the start of an era of sustained attack on comprehensive education marked by publication in the *Critical Quarterly* of the first two of the so-called 'Black Papers' (Cox and Dyson, 1969). Written largely by right wing academics, they were highly critical of comprehensive schooling in general and non-selective teaching in particular and, despite questionable intellectual integrity, provided ammunition and a source of courage for elitist elements in universities, colleges and the educational establishment. The media were presented with a gift-wrapped opportunity when Ted Short, the Labour government's Secretary of State for Education and Science, told the National Union of Teachers soon after the first was published that this marked 'one of the blackest days in education for over one hundred years' and claimed that a backlash against progressive education had created 'the crisis of the century'.

16 The limitations of craft courses consisting only of woodwork and metalwork were beginning to be recognised but this was before the methods and concepts of craft, design and technology (CDT) and design technology had been more fully developed and popularised. 'Technical Studies' implied some widening of traditional course content together with emphasis on design as well as making. Mixed classes of boys and girls were introduced long before they became the norm — indeed in many schools the respective courses were still known as 'boys crafts' and 'girls crafts'. Ryhope's two heads of department described the experience of changing to mixed technical studies and home economics classes in an article 'Mixed Classes for Craft Subjects: Developments in Home Economics at Ryhope School' in the *Journal*, a termly magazine of the Institutes of Education of the Universities of Newcastle upon Tyne & Durham (Franklin and McGeough, 1972). Their account presents a fascinating piece of social and educational history.

17 A forceful debate on the relevance of 'modern maths' in the school curriculum was pursued vigorously in professional and media circles. Separate syllabuses for modern maths appeared together with textbooks and teaching materials. Today, the national curriculum requires all students to study topics such as probability and statistics, patterns and symmetry which first appeared in schools as modern topics. However, many teachers and advisers think that students should have the opportunity to study other modern topics which would help them to think and reason but which may have been prematurely jettisoned.

18 At the time, in Sunderland, all appointments to senior posts, including heads of major departments, were made by a sub-committee of the Education Committee.

19 'Little and often' for languages was usually interpreted as one 35 minute lesson (less end-effects) each day. Those who held that languages could only be taught in this way ignored the effects of weekends and holidays and, more pertinently, the practice in adult education where most language courses involve one two-hour or even longer session per week. By the later years of the school, and especially under the dynamic leadership of a head of department who made Spanish a most

successful first foreign language, the wheel had turned full circle and language teachers were strong supporters of the longer periods.

20 The *Ideas* article omitted a heading '4th and 5th year Curriculum' which should have appeared immediately before the final paragraph of page 39.

21 Certificates awarded for success in the City and Guilds Foundation courses were attractive and informative. With assessments (pass, credit and distinction) for both written and course work in each of the four components of each course, the certificates emphasised achievement. They proved popular with recipients and were well received at interviews for jobs or further education courses.

22 With fifth year classes the careers teacher and a colleague were timetabled together so that it was possible to provide individual or group advice and career counselling together with the normal programme of careers lessons (Chapter 7). I needed considerable persuading to agree to this arrangement — careers education lessons were innovative enough, let alone two teachers to a class — but never regretted it; the service proved highly successful and much appreciated by the students.

23 Examination results are important but must not become a fetish (Chapter 6, note 21). A member of staff once said to me after I had suggested something that might be done in the fifth year 'Oh but the fifth year is the examination year'. I thought 'Oh dear! At this tremendously sensitive and exciting age, 15 to 16, where young people are developing their ideas and thoughts, deepening their experiences and growing rapidly into adulthood someone sees this stage as just 'the examination year'. Yet with so many pressures it is easy for examinations to dominate all other priorities both in a school as a whole and in the classroom.

24 The Department of Education and Science defined a higher grade pass as a GCE at grade A, B or C (grades 1-6 prior to 1975) and CSE grade 1. Statistics involving higher grade passes (today grades A* to C in the GCSE) give only part of the picture although they are the most frequently quoted nationally. Unfortunately, we did not find a feasible method of satisfactorily quantifying CSE grades 2 to 5. Students who gained seven or eight CSE grade 2's but no higher grade passes were understandably disappointed, yet their overall performance was often better than that of a student who obtained one or two higher grade passes and lower CSE grades in the remaining subjects. Similarly, results of Royal Society of Arts typing certificates and City and Guilds Foundation Certificates do not appear in analyses confined to higher grade passes.

25 If a student took an examination at both O-level and CSE and obtained an O-level grade A, B or C and a CSE grade '1', that naturally counted as one higher grade pass.

26 At the A-level stage numbers were much smaller and varied considerably from year to year precluding a comparative analysis.

27 Young people achieving pleasing examples such as this were sometimes referred to as 'late developers'. However, this term encourages the suspect notion that the outcome of educational experience depends overwhelmingly on the inherent potentialities of the student. A scientific description would give full acknowledgment to the determination and perseverance shown but point to the

complexity of the social forces and educational experiences which people must learn to utilise and contend with. With such considerations in mind it is vital that access to A-level and other courses in further education should not be restricted by arbitrary entry requirements. Open access to courses should be maintained and opportunities for extra supportive studies provided where necessary.

Chapter 11. Activities and Quality of Life

1 Many teachers at the time, especially those working in primary or secondary modern schools, had qualified for teaching through two or three year non-graduate courses at colleges of education. Later these were replaced with degree courses.

2 'Miss' is of course, the female equivalent used by school students to describe women staff irrespective of their marital status. The only exception is when they bestow an honorary title of 'Mrs' on an older and venerable member of staff, again without reference to her marital status.

3 I made a similar statement dissociating myself from corporal punishment at interview for my previous post as deputy head of Wyndham School in Cumberland; corporal punishment was never used.

4 So-called 'extra-curricular' activities lie not only outside the formal curriculum but also outside teachers' contracts of service. They are, therefore voluntary and, strictly speaking, candidates for appointment should not be asked questions about them unless they volunteer information.

5 Before travel to work by car became the norm most teachers lived within a relatively short distance of their school.

6 Like many worthwhile activities in school, Radio Ryhope had a limited life. After three or four years the originator moved on and problems of security became increasingly difficult as the studio was away from the main building. Little would be achieved in school, however, if semi-permanency was a criterion for starting.

7 Four years later the director went on to Tyne Tees Television where he produced 'The Tube', a nationally popular rock music show. He moved to London and further television fame and is now managing director of a major film and TV production company. He was accompanied to Tyne Tees by two Ryhope School students who had been closely involved in the shows. Both did well and one is currently producer of BBC 1's 'Top of the Pops'.

8 Drugs were a taboo subject for schools in the early 1970s.

9 'Aquarius' was eventually replaced by 'The South Bank Show'.

10 'Self-concept' is a psychological term meaning 'one's concept of oneself'. It is not related to selfishness.

11 The single governing body for all schools in Sunderland operated until 1985. At the time of intense action concerning the school in the autumn of 1982 it served over 168 separate schools.

12 Elected parent governors were established under The Education (No. 2) Act of 1986 but, in many schools, very few parents are able and willing to serve in this

manner. Also, however conscientiously individuals may attend to their duties, they do so primarily as individuals because of the virtual impossibility of ascertaining the views of their 'constituents' as a body.

Chapter 12. Records and Assessment

1   Some information should remain confidential to a very small number of staff who need to know in case of emergency. This may be of a legal or medical nature or concern a young person deemed at risk by Social Services or a voluntary agency.

2   Despite a name which produces visions of video recorders and overhead projectors, courses with the title 'Educational Technology' are mainly concerned with curriculum development, teaching techniques and assessment.

3   The stannine scale is based on the so-called normal distribution curve which assumes that more students will attain about average than at either extreme. On the stannine scale, just over half receive scores of 4,5 or 6; just under a quarter 1, 2 or 3 (low), and a similar proportion 7, 8 or 9 (high).

4   Hopefully, the requirements of the national curriculum have eliminated a not uncommon preference among teachers, especially of younger students, to be influenced by neatness and docility before depth of understanding.

5   Z-scores (another statistical quantity) retain the advantages of stannines without assuming a normal distribution. The scores standardise the spread of marks or grades so that if, as is common, marking in subjects like mathematics and science (where 0 and 100% are both possible) shows a wider range than in English and humanities, valid comparisons can still be made. I used the system on an experimental basis in a streamed situation at Riddings Secondary School (Copland, 1962b) but the manual calculations were tedious. With computers there is no problem.

6   This key responsibility of the group tutor was described in the first edition of our staff handbook and continued throughout the life of the school. The primary role of heads of year and their assistants was to 'coordinate the work of the year as a whole'.

7   Juvenile Court reports are concerned with a young person's school career and not the offence with which he or she is charged. If found guilty, the school report was usually read out before sentencing and almost all magistrates said that they attached considerable importance to it. It was essential, therefore, to try to be fair both to the young person and the authorities by being as objective as possible and to describe attributes as well as deficiencies. This task was not made any easier in the Sunderland area (and I suspect in others as well) by a stereotyped but compulsory form. As well as factual information such as a record of attendance, it contained many questions of the type 'Is he obedient?...'; 'Truthful? ...' and 'Does he resent correction? ...' The small space provided for a response obviously anticipated only one or two words, thus negating the purpose of the report. Our returns included many comments such as 'usually', 'sometimes' and 'see over' as we invariably added a more balanced picture on the reverse side. To make a

professional job of the report was often a frustrating and time consuming experience both for the head of year who prepared an outline and myself who agreed the final wording before signature. Despite several efforts to have the forms improved they remained intact until 1985. When I started to put a line through the assessment of character sections with a note that the specific questions were dealt with in a full report on a separate sheet, I soon received a visitation from the chairman of the Bench and a request to help the due process of law by filling in the form as constituted! Following the Criminal Justice Act of 1982, things began to change for the better and, in 1985, much improved forms were introduced in Sunderland. A year later, Sunderland's Juvenile Crime Consultative Group made a welcome recommendation that 'the information in the school report should be discussed with the juvenile and family prior to a court appearance'.

8   Assessment based on previous performance is known as student-referenced or ipsative and, when involving the performance of others, as norm-referenced. Despite original intentions to base assessment in the national curriculum on actual achievement (criterion-referenced) each student's performance is converted to a level on an 8-point, scale with national norms heavily emphasised.

9   Design work for the progress reports occurred some 17 or 18 years before desk top publishing was an affordable option in schools. Nevertheless, even with the most sophisticated technology, the final result is limited to the quality of the original design. For six years in the early 1980s, Ryhope was fortunate to have a gifted designer on the staff and he willingly lent his talent to many projects. The results, ranging from letter headings to a brilliant PE certificate, had a touch of class and raised the morale of those who used and benefited from them.

10 The nickname 'ticky boxes' is of more recent origin. Its slightly cynical, connotations are doubtless associated with assessment in the national curriculum which generated so many previously undreamed of varieties of the genre.

11 Fourth and fifth year reports included estimates of public examination performance even though, in many cases, final decisions concerning entry for GCE or CSE were made as late as possible. The letters PQRS gave an estimate for either examination 'based on your standard of work, interest and approach to study so far'. P predicted a high grade in GCE or a grade 1 in CSE whilst S indicated 'successful (at least grade 4)' in CSE but 'only an outstanding effort can give any chance of success' for GCE. The PQRS system remained until the replacement of the dual system with GCSE.

12 Later work by Stansbury in Devon led to the name 'Record of Experience'.

13 In Swales' report on records of achievement individual schools are not identified but Ryhope's work is summarised in Table 18 where it is the last school entry (pp. 84-85).

14 When records of achievement are used over several years as part of the learning process, they are called formative documents. Single, end of course records, such as the one at Ryhope, are referred to as summative. The distinction has been explained as follows: formative records assist and inform students while they are learning; summative records inform others at the end of the period. At Ryhope,

Easter leavers completed their personal achievement files during the spring term; the remainder either early in the summer term or after finishing their public examinations.

15 At Ryhope the aims within each subject were the same for all students reflecting the non-selective teaching in the school. Perhaps the national curriculum should be similarly defined by brief statements of intent leaving the detail, suitably monitored, to be developed at local authority and school level. After all, the national curriculum was introduced as a common curriculum for all even though this essential feature was quickly lost sight of in the secondary years.

16 A small volunteer group of teachers provided guidance for students preparing their files. They offered ideas to think around while planning and help with ways of accurately expressing sentiments and opinions. They made every effort, however, to avoid influencing students to transpose their genuine expressive writing into adult transactional prose. (The terms are explained in Chapter 7). For those who did not rate their handwriting too highly, members of the typing option offered a welcome service whilst, for subjects which had not appealed, the advisory teachers normally suggested constructive criticism. This produced some realistic and helpful accounts showing insight into both the student and the curriculum. Failing that, students were recommended to omit the sheet altogether. Comments such as 'The lessons were boring ...' with little else to add hardly reflected the positive theme of a personal achievement file!

17 The 'good wishes' sheet could always be removed from the personal achievement file before interview if a candidate felt that a light hearted and informal touch might not be fully appreciated by the interviewer.

18 Graded tests in foreign languages were popular in many parts of the country but details varied from district to district. In Sunderland emphasis was on the practical skills of reading, listening and speaking with an optional test in writing at grade 3. One of the aims was mastery at the appropriate level, a credit requiring a score of 90 per cent.

19 Study of the life and customs of Spanish-speaking people provided important educative opportunities based on the extensive use of the language in the world; this was one of the reasons for its selection at Ryhope as the first foreign language.

20 Several tutor groups made it their goal to help all their members obtain at least a level 1 certificate in Spanish. Students encouraged group members who were having difficulty and provided informal and intensive help before the test. There was a most encouraging sense of collective achievement when all were successful — indeed the tutor group was acting as a collective in the sense described by John Fraser (1994) in an article in *Education for Tomorrow*.

21 Testimonials were given to almost all students except in a few cases where attendance or approach to school life did not enable us to offer an open testimonial which would be of value. The reasons for the decision were explained individually sometimes with an example of what we should have had to write. In all cases the head of year and I were willing to act as referees and to deal with specific enquiries as constructively and helpfully as possible.

22 Imperfections in testimonial writing are many and varied:

A is well mannered and courteous — Value laden; a crawler perhaps?
B can take initiative but prefers guidance — Mixed: not clear what is meant.
C is reluctant to try new ideas — Generalised statement lacking context.
D has distinct management ability — Non-operational: what use is the remark?

23 The second project involved mainly younger students and centred around the preparation of a 'Time Capsule' deposited at Sunderland Museum for 50 years.

24 The Pilot Records of Achievement In Schools Evaluation was established and funded by the Department of Education and Science.

25 For many years records of achievement were also referred to as profiles.

26 The scope of the Newsom Report is outlined in Chapter 1.

27 The following example shows how the quota was calculated for, say, geography. Assume that on average each student took 8 subjects (the precise figure was not critical) and that students taking geography obtained a total of 120 higher grade passes from all their subjects. The quota for the subject was $120 \div 8 = 15$. If the geography results produced 18 higher grade passes the subject would have achieved $18 \div 15 = 120$ per cent of its quota. The method is independent of the number of students taking geography and provides a performance indicator for results in that subject. Today, it might be possible to draw up quotas based on different criteria at the start of courses in year 10 instead of retrospectively after results are known. The national tests at the end of Key Stage 3 are taken at the right time but their use for such a purpose needs critical examination. GCSE grades A*, A, B and C would replace higher grade passes.

28 The correlation coefficient is a statistical quantity which compares the relationship between two variables. The coefficient (or value) can vary between 1 and -1. A correlation coefficient of 1 indicates a one-to-one relationship (ie if the value of one of the quantities doubles so will that of the other); 0 indicates that the two quantities are independent of each other (ie there is no correlation); a negative value between 0 and -1 signifies that if one quantity increases the other decreases.

The analysis shed some light on an imbalance of results between girls and boys for which we had found no obvious explanation at the time. During the years 1978-1988 girls gained 1.5 higher grade passes for every 1 by boys. Over the corresponding period the analysis showed a similar imbalance among higher scoring students in AH3 tests. The ratio of girls to boys gaining stannine scores of 7, 8 or 9 was 1.4: 1. For the highest scoring eleven per cent (stannines 8 and 9) it was 1.8: 1.

29 Analysis of Sunderland schools' GCE and CSE results commenced in 1978. Ryhope's results in this and the following year were almost exactly average for the categories of total higher grade passes and numbers obtaining five or more HGPs. In later years, the school had a reduced proportion of high attainers which was reflected in results.

30 My letter to parents was to give positive information following a local Conservative campaign aimed at Ryhope School (Chapter 14). However, the director of

education saw my letter as a 'claim that Ryhope has an above average record of employment'. Much administrative time must have been spent to comb the figures and come up with 'some minor errors' (almost inevitable by the nature of the exercise). However, he also pointed out that we had used an incorrect number on roll. Acknowledging this in my reply, I noted that we had used a figure 'from the statistics brought to me a few days earlier by the senior inspector in connection with examination performance' but assured him, no doubt with a smile as I wrote, 'I shall use school figures in future calculations'. Recalculating and re-scrutinising the data, I decided that 'a percentage in the upper half of the eighties' — still an excellent result for the times — would best reflect the constantly changing details.

31 Between 1978 and 1984, for example, four deputy heads were promoted to headships.

Chapter 13. Defending Gains

1 From information I received later and by subsequent deduction I formed the opinion that a group of five or six teachers opposed to the general direction of the school had 'had the ear' of the senior inspector for some time.

2 In the mid- to late-1970's damage to school buildings including arson attacks was a wide spread problem not least in the north east.

3 In the 1970s new arrivals to comprehensive school staffs included a high proportion of newly qualified, mainly young teachers. Student training places had increased in response to a population bulge, raising the school leaving age and to meet the requirements of the new comprehensive schools. At Ryhope additional vacancies occurred as some teachers, especially from the grammar school, obtained posts in more traditional schools whilst others were in demand for more senior posts at other comprehensive schools. The local inspector's report claimed to have identified 'excessive staff movement' after comparison with two unnamed schools in the borough.

4 The relevant sections of the Articles of Government current at the time were:

8(a) The Local Education Authority shall determine the general educational character of the Schools ... Subject thereto, the Governors shall have the general direction of the conduct and curriculum of the school.

8(b) Subject to the provision of these Articles the Headteacher shall control the internal organisation, management and discipline of the school ...

5 Positive outcomes of the staff working party included generally improved mutual understanding and the establishment of an improvement centre where students who persistently disrupted lessons could be taught and supervised on an individual basis normally for a week. A constructive discussion on the roles of students and staff based on a paper prepared by a head of department was later extended to involve students discussing their role.

6 In a closely integrated process such as education one person's choice will always

influence the opportunities for others to develop in their own preferred ways. For example, in schools where some teachers used corporal punishment others who choose not to could be perceived as weak — a particular problem for newly qualified teachers who had yet to establish their principles and methods with their students.

7 A lobby for the abandonment of 70 minute lessons emerged in the wake of the report by the local inspectorate; this would have curtailed opportunities for teachers to use preferred teaching methods which needed a substantial period of time (Chapter 10).

8 The tone of the HMI visit was entirely different from that of the local one. At its conclusion there were oral reports to subject staff and the leader of the group reported on more general management matters to myself and senior colleagues. The visit combined acknowledgement of good work with constructive criticism and the opportunity to engage in educationally useful dialogue. Even so, HMI did not address the relationship of non-selective methods to the aims of comprehensive education. By 1977 any moves, never predominant, towards consensus concerning comprehensive education had weakened nationally. A key reason was the lack of political commitment to the principle of the comprehensive school as the secondary school for all requiring a broadly common curriculum for its students.

9 In the staff working party the authority of a director of education to make a decision on timetabling appeared contrary to the Articles of Government even though the ruling to continue with the existing arrangements was a correct, if reluctant, one. The counter-decision of the governors a few months later, no doubt prompted by the director, produced many problems over the next few years though we endeavoured to maintain some flexibility in lesson length. Soon, however, there was a cost as the changes affected other curricular objectives. In September 1982, nearly five years after the first changes, we resumed the simplicity of two 70 minute lessons in the morning and two in the afternoon with widespread staff agreement; the diversion had not been without effect on the process of coherent curriculum development.

10 At the time modern languages were set from the second year. Later, a new head of department developed non-selective teaching throughout the school and generated much increased interest and involvement among students.

11 Interviews for the second deputy head were not due until March for appointment in September.

12 The director consulted me during the preparation of his report both on matters of fact and on interpretation. He incorporated several of my recommendations and I was invited to submit my own report to the same meeting of the governors. Whilst there remained several key points with which I disagreed, I have no complaint about the manner in which it was prepared and presented with staff able to see copies of both the director's and my own reports. The replacement of the original emphasises that, because such a document has the name 'Inspector' attached to it, this does not mean that it contains infallible truth. Valid questions to ask concerning any inspection are: Have the inspectors a hidden curriculum? and Who

inspects the inspectors?

13 Throughout the period of Ryhope School I met union representatives on a regular basis to discuss informally any matters of concern. Final decisions, of course, lay with members of the individual unions.

14 The next day a clergyman representing the Church of England on the Education Committee wrote a kind and appreciated letter to me. 'I thought you were very brave last night and I now know how "lynching parties" must be and operate! I hope things work out — you are not friendless I am sure!'

15 Although voting figures are not known, majorities were substantial. However, the NASUWT motion to inform the press probably received less support than others. The AMA/AAM later became the Assistant Masters and Mistresses Association (AMMA) before, in 1993, changing its name to the Association of Teachers and Lecturers (ATL). It has never sought affiliation to the TUC.

16 The principles guiding disciplinary action were described in Chapter 9. It is no easy task to be constructive with those students, of which Ryhope had a full share, whose behaviour causes serious concern. The school had teachers of all levels of seniority who were gifted in gaining the confidence of such students and willing to spend time helping them to maintain acceptable standards. There were failures as well as successes but, as it was put to me by a visitor with experience in the field, the community of a comprehensive school may offer many errant young people their most favourable environment for developing in self-esteem and responsibility. Headteachers have a duty to both parents and teachers and anyone may disagree with particular actions and outcomes but I strongly rejected the reference to lack of support.

17 At least one union considered that job specifications had implications for conditions of service and it proved difficult to formulate them in a manner agreeable to all concerned.

18 The advice of the regional official of the NUT was sound. The two clauses of the Articles of Government read as follows:

8c(i) There shall be consultation at all times between the Headteacher and the Chairman of the Governors.

8c(iv) There shall be full co-operation between a Headteacher and the Director of Education on matters affecting the welfare of the School.

Chapter 14. Politics, Inspections and Parental Preference

1 The Council leader had made at least two previous appeals for calm, the first in response to a well publicised announcement by a Silksworth resident to refer the school to the local Ombudsman. The complainant favoured a traditional grammar school ethos and curriculum and had been sniping at me in the press for some years. The second occurred in a public announcement describing the decisions of the governors at their meeting of 18th April. This support, welcome as far as it went, must be seen in the context of the same person's conduct of the parents

meeting in the previous March and his press statement after the meeting of governors in November 1977 following the leak of the local inspector's report (Chapter 13) 'It is fair to say that the views of the headmaster of the school on education do not coincide with mine or with those of the majority, if not all of the Education Committee'.

2   Numbers transferring to Ryhope were affected by the decisions of particularly popular and capable pupils (Chapter 9, note 17), personal friendships and the influence of their primary school teachers.

3   A few weeks earlier Sunderland Conservative councillors had commenced a campaign to obtain access to individual schools' examination results and, surprise, surprise, linked this to Ryhope School in particular. At the time all Sunderland schools including Ryhope published the names of successful students in public examinations but did not give further details those being considered as personal to the individual student. My letter to parents referred to career destinations of the previous fifth year students which produced much activity from the director (Chapter 12, note 30). The reference to Gordon Bagier, the local Labour MP, is a mystery.

4   The Conservative councillor was later identified as a former resident of Silksworth now representing another ward.

5   There were indications of pre-conceived ideas concerning the school which inspectors brought with them.

6   Ken Masters (1983), headteacher of St Kevin's Comprehensive School in Kirby, has given his impressions of an HMI inspection:

> Where individual departments had received glowing verbal reports from individual inspectors the written report tended to the bland. Criticism, however, in both verbal and written reports was always forthright.

Well-merited matters for praise at Ryhope included the work of the careers department which was considered outstanding and the value of the school's activities such as visits, charity work and sport reflecting the work and commitment of the teachers concerned. Whilst this was welcome, the report for social studies illustrated one of many missed opportunities. Although the subject was a vital component of the school's common curriculum in the fourth and fifth years, no specialist inspector in this field was included in the team so the subject was shared by those responsible for history, economics and so on. Nevertheless, the inspector covering the subject in the fourth and fifth years congratulated the head of department with words to the effect of 'You've got it just about right here'. The written report had, indeed, some complimentary things to say but immediately qualified them with questions concerned with teaching all-ability groups — the concept around which the course was built!

7   Three years later, when the results of HMI inspections were published, it became clear that statements that the needs of all-ability teaching had not been fully met were a common theme in many reports. These carried with them an implicit assumption that non-selective teaching was a deviation from a norm of selectivity

which apparently required much less justification. At Ryhope the inspectors noted that the arguments for non-selective teaching had not been accepted by all involved but I know of no HMI report which used a corresponding argument to cast doubt on banding and streaming in schools.

8   Experimentation, with its connotation of lack of concern for the interests of students, is not acceptable. However, innovation, development and consolidation, far from being alternatives, are all indispensable if schools are to meet the changing needs of society. As we have seen in Chapter 10 the need for curriculum development was urgent and whilst planning and preparation are essential this must never provide an excuse for long term postponement; learning through experience concentrates the mind on essentials.

9   The graffiti clear-up did not solve the long-term problem at nights and weekends and later we had much more success with a small volunteer group of students working under the guidance of a senior teacher removing graffiti within a few hours of its appearance.

Wider issues involving care of the environment had also been raised by the inspectors. They noted that students generally responded well to teachers and to each other when they were under direct supervision but named as one of the school's major problems the position when not directly supervised. This illustrated a dilemma. The mature and friendly atmosphere in the school noticed by many visitors depended on a vital balance between encouraging personal and group responsibility (with most young people not needing to be watched every minute of the time) yet reducing to a minimum opportunities for graffiti, litter and vandalism which were all prevalent in the district at that time. The inspectors recognised the problems of supervising the buildings and site and I agreed that further action was necessary but regarded an implication in their report that the standards of behaviour required of students had not been set sufficiently high as a travesty of the situation. Aiming high is a prerequisite for developing responsibility for a lasting effect through life — an objective in which the school was remarkably successful according to the testimony of many former students and their parents.

10 Publication of HMI inspection reports showed that lack of pace in the early years of comprehensive schools was also a common theme of the period — but such information, which would have been helpful to school staffs planning improvements, was never revealed during inspections. Each school a separate unit (divide and conquer?) was apparently the tactic.

11 Demands for the services of senior staff in the older years, always heavy, had been accentuated with the raising of the school leaving age and the need for curriculum development to replace unsuitable curricula.

12 Two months later, in January 1981, the local authority approved the first of a series of consultative documents 'Falling Rolls in Secondary Schools' prepared by the director and followed by public meetings at each of the secondary schools. This report set out four main options including the one eventually adopted for 11 to 16 comprehensive schools followed by tertiary colleges for all students over 16. Although there were no specific proposals, school closures were now openly

on the agenda.

13 I understand that the school representative for the NASUWT, standing in for a year while the regular member was on secondment, received a brusque response from the local secretary when he learned of the resolution two or three months later. Nevertheless members kept to their decision.

14 Although the catchment area for Ryhope included the whole of Silksworth two of the more prestigious comprehensive schools in Sunderland were at least as easy to reach from many parts of the district. The schools were banded but parents and children were used to selection as the local junior school continued to be the only primary in Sunderland to practise streaming. Although a higher proportion of parents from Silksworth opted for alternative schools than in other areas there was no shortage of strong supporters for Ryhope among Silksworth students and their parents.

15 By this time the chairman who had conducted the parents' meeting in 1978 (Chapter 13) was concentrating on his duties as leader of the Council. His replacement was a councillor with a long record of service in the labour movement. The leader retained his interest in education.

16 The leader was quoted in the *Municipal Review* in February 1978: 'To talk carelessly about closing schools because parents have voted with their feet is assuming that these parents are able to make value judgments about the schools, whereas in fact many of such judgments are based on rumour, hearsay and even political consideration. Just because some parents know how to play the system, what happens to those who don't?'

17 School size is often indicated by the number of classes in each year with each class assumed to contain thirty students. Thus four form entry means 120 students in each year group or 600 in total for the five years covering ages 11 to 16. Sunderland was already considering a move to make all its comprehensive schools 11 to 16 followed by tertiary colleges (Chapter 5, note 4).

Chapter 15. Sustained Attack

1 The parent had cause for concern following harassment of his sons by other boys, two of whom were excluded pending discussion with their parents and guarantees concerning future behaviour. Subsequently I reported to the director that I had apologised to the parents of the boys on the receiving end for a lack of vigilance on our behalf and the father had apologised for the tone of certain aspects of his letter which had been written in a period of frustration. Happily I was also able to report that I was confident that the boys were now 'developing good friendships with other pupils in their classes and are becoming well liked and accepted'.

2 It was not clear on what criteria the Secretary of State based his instant assessment of Ryhope School. Our designated HMI had made no comment since the full inspection two years previously and the director of education had expressed satisfaction with progress made (Chapter 14). Was Ryhope on some Department of Education and Science special list of schools which must be watched? Or was there

a hidden agenda concerning the school in the regular contacts between the director of education for Sunderland and the DES?

3   There was also regular coverage in the Newcastle *Journal* and *Evening Chronicle*; the Darlington-based *Northern Echo,* and on local radio and television.

4   The attacks on Ryhope School were essentially political rather than educational although, in the public arena, educational and management issues were more prominent. The formation of the support group recognised the need to organise in defence of important values not just for one school but also in a wider context.

5   Later I received a letter of thanks for the school's handling of the situation from one of the parents who had reported the lighter fuel incidents. On 29th October, another request came from the deputy director, this time following a report from the local authority's senior educational psychologist concerning a student's learning difficulties. Our staff had, once again, acted in an effective, understanding and highly professional manner but again there was an implication of laxity.

6   A doctor who lived and worked locally also wrote to Sir Keith. Reminding him of his recent statement that the curriculum needed to be planned as a whole and not simply centred around the needs of the more successful pupils, she said 'Ryhope School follows your advice'. She remarked that she knew many of the children and their parents. 'They are all very happy and strong supporters of their local school. The children are responsible and can converse maturely about the aims and achievements of their school'.

7   On matters of behaviour, for example, if a school attempts to be constructive though not permissive with students who present problems this will make demands on the professional expertise of teachers over considerable periods of time. Problems are not solved instantly but the aim is to achieve durable results in as many cases as possible. It is not just a matter of reducing the number of problems at any price.

8   The role of the morning circular is described in Chapter 16. Teachers were asked to explain and discuss items in the circular in a manner suitable for the age of their group.

9   My message to students on this occasion first mentioned the recent governors' meeting and the decision to hold another and that the *Echo* would have a major item that evening. 'As in the past people will say all sorts of things and I know that this can be upsetting for pupils, teachers and parents alike. It is very important that everyone's education continues at the highest possible level — each of us has only one education at school and we must make the most of it at all times. Your teachers will help you in every way to see that we keep a high standard in the classroom and outside. Each of you can also do much to see that all goes as it should. Here are a few hints: Be on time for your lessons ... Be extra helpful to your teachers ... and most important of all continue to be polite, cheerful and friendly to each other and to teachers, non-teaching staff and visitors. These are qualities for which Ryhope pupils are known and respected. Outside school be sure your behaviour always shows consideration for others ... If anyone passes a remark about the school the best answer is to say firmly but politely that you are working hard and behaving as

you should'. In the staff section I emphasised that the message was designed to 'encourage a purposeful and constructive approach from everyone in this period ... Its success will depend entirely on how successfully we can interpret the message to them, and I am confident that a good job will be done by all.'

'Stay cheerful, urges head' was the *Journal*'s heading following an interview with me.

10 My statement commenced: 'The opposition to the school from inside and outside education appears now to have been successful. Yet so many pupils, parents, teachers and friends of Ryhope School have recognised and supported its personal and constructive approach to the education of each individual student'. The concluding sentence, used by the *Echo*, was: 'I regret that there is, as yet, no indication of how the future can be built on the firm and widely recognised strengths which have been established over the years'.

11 The exception was the clergyman who sent me the kind letter after the parents' meeting in March 1978 (Chapter 13, note 14), who had continued his interest in the school.

12 The words of the song were reproduced in the *Echo* and I include them here to help to give a picture of the time: '*Copland we love you, Copland we do/ Even when you're far away we think of you/ And one day when we're older, We'll look back and say/ There is no-one quite like Copland Who has helped us on our way.'/*

13 About thirty students had gone out to nearby streets but teachers quickly brought them back.

14 When asked later by a reporter why they supported their head they replied 'You can talk to Mr Copland and you know he will understand' — a much appreciated compliment.

15 By this time in the life of the school, students were welcome to accompany their parents at evenings to discuss work and progress. Some parents, understandably, lacked confidence on their own when meeting unknown people in strange surroundings.

16 The *Journal* described me as reacting strongly to the teachers' attack and saying that lack of obvious support for the school from some official quarters 'has helped to foster a feeling of uncertainty amongst some teachers at the school'. The resolutions were a symptom of this uncertainty 'which was particularly strong in the present climate of falling pupil numbers and school closures. They will become a thing of the past when the true values to which Ryhope is working are more widely understood and supported.'

17 My information is from eyewitnesses and the press as I did not attend personally.

18 'A difficult [school] to teach in' is doubtless fair comment but the friendliness and approachability of so many of Ryhope's teachers, often remarked on by parents, students and visitors alike, suggests that most of the staff had successfully overcome any latent difficulties.

When a school is perceived to be 'working class' — so easy to stereotype from outside — this has a considerable influence on parental preference. Stereotyping is always easier at a distance where it helps to create misleading images.

19 In fact, the version of the pamphlet received was an early draft which contained an even more explosive comment already deleted for the final version. Referring to the teaching staff in general, it said 'We call on the disaffected staff at Ryhope to move on to educational pastures which suit their more conservative tastes. Don't stick around and disrupt what is good, decent and progressive at Ryhope'.

20 The full question, which was handed to us in writing, was as follows:

At this point in time regardless of the rights and wrongs of the situation and the merits and demerits of all the arguments and statements in the media recognising the natural concern of parents, pupils, staff, the community at large, the governors and yourself and regardless of your own personal principles would you be prepared to carry out a programme of measures approved by the governors and which they consider necessary to:

1 Improve the standards of pupil behaviour

2 Improve the organisation and administration

3 Restore confidence in the school's policies and its capacity to carry them out and its standards of performance

4 Improve staff morale

The progress of such programme to be reviewed at the end of each term.

21 The full text of the reply was as follows:

I am willing to answer the question now. The answer is yes. However, it is 'yes' with the understanding that any particular measure within the programme will be fully discussed with me prior to adoption. I would contend that under the Articles of Government the governors can quite properly lay down a programme. Equally as headteacher in charge of the day-to-day management of the school I would need to be consulted and indeed convinced of the efficiency and practicality of the proposals. I am not sure what happens now that I have given this answer. I would, however, whatever the position wish to have the opportunity to make some comment on the report presented by the director as in all professional conscience and as a matter of natural justice I feel it would be wrong to have the report presented without my comments being at least noted. I do not accept fully the possible inferences behind the four points in the question and though, I, and I am sure the governors, would like to see improvements in many areas I cannot accept that the areas mentioned are of such concern as the director's report would indicate.

22 The second question from the governors was:

What would you do if after being consulted, in accordance with the Articles of Government, you were not convinced that you should carry out a requirement of the governors?

After joint preparation with the NUT regional officer, I replied:

Despite the prior consultation and assuming the requirement was in line with the Articles of Government I should make alternative proposals to the same end as the governors. Nevertheless, if the governors insisted and the proposal was one which professionally I could not accept I would consider discussing with the directorate the possibility of termination of contract. After thirteen years of what I consider loyal and highly effective service to the local authority whose educational aims I have always endeavoured to promote I should take such a step with the deepest regret and believe that the governors and I should make every effort to see that such a situation does not arise. I believe it need not if the strengths of Ryhope School are built on.

23 The DES aims were described by another Sunderland headteacher as having 'an anonymity and a neutral generality' which did not provide a sound basis from which to derive more specific objectives and practices.

24 For example, much curriculum development was initiated in schools within subject departments and then agreed between heads of department concerned and an appropriate member of the senior management team. One of the 18 points required a new policy making procedure which involved setting up a senior staff council (There was no mention of our existing school policy committee described in Chapter 8). Under the proposal not only were all curriculum developments to be submitted in the first instance to the senior staff council but the head was to report all proposals to the governors and include 'the views of his staff council who *shall sign it'* [my emphasis].

25 For example the programme required a core curriculum in the first three years consisting of a list of subjects which we already taught whilst another of the points was to establish a system of diagnostic testing in the first term of the first year — a topic on which we had done much development work particularly in the previous two years.

26 Meetings of the staff council were open to all teachers but I chose not to attend them.

27 The size of the vote may have been partly influenced by the deputy head's unexpected support for the motion. I know that he felt very pessimistic at that stage.

28 The remainder of the item read: 'The organisation of teaching groups will be considered by the headmaster, appropriate staff of the school and the Director of Education (or his representative) and proposals will be submitted to the Governors for their decision.'

29 Two studies for degree courses give interesting background information on the period covered in this chapter. Pauline Green (1983), head of fourth year in another Sunderland school, asked permission to evaluate a social responsibility course which Ryhope had introduced for students whose behaviour had consistently been of an anti-social or inconsiderate nature. Most of her interviews occurred during the term which is the subject of this chapter. She gained the confidence of both students and teachers associated with the course as shown in

the extracts from interviews and discussions which she reports. She identified markedly different visions and approaches to the course by teachers and, in her study, supports the need for in-service training in such matters. Interestingly her husband was deputy to Sunderland's senior inspector of schools.

Neil Reed (1987), a senior teacher at Ryhope, undertook an inquiry into the attitudes of former Ryhope School students to the Youth Training Scheme (YTS) and their preparation for it. He interviewed a group of YTS trainees who represented a cross-section of former students whom he had known well as head of year for their last years at school. They had entered the school in September 1981 so were in their second year during the period covered by this chapter. His dissertation contains interesting background to Ryhope School from the point of view of former students as well as himself.

Chapter 16. Final Phase

1 At this governors' meeting held on 11th February I was concerned at an unexpected air of hostility from the director to the reports which had been prepared in accordance with both letter and spirit of the Governors Programme. Following subsequent correspondence between myself and the director the situation improved greatly as the year progressed.

2 Time constraints were sometimes so severe that it was only possible to discuss the final versions of reports with the director before the meeting but at least we were able to explore potentially contentious ground in advance. For a meeting in April there were only six working days from the previous meeting to prepare reports on three further items of the programme. True, some of the work was already in hand but demands such as this made it almost impossible to also give full and necessary attention to normal school affairs.

3 The HMI visit in June was not a success: firstly it seemed to be a half-way house between a routine visit and formal inspection with unclear guide lines; secondly I gained the impression that it was weighted towards justifying the findings of the 1980 general inspection report. Last but not least, the school had one of those 'off' days when little seems to go according to plan. The visit in November, which included one of the inspectors who had come in June, was entirely different. I raised with them my concerns over the June meeting and was pleased to find that, on this occasion, the inspectors had positive comments to make in almost all areas of school life. These were confirmed in their subsequent discussion with the director who prepared a report for the Governors.

4 The director wrote to me on the day he received the letter from the Department of Education and Science enclosing a copy and adding 'I have no doubt that you will be as pleased as I am to have this reply.' I was!

5 In 'A Review of Progress at Ryhope School' the local inspectors noted that 'The staff seem presently to possess a greater degree of collective will than ever in recent years.'

6 Heads of home economics at Ryhope School generously agreed to requests to

involve their students in matters of hospitality providing this was never taken for granted; they correctly and vigorously guarded their work as an important part of the curriculum and education of both girls and boys.

7 At the time 23 per cent of our first year students and an average of 15 per cent over all years were receiving help and guidance from the special needs staff.

8 In September 1985, despite the likelihood of closure, there were 72 admissions to Ryhope representing 41 per cent of the nominal number in the old catchment areas of Ryhope and Silksworth. Almost exactly the same total and percentage applied to the combined entry of two other schools which were to be amalgamated.

9 We met the chairperson of the Parents' Action Group in Chapter 11 as the writer of a letter in support of the school's equal opportunities submission to the Fawcett Society.

10 Here is an extract from the transcript of the discussion between a Ryhope parent (T) and Sir Keith Joseph (J):

T: You have always been a keen advocate of progressive education in schools. Am I correct?

J: I don't know about progressive education, it's a dangerous word Mr T — means many things to all people.

T: Well progressive in the sense that the standard is to be higher. That's what I meant by progressive.

J: Oh yes, yes, if that's what you mean. Passionately so.

T: Now you're dead keen, you're very keen for schools to come up to this standard that you advocate. Right?

J: Not only in exams but in behaviour and understanding, Mr T.

T: The whole school.

J: That's right. The whole child.

T: Well here in the Sunderland area, in Ryhope ...

J: And all abilities.

T: Yeah ... we have such a school which has that variety of courses and a wide-ranging curriculum which is actually following very closely the guidelines that you've always advocated, you know.

Mr T was able to get in the name of the school a couple of times and the intended closure before time was up.

11 Publicity accompanied the announcement of Ryhope's first Governing Body when it was learned that the minority parties on Sunderland Council (in effect the Conservative group as the Liberals denied involvement) nominated not only the upholder of traditional grammar school values (Chapter 14, note 1) but also the independent socialist councillor for Silksworth who had reported the school to the Secretary of State. Following a vigorous debate at a full council meeting and a letter from members of the action group, the Labour leader of the Council said 'It appals me that because people have particular views about anything they are regarded as unfit to be governors. That, in my opinion, is totally unjustifiable.' In the event their presence on the Governing Body proved a low key affair.

12 I reached the meeting with heads and the director a little late but having had time to

collect my thoughts. I took an immediate opportunity to express my feelings concerning the right of staff and students to hear such news from the person directly responsible for their well-being rather than the local newspaper. Although I accepted the director's assurance that no discourtesy to the members of the school had been intended — he thought that all schools (including others destined for major changes) would learn the news together — I felt very strongly and understand that my short speech made a notable impression on those present.

13 At first I thought that the newsletter could operate like the morning circular where teachers handed in items in the office which were typed in order of receipt with the only rules being full sentences, full names of students, sober entries (though with occasional humour) and the signature of the teacher responsible for the item. Students could include items if they obtained the agreement of an appropriate teacher. In contrast, a newsletter needed an editorial policy and a distinctive style.

14 A typical edition would contain four to eight items varying in length from 70 to 200 words. Occasionally rather longer items were included.

15 Occasionally a school student was profiled but only if he or she agreed.

16 Legislation on conditions of service provided five days in each school year (nicknamed 'Baker Days' after the Secretary of State at the time) for staff planning and associated in-service training. All teachers were expected to work for 1265 hours annually during what was referred to as 'directed time'. Although this latter requirement was ill-thought-out and issued without consultation with the teacher unions it did enhance the effectiveness of activities such as after school meetings and parents evenings when all teachers concerned were now present. Previously schools relied entirely on goodwill with, in most cases, a remarkably good response. Nevertheless the voluntary nature of the system tended to add to the work load of the most conscientious teachers and limit the scope for important developments. The idea needed sensitive planning and negotiation with unions so that requirements were reasonable and purposeful and did not underestimate the importance of time spent by teachers in organising extra-curricular activities and in preparation, marking and keeping up to date. Overall the intention should have been, through greater efficiency and effectiveness, to decrease rather than increase the load on teachers.

Chapter 17. Current Issues and Campaigning Strategies

1 An alternative to hard-to-justify specialist schools is provided by the type of enhanced educational experience put forward in Chapter 5. Specialist facilities would then be available on a broad and equitable basis.

2 The influence of business is to be seen in all types of school. Sums involved may be large or small with many firms welcoming relatively small scale sponsorships. In exchange firms receive access to advertising and other marketing activities which can be found on exercise books, folders, wall displays, sports kit, concert programmes and similar locations.

3 In business and industrial management circles there is currently much interest in a

process (elevated by enthusiastic proponents to the status of a philosophy) known as Total Quality Management. One of the virtues claimed for TQM is its emphasis on seeing that components are correct at source (Right First Time in the jargon) rather than faults being discovered by inspection at a late stage of the production process. Authors such as John West-Burnham (1992) and Malcolm Greenwood and Helen Gaunt (1994) have endeavoured to apply the ideas of TQM, particularly those involving processes, to the very different world of education. Such adaptations must be treated with great caution and certainly some of the ideas clash with important principles examined in this book. Nevertheless this is not true of all aspects of TQM and, in particular, one may ask why we still rely so heavily on such an inflexible, unrealistic and, ultimately, unhelpful form of quality assurance as the school inspection. As the founder of TQM, W. Edwards Deming, put it in the third of his fourteen points for management: 'Cease dependence on mass inspection; build quality into the product in the first place'.

4   As well as making the national curriculum work at any level, teachers also found time and energy to adapt and develop the best of its ideas and thus maintain the interest and enthusiasm of their students.

5   The White Paper also contains proposals for two types of comprehensive school: 'community' maintained by local authorities and 'foundation' comprising most of the former grant maintained schools. The proposal is divisive and totally unnecessary. There is also a category of 'aided school' for schools with a religious basis whilst a section, ominously headed 'Modernising the comprehensive principle', states 'By 2002 we will have schools setting pupils according to ability and further development of innovative approaches to pupil grouping'.

6   Strong and effective trade unions, being essential for the health of public education, are in the interests of all parents and students. Trade unions, both for teachers and for other workers, have a particular concern for ensuring high standards in the quantity and quality of teaching and support staff; in salary levels and structure, and in conditions of service. These matters are vital to the effectiveness of education policies.

7   This was Circular 10/65 (Chapter 3).

8   In the absence of an adequate definition of comprehensive education there was justified criticism that, fundamentally, most comprehensives reorganised the tripartite system under one roof (Chapter 8, 'Comprehensive Challenge').

9   Distinctions between theory and practice must be treated with caution. For effective action, theory and practice must develop in step, each interacting with the other in the light of developments and experience.

10 Benn and Chitty (1996) investigated grouping of students in comprehensive schools in their survey *Thirty Years On: Is Comprehensive Education Alive and Well, or Struggling to Survive?* In the year 1993-94 (when the data was collected) 50.5 per cent of comprehensive schools grouped their students non-selectively for all subjects in year 7 (p 255). The figures fall sharply in the next two years though markedly less so in Scotland (p 259). In years 10 and 11, immediately prior to GCSE, it is encouraging to learn that, despite the climate and pressures of the time,

three schools in every hundred were continuing to show what can be done without resorting to selection in any subject. A further 8.7 per cent in these years had mainly non-selective groups with not more than two subjects setted (p 276).

11 In Chapter 16 we noted the much improved situation at Ryhope School after the working through of the Governors' Programme. Despite the Programme's imperfections, this is an example of how much progress can be made when more equitable, detailed policies have been adopted at education committee and governing body level following staff involvement and with advice and support from advisers and inspectors.

12 In 1996 an action group Professional Unity 2000 was formed. Its membership is open to associations of the ATL (Association of Teachers and Lecturers), NAS/UWT and NUT; also to school groups. It has the full support of the NUT Executive and its objects are 'to achieve a single union for all primary and secondary teachers in England and Wales by the Year 2000 AD; and thereafter to explore the possibility of widening that union to embrace all professionals in education'.

13 We must never ignore effects of the private sector on state education — a matter largely neglected in the last half-century. Simon (1991:43), referring to a period shortly before the 1944 Education Act, notes that proposals for public schools to be brought into the popular system were 'now advanced across a wide front not only by organisations of the labour movement'. One of the most strongly critical statements of the position of the public schools came from the Association of Directors and Secretaries of Education (the chief officers of the time).

14 The City Technical College scheme failed to attract financial support from all but a handful of industrial and business organisations. Reasons include the very substantial sums expected but also, as a result of vigorous campaigning, reputable firms came to realise that they risked alienating good relations with main stream schools. (The subsequent proposals for technology and other colleges required less money from individual firms, was introduced with a much lower profile and had greater success).

References

Adey, P. (1991) 'Better Learning'. Report from the Cognitive Acceleration through Science Education (CASE) project. London: Centre for Educational Studies, King's College.

Aldrich, R. (1989) 'The lessons of history', *The Times Educational Supplement*, 22 September.

Amphlett, D. (1990) *Flexible Learning in Schools: The Oxfordshire Experience 1988-90*. Oxford: Flexible Learning Access and Guidance Unit.

Association for Science Education (1975) *Non-Streamed Science - A Teacher's Guide*. Hatfield: Association for Science Education.

Association for Science Education (1976) *Non-streamed Science: Organisation and Practice*. Hatfield: Association for Science Education.

Bahro, R. (1978) *The Alternative in Eastern Europe*. London: New Left Books.

Ball, S. (1987) *The Micro-politics of the School: Towards a Theory of School Organisation*. London: Methuen.

Banks, B. (1991) *The KMP Way to Learn Maths: A History of the Early Development of the Kent Mathematics Project*. Available from the Mathematics Centre, Kent County Council Education Department.

Barker, B. (1986) *Rescuing the Comprehensive Experience*. Milton Keynes: Open University Press.

Barrell, G. (1963) *Teachers and the Law*. (2nd edition) London: Methuen.

BBC (1971) *ROSLA and After: Book 2*. London: British Broadcasting Corporation.

Bell, V. (1950) *The Dodo: The Story of a Village Schoolmaster*. London: Faber and Faber.

Benn, C. and Simon, B. (1972) *Half Way There*. (2nd edition) London: Penguin.

Benn, C. and Chitty, C. (1996) *Thirty Years On: Is Comprehensive Education Alive and Well, or Struggling to Survive?* London: David Fulton.

Berg, L. (1968) *Risinghill: Death of a Comprehensive School*. London: Penguin.

Best, R. (1991) 'Support teaching in a comprehensive school: Some reflections on recent experience', *Support for Learning*, 6, (1).

Blishen, E. (1965) 'Forum Visits the German Democratic Republic', *Forum*, 7 (2), 68-71.

Board of Education (1931) *The Primary School*. London: HMSO, quoted in Dent, H. (1970) *1870-1970, Century of Growth in English Education*, page 102. London: Longman.

Board of Education (1943) *Report of the Committee of the Secondary Schools Examination Council on Curriculum and Examinations in Secondary Schools* (The Norwood Report). London: HMSO.

Booton, F. (1985) *Studies in Social Education. Vol 1: Work with Youth.* Hove: Benfield Press.

Bruner, J. S. (1972) *The Relevance of Education.* London: Penguin Education.

Bush, T. (ed.) (1989) *Managing Education: Theory and Practice.* Milton Keynes: Open University Press.

Capra, F. (1983) *The Turning Point: Science, Society and the Rising Culture.* London: Fontana.

Chitty, C. (1989) *Towards a New Education System: The Victory of the New Right?* London: Falmer.

Colls, R. (1976) ' "Oh Happy English Children!": Coal, Class and Education in the North-East', *Past and Present,* 73, November.

Community Education Association (1991) Leaflet giving a broad statement of policy in 'Access' insert, *Network* 11, (10).

Copland, R. (1962a) Letter in *The Listener,* 25 January.

Copland, R. (1962b) 'Testing, Marking and Assessing', *Mathematics Teaching,* 20.

Copland, R. (1966) 'School Reports', *Educational Research* 8 (3).

Copland, R. (1975) 'Towards Comprehensive Education: Ryhope School, Sunderland 1969 to !975', *Ideas,* 31.

Copland, D. (1986) 'Enterprise Redefined', *Curriculum* 7 (1).

Copland, D. (1989) 'Britain-GDR Youth Exchange. Background and Opportunities', *Youth and Policy,* 27.

Corrigan, P. (1979) *Schooling the Smash Street Kids.* London: McMillan.

Cox, C. and Dyson, A. (eds) (1969) *Black Papers on Education.* London: The Critical Quarterly Society.

Daunt, P. E. (1975) *Comprehensive Values.* London: Heinemann.

Dent, H. (1968) *The Education Act 1944.* (12th edition) London: University of London Press.

Department for Education and Employment (1997) 'Excellence in Schools'. London: The Stationery Office.

Department of Education and Science (1967) *Children and Their Primary Schools* (2 vols) (The Plowden Report). London: HMSO.

Department of Education and Science (1975) *A Language for Life* (The Bullock Report). London: HMSO.

Department of Education and Science (1977) *Ten Good Schools: A Secondary School Inquiry.* London: HMSO.

Department of Education and Science (1978a) *Mixed Ability Work in Comprehensive Schools.* London: HMSO.

Department of Education and Science (1978b) *Special Educational Needs: Report of the Committee of Enquiry into the Education of Handicapped Children and Young People* (The Warnock Report). London: HMSO.

Department of Education and Science (1979) *Aspects of Secondary Education in England*: A survey by HM Inspectors of Schools. London: HMSO.

Department of Education and Science (1988a) *Secondary Schools: An Appraisal by HMI.* A report based on inspections in England 1982-1986. London: HMSO.

Department of Education and Science (1988b) *Education Reform Act.* London: HMSO.

Douglas, J. W. B. (1964) *The Home and the School.* London: MacGibbon & Kee.

Entwistle, H. (1979) *Antonio Gramsci: Conservative Schooling for Radical Politics.* London: Routledge Education Books.

Fletcher, C. (1983) *Challenges of Community Education: A biography of Sutton Centre 1970 to 1982.* Nottingham: Department of Adult Education, University of Nottingham.

Fletcher, C., Caron, M. and Williams, W. (1985) *Schools on Trial: The Trials of Democratic Comprehensives.* Milton Keynes: Open University Press.

Forum (1967) 'Non-streaming in Comprehensive Schools', 9 (2) and 9(3).

Franklin, J. and McGeough, A. (1972) 'Mixed Classes for Craft Subjects: Developments in Home Economics and Technical Studies at Ryhope School', *Journal*, 23, (117). Newcastle: The Institutes of Education of the Universities of Newcastle Upon Tyne & Durham.

Fraser, J. (1994) 'The How and the Why', *Education for Tomorrow*, 41.

Freeman, J. (1991) *Gifted Children Growing Up.* London: Cassell Educational.

Galton M. (1994) *Crisis in the Primary Classroom.* London: David Fulton.

Galton, M., Simon, B. and Croll, P. (1980) *Inside the Primary Classroom.* London: Routledge and Kegan Paul.

Goslin D. (1963) *The Search for Ability: Standardized Testing in Social Perspectives.* New York: Russell Sage Foundation. Quoted in Krutetskii (1976).

Green, E. (1976) *Towards Independent Learning in Science.* St Albans: Hart-Davis Educational.

Green, P. (1983) *An Evaluation of a Social Responsibility Course in a North Eastern Comprehensive School.* A study for the B. Phil. at the University of Newcastle-upon-Tyne.

Greenwood, M. and Gaunt, H. (1994) *Total Quality Management for Schools.* London: Cassell.

Gregory, J. (1987) 'Comprehensive Comrades', *The Times Educational Supplement* 6 February.

Guardian (1975) 'Sir gonna make you a star', 22 August.

Hall, S. (1983) 'Education in Crisis' in Wolpe A. and Donald J. (eds) *Is There Anyone Here from Education?* London: Pluto.

Hart, K. (ed.) (1981) *Children's Understanding of Mathematics: 11-16.* London: John Murray.

Hayes, J. and Hopson, B. (1971) *Careers Guidance: The Role of the School in Vocational Development.* London: Heinemann Educational.

Holmes, G. (1977) *The Idiot Teacher.* Nottingham: Spokesman (for the Bertrand Russell Peace Foundation). First published by Faber and Faber (1952).

Holt, J. (1964) *How Children Fail.* New York: Pitman.

Hoyle, E. (1986) *The Politics of School Management.* London: Hodder and Stroughton.

Hughes, M. (1993) *Flexible Learning: Evidence Examined.* Stafford: Network Educational Press.

James, C. (1968) *Young Lives at Stake: A Reappraisal of Secondary Schools.* London: Collins.

Jennings, A. 'Out of the Secret Garden' in Plaskow, M (1985).

Joint Matriculation Board Examinations Council (1977) *Annual Report 1976-77.*

Manchester: JMB.

Joint Matriculation Board Examinations Council (1981) *General Certificate of Education Regulations and Syllabuses.* Manchester: JMB.

Joint Matriculation Board Examinations Council (1983) *General Certificate of Education Regulations and Syllabuses.* Manchester: JMB.

Joseph, G. (1994) *The Crest of the Peacock: Non-European Roots of Mathematics.* (Revised edition) London: Penguin.

King, R. (1964) 'A Visit to the German Democratic Republic', *Forum*, 7 (1).

Krutetskii, V. (1976) *The Psychology of Mathematical Abilities in School Children.* Chicago and London: University of Chicago.

Labour Party (1926) *Report of the Twenty Sixth Annual Conference*, page 333. London: Labour Party.

Labour Party (1993) 'Opening doors to a learning society' (Green Paper). London: Labour Party.

Labour Party (1995) 'Diversity and Excellence'. London: Labour Party.

Labour Weekly (1979) 'Keep them in their place', 9 March.

Lacey, C. (1966) 'Some sociological concomitants of academic streaming in a grammar school' in *British Journal of Sociology* 27 (3).

Lacey, C. (1970) *Hightown Grammar,* Manchester: Manchester University Press.

Lenin, V. I. (1920) 'Tasks of the Youth Leagues'. English edition (1953) in *Selected Works.* London: Lawrence and Wishart.

Levitas, M. (1974) *Marxist Perspectives in the Sociology of Education.* London: Routledge and Kegan Paul.

Levitas, M. (1986) 'The Educational Ideas of Antonio Gramsci', *Education for Tomorrow*, 1 and 2.

Little, C. (1991) 'Straitened Circumstances', *The Times Educational Supplement*, 21 February.

Luria, A. and Yudovich, F. (1971) *Speech and the Mental Development of the Child.* London: Penguin.

Maclure, J. Stuart (1968) *Education Documents of England and Wales 1816 - 1967.* London: Methuen Educational Paperback. Originally published (1965) London: Chapman and Hall.

Masters, K. (1983) 'The real St Kev's?', *The Times Educational Supplement*, 14 October.

Ministry of Education (1944) *Education Act*, section 8. London: HMSO. The passage concerning variety of provision is reproduced and discussed in Dent, H. (1944) *The Education Act 1944.* London: University of London Press.

Ministry of Education (1945) *Youth's Opportunity.* London: HMSO.

Ministry of Education (1947a) *The New Secondary Education.* Ministry of Education Pamphlet Number Nine. London: HMSO .

Ministry of Education (1947b) 'Circular 144, 16th June 1947' quoted in Simon B. (1971), page 272.

Ministry of Education (1960) *The Youth Service in England and Wales* (The Albermarle Report). London: HMSO.

Ministry of Education (1963a) *Half Our Future* (The Newsom Report). London: HMSO.

Ministry of Education (1963b) *Report of the Committee on Higher Education* (The Robbins Report). London: HMSO.

Moon, B. 'Stantonbury Campus, Milton Keynes: Buckinghamshire, a Study in Teacher Response to Motivation' in Moon, B. (ed.) (1983) *Comprehensive Schools: Challenge and Change.* Windsor: NFER-Nelson.

Mulloy, M. (1990) 'Open Door: Teachers report their success with SMILE', *The Times Educational Supplement,* 2 November.

National Association for the Teaching of English (1976) *Language across the Curriculum: Guidelines for Schools.* London: Ward Lock Educational.

Newell, P. (ed.) (1972) *A Last Resort? Corporal Punishment in Schools.* London: Penguin Education Specials.

Newell, P. (1989) *Children are People Too: The Case Against Physical Punishment.* London: Bedford Square Press.

New Musical Express (1974) 20 July.

Nottinghamshire (1991) *Pupil Exclusions from Nottingham Secondary Schools: Full Report.* Nottingham: Nottinghamshire County Council.

Open University (1976) *A Study in Management: Sydney Stringer School and Community College.* Management in Education Open University Course E321 2. Milton Keynes: Open University Press.

Payne, T. (1991) 'It's Cold in the Other Room', *Support for Learning,* 6 (2).

Peel, E. (1956) *The Psychological Basis of Education.* Edinburgh: Oliver and Boyd.

Pedley, R. (1956) *Comprehensive Education: A New Approach.* London: Gollanz.

Pinder, R. (1966) 'Non-Streaming in Comprehensive Schools'. Conference Report in *Forum,* 9 (1).

Plaskow, M. (1985) *Life and Death of the Schools Council.* London: Falmer.

Politzer, G. (1976) *Elementary Principles of Philosophy.* London: Lawrence and Wishart.

Pyle, D. (1979) *Intelligence: An introduction.* London: Routledge and Kegan Paul.

Reed. N. (1987) *An Inquiry into the Preparation for, Participation in and Views on the Youth Training Scheme.* Dissertation for B. Ed. at Sunderland Polytechnic (now University of Sunderland).

Reynolds, D. and Sullivan, M. (1987) *The Comprehensive Experiment.* London: Falmer.

Roberts, D. (1982) 'Our Single and most Significant Decision' *Forum* 24 (3).

Rowe, A. (1971) *The School as a Guidance Community.* Hull: Pearson Press.

Saad, L. (1957) *Understanding in Mathematics.* Birmingham: University of Birmingham.

Schools Council (1973) *Patterns, Teachers' Handbook.* London: Longman.

Schools Council (1976a) *Framework.* London: Longman.

Schools Council (1976b) *A New Look at History.* Edinburgh: Holmes McDougall.

Schools Council (1976c) eg *History Around Us.* Edinburgh: Holmes McDougall.

Schools Council (1977) *Work Part 1: Framework 1-8, Teachers Guide.* London Longman.

Schools Council/ London University Institute of Education (1973a) *From Information to Understanding*. London: Ward Lock Educational (originally published by the Project).

Schools Council/ London University Institute of Education (1973b) *Why Write?* London: Ward Lock Educational (originally published by the Project).

Schools Council/ London University Institute of Education (1974) *Keeping Options Open: Writing in the Humanities*. London: Ward Lock Educational (originally published by the Project).

Secondary Schools Examination Council (1947) *Examinations in Secondary Schools*. London: HMSO.

Sharp, J. (1973) *Open School*. London: Dent.

Simon, B. (1965) *Education and the Labour Movement 1870 - 1920*. London: Lawrence and Wishart.

Simon B. (1971) *Intelligence, Psychology and Education: a Marxist Critique*. London: Lawrence and Wishart..

Simon, B. (1974a) *The Two Nations and the Educational Structure 1780-1870*. London: Lawrence and Wishart. Originally published (1960) under the title *Studies in the History of Education 1780 - 1870*.

Simon, B. (1974b) *The Politics of Educational Reform 1920-1940*. London: Lawrence and Wishart.

Simon, B. (1985) *Does Education Matter?* London. Lawrence and Wishart. The chapter 'Why No Pedagogy in England?' appeared originally in Simon, B. and Taylor, W. (1981) *Education in the Eighties: The Central Issues*. London: Batsford Academic and Educational.

Simon, B. (1991) *Education and the Social Order 1940-1990*. London: Lawrence and Wishart.

Smail, David (1991) *When I Was Little: The Experience of Power*. Durham: University of Durham School of Education.

Smith, Sir A. 'The Review' in Plaskow (1985).

Socialist Education Association (1985) *Handbook for Labour Governors*. (2nd edition)

Southall Black Sisters (1990) *Against the Grain*.

Stansbury, D. (1992) 'A Loss to Comprehensive Education', *Forum*, 34 (3).

Stone, M. (1985) *The Education of the Black Child in Britain* (second impression). London: Fontana.

STOPP (1978/79) *Abolition Handbook* (ed. Peter Newell).

STOPP (1980) *The European Example: The abolition of Corporal Punishment in Schools*.

STOPP (1984a) *Catalogue of Cruelty: a dossier of child-beating incidents reported to STOPP*.

STOPP (1984b) 'County's Horrendous Child-Beating Statistics'. Press release.

STOPP (1986) 'Victory', *STOPP News*, 2 (3).

Sunday Telegraph (1978) 16 April.

Sunday Telegraph (1979) 4 March.

Swales, T. (1979) *Record of Personal Achievement: an independent record of the Swindon RPA Scheme*. London: Schools Council.

Talyzina, N. (1981) *The Psychology of Learning*. Moscow: Progress Publishers.

The Teacher (1978a) 'Control of Curriculum', 31 March.

The Teacher (1978b) 'TUC charter for women at work', 7 April.

The Times Educational Supplement (1945) 15 December, quoted in Pedley (1956), page 18.

The Times Educational Supplement and *The Times Higher Education Supplement* (1974) 'Teachers in the British General Election of 1974'. London: Times Newspapers.

The Times Educational Supplement (1982) 'Ryhope: past imperfect, future conditional'. Report by Sarah Bayliss, 26 November.

The Times Educational Supplement (1985) 'The Full Course'. Report by Virginia Makins, 26 July.

The Times Educational Supplement (1990a) 'Multicultural links cut from English report'. Report by Ian Nash, 8 June 1990.

The Times Educational Supplement (1990b) 'Fears for minority grants'. Report by Diane Spencer, 8 June.

The Times Educational Supplement (1990c) 'Race posts may be cut'. Report by Nicholas Pyke, 26 October.

The Times Educational Supplement (1991a) 'Hungry to Learn'. Report by Angela Neustatter, 5 July.

The Times Educational Supplement (1991b) 'Too many hairline fractures'. Report by Nicholas Pyke and Yvonne Taylor, 23 August 1991.

The Times Educational Supplement (1991c) 'Young minds need a sense of awe'. Report by Ian Nash, 30 August.

The Times Educational Supplement (1991d) 'Changing lives', 30 August.

The Times Educational Supplement (1991e) 'Drawn by horsepower' (Knighton School, Dorset) and 'No longer such a cloistered life' (Rodean)'. Reports by Elizabeth Heron, 27 September.

The Times Educational Supplement (1991f) 'Good, bad and gifted'. Report by Virginia Makins, 27 September.

The Times Educational Supplement (1991g) 'Children make the secondary choice'. Report by Neil Merrick, 1 November.

The Times Educational Supplement (1991h) 'Absurdly low ceilings'. Report by Maureen O'Connor, 29 November.

The Times Educational Supplement (1992a) 'Merit points provide no incentive'. Report by Nicholas Pike, 21st February.

The Times Educational Supplement (1992b) 'Opt-out floodgates open'. Report by Clare Dean, 17 April.

The Times Educational Supplement (1992c) ' "Passport to life" issued'. Report by Diane Spencer, 18 December.

The Times Educational Supplement (1992d) 'Choice widens class divide'. Report by Susan Young, 2 October.

The Times Educational Supplement (1993) 'The Balcarras Experiment'. Report by Maureen O'Connor, 14 May.

The Times Educational Supplement (1994) 'Beware the perils of parental power'. Report by Susan Young, 6 May.

The Times Educational Supplement (1997a) 'Tories facing poll revolt'. Report by Clare Dean, 21 March.

The Times Educational Supplement (1997b), 'Let pupils choose their own lessons'. Report by Mark Whitehead, 6 June.

Trades Union Congress (1962) 'Report of the 94th Annual Trades Union Congress'. London: TUC. See 'Memorandum of Evidence to the Central Advisory Council for Education (England)', 162-172.

Trades Union Congress (1977) 'Report of the 109th Annual Trades Union Congress'. London: TUC. See Annex 3: 'The Government's Consultative Paper "Education in Schools" ', 346-356.

Trades Union Congress (1980) 'Report of the 112th Annual Trades Union Congress'. London: TUC.

University of Sheffield (1980) *Faculty of Materials Prospectus.*

Warwick, D. (1971) *Team Teaching.* London: University of London Press.

Watts, J. (ed.) (1977) The Countesthorpe Experience: The First Five Years. London: Unwin Education Books.

Watts, J. (1980) *Towards the Open School.* London: Longman.

West-Burnham, J. (1992) *Managing Quality in Schools.* Harlow: Longman.

White, J. (1997) *Education and the end of work: towards a new philosophy of work and learning.* London: Cassell.

Williams, S. (1991) 'English by design', *The Times Educational Supplement,* 18 October.

Wiseman, S. (1964) *Education and Environment.* Manchester: Manchester University Press.

Young, Lord D. (1990) *The Enterprise Years.* London: Headline.

Terminology explained

Most specialist terms and acronyms are described when they first arise in each chapter but, to avoid unnecessary repetition, some of the most frequently occurring are described here.

Year Groups

The Education Reform Act (ERA) rationalised the numbering of school year groups from 1 to 11. Previously, one referred to first year juniors, third year secondary and so on. To avoid ambiguity, I have used the terminology of the time when referring to specific events before the ERA (eg 1st year) whilst, from September 1989, the current system is used (eg. 'year 7'). The secondary stage equivalents are as follows:

Pre ERA	Secondary Stages	From 1989
1st year	New entrants at age 11+	year 7
2nd		8
3rd		9
4th	Main options commence	10
5th	Last year of compulsory schooling. GCSE normally taken	11
6th	Also called lower sixth	12
7th	Also called upper sixth. GCE A-levels normally taken	13

Key Stages

The Education Reform Act also introduced the concept of key stages for the compulsory years of schooling. These are:

Key Stage	School	Years
1	Infants	1 — 2
2	Junior	2 — 6
3	Secondary	7 — 9
4	Secondary	10 — 11

The Department for Education and Employment

The name of the government department and its chief minister have changed on several occasions:

Date	Department	Chief Minister
1899	Board of Education	President of the Board of Education
1944	Ministry of Education	Minister of Education
1964	Department of Education and Science (DES)	Secretary of State for Education and Science
1992	Department for Education (DFE)	Secretary of State for Education
1995	Dept for Education and Employment (DfEE)	Secretary of State for Education and Employment

The titles at the time of an event or publication are used throughout the book.

Gender

Several quoted documents, particularly those pertaining to Ryhope School in Parts 4 and 5, were written when it was still regarded as correct practice to use the masculine form of a word to include the feminine where the sense dictated. The original wording has been retained for accuracy although its use would be unacceptable today.

Pupils/School Students

Similarly, although I have came to prefer 'school student' or 'student' at the secondary stage to the more common 'pupil' I have retained the latter in quotations from school documents and where the comments specifically refer to primary and middle school children.

Examinations

GCE O-level — General Certificate of Education Ordinary Level
This examination operated from 1951 to 1987. Candidates could gain the certificate in any number of subjects taken on one or more occasions at any age. In schools, most entered at the end of the fifth year. Results were originally in grades 1 to 9 and then, from 1975, grades A to E plus an unclassified category. Grades 1 to 6 and A to C were regarded as 'passes', meeting entry requirements for certain courses in further and higher education. GCE O-level replaced the School Certificate which was an examination which required success in a group of subjects though at a lower pass standard for each one.

CSE — Certificate of Secondary Education
CSE was planned in the late 1950s before the period of rapid expansion of comprehensive education. Intended for a selective system, it was first examined in 1965 and soon adapted by schools to serve a much wider purpose. The certificate was awarded on a single subject basis, like the GCE, in grades 1 to 5 and unclassified. Grade 1 was equivalent to GCE Ordinary Level 1 to 6 (later A to C) whilst grade 4 represented the standard obtained by a student of average ability who had worked steadily.

GCSE — General Certificate of Secondary Education
This certificate, first examined in 1988, replaced the unsatisfactory dual provision of GCE O-level and CSE. It is a subject examination like its predecessors and is awarded in grades A to G with an additional A* grade, introduced in 1994, for exceptional merit. GCSE grades A to C are equivalent to the corresponding O-level grades and work below the standard of grade G is ungraded.

GCE A-level — General Certificate of Education Advanced Level
Candidates normally take A-levels in one to four subjects at the end of a two year sixth form course (year 13) or at college where they may be taken

at any age. The pass grades are A to E. Admission requirements to degree courses via the A-level route vary according to the popularity of the course and of the institution on a supply and demand basis. The minimum is two A-levels in appropriate subjects at any pass grade up to three or more at grade 'A'.

Vocational and Pre-vocational Qualifications
The City and Guilds of London Institute and Royal Society of Arts are both long established bodies whose qualifications were originally awarded for technical and vocational skills obtained at work and in colleges of further education. They became active in the school sphere from the early 1970s and were followed by the Business and Technician (later Technology) Education Council (BTEC). The qualifications of all three bodies are well known and held in esteem in industry and business. They became popular in comprehensive schools for students who wished to supplement the prospect of modest grades at O-level and CSE with something more marketable. In the late 1980s, the Council for National Vocational Qualifications was established with one of its main objectives to bring some order and rationalisation into this expanding but now diffuse sphere of vocational and pre-vocational qualifications. Before being incorporated into a new Qualifications and Curriculum Authority from October 1997, it was responsible for national vocational qualifications (NVQs) and the more broadly based general version (GNVQs). Vocational and pre-vocational qualifications, at appropriate levels, provide an alternative entry to degree courses.

INDEX